TEACHING THE CHILD TO READ

FOURTH EDITION

Teaching
the Child
to Read

Guy L. Bond
University of Minnesota

Eva Bond Wagner
Newark State College

THE MACMILLAN COMPANY, NEW YORK
COLLIER-MACMILLAN LIMITED, LONDON

Fifth Printing, 1968

Earlier editions © copyright 1943, 1950, and
1960 by The Macmillan Company.

Library of Congress catalog card number: 66-10589

THE MACMILLAN COMPANY, NEW YORK
COLLIER-MACMILLAN CANADA, LTD., TORONTO, ONTARIO

PRINTED IN THE UNITED STATES OF AMERICA

To Freddie

PREFACE

Teachers in training and in service must understand and appreciate the teaching of reading, so that their students may learn to read more easily and with greater comprehension. The purpose of this book is to translate related research in reading, child development, learning, and science of language into instructional practice.

Nearly twenty-five years have passed since the first edition of *Teaching the Child to Read* was published, and it has been gratifying to the authors that many teachers have found the book useful and inspirational. During these years, the growth and understanding of the teaching of reading has been vast, exciting, and productive. Great contributions have been made by workers in education and allied fields to the knowledge of what constitutes a scientific approach to the teaching of reading. It thus became clear to us that the book should be rewritten to recognize the dynamic nature of today's reading instruction and to incorporate these advances in information about children, their educational needs, and the reading process itself.

The major difference between this edition and previous ones is increased emphasis on certain areas, rather than a fundamental change in point of view. The introductory sections have been condensed to include only those elements necessary for an overall understanding of the basis of a modern reading program. Actual classroom procedures have been integrated with the underlying principles of effective instruction. Adjustment to the great variety of classroom challenges that daily confront the teacher has been carefully considered throughout. The concept of diagnostic teaching by the classroom teacher is discussed in appropriate places and is given special attention in the final chapter.

In summary, the purpose of this book is to help teachers make the transition from theory to classroom teaching, and to furnish them with a learning guide while in training and a reference when in service.

G. L. B. *and* E. B. W.

ACKNOWLEDGMENTS

The photographs of children engaged in reading activities were taken by Dr. Douglas W. Tatton at the Campus School of Newark State College, by Miss Diana Knight at the University of Minnesota Elementary School, and by Principal Robert G. Payton at the Hartshorn School in Short Hills, New Jersey. We are grateful to them for permission to use the photographs, to the teachers and children of the schools where the pictures were taken, and to Dr. Franck Darte, Principal of the Campus School of Newark State College.

We are indebted to many scholars of the teaching of reading, including our own master and doctoral students, and to our coworkers over the years for insights and concepts embodied in this discussion of teaching the child to read.

Special gratitude and appreciation go to Fredericka Hoffa Bond, wife of the senior author, and to Ray J. Wagner, husband of the junior author, for patience, help, and encouragement.

G. L. B. *and* E. B. W.

CONTENTS

IV. THE TEACHER ENCOURAGES THE USE OF READING

V. THE TEACHER RECOGNIZES INSTRUCTIONAL NEEDS

TEACHING THE CHILD TO READ

I

THE TEACHER
INITIATES INSTRUCTION

Teacher Incentives

It is the first day of school. The preparations for this day have been long and involved—and enlightening—because this is the first year of teaching for Mr. Clark, a newly certified teacher.

As one of the new teachers in the school system, Mr. Clark has had during the preceding three days a brief orientation about the school, its objectives, and its procedures and about the objectives, methods, and materials of the teaching of reading, mathematics, science, and other content areas. His rich academic study and the preparatory work he has had in reading methods have given him an insight into the aims of the school. Now at last he feels ready to meet his fourth-grade class.

The Teacher Studies His Class

Mr. Clark looks about the classroom that is to be the school home of the children for so many hours of each day, hoping it will seem attractive and comfortable to the 30 children whom he will teach, guide, and perhaps even inspire. The many windows provide ample light for the activities of the school day. The desks and chairs are movable in order that their arrangement may be changed to suit the occasion. Mr. Clark is pleased with the number of chalkboards and bulletin boards and with the amount of cupboard space. There is a sink and a hot plate for work in science. Nearby Mr. Clark has on display the materials required in the first science experiment. That corner of the room will shortly be named "The Science Corner," where at all times there will be set up interesting scientific displays.

Another corner of the room has a table, chairs, bookcases, and a collection of books. This corner will soon be called "The Reading Corner." When their other work is finished, the children will be encouraged to move freely to these two corners and follow their personal interests or study their reading, science, or social studies units. The classroom collection has a variety of basal reader materials, other textbooks on several reading levels, trade books of many sorts, an encyclopedia, and other reference materials. To the collection that was already in the room Mr. Clark has added other books to round out the resources to meet the reading levels of the children, to expand the topics to be studied, and to meet the personal interests of the children, to the extent that he knows them at this time.

In the attempt to know each pupil and his unique needs, Mr. Clark has studied the individual folders that have come to him from grade three. Included in each folder are an interest questionnaire that was filled in during the preceding year, the results of a mental test and reading tests given at the beginning of grade three, a health history, and a number of anecdotal records on each child. Even before Mr. Clark has seen the 30 children he feels he has acquired some acquaintance with them. He plans, in the first several days, through observation, conference, and testing, to learn much more about them so that they will all soon be friends. These appraisals will occur continuously throughout the year, for children have different rates of growth and achievement.

On the first day after the summer holiday most of the children are happy to return to school. They meet their new teacher and are pleased with him. Mr. Clark takes special care to talk individually with each child at some time during the day. When the day ends and all the children have departed, he thinks over its happenings. He realizes that he knows far more about the children and about teaching than he knew at nine o'clock that morning. Lucile is shy, Steve is somewhat boisterous, Mary is proper, Roger's absorbing interest is sailboats, Brad is a leader, and Susan is thoughtful and helpful. Pat volunteered to read aloud and reads excep-

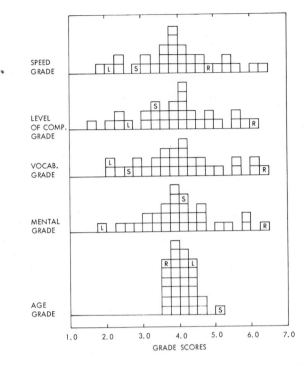

Figure 1 *Results of mental test and reading test of a fourth-grade class recorded in quarter-grade units.*

tionally well. Anne is inattentive and seems preoccupied. Perhaps, though, the inattentiveness is due to an inability to hear well. Mr. Clark has learned a great deal more about the children who yesterday had been merely names attached to records. Today they are personalities to him.

Before the week is out Mr. Clark gives, scores, and records the results of a group mental test and a reading test. He wishes to have normative data, in addition to the findings of interview, observation, and informal appraisal, upon which to base the decisions concerning which of the reading groups is the appropriate one for each of the 30 children.

The standardized test results are shown in Figure 1. The scores available to Mr. Clark include: age, recorded in quarter-grade units; mental age, on the basis of the group mental test, recorded in quarter-grade units; and vocabulary, level of comprehension, and speed scores in quarter-grade units, obtained from the Gates Reading Survey Test. Each block in the chart represents a child. The first initials of three children are included so that they may be identified for later discussion.

Mr. Clark concludes, from a study of these results, that his class is progressing satisfactorily in reading and that, by and large, good teaching has been done. In vocabulary and level of comprehension, the class as a

5

whole is about where it would be expected to be in view of age and mental ability.

The children are essentially homogeneous in age. This homogeneity is the result of continuous promotion; nearly all children of the same age are passed along each year from grade to grade. Steve, represented by S in Figure 1, is the only child outside the age range that would be expected for a fourth-grade class. When Steve was eight years old, his schooling was interrupted. He and his family spent two years in rural Argentina.

In mental ability, these children vary considerably, which is typical in most classrooms. In mental age, there is almost a five-year spread among the children within this fourth-grade classroom. Mr. Clark thought: "On the basis of mental age, one child is scarcely able to begin reading, and another child has the ability of a child entering junior high school. Although the children are homogeneous in chronological age, they are decidedly heterogeneous in mental age." Many adjustments will be required to meet the needs of children demonstrating so great a variability in intellectual development.

The various reading capabilities measured also show a wide range. In certain of the reading attributes tested, several children seem, at best, to be beginning second-grade readers, and others are as mature in these reading attributes as the average sixth-grade child.

Even though the class seems to be progressing nicely in reading achievement, with a fairly uniform reading pattern, Mr. Clark nonetheless has a wide range of talent to deal with. Wide variations could also be expected in whatever attribute or part of reading was considered. The problem of adjusting instruction to meet the needs of the pupils within this class is a challenging one. The same thing can be said for any class at any grade level as far as reading instruction is concerned.

The results of the mental test indicate that Steve's mental potential is slightly above average. His vocabulary score is among the lowest of the class, reflecting slow English language achievement due, probably, to having spent two of his ten years (two of his four years of schooling) in Argentina, where he heard and spoke only Spanish. He scored somewhat higher on the level of comprehension test, although below the class average. These three results considered together, caused Mr. Clark to believe that the group mental test result is a minimum estimate and that he might expect Steve to make insightful contributions to class discussions and to progress in English language development somewhat rapidly. Possibly by the time Steve reaches high school he will have overcome in large part the English language handicap he is now laboring under.

Neatly dressed Lucile, represented by L in Figure 1, is small for her age. She tries hard and is eager to please. She raises her hand frequently but when called upon fails to answer correctly. Her vocabulary score is the lowest of the class, and her level of comprehension score is one of the lowest. However, when her mental potential is considered, Lucile is progressing as well as could be expected. Mr. Clark will see that she has opportunities to do concrete rather than abstract thinking, that she is given needed help in word recognition, and that she is rewarded by gesture or praise when she makes achievements, however little, for he knows her progress will be slow and her need to do well is large.

Roger, represented by R in Figure 1, is liked by his classmates, who look to him for leadership. They elected him class president. Although he is one of the youngest children in the class, he does not appear so, because he is large for his age. He scored above the sixth-grade norm on the mental test and on the level of comprehension and vocabulary subtests of the Gates Reading Survey Test. Judging by the rest of the results, Roger evidently needs some help to enable him to read more rapidly. He has many good ideas, he has a quick sense of humor, and he is energetic and cooperative, making him a resource pupil both for the other children and for Mr. Clark.

Many differences are obscured by the fact that few attributes of reading have been measured and that the class is being considered as a whole. Of course, Mr. Clark, through class observation, has learned even after so short an acquaintance with them that the children of this class vary in their attitudes toward reading, in variety of interests, in intensity of those interests, and in level of tastes. He knows that some of the children are independent workers and finish the tasks they undertake, and others do not demonstrate such mature work habits. He has noticed that some can locate quickly materials on topics and can interpret graphs and charts well, and others find these materials so difficult to decipher that they skip over them with the briefest inspection and with little comprehension. In this class the variation in reading in all its attributes is great indeed, but Mr. Clark knows it is not different from individual differences found in any classroom at this level. He feels fortunate that the children have progressed through three years of instruction directed toward the same objectives upon which his instruction will be focused. He is aware of his responsibility for continuing the children's growth in each of the major objectives of reading instruction and also in preparing for the program the children will meet in succeeding years. The continuity of development toward maturity in each of the major objectives is essential in the reading development of each child.

The Major Objectives of Reading Instruction

In an educational scene in which the objectives are many, everyone agrees that the development of reading ability is one of the important goals of education. All people concerned with education know that reading is a dominant means of communication. They recognize that education will not have fulfilled its responsibility if it does not develop the ability necessary for readers to communicate with authors of a variety of materials. Reading instruction, therefore, must always have an important place in the school curriculum.

The unique characteristics of reading enable the person: (1) to be more critical; (2) to reflect more adequately; (3) to organize more effectively the contributions from many sources; (4) to be more rigorous in thinking with the content of the material; (5) to demand that the authorities consulted be well qualified to express opinions; and (6) to select authorities with which the reader would like to communicate to fulfill his own immediate needs.

FACTORS TO CONSIDER IN SETTING UP OBJECTIVES

In discussing the objectives of reading instruction, there are two extremes that must be avoided. First, the objectives can be given in such general terms that they have little instructional meaning. Second, the goals can be given in such specific terms that they become little more than a list of day-by-day tasks that would vary with the approach to reading and with the total educational program in which the reading is to be nurtured. This presentation will discuss well-defined objectives that are of sufficient importance to reading growth that they must be considered in formulating any well-rounded reading program at all levels.

Reading instruction must be broader and more inclusive today than in the past if it is to meet the increased demands that are made on the reading abilities of every student. As Tooze [267]* has pointed out: "Reading gives information which leads to knowledge which may lead to wisdom; reading is a time saver; reading is relaxation; reading is fun; reading is adventure; reading is a problem solver; reading may be an aesthetic experience, as is listening to music or looking at pictures."

The reading program must do more than develop basic skills and techniques, although the broader objectives of the reading program depend

---

* Throughout the text, numbers in brackets refer to the bibliography at the end of the book.

upon these basic skills and techniques. It must develop more than the ability to group words into thought units, even though such grouping enables an individual to be a more fluent and understanding reader than would otherwise be possible. It must develop more than the ability to note details and follow directions, although such comprehension abilities allow the reader to use printed material in a purposeful manner. Instruction must develop more than such basic study skills as the ability to read maps, graphs, and charts and to find references.

The program must, in addition, develop the attitude of wanting to find the references, develop broad interests in reading to gain information in many fields, and develop a taste for reading so that the reader can choose material wisely. The program must develop an independent reader—one who can rely on his own resources, one who will employ self-initiated reading activities, and one who can appraise the reading problems and adjust to the many purposes for reading. It must develop readers who can locate relevant and discard irrelevant material. It must develop readers who are able to see the relationships between things read and the problems they face. The program must develop individuals who can rely on many sources for getting information and who are able to organize the findings from these many sources. It must develop readers who can distinguish facts and opinions and detect propaganda or prejudice if critical judgments are to be made. It must develop readers who can draw conclusions from what has been read. It must develop readers who are able to relax and enjoy reading, and gain from their leisure-reading activities a degree of personal development and satisfaction. It must develop readers who can share interesting material with others through interpretive oral reading and discussion.

These, then, are some of the characteristics of a reading program that will develop readers who can respond effectively to authors. These characteristics give direction to reading instruction and guidance in setting up objectives of instruction that should be considered when organizing reading programs.

One other factor it would be well to consider in formulating objectives of reading instruction is the nature of reading growth itself. Fortunately reading growth is developmental. The developmental nature may be appreciated by considering three fundamental aspects of reading growth. In the first place, the more mature a reader becomes, the abler he is to read materials of increasing complexity and that require broader backgrounds, more extensive and refined knowledges, and more careful reorganization of these knowledges in order to get new concepts from reading. Second, the more mature the reader is, the more effectively he reads materials of increasing subject-matter specificity that require greater adjustment of reading techniques, more highly specialized and well-defined vocabularies, and more diversified application of comprehension abilities. Third, the more mature the reader becomes, the more he increases the speed and efficiency with which he fulfills his reading purposes. Fundamentally, however, the maturer reader uses reading in much the same manner as the child who is just beginning to learn to read. The characteristics of the mature reader have their start in the early reading experiences of the growing child.

PURPOSE OF READING INSTRUCTION

The fundamental purpose of reading instruction is to aid each individual to become as able and as diversified a reader as his capabilities and the instructional time will allow. In order to meet this major responsibility, teachers at all levels must focus their attention on some specific subgoals that are equally important basic goals of reading instruction. Keen attention must be given to these goals at every level of instruction if reading is to make its contribution to the educational objectives, to which all means of communication must relate.

A study of the goals of reading instruction will show that they are started during the child's early reading experiences and continue to grow as he matures with each succeeding reading experience. Goethe implied continuous growth when he wrote: "The dear people do not know how long it takes to learn to read. I have been at it all my life and I cannot say I have reached the goal."

It should be recognized that there is an interdependence among the goals of reading instruction. Word recognition, for example, makes comprehension possible; and diversification of comprehension abilities makes adaptation to the materials of the content fields possible.

1. Maturity in Word Study

The reading program must develop maturity in word study. Word study involves three interrelated tasks: building an ever-increasing meaning vocabulary; developing word-recognition techniques; and accumulating words that can be recognized instantaneously. From the very start, the teacher focuses a major portion of the reading instruction upon these three aspects of word study. In every lesson, the teacher endeavors to make sure that each child has clear, accurate, and vivid meanings for the words he is to encounter. Also from the start, the teacher directs instruction toward building adequacy in word-recognition techniques. This instruction is designed to help the learner develop those skills that enable him to recognize words rapidly and with minimum effort so that he may attend to content. This set of skills makes it possible for the reader to work out the pronunciation and understanding of new words so that he can continue to grow in this and the many other aspects of reading ability. In addition, the teacher gives the child experiences that reuse words, so that he becomes sufficiently familiar with them to recognize them immediately without the need for detailed study. Thus, the teacher helps the child develop a sight vocabulary upon which fluency of reading depends.

2. *Maturity in Comprehension*

Reading-comprehension ability is the major goal of reading instruction. Basic skills underlying all types of comprehension include: (1) selecting the appropriate meanings for words; (2) grouping words into thought units; (3) sensing sentence meaning and organization; (4) sensing paragraph meaning and organization; and (5) understanding the inter-relationships among the parts of a selection so that the whole can be understood. Comprehension ability is also made up of diversified types of comprehension that may be classified roughly into five highly inter-related categories: (1) factual reading; (2) interrelated reading; (3) evaluative reading; (4) reflective reading; and (5) appreciative reading [223].

At this time, growth in the ability to read evaluatively, an ability usually put off till later, will be considered by way of illustrating that these comprehension abilities are ever-present goals of reading instruction and that it would be unfortunate to leave any of them to be developed at more advanced school levels. Evaluative reading includes being able to differentiate factual concepts from fanciful ones, to distinguish fact from opinion, to judge the reasonableness of content, to determine the relevancy of content, and to read critically.

If children at all levels do not work constantly toward greater maturity in evaluative reading, the printed page could easily become a tool of pressure groups. Ability to detect propaganda or prejudice or to judge the reasonableness of content is often difficult to achieve and should be started early. The teacher, for example, who asks children, "Do you think this could really happen?" when they are reading a story about a fox that puts an ox in a bag, throws the bag over his shoulder and walks away, is teaching the children to read to evaluate. Or again, the teacher is developing evaluative reading when he queries whether the father in the story was speaking about a known fact or just an informed opinion when he said that he believed that the lost dog was at the neighbor's house, because the dog frequently went there to get a bone. When the child finds, as he continues to read the story, that the father's informed opinion was wrong, he begins to sense the difference between fact and opinion no matter how well intended the opinion. This type of comprehension ability is developed also when children discover that authors disagree in describing the homes of people of various countries or in their concepts of the bravery of wolves, especially when the children follow the reading with discussion about which author or which treatment was the more accurate.

When children appraise the meanings and overtones of words as well as the propaganda value of certain words and phrases, they are developing a higher level of ability in evaluative reading. Growth toward the goal of achievement in many sorts of comprehension, all developmental in nature, must be equally carefully nurtured throughout the reading program if a good level of ability is to be achieved.

3. Maturity in Adjusting to the Reading Demands of Each Discipline of Human Experience

Each of the disciplines develops ways of writing suitable to the content to be handled by the authors within that field. It is necessary for the child growing in reading proficiency to learn how to adjust his reading to the characteristics of the writing and the demands of the type of material he is reading. Such adjustment grows out of a fine coordination between the various basic study skills and the various comprehension abilities. These adjustments must be taught, and so they constitute one of the goals of reading instruction. The young child reading the science textbook or a science unit in the basal reader starts the development of a differentiated attack upon various types of reading material found in the content fields. He should be helped to make the necessary adjustments. As he goes up through the reading program and becomes a more mature reader, the child finds that there is an ever-increasing specificity in types of material to which he must adapt. Developing a differentiated attack, then, becomes a goal of reading instruction at all instructional levels.

4. Maturity in Basic Study Skills

This goal includes efficiency in the skill of locating information through such various aids as table of contents, indices, card catalogues, and the like. The first-grade teacher who says, "Our next story begins on page eight," and writes the number 8 on the chalkboard, is starting the child on the long road that could conceivably end one day in a degree of proficiency that will enable him to become a reference librarian in the Library of Congress.

Another group of basic study skills includes those needed for adequate use of general reference material. The primary teacher who has a picture file of animals classified alphabetically and who encourages the child to locate in that file the picture of the animal he wishes to know about is fostering the child's growth toward maturity in efficient use of general reference material.

At some points in the reading continuum, as in the illustration just cited, progress toward the goal is in the nature of readiness for more intensive training to be given at a later date. At other times, it is in the nature of further experience with and refinement of the skills that have been previously introduced. But all teachers at all levels are concerned with developing more effective use of general reference materials.

A third group of basic study skills consists of interpretation of maps, graphs, charts, and other pictorial material. As in all other reading development, the start toward the goal of competence in reading this sort of material is begun early. A health chart in the kindergarten, indicating children who have dental certificates; a weather graph on the bulletin board of a first-grade class that follows the noonday temperatures for a given week; a map of the neighborhood, showing where the police boys are stationed for safety in crossing streets—all these indicate the use of this goal of reading instruction in the very first days of school.

A fourth set of skills involves techniques of organizing materials. Examples of ways of organizing include the mechanical aspects of outlining, mechanical means of classifying material under a two-way arrangement, the preparation of time lines, and the like. The development of these skills has its start in the tabulation of class plans resulting from teacher-pupil planning, writing experience charts in sequential order, and classifying pictures in sequence in the prereading program. These illustrations from early reading experiences indicate that skill in organization is one of the important basic study skills continually being developed. Efficiency in using study skills becomes increasingly important as a goal of reading instruction because of the wider use today of reading as a tool of finding out about the world and its people as well as a tool of problem solving.

5. Maturity in Oral Reading

Another goal of the reading program is to develop capability in the communicative art of oral reading. The reader must be able to read orally in such a way as to interpret to others the meanings and feelings contained in passages he wishes to share with them. Development toward this goal, like all others, starts from the very beginning of reading instruction and continues throughout the entire program.

6. *Maturity in Independent, Efficient Reading*

The reader of today must be versatile and effective. He must read many types of material, and he must read for many purposes. Often, he must read at a very rapid rate. He appraises problems in order to know when reading is an effective tool and when it is better to get the information through other sources. Independently, he locates material that discusses the problem at hand, and he rapidly finds the part of the discussion than enables him to meet his goals. Thus, if the child is to be a good reader, he must be well equipped with reading abilities, skills, and techniques and must be versatile in using them.

If the child is to become a good reader, it is evident that much growth in reading ability will have to take place between the time he enters school, unable to read, and the time when he leaves school and has developed into an independent reader. He must learn to adjust his rate of comprehension to his purpose in reading, the difficulty of the material, and his familiarity with the content he is reading. Versatility in reading is necessary in order to meet the many reading demands met by the pupil in his schoolwork and by all literate adults.

Independent and efficient reading abilities are not easily acquired. These abilities are the result of good reading instruction by all teachers, instruction that provides opportunities for the gradual development of the characteristics possessed by a mature reader.

7. *Maturity in Reading Habits, Attitudes, Interests, and Tastes*

The child starts early in his development of habits and attitudes toward reading and continues to grow in them as long as he is growing in reading ability. He soon learns to appreciate books and develops habits of caring for them. He establishes the attitude of intellectual curiosity and the understanding that reading matter can help him satisfy this curiosity. Such an attitude progresses as he uses reading to solve individual and group problems, as he becomes an individual contributor to class enterprises, and so on. By these means, the child gradually realizes that reading is a part of written communication and develops the attitude of wanting to share the author's experiences, his factual information, his expression of point of view, and the stories he has to tell.

The habit of tending to words and word meanings is carefully nurtured in a well-rounded reading program. It starts early—when the child notices, for example, that the word *trunk* is not only a part of an elephant but also part of a tree or something in which to put clothes for traveling. The habit of attending to words and demanding an understanding of their meanings is something that all teachers should encourage at all levels. The habit of relying on one's own resources and of energetically attacking material should be started early and developed throughout the reading program.

The development of reading interests and tastes needs little discussion as a goal. Quite obviously, there is little to be gained in teaching efficient reading habits, attitudes, and abilities if the reader is to employ them on relatively inconsequential materials or if he is to use them in completely restricted areas. Therefore, interests and tastes should also be given consideration throughout the reading program.

Selected References

DeBoer, John J., and Martha Dallmann. *The Teaching of Reading,* revised edition. New York: Holt, Rinehart and Winston, Inc., 1964, Chap. 2.

Harris, Albert J. *Effective Teaching of Reading.* New York: David McKay, Inc., 1962, Chap. 1.

New York State Education Department. "Miss King's First Grade," *That All May Learn To Read.* Elementary School Aids to Teaching Language Arts, Leaflet No. 3. Albany, New York: Bureau of Curriculum Development, Division of Elementary Education, 1949.

Russell, David H. "Continuity in the Reading Program," *Development In and Through Reading.* The Sixtieth Yearbook of the National Society for the Study of Education, Part I. Chicago: The University of Chicago Press, 1961.

CHAPTER 2

Preparing the Child
for Instruction

An understanding of readiness on the part of his teachers will do much to facilitate the child's reading growth. Reading growth is the process of development in which the skills and abilities in reading are gradually learned throughout the school years, as was pointed out in the previous chapter. Actually, the child has been making necessary prerequisite learnings since birth. He started to learn to read when, in the first year of life, he made his first visual discriminations and, in his second year, he coupled words with objects in his listening and spoken language [109].

Throughout the preschool years, the child learns many things that contribute toward growth in reading. He develops the beginnings of an understanding of the world about him and his place in it. He learns to associate with other children and adults. He begins to know himself as a person and to build his own individuality. Learning these and other important matters continues concurrently with growth in reading throughout his school years. Readiness will be an ever-present concern of all his teachers in every learning situation. Much of what he learns he will learn only when he is sufficiently advanced.

Reading readiness, thus, is not the concern of the first-grade teacher alone but of all who wish to encourage growth toward reading proficiency. The basic readiness concepts are quite similar at every point in the educational continuum. The differences are matters of emphasis rather than of pedagogical practice.

In general, readiness has three interrelated components: motivational, maturational, educational.

1. *Set.* The pupil must accept the goal of learning and the intermediate goals necessary to reach the ultimate goal. In the beginning stages, the child must want to learn to read. At higher levels, he must want to improve his reading. That is, he must accept the tasks of learning as well worth the effort required.

2. *Maturity.* The pupil must have matured sufficiently to involve himself in the act of learning. At the outset of learning to read, maturity considerations include sensory, mental, emotional, and social development.

3. *Learnings.* The child must have the prerequisite learning to achieve the new reading accomplishments expected of him [120]. Educational readiness is an area of major concern to every teacher at every level of instruction.

Let us consider an example. To read the sentence *The cat likes to eat* the child must be able to distinguish visually the difference in the word patterns *cat* and *eat*. Ability in visual discrimination can be taught and can be learned.

At the third-grade level, prior to teaching the ability to break words into syllables, the teacher prepares the child by showing him that words are made up of syllables and by giving him experiences in detecting auditorily the number of syllables contained in lists of words. Not until the child can hear the number of syllables within a specific word can he be expected to separate visually the word into its syllabic parts.

In the intermediate years, the teacher might give the child practice in listening to words before teaching accent and corresponding dictionary skills.

Five Approaches to Limitations

At any level of instruction there are five possible approaches to working with children who lack readiness for instruction: (1) waiting until readiness develops; (2) recognizing the limitation, correcting it, or adjusting to it; (3) providing readiness instruction; (4) providing corrective readiness instruction; (5) developing readiness concurrently with instruction.

DELAY INSTRUCTION

At times it is wise to delay instruction until the child develops through normal growth processes the necessary maturity to undertake a new learning [259]. At the outset of reading instruction, the procedure usually is to wait for a certain age level before introducing reading instruction. It is not that children cannot be taught at earlier ages [80, 81, 123, 179, 213, 219]. Rather, for efficiency in group instruction, certain developmental characteristics are needed. Granted many children can be taught to read as early as three or four years of age. Indeed many deaf children are. For the usual child it is questionable whether such early instruction is wise educationally [103, 230, 271]. Certainly, it is economically and educationally inadvisable usually. In the United States, for the most part, beginning first grade has been selected as the most advantageous time educationally, socially, and economically at which to start instruction in reading for the vast majority of children.

ADJUST TO KNOWN LIMITATIONS

For some children with known limitations, instruction is begun and then adjusted to those limitations. There are children with poor vision, limited hearing, low mental ability, psychological immaturities, or limited physical energies. In many instances the limitations can neither be corrected nor altered by training. In such cases, at any level, the instructional program must be modified to enable the child to be a more effective pupil than he would otherwise be. For the child of low mental ability, for example, the reading program must proceed more slowly, more concretely, more repetitively than is suitable for the child with more rapid learning capacities.

PROVIDE READINESS INSTRUCTION

At the outset all children profit from general and specific preparatory programs. Time spent in acquainting the child (whether he is a beginning schoolchild or one just transferred to the school) with what is expected of him, in allowing him to become familiar with the school routines, and in encouraging him to make friends is time well spent. The child must be at ease if the most effective learning is to take place. It is not enough that the child have the requisite abilities and learnings upon which to base new learnings; he must have also an emotional acceptance of the entire learning situation [11].

During the period when the classroom adjustments are being made, other phases of preparatory instruction may be initiated. While the children develop in readiness to learn, they may also engage in activities specifically designed to prepare them for their first formal lessons in reading. Although all children have been exposed to printed matter prior to their entering school, it is the unusual child who has the ability to recognize more than his own name in print. Most first-grade children in the initial days of school fail to recognize the word *STOP* when it is disassociated from the octagonal traffic sign they so glibly "read" when they see it on the highway. They fail to recognize other words common to their daily living, such as *OFF, ON, MILK.* Many children cannot find the word that is different in series of words such as this:

WALK   WALK   TALK   WALK

Many children cannot even distinguish words from groups of numbers or groups of geometric symbols [47].

PROVIDE CORRECTIVE READINESS INSTRUCTION

Children who are lacking in some aspects of educational readiness can be helped to overcome their deficiencies by direct specific remedial teaching. At the first-grade level, for example, a child limited in attending to and carrying out directions may be systematically taught by giving him classroom responsibilities to attend to, tasks involving two or more directions. Such a child will need a number of experiences in attending to and carrying out directions before he is prepared to follow through with the instructions necessary to learn even the initial phases of reading. Again, at the fourth-grade level, the teacher, desiring to introduce the way the prefix *dis* alters the meaning of such words as *connected* and *continued,* and realizing that a given child may not be able to recognize immediately the root words, first teaches the child to recognize the stem words before introducing the prefixes and their modification of meaning. That is, the teacher provides remedial instruction designed to prepare the child for the new learning.

BUILD READINESS CONCURRENTLY WITH
DEVELOPMENTAL INSTRUCTION

Much readiness instruction may proceed at the same time that reading instruction is taking place. In first grade, for example, the teacher may give training in identifying initial sounds auditorily before presenting the letter that represents a given sound. Teachers frequently find it expedient to have the children listen for and detect in a list of spoken words those that start with the sound of the symbol that is to be taught. If the relationship between auditory knowledge and the symbol *r* in such words as *run, ride,* and *rat* is to be introduced, the teacher may have the children locate all the words that begin with the same sound as *run* in a dictated list, such as: *come, ride, car, rat, ring, song,* and *red.* In this case it is not that any given child is necessarily limited in auditory capability; it is that this review enables the new learning to take place more efficiently than would otherwise be possible.

Appraising Readiness

In order to know more about the strengths and the weaknesses of a group of beginning first-grade children, certain information about them should be collected. Many of the appraisals can best be made by the teacher over a period of time. For example, he can watch the children at work to determine their methods of work. Some children, he will find, have systematic ways of going about classroom activities and are efficient workers. Others display less efficiency in the way in which they attack their problems. The teacher, through observing the children, can make many fairly reliable subjective judgments. There are standardized tests that measure many of the factors that make up readiness [129, 138, 156, 175, 201]. Wherever possible, standardized tests should be used, because with them the appraisals can be made much more rapidly and objectively [30]. There is no one standardized readiness test that gives data on all factors in readiness, nor does any combination of standardized tests give all the data. So whatever the program of standardized testing, it must be supplemented by teacher appraisals.

Coupled with the results of teacher appraisal of the educational factors in readiness, the results of a battery of measures—including mental ability, reading readiness, sensory acuity, health, and social- and personal-maturity assessments—provide the teacher with information helpful in determining individual readinesses for reading. The battery of tests should include a group mental test and one or more readiness tests. Visual, auditory, and health factors should be appraised by teacher observation for screening and by medical means whenever needed. Teacher appraisals should include assessment of factors in educational readiness, such as backgrounds of understanding, vocabulary, quality and accuracy of speech, ability to attend, desire to read, ability to handle equipment, ability to sense a sequence, and ability to follow directions.

The results of standardized tests and teacher appraisals, in the beginning, form the basis for gaining an understanding of the children and for making adjustments in the instructional program [156]. These appraisals should do much more than give an estimate of which children are going to have trouble with reading and which ones are not; they should tell wherein the sources of difficulty are likely to be. The appraisals, then, should be thought of both as predictive and diagnostic in nature. They should help the teacher gain insight into the instructional adjustments to be made and the readinesses to be built.

APPRAISING MENTAL ABILITIES

Intelligence is related to successful achievement in reading, as it is to successful achievement in all other learning. In a program of developing readiness for reading it is important to have as accurate estimates as possible of the mental abilities of a class group so that the teacher may better know the pupils and so that teaching adjustments may more effectively be made. The results of a group test of mental ability are informative and useful to the teacher in judging the intelligence of the children in his class. Without the help of information obtained from a well-chosen standardized mental test a teacher's estimate of the scholastic aptitude of his class members is an inaccurate assessment of the existing facts.

There is much research evidence to show that the relationship between intelligence and reading success becomes increasingly more pronounced as populations are sampled at succeedingly higher grade levels [21, 196, 253]. The correlation between mental age, as measured by individual Stanford-Binet tests, and reading comprehension at the end of the first grade is approximately .35; at the end of the fifth grade it is approximately .60; during the high-school years it approaches .80. The size of these relationships indicates that factors in addition to mental age are markedly influencing the child's success in reading. Inasmuch as the relationship becomes more marked as the children progress through school, it is apparent that some children who start out relatively slowly in the early phases of learning how to read will later have increased in rate of learning and have outstripped some of their contemporaries. Early success, therefore, is not necessarily an indicator of ultimate reading capability. The mere fact that the child has high intellectual capability does not in and of itself guarantee that he will be successful in reading, especially in the early years.

In those cases where he has questions relative to the results of a group test of intelligence, the teacher should request that an individual test, such as the *Stanford-Binet Test of Intelligence* and the *Wechsler Intelligence Scale for Children,* be given by the school psychologist or other expert in mental testing. It would be advantageous, indeed, if results of such an individual mental test were available to all teachers for all of their pupils. There is little likelihood that so utopian a situation will ever arrive. But in the case of a child about whom the teacher questions the accuracy of the group mental test result, the result should be checked by individual mental testing.

READING READINESS TESTS

Although readiness tests vary, most of them measure the following factors: ability to interpret pictures, follow directions, and work in small groups; linguistic maturity; information about common objects; auditory and visual discriminations, ability to read and name letters and numbers; and motor control. For the most part the tests are group tests. In the case of some of the most widely used tests, one or more subtests are designed for individual administration.

Standardized readiness tests may be administered and scored and the results interpreted by the teacher. Gates [100] has said that standardized readiness tests that have diagnostic and predictive value can be given satisfactorily by a teacher who is skilled enough to give good instruction in reading. The directions for administering, scoring, and interpreting the various readiness tests are so explicit and so well standardized that the teacher should have no difficulty in using such tests.

Many of the children in a first-grade class are not ready to take a readiness test until two or three weeks after they enter school. This is especially true of the children who have not had the advantage of kindergarten experience. In order to take most of the various readiness tests, the children must have had experience in working in groups with other children. They must be able to attend to the teacher as he gives the necessary directions, and they must have some degree of ability to follow directions. In the manuals for readiness tests, it is suggested that the tests be administered toward the end of the first month of school. Here again, however, it is necessary for the teacher to appraise the development of the children in his class to determine when the readiness test should be given. It may be that the class will be divided into groups on the basis of observation and judgment so that the readiness test may be administered to the various groups at different times. Then the test could be given to the children of a group when they have shown sufficient growth in the use of crayon or pencil, in attending, and in working in groups—all necessary for taking the test.

TEACHER APPRAISALS

The teacher's careful and systematic observations of the child are among the most important appraisals to be made, and they must be done by the teacher himself. For example, the *desire to read* is a readiness factor for which there is no standardized readiness test. Therefore, if any appraisal is made of the child's attitude toward learning to read, it is the teacher who makes it. He does this by appraising the child's attitude toward reading when reading situations are present. One child may ask no questions concerning what the print says; he may show no interest in the print on posters, on name cards, or in what signs say; he may show little or no interest in picture books; and he may pay little or no attention to stories read by the teacher. When the teacher has ascertained these facts, he will know that he must develop an interest in reading in this child before, or as, he begins to teach him to read. He makes informal appraisals of the other children by noting their attitudes toward reading when reading situations arise. He will find that some children have very good attitudes toward reading in various reading situations, and he will rate them as *very good* in the readiness factor *desire to read*. Others will seem to the teacher to exhibit *good* attitudes toward learning to read; he will so record their ratings. Still others will seem to him to be *average* in their attitudes toward reading; others will have poor attitudes; and possibly others, such as the child described above, will be rated *very poor* in this readiness factor, because they show little or no interest in reading. Differences in attitudes toward reading reflect the home environment, such as little contact with printed material, unsuccessful early attempts by parents to teach the child reading, or the child's fear that he will lose his oral-reading associations with adults should he become able to read. These ratings, based upon informal observations, enable the teacher to know for which children he should plan instruction to awaken and develop an interest in reading, and they enable him to know the children for whom no such instruction is required.

Questions illustrating those that teachers at various levels of instruction should ask with regard to each child and his readiness are listed below. Any area of immaturity or inadequacy must be adjusted to or corrected in those instances where the answer to a question is negative.

A. Personal Adjustment
  1. Is the child adjusted to the new surroundings?
  2. Does the child feel comfortable in the classroom?
  3. Has the child become acquainted with the demands and customs of the school?

B. Social Acceptance
  1. Is he accepted by his schoolmates?
  2. As his teacher, am I to him an individual worth knowing?
  3. Does he have friends?
  4. Is he invited to share experiences and work with groups in the classroom?
C. Educational Maturity
  1. First grade
     a. Has the child developed the ability to listen?
     b. Can he understand and carry out directions?
     c. Does he enter into class activities and discussions?
     d. Is he able to follow a sequence of ideas?
     e. Does he have the necessary language facility?
     f. Is he interested in learning to read?
     g. Has handedness been established?
     h. Can he use the materials of instruction, including scissors, crayons, paste? Can he hold a book?
  2. Second grade
     a. Has he developed an appreciation of reading as a means of sharing experience?
     b. Does he demand meaning from the printed page?
     c. Has he built a usable sight vocabulary?
     d. Does he anticipate words from context?
     e. Has he noticed that words are made up of sound elements?
     f. Does he consistently read from left to right?
     g. Does he find reading interesting?
  3. Third grade
     a. Has he established feelings of confidence and security in reading situations?
     b. Has he indicated a desire for self-initiated reading activities?
     c. Has he developed a sense of responsibility for contributing to group enterprises?
     d. Is he becoming independent in reading?
     e. Is he able to read orally so that others enjoy his oral interpretation?
     f. Has he started to use previously learned common initial phonetic elements and word endings in recognizing new words?
     g. Is he phrasing adequately?

Many of these questions should be asked and answered about children in grades four, five, and six, as well as additional questions dealing with readiness concepts appropriate to those levels of instruction. The questions, listed above, merely suggest queries about readiness teachers must raise and appraise.

Readiness Factors

A considerable amount of research on reading readiness has been done that is helpful to the teacher [36, 37, 89, 133, 181, 210]. Many factors that make for reading readiness have been isolated and carefully studied [207]. Although this discussion for the most part indicates the relationship of these factors to initial instruction, the teachers at others levels will recognize that the factors are pertinent at their levels of instruction also. Adjustment to these factors at more advanced levels will be a major concern of the treatment of reading growth as discussed in the succeeding sections of this book.

Readiness factors will be grouped and discussed under the headings *mental, physical, social and emotional,* and *educational readiness.*

MENTAL READINESS

In a first-grade class, there is likely to be a wide range in the mental capability of the children, necessitating an adjustment of materials, teaching methods, size of groups, and amount of preparatory work before beginning reading. The bright children can and should be expected to develop faster in learning to read than can the children mentally less well endowed. The amount of preparatory work for some children may be reduced to a minimum [41].

The children of low mental capability can profit from reading instruction, but their growth may be expected to be less rapid and somewhat limited, compared to the reading growth of the brighter children. The amount of preparatory work for them may be extensive, and the length of the delay before beginning formal reading may be long.

The question is often raised, "At what mental age should the child begin reading?" In a few countries where English is the native language, children begin to read soon after the age of five. Is a mental age of five the appropriate one? Throughout the world the more usual practice is to begin teaching reading at six or seven or later. It should be recognized that the earlier instruction is started, the more expensive is the training and the greater are the hazards [44].

Gates [103] has shown that the important question is, "How and what is the pupil to read?" Therefore the problem of mental age really resolves itself into this: "How can the teacher adapt materials and methods to suit the differences in mental functioning found in any first-grade class?"

Briefly, adjustments to differences in mental capability will be made by:

1. Varying the length of readiness instruction, so that some children have almost no instruction, others a month or so of instruction, and others a more prolonged period of instruction.
2. Providing variation in instructional materials, so that for some children the materials would be somewhat demanding, and for other children they would be far less so.
3. Varying instructional procedures, so that for some children the methods would be highly repetitive, concrete, and slowly paced, and for other children the methods would be paced more rapidly and would be more abstract, requiring reflection and reasoning.

PHYSICAL READINESS

The relationships of various physical factors to ability in learning to read are frequently recognized [155]. Among these factors are the sensory capacities of *vision* and *hearing*. If a child has poor vision, he cannot be expected to get clear visual images of words, and therefore is likely to have difficulty in learning to read. If he has hearing difficulties, he may not hear the word patterns well or accurately, and he may therefore get into trouble learning the words.

Among the physical factors less obviously related to learning difficulties, but nonetheless important, are *speech defects* and *health factors,* such as poor physical stamina, faulty nutritional and glandular conditions, recurring illnesses, and unfortunate neurological conditions.

If such physical handicaps could improve merely through the passing of time, it would be well to delay reading instruction until they did improve; however, they do not improve that way. Gates and Bond [108] found that in some physical factors no improvement took place during a period of a year, and in some factors the physical difficulties grew worse. They emphasize the importance of recognizing and adjusting to individual limitations and needs before and after beginning reading, rather than merely changing the time of beginning reading.

1. Visual Difficulties

Visual difficulties of one sort or another are often at the root of failure to learn to read [13, 17, 46, 86, 87, 90, 217]. Children with poor vision, however, do not inevitably become poor readers [95]. Many children with defective vision learn to read very well indeed, whereas children with no visual defects have difficulty in learning. It cannot be said that the child with poor vision will become a poor reader or that the child with good vision will become a good reader. Of course, the child with poor vision is more likely to get into difficulty while learning to read; the teacher should, therefore, be on the alert to detect signs of visual trouble. He should watch for such signs as constantly readjusting the material, squinting, rubbing the head, and giving unusually close attention to the bulletin board or chalkboard to see the pictures or other material. When a defect in vision is suspected, the teacher should recommend a thorough eye examination for the child, including binocular vision. Frequently, more than just the routine visual examination is needed in order to detect a visual difficulty that may become associated with a reading defect.

The teacher should also make certain classroom adjustments. For example, he can give the child with poor vision a seat in the classroom where the light is good and from which the chalkboard and other visual aids to learning are seen easily. He should recognize, too, that reading for such a child may be more fatiguing than for the child with more normal vision. He should be on the alert for signs of fatigue in order to prevent the child from continuing too long with a task requiring close visual application.

2. Visual Discrimination

The ability to distinguish between visual word symbols, such as *horse* and *house,* is essential for effectiveness in reading. The child engages in no other activity that requires as high a degree of visual discrimination as does reading. Although it is true that there are many primary-grade children who find such discriminations difficult, it is fortunate that instruction directed toward systematic observation is effective.

Direct training should be given in seeing likenesses and differences in pictorial and geometric patterns and letter and word configurations. The pictorial and geometric configurations may range all the way from those

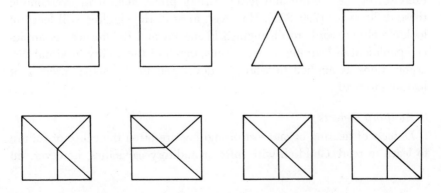

in which the likenesses and differences are very apparent to those in which they are somewhat subtle, as the two series shown on page 27.

The series of letter and word configurations should also range in difficulty from those in which the likenesses and differences are very apparent to those in which they are far more subtle, as:

m	m	o	m
e	e	e	c
b	d	b	b
h	h	n	h

dog	dog	dog	cat
ball	ball	doll	ball
no	no	on	on

Most reading-readiness books contain exercises to develop this ability. The exercises are carefully graded in difficulty. These commercially prepared materials are the work of experts in the teaching of reading; they have been carefully graded in difficulty, and have been critically formulated to give varied experience in visual discrimination. The teacher can prepare additional exercises of the types illustrated above. A more profitable use of teacher time is that of giving help to individual children rather than replacing with material of his own making that which has already been developed. On occasion a teacher may prepare material designed to meet the needs of a specific child or a small group of children to supplement that supplied by the school.

Word discrimination may also be developed by calling attention to likenesses and differences in word and letter configurations of the words in signs, on the bulletin board, and in the stories the teacher reads aloud. The ability to distinguish similarities and differences among items is best developed through making such discriminations in meaningful and important situations.

For some children who have poor visual discrimination, additional exercises of the picture and letter variety prove helpful in overcoming these deficiencies [200, 233]. However, most of the children will learn to look closely at words to distinguish likenesses and differences, as an accompaniment of learning to read. Thus, much of the ability in visual discriminations as applied to words is developed in the actual process of learning to read.

3. Auditory Defects

Defects of hearing of one sort or another are often the cause of failure to learn to read. Children with inferior auditory capacities, however, do not inevitably become poor readers [22, 134, 216]. The responsibility of the teacher is again one of detection. As in the case of vision, he should be alert to the possibility that some of the children have hearing defects. Such actions as inattentiveness, signs of fatigue, turning the head, many requests for repetition of directions, and frequent misunderstandings are signs of hearing trouble. Whenever a hearing defect is suspected, the teacher should recommend a thorough examination of the hearing of the child. He should give the child a favorable seat in the room—one in the center and in about the second or third row. Moreover, he should be sure that the child hears all the directions and explanations. When instruction begins, he should depend more on workbooks and other teaching-testing material with such children than he does with other children.

4. Auditory Discrimination

Most children living in an environment that includes spoken words have developed the ability to make fine auditory discriminations. However, many children have not developed the degree of auditory discrimination necessary for learning to read. They have not, for example, learned to isolate specific sound elements to the degree necessary to find the rhyming words in jingles or to isolate from a group of words those that begin with a specific sound. Such a degree of familiarity with word-sound elements is needed to profit from oral word study and phonetic training.

Inasmuch as the ability to make fine discriminations in the auditory patterns of words is needed, some training in oral word discriminations should be given before or during initial instruction in reading. Here the tasks are to teach the children that words are made up of sounds and to get them to be alert to and to attend to similarities and differences in the sounds of words [54].

The materials are as extensive as the words, rhymes, and jingles that are the common heritage of children. Indeed, the whole vocabulary of the children is the material to be used. As in the case of visual discriminations, the exercises should progress from large gross differences, such as *light* and *lamp* to the more fine and detailed differences found in words of very similar sounds, such as *which* and *witch*. Much of the training in sound perception can come as a concomitant of the games and rhymes that the children encounter in the kindergarten and prereading periods. There are, however, exercises that give drill for children who need additional work. The degree of similarity, and consequent fineness of discrimination, that needs to be employed should be determined by the level of ability of the child. He should in this learning, as in all others, be taken by gradual steps to the level of accomplishment desired. Examples of exercises that have proved helpful in building sound discrimination are:

1. Identifying the wrong word in a series of rhyming words.
   may   play   mat   day

2. Identifying the wrong word in a series of words similar in initial sound.
   hat   has   land   hand

3. Selecting the correct word to complete a rhyme from three or four words.
   The man fed the pussycat
   A little piece of bacon
   meat   fat   rind

4. Finding the words that sounds most like another word, for example, *string*.
   ring   home   play   rat

5. Telling in what way words sound alike.
   run   ring   rat   row
   ball   fall   call   tall

6. Telling a word that rhymes with another word.
   i.e., *dog*

7. Telling a word that begins like another word.
   i.e., *cap*

Such drills are interesting, and children like them. The objective is to get the children to notice the sounds of words in actual conversation and in other meaningful language. Therefore, exercises using pleasant-sounding words in conversation and humorous jingles, and the like, are in reality more effective than the drill devices suggested above.

> Little Miss Muffet
> Sat on a tuffet,
> Eating of curds and whey;
> There came a big spider,
> And sat down beside her,
> And frightened Miss Muffet away.

These exercises as well as the drills should deal with only the most common word-sound elements. Their motivational force is lost when they are used too often or for too long a period of time. In presenting these exercises, all words should be spoken in the normal manner. The words should not be broken up into their phonetic elements, because difficulties in sound blending may result from too great stress placed upon isolated word sounds.

5. *Speech Defects*

The role of speech defects in causing difficulty in learning to read is somewhat uncertain [22, 59, 216, 269]. When the oral reading method of the teaching of reading is given an undue emphasis, the child with speech defects will be handicapped in learning to read. When, on the other hand, oral reading is used in the composite method of teaching, the child with speech defects is not handicapped. Obviously, whenever a child has a speech defect, positive efforts should be made to correct that defect. In the meantime, the child with speech defects, if otherwise ready for reading, should start to learn to read. There is, however, a problem of adjusting the method of instruction, and the methods used with children who have speech handicaps should include those that place oral word study at a minimum.

6. *Accuracy of Speech Patterns*

The major speech defects, such as cleft palate, stuttering, and the like, have been assumed to be more physical and emotional than educational, although some such defects are probably both. There are some minor speech difficulties that are the result of faulty learning. These will be discussed here, although from an organizational point of view they do not rightly belong in a discussion on physical readiness.

Among the more common speech difficulties attributable to faulty learning are habits of poor enunciation, inaccurate pronunciation, and immature speech. Frequently, difficulties in enunciation are transitional. They are caused by the change from deciduous to permanent teeth. Enunciation faults of this sort are remedied automatically when the permanent teeth are well developed. Focusing attention upon them during the transitional period is likely to cause self-consciousness.

As contrasted to those children who have slovenly or lazy speech, children who articulate distinctly are naturally better prepared to continue language development. Often, though, poor enunciation is a pattern of speech assumed because of lack of security in verbal situations. Here, the problem is one of enabling the child to feel secure in the group oral situation. Obviously, such difficulties of articulation should be corrected.

Habits of inaccurate pronunciation include habits of omitting and transposing parts of words, adding word elements, and accenting faultily.

Of course, all children make errors of pronunciation; some, however, are so seriously handicapped by inaccurate pronunciation that they experience difficulty with beginning reading [22]. It is too often true that habits of mispronunciation are fostered and trained by parents and other adults who encourage the use of baby talk. Many first-grade children have immature speech. Faulty pronunciation and faulty use of words as a result of prolonged baby talk should be corrected during the first months of school, and so also should other difficulties in pronunciation, as far as possible, without upsetting the child.

Poor enunciation and pronunciation, under certain methods of instruction, have deleterious effects upon reading. Under methods that lean heavily on oral reading, on the sounding out of words, and on phonetic analysis, the child with minor speech difficulties may get into confusions that cause trouble in learning to read.

Most of the teacher-training institutions of the country have departments of speech where the prospective teacher is given training in speech, for it is realized that the teacher becomes the model after whom all the children pattern their speech. Errors of enunciation and pronunciation are corrected. Attention is given also to other aspects of speech, such as pitch of voice. Speech training should be provided the prospective teacher in order that he may speak distinctly in a well-modulated voice and that he may enunciate and pronounce words correctly.

The unfortunate truth is that some children grow up in homes where words are often mispronounced and frequently poorly enunciated. In such cases, the teacher helps the child with the words with which he has trouble by saying them for him and by helping him check his own errors. Also, during these first days of school he builds in each pupil an attitude of speaking in such a way that the rest of the class can hear and understand what is being said.

In other phases of their preparatory instruction the children learn to discriminate between sounds and to note similarities and differences in the ways that words sound. The alertness to sounds, and how words, parts of words, phrases, and sentences sound, help in making the speech patterns more accurate.

Often, the youngster with inaccurate speech patterns does not know how his speech sounds to others. Where a tape recorder is available, the child may learn of his speech inaccuracies in a dramatic way. Inaccuracies may be pointed out, and a better understanding of the needed correction may be achieved. A recorder has many uses in a school, and it is a valuable piece of equipment for a school system to acquire. Where a tape recorder is not a part of the equipment of the school, one may be lent to the school by a parent for a few days in order that the motivational aid to good enunciation and pronunciation be utilized at this stage of learning to read. Even though a recorder may not always be available, clarity of speech can be encouraged through the use of a mock microphone. The children may give informal accounts of the day's experiences or dramatize a story they have heard or created. The presence of a microphone will tend to encourage them to emulate the clear speech patterns heard over television and radio. It will emphasize the responsibility of communicating distinctly with an audience. At such times, under careful guidance, suggestions may be made to a particular child in order that he may have an evaluation of his growth. The attention of the children may be directed to listening to the enunciation and pronunciation of television and radio performers and public speakers as another way of creating a desire in them to speak clearly and distinctly.

7. Health Factors

The healthy child is better prepared to learn than the unhealthy child. The child who is easily fatigued does not have the energy necessary for continued application to a task. His attention wanders, and his drives toward his goal are not very forceful and not sustained. He is more easily discouraged, and reading, along with other learning, suffers. The various phases of the day's work in learning to read seem unduly arduous to him. If a child is listless and easily fatigued, he should be recommended for a medical examination, and remedial health measures should be undertaken to correct any deficiencies. A medical examination with the prescribed remedial health measures should be recommended for the children who show other evidences of poor general health. For such children, the length of the periods of work should be shortened. Instruction in beginning reading should be delayed until the time that the teacher, in consultation with parental and medical authority, should decide that the tasks will not be too arduous [107].

8. Neurological Limitations

As Bond and Tinker [32] have indicated, there are some children with neurological limitations, such as epilepsy, spastic conditions, chorea resulting from rheumatic or other high fever, and brain damage, who cannot be expected to develop reading capabilities as rapidly as other equally intelligent but neurologically sound children. These limitations are difficult to detect and often come to light as a result of unexplained unsatisfactory results in good reading programs. These conditions constitute a medical problem in addition to an educational problem, and such children should receive medical aid. The teacher must be satisfied with less than usual results. These children should not be kept under sustained visual work [13]. They should be encouraged to relax visually even though that relaxation is only looking up from the printed page every few minutes. Most of these children actually need careful instruction and should be required to do a minimum of reading acts within the classroom.

SOCIAL AND EMOTIONAL READINESS

Not all children who enter school and set about the task of getting ready to read have had serene and happy preschool years. Not all have had wise and consistent parental discipline. Many, having had over-solicitous parents, are far too dependent. Others have been subjected to constant nagging and to frequent thwartings. Other children, having perhaps been deprived of affection or rejected by their parents, have had little chance for becoming personally well adjusted. There are some children who are so mature socially that they adjust easily to the strangeness of the room, to the large group of new boys and girls, and to the teacher. These children feel secure and unafraid. There are others, immature emotionally, who are poorly equipped to adjust to so new and difficult an experience. Of course, the personality development of still others will range between these extremes.

For the child who is emotionally or socially immature and for the child who is insecure for any reason, reading will suffer along with other learnings [102, 128, 216]. Time must be allowed the child to get acquainted with his surroundings, to establish himself in the group, and to become adjusted to the teacher. For many children, these adjustments, along with success in learning to read, are all that are needed. Other children will have to be carefully studied by the teacher. He should not expect to be able to help all these children to obtain social and emotional maturity during the time they are under his guidance. Rather, he can appraise their social and emotional growth and can provide and adapt teaching procedures that will lead them to a better personal adjustment. He can select or prepare situations in which they will have opportunities for successful achievement. He can help them acquire new skills and build toward new learnings so that they will feel greater security and will become surer of themselves and of their capabilities.

EDUCATIONAL READINESS

Children entering school have come from six years of environmental experiences that have given them varying degrees of proficiency in abilities that are related to learning in the initial reading program [107]. Among these experiences are the following:

1. Picture interpretation.
2. Orientation to the printed page.
3. Backgrounds of understanding.
4. Extent of vocabulary.
5. Quality of spoken language.
6. Ability to attend.
7. Ability to sense a sequence of ideas.
8. Ability to follow directions.
9. Ability to handle equipment.
10. Desire to read.

These factors will be discussed in the following paragraphs.

1. Picture Interpretation

Children come to their first day of school with the knowledge that pictures have stories to tell. Their ability to interpret pictures fluently varies considerably, however. They have been to movies and have sensed the sequence of events that the pictures tell. They have watched pictures on television. They have looked at the family photographs and have heard discussions about them. They have followed the illustrations as stories have been read to them. They have been keen students of the pictures in the magazines spread out on the floor before them. Frequently, by the way, they have studied those pictures upside down. They have followed sequences of pictures as comics have been read to them, but have had little opportunity to reconstruct the stories the series of pictures present. Inasmuch as modern reading programs in the early stages depend upon pictures to relate some of the plot and action of the stories to be read and inasmuch as these programs depend upon picture clues to aid in word recognition, the children must develop proficiency in oral interpretation of pictures. Growth in future reading comprehension abilities is begun as the children grow in ability to interpret pictures. Children learn to organize pictures into the proper sequence, they learn to predict what will happen next, and they learn to recall specific information; and, as they do so, they learn comprehension abilities that will be useful to them throughout their lives. Learning to read is developmental. These lessons in picture-story reading are important ones, for they are early learnings in comprehension abilities. From these learnings later ones will be developed in step-by-step sequence.

The prereading program offers many opportunities for developing the ability to interpret pictures. As the teacher reads a story, he displays the accompanying illustrations and encourages the children to discuss them. The children bring, to discuss with other children, pictures they have found in books, magazines, pamphlets, and newspapers, as well as pictures they themselves have drawn. As they grow in ability to get meaning from pictures, they tell the story depicted by a series of pictures. Storybooks from the book corner, such as an illustrated edition of *The Tale of Peter Rabbit* or *Pretzel and the Puppies,* are used for picture-story reading. The children also may develop picture-story sequences of their own. In speaking of interpreting pictures, Lamoreaux and Lee [168] suggest:

> Hand in hand with this experience in interpreting pictures should go the experience of telling a story by means of pictures. Many of the art media may be used, coloring, painting, drawing, cutting and pasting, modeling and others. After the children have an experience of some sort, the natural reaction is to "tell about it" through making pictures if the media are available. It gives them another means of expression, develops their thinking about the subject and is their first means of putting an idea or experience in objective form which may be "read back" by others.

Most modern prereading materials provide many opportunities for picture-story reading. By means of a gradual development, these materials enable the children to become efficient not only in telling a story in sequence, but also in predicting outcomes, in organizing a logical order of events, in classifying information, in distinguishing between fact and fanciful material, as well as appreciating the humor, characterizations, and plot of picture stories.

2. Orientation to the Printed Page

The child may come to school with habits of observing objects and pictures in a random manner. The transfer of these random habits of perception into the reading situation is apt to cause confusion. Reading is probably the only activity in which the child engages that requires a left-to-right orientation.

Most children entering the first grade have difficulty in maintaining the degree of orientation that is necessary to be effective with printed material. Some children find it difficult to keep their orientation even in picture work and in drawing. They have little notion of the fact that the printed page must be read from top to bottom. If, for example, unselected first graders are asked to color a series of four unrelated pictures on a page, it makes no difference to them which they color first. Children versed in reading are more apt to proceed systematically through the page. Such orientation is essential to reading and must be developed.

First, the child must learn to distinguish his left hand from his right.

Personal orientation can be encouraged by playing simple games, such as Looby Lou, marching games, and various other games of direction.

The teacher can help materially in establishing orientation by swinging his hand under the print from left to right as he reads to children. Picture-story sequence material is arranged, of course, to encourage left-to-right orientation. When children draw, paste, and mount stories of their own, care on the part of the teacher may insure a left-to-right orientation. It is helpful, too, to call attention to the sequence as bulletin board pictures, notices, and objects are labeled, as *Our Fish Pond* and *Our Flower Pot*. The *Directions of the Day* notices provide an opportunity for developing a sensing of left to right. The teacher, both when writing information on the chalkboard and when reading it to the children, indicates that they go from left to right and from top to bottom. The teacher should be ever on the alert to see that the children proceed at all times in all their prereading and early reading tasks from a left-to-right and top-to-bottom fashion.

The use of experience charts during the transition from prereading to reading activities is beneficial in developing left-to-right and top-to-bottom orientation. As the children dictate accounts of experiences, they see the teacher writing the experience charts with the proper orientation. In such dictated experiences, they can be easily led to observe that words at all times are written from left to right. The exercises in prereading materials that accompany basal programs are arranged to encourage the proper orientation to printed materials.

3. Backgrounds of Understanding

From the first lesson to the last, reading should be a meaningful process. Instruction must lean heavily upon the backgrounds of experience that the children have. With television, motion picture, radio, and extensive travel, children today come to the first grade possessing vast and rich sources of information and understanding [62]. They have been adding to their understandings daily—even hourly—throughout their lives. They have been refining and enriching their understandings. Of course, many of their understandings are inaccurate, incomplete, and prejudiced.

It would take but a casual overview of the environmental surroundings in which children have lived to show that they have had quite different opportunities to build backgrounds. Anderson and Dearborn [5] draw attention to the difficulties children encounter in learning to read when they have not had the support of a good language atmosphere in the home. Of course, some children in poor environments tap most of the resources and thereby gain a fairly large background of understanding, even though that background is somewhat narrow in scope. Other children in environments of many opportunities have meager and limited backgrounds of understanding, for they may not have had the capacity to avail themselves fully of their opportunities. Obviously, the children in the favorable environments generally stand greater chances of developing broad and meaningful backgrounds. Thus, children of six years of age vary greatly in the extensiveness and usefulness of the concepts they possess. The teacher should learn where any given child is limited in essential concept, because he may then know, in terms of the topics to be handled, what areas need developing throughout the year.

For the class that is limited in any area, it is important to provide opportunities to build knowledges in that area. When each new topic is introduced in the reading program it is a good plan to take time to build concepts necessary for understanding the materials of that topic. Such techniques as the following can be used for building and increasing understandings.

Firsthand Experiences. The understanding the child has acquired has been gained chiefly from his many firsthand experiences. The teacher will find actual experiences very useful in building concepts. Firsthand experiences may be of many and various sorts; for example, the trips that the children take about the school to see the furnace room, the mimeograph machine, and the like; the larger excursions to the neighborhood fire station, the post office, or the village water supply; the experiments conducted in the classroom, taking care of plants, keeping the aquaria, and building a pen for the rabbit so that it can be out in the sun; the experience of seeing the rainbow and feeling the rain, of noticing the leaves fall off the trees, of noting the cocoons and caterpillars; dramatizing an activity, as, for example, selling flowers and plants in school, collecting paper, making the schoolroom attractive, and the thousand and one things that are done around school—around all schools in which children have an active part. It is not implied here that every experience should be directly related to the next reading lesson, but it is implied that the teacher should make fairly certain that among the firsthand experiences will be some that directly build background for topics about which the children will read. Then again, all such experiences contribute to the broad background that is indispensable if reading is to be worth while in the completer sense.

Class Discussions. Discussions in the classroom are helpful in building background. Talking about things has a twofold use: it is a means of building broad general understanding, and it is also a means of building the more specific background that is preparatory to reading on a given topic. Let us suppose the next unit in the reading material is to be "Pets." Before the reading is begun, the teacher starts a discussion about pets the children have known. Not only does this build incentive for studying the unit, but it also has the further merit of promoting the interchange of ideas about the habits, customs, and actions of the pets and descriptions of them. Through the cumulative effect of the many and different experiences that the members of the class have had, the background of understanding pets is increased for the class as a whole and also for each member of that class, including the teacher. Furthermore, such discussions call to mind and make real again experiences that have grown somewhat dim with the passing of time. Children who have discussed, recalled, and relived experiences with pets—their own and others—will be much better prepared to read descriptions of and stories about animals than they would have been if no discussions had taken place.

Reading by the Teacher. The reading of stories and other materials by the teacher is a means of building understanding that every teacher has used to a greater or less extent. This method is among those recommended for building backgrounds for children in the primary grades and is of especial value in the prereading period, when the children cannot yet read for themselves. Teachers at all levels, however, have found that reading interesting and pertinent materials to students is an effective means of building concepts. Teachers should accumulate interesting materials suitable for building understanding.

Visual and Auditory Aids. Such aids as television, motion pictures, slides, pictures, and radio provide excellent means of building background. Many teachers keep a file of interesting and instructive pictures for the children in their classes. Each new group of children contributes to the file. Understanding is gained as the children study the pictures, talk about them, and clarify their ideas and generalize from them. Prereading materials for building meaningful background lean heavily upon the use of pictures and upon discussions and stories about pictures.

Television and radio are valuable media for building concepts. So too are films. Probably the best sources of films for a specific teacher are those listed by state, county, and local audiovisual departments.

Reading. The act of reading itself is an important means of increasing understanding. As the reading ability becomes more effective, this means of building understanding becomes obviously more useful. As the children progress through the grades, therefore, a greater dependence may be placed upon building background by reading. One of the chief ways

that adults have of growing in knowledge and understanding is by reading widely and well.

It can be seen that the building of readiness background is not a task
unique to the teacher of six-year-olds alone but applies as well to teachers
of pupils of any age. It is also the task of the teacher introducing any
topic to be read about.

4. Extent of Vocabulary

Some children come from homes where they hear a wide range of well-
chosen words. They have had many opportunities to talk with others in
their homes, Sunday schools, and play and other social groups. Stories
have been read to them; they have learned nursery rhymes; and they have
been encouraged to handle their ideas in a verbal fashion. As a result,
many words are familiar to them. Their vocabularies are ample for the
reading situations in which they find themselves [105, 106]. On the
other hand, there are children who come from environments of limited
vocabulary. It may be that most of the conversation is carried on in a
foreign tongue, so that the English words they hear are few in number
and often misused. Or it may be that the child is not encouraged to talk.
The home may be one in which the child is to be "seen and not heard."
Such children come to the task of reading with limited vocabularies, often
so limited that the small size of the vocabulary interferes with learning
to read. For all children, continued growth in vocabulary is important.
For some, direct instruction in vocabulary building is imperative.

Most children have oral-recognition vocabularies considerably in advance of the vocabulary needed to understand the initial reading lessons
[164, 197]. As a matter of fact, Anderson and Dearborn [5] comment
that knowledge of the spoken word comes first and sets the standard of
reading achievement that can be reached. This fact is particularly important in the beginning days of reading. Children have been eager students of words and their meanings during their preschool years. It is
incumbent upon the school program to nourish this zest for word understanding. In the initial reading lessons there must of necessity be a control of the words to be recognized visually. This needed control of printed
words is a problem completely apart from the enrichment of meaning
vocabularies. The teacher must do everything possible to keep the children's interest in spoken language alive and expanding while visual
recognition of words is first being made. It must be seen that the teacher
and the children are working in two verbal situations: the first situation
is one of spoken language, where the aim is to make the environment as

expansive as possible; the other, is the one in which there is a controlled, careful development of the new language of printed symbols.

Direct instruction designed to extend knowledge and use of words must be undertaken during the prereading and initial reading stages. The situations provided to build a background of understanding also afford opportunities to increase knowledge and understanding of words. During class discussions, words should be used upon which the attention may be focused and about which the teacher and children may talk. It is in this way that the teacher arouses the *desire to know more about words.*

The skill and art of the teacher of six-year-olds is nowhere more clearly seen than in the ways by which he encourages children to attend to words and to ask questions about them. The skillful teacher builds an awareness of words—a desire to know more about, to understand, and to use the words that are heard.

The oral reading of the teacher gives many chances for increasing a knowledge of words. In fact, many of the passages and stories are selected for the purpose of extending knowledge for specific words and specific concepts. Unusually expressive words may be discussed, as in the conversation between *Christopher Robin* and *Pooh,* in the story *Winnie the Pooh:*

> "I think the bees *suspect* something!"
> "What sort of thing?"
> "I don't know. But something tells me that they're *suspicious!*"*

5. Quality of Spoken Language

The ability to handle ideas in simple accurate sentences is an important requisite of learning to read. This is especially true when the method of instruction leans heavily upon context clues and meaningful reading. The child who is in the habit of confusing the use of the words *come* and *came* would have more difficulty in using the context to help him recognize *came* in the sentence *The girl came to school* than would the child who had no such language confusion. Any first-grade teacher knows that the speaking patterns of children vary greatly. Discussing variability of children in spoken language. Monroe and Rogers [197] say: "The teacher of beginning reading can be sure that her group will include boys and girls of just about every level of linguistic development and that not one of them will conform completely to any rigorously outlined growth pattern. She must become acquainted with each individual boy and girl in

* From the book *Winnie the Pooh* by A. A. Milne. Copyright, 1926, by E. P. Dutton & Co., Inc. Renewal, 1954, by A. A. Milne. Reprinted by permission of the publishers.

her class and learn especially the particular level of linguistic ability which has been reached by each. Only when she knows this can she *start where they are* in leading them from their oral language skills into the skills of understanding printed language." The fact that faulty English is closely associated with trouble in learning to read gives another reason for attempting to improve linguistic facility.

In developing quality of spoken language, the teacher becomes the model for all the children. Again, we find the many opportunities for oral expression provided in a program rich in activities, discussions, and storytelling comprise the materials through which a very important phase of reading readiness is developed. It is through the oral activities within the classroom that the quality of oral English can best be improved. But merely putting children into oral situations will not in and of itself correct gross errors unless language patterns and standards of accuracy are recognized by the children.

The oral instruction should be carried on in an informal fashion. As the desire to improve oral composition develops and as the children accept the responsibility for their own improvement, the quality of their English improves. Neither a completely accurate nor mature pattern of linguistic expression is to be expected. Children should be encouraged to talk in logically organized, complete sentences. Of course, this type of encouragement is a responsibility of all teachers at all levels of instruction. The teacher of first-grade children should not demand more than simple sentence construction. Strickland [258] has found that a wide variety of language patterns are used by first-grade children. Through many oral experiences, coupled with the guidance and example of the teacher, improvement may be expected to be somewhat rapid among children of limited language development.

6. Ability to Attend

In learning to read, it is necessary to be able to attend to what is being done. This implies the ability to look at, to listen to, and to concentrate upon what is being taught. Children differ greatly in their ability to attend. Some children find it difficult to listen to what is being said for more than relatively short periods of time. The same children find it difficult to work with the materials for more than a few minutes at a time. Some children have not yet established habits of applying themselves closely to the task at hand. Other children have not learned to pursue a task to its completion. When a task becomes difficult, they turn to some other activity or they seek aid from an adult. Such children must be trained to follow through with a task even when the task is difficult for them. Often, however, lack of attention is due to the fact that the task is too great or the explanation too involved or because there are distractions in the classroom. The poorer the habits of attention of the child, the greater will the distractions affect learning. Reading, along with any other kind of learning, will be influenced by the amount of attention the child is able to apply to it. If the child is to become an effective reader, his tasks should be well suited to him, the atmosphere of the classroom should be conducive to work, and habits of attending should be developed.

Conditions in the classroom should be such that they foster habits of attention rather than habits of inattention. The room should be free from the distractions of extraneous noises and interruptions, because it is possible to build habits of inattention just as it is possible to build habits of attention.

Teaching procedures too can foster habits of attention; and they can, unfortunately, foster habits of inattention. The procedure, for example, that stops an activity before it is completed or before there is a logical breaking-off point is irritating to children. In fact, such interruptions defeat the goal of attending to an activity until a unit of it is completed or the activity itself is finished. Completing tasks once begun is a habit fundamental to adjusting to the demands of living. It is a habit conducive to learning to read. There are many chances to give positive training in this habit in the daily living of the child in school. Putting away equipment, serving on the committee for feeding the fish, straightening The Book Corner, or any of the numerous duties that should be the responsibility of the children offer such opportunities. The teacher has careful judgments to make. He must nicely balance the difficulties of the task with the capability of the child, so that completion of the task may reasonably be expected.

Another aspect of the ability to attend is that of listening [73]. To make all the children attend to what he says, the teacher will find it helpful to draw the children near him. It is far easier for children to attend by having them sit in a semicircle around him while listening to a sequence of ideas or directions than by having them sit in rows behind desks. The teacher will also find that a calm, low, and well-modulated voice fosters attitudes of attention, whereas a shrill and excited one does not.

It is imperative, when the child is called upon to attend to something either visual or auditory, that the purpose be acceptable to him and that he understand what is expected of him. It is well, when there is evidence of lack of attention, to watch for signs of fatigue. If the children are fatigued, they should not work at activities that call for close attention, because they will give only intermittent attention to the task and thereby actually develop habits of inattention.

Previous sections of this chapter have discussed methods of fostering attention on the part of the child to the sounds of words and to likenesses and differences in the way words look. In the two sections to follow, it will be seen that attending is the first step in sensing a sequence and in following directions. Other activities can be used to further growth in these factors of readiness, and also in countless other activities and incidents of the day: training in looking, listening, and concentrating. For example, when a child digresses in conversation, he may be brought back to the topic at hand. Responsibilities that call for doing or making something may be given to a child, and when it is seen that he digresses, or is about to digress, he can be told to finish the task. After directions have been given to the group, the teacher can rather frequently ask the child who needs practice in attending to repeat the directions to the group. Another useful technique in fostering development of the ability to attend is as follows: before reading a passage or story the teacher may list for the children two or three "things to listen for." The children are instructed that when they know the first "thing to listen for," they are to raise their hands for the teacher to see. When they have listened and heard the second, they are again to raise their hands. Many variations of this procedure, which is often successful in securing the close attention of all the children, may be used.

7. *Ability to Sense a Sequence of Ideas*

In addition to the ability to attend, it is necessary for the child to be able to keep ideas and happenings in a logical order. This ability to sense the sequence of events is important for remembering what has been read and for anticipating what is to be read, both of which are important for maximum comprehension. The ability can be made an outcome of many of the activities commonly used in the early grades. It should be pointed out at this time that the ability to sense a sequence is not matured in its complete form in the early years of the elementary school but continues to grow to the extent that more complex and subtle relationships can be sensed and organized as the child progresses through the educational system. Before the child reads, however, he should be taught to keep simple and logical sequences in mind in order to be able to reproduce such sequences. He should, for example, be able to relate the excursion taken by his class in the order in which things happened. That is, he should tell how they planned to go, how they got there, what they saw, and how they got back to school again.

This ability can be developed in many ways. The telling of experiences, under the direction of the teacher, who may say, "Did that happen next?" or "Didn't something else happen before we did that?" is an effective means of building the ability to sense a sequence.

Another means that has proved to be effective is to have a group who need such practice make up a series of pictures to illustrate the sequence of an experience or a story. These pictures may be held up before the class, one by each member of the group, in sequential order, so that the rest of the class can see them. The child with the first picture tells about his illustration, and when he is finished, he may say, "And then," at which time the story is taken up by the child who has the next picture. Through planning and organizing which event comes first and which second, the children get a great amount of experience in this readiness factor. At another time, pictures may be pasted on a long scroll of paper that is unwound as the story is related by one or more children. This device, often called "class television" by children and teachers, is interesting to the children and gives training in sensing a sequence. A variation of the above device is to paste large illustrations of commonly known stories, such as *Goldilocks and the Three Bears,* on separate pieces of cardboard. These pieces may be first arranged in sequence as the story is told to the children. Then the pieces may be disarranged for children to re-arrange on the chalkboard ledge in sequence, each child having responsibility for one picture. (This exercise also develops the ability to attend.) The experience gives practice in completing a task cooperatively.

Finishing a partially told story gives training in sensing logical sequence, as does also retelling or dramatizing stories that have been told or read by the teacher. One of the best ways of developing the sense of sequence is to be found in planning the day's activities and in remembering what was to take place first, what second, and so forth. The readiness books of the basal series have many picture sequences for the children to study and discuss.

8. Ability to Follow Directions

In order to follow directions, one must be able to attend to them and to sense their sequential order. Moreover, one must know how to put them into operation. Many directions are given in reading instruction. Therefore, ability to follow directions becomes a part of learning to read. Some children are well prepared in this attribute when they enter school, for they have had responsibilities around the home. They have worked with their fathers and mothers in various activities, such as, for example, planting a garden, wherein they have developed the ability to follow directions. This learning, in many cases, has come about as a result of allowing the children to participate in interesting activities around the home.

The situations in the typical classroom that require the children to follow directions are numerous—far too numerous, in fact. The teacher does not have the task of planning and introducing activities that foster this factor in readiness, for it is all too often necessary that the children follow directions as a concomitant of living and working with others in school. Here the task of the teacher is to be sure that the activities of the children are circumscribed by directions and regulations only so much as is necessary. He should be certain that the directions are not so complicated that they cannot be understood and carried out by the child to whom they are given. Then he should be sure that the directions are attended to, that their sequence is understood, and that they are followed.

The teacher can readily see when the child who is following directions in construction activities gets into difficulty and can ascertain wherein the difficulty lies. It may be that the directions were not fully attended to, or that they were too many or too complicated for the child, or that the step-by-step sequence was not understood, or that the motor coordinations needed to complete the task were not within the child's capabilities. When he has ascertained the cause of the difficulty, the teacher can make necessary adjustments to enable the child to carry the project forward to its successful completion.

9. Ability to Handle Equipment

Much equipment is used in teaching reading. The children must be able to handle the usual classroom equipment. They must be able to handle a book; they must be able to use crayons, pencils, chalk, paper, scissors, paste, and other materials. These, of course, are skills that children have acquired to varying degrees and that can be taught. The teaching is more difficult and will take more time in the case of the child who is severely handicapped physically.

In every classroom there are many tools of instruction, many pieces of furniture, and other equipment and supplies that are new to the child. A child could easily become so confused and overwhelmed by this environment, which requires the handling of new equipment and supplies, that he could easily cease being an effective member of the group. This is true especially when it is realized that the various types of equipment and supplies are aids to learning. Because of this, a certain degree of ability in handling materials is a prerequisite to learning to read. Time should be taken to introduce the child to such equipment and supplies as chalkboard, chalk, and crayons, because many children have never had the opportunity to use these materials. Equipment for construction activities will also be new to many of the children, and it will be necessary to teach them how to use such tools as hammers and saws. If the room has movable chairs, the children must learn how to move them about the room quietly and where to place them. The children should be taught that the materials are best used when not wasted, how to put materials away, and how to clean up after themselves, and they should be made to feel a sense of responsibility for the proper use and conservation of materials.

Books are among the universal materials that children should be taught how to use. The attitude that should be developed toward books is that of treating them like friends who are worth knowing and are not to be injured. The instruction in handling books can be conducted in such a way as to make the child feel at home with books without being afraid of hurting them while at the same time being careful with them. The teacher may get a small group together, explain how to hold the book, how to open it, and how to leaf through it. Through the use of The Book Corner, with its classroom collection, the children may be given experience in handling books.

It must be recognized that certain children are immature in motor coordination. They have good attitudes toward handling equipment; they know what the equipment is for; but they do not have the motor coordination required to handle it well. In the case of such children, rhythm games should be used, the gross activities becoming finer and finer as the children develop coordination. Most children beginning first-grade can readily be taught to handle the materials by showing them how to go about using them, even though they have not previously used similar materials.

10. Desire to Read

Most children come into the first grade with the desire to read. In fact, they come to school with the idea that the task of school is to teach them how to read. Although their appraisal of what school is for is fairly accurate, there are differences among the children in the intensity of the desire to read. Some of them will continue to try even though the task is difficult; for others, the motivational force is not so strong. There are, of course, a few children who have little or no desire to learn to read; in these cases, the teacher's task is to make reading ability seem attractive enough to be worth the effort to learn.

Some children have had unfortunate emotional experiences, prior to school entrance, due to unsuccessful attempts to learn to read before they were ready for reading. Many such children have already rejected reading. Children of these types may require some direct help in establishing a desire to learn to read. The class environment almost automatically stimulates such a desire. There are bulletin board notices and other signs in and about the school and classroom that have something of importance to say. Children want to know what these notices say. In school, when they wish to make something, they see the teacher read directions in order to find out how. When they want to know more about some question of interest, they see their teacher use reading as a means of gaining information. They get enjoyment from the stories the teacher reads to them. At times he reads a part of the story and asks, "And what do you suppose happened next?" Then he continues to read so that they may all find out. An older boy or girl from another class may at times come into the classroom to read to them. They like that. They see their own classmates, who know how to read, go immediately to The Book Corner to read whenever they have the opportunity. They themselves look at picture books with enjoyment. They look forward to the day when they can "really" read and do not have to explain, "I'm not really reading, I'm just looking at the pictures and remembering what was read to me."

As the child progresses through the first grade, he grows in his appreciation of the value of reading ability; he realizes that he uses reading as a means to learning in other school subjects. And as he progresses through the elementary school, the secondary school, and college, he continues to grow in his understanding of the role that reading plays in learning. However, individuals vary tremendously in the use that they make of reading and in the understanding of its worth to them. It is the task of every teacher at every school level to help his pupils develop a fuller realization of the usefulness to them of reading throughout their lives.

Selected References

DeBoer, John J., and Martha Dallmann. *The Teaching of Reading*, revised edition. New York: Holt, Rinehart and Winston, Inc., 1964, Chaps. 4 and 5.

Dolch, Edward W. *Teaching Primary Reading*, third edition. Champaign, Illinois: Garrard Press, 1960.

Gunderson, Doris V. *Research in Reading Readiness*. Washington, D.C.: Superintendent of Documents, Government Printing Office, Catalog No. 5.230:30013, 1964.

Lee, Dorris M., and R. V. Allen. *Learning To Read Through Experience,* second edition. New York: Appleton-Century-Crofts, 1963.

Meeker, Alice M. *Teaching Beginners To Read,* Rinehart Education Pamphlets. New York: Holt, Rinehart and Winston, Inc., 1958.

Monroe, Marion, and Bernice Rogers. *Foundations for Reading.* Chicago: Scott, Foresman and Company, 1964.

CHAPTER 3

Introducing Book Reading

The transition from the prereading period to the book-reading period must be a gradual one. It is during the period of transition that groups are formed, that the teacher studies the factors to be considered in grouping, and that the children are trained in the ability to work in small groups relatively independent of the teacher.

It is also during this time that the children are led gradually from the comparatively easy reading of pictures to the much more difficult reading of print. Experience charts are especially valuable in helping the children to make this transition. Therefore, such charts should be used extensively during the latter phases of the readiness program and the initial phases of the preprimer program.

An illustrative experience chart, as dictated by a group of first-grade children, is shown below.

> Our teacher brought some fish to school.
> We put them in a glass box.
> The box is called an aquarium.

Alice and Jim got the water for the aquarium.
Jane and Tom fed the fish.
We saw the fish swim.
We like our fish.

Fish Swim in the Aquarium

During the readiness period the children have learned to look at and interpret pictures. They know that a series of pictures can tell a story. They have read many such picture stories. During the transition period, it is especially beneficial to the pupils for the teacher to read some print to them that they are not expected to read, but which they follow as the teacher reads. In this way the children may learn that reading material tells something more about the story than can be found in the pictures alone. The pictures, for example, cannot tell the conversation of the people pictured. They can depict only sequential actions, descriptions, and the like. The print too may expand the action and in other ways tell more about it than can be shown in the pictures alone. The teacher can demonstrate to the children that print reading has something more to contribute than does picture reading. The children will begin to want to read print as well as just look at the pictures. So it is with other transitional activities.

Handling the prereading readiness books and picture books from the classroom collection will have helped in developing abilities to handle books and materials to the degree required for instruction in book reading. The concentration of the children has been developing, so that they can work for longer periods of time and with less susceptibility to distraction than they could when they first entered school.

Thus, some of the children will have developed the requisite abilities for beginning reading. They will have developed backgrounds of knowledge, ability to look at and read pictures, and a certain amount of ability to work independently in small groups. All of these abilities will be very helpful to successful achievements during initial instruction in reading. Some children will not be ready for systematic instruction as soon as others. They will not have developed enough of the requisite learnings. They will need to have a continued readiness program. Others, who have a fair background of learning, will have to be led into the program of initial instruction more gradually than the group that is most ready. For this middle group, the teacher will have to be concerned about continued growth in readiness factors as well as initial instruction in reading.

Grouping Pupils for Preprimer Instruction

There are differences in the extent to which children have the abilities necessary for initial instruction in book reading. There are no clearly defined dividing lines among the members of a class that enable a teacher to say. "This group is ready," "With this group I must proceed slowly," and "This group is not yet ready." Unfortunately, reading readiness is not a simple state of affairs but is made up of many factors. In considering whether a child is ready for initial instruction in reading, the teacher must have weighed his progress in the many characteristics discussed earlier.

One child, for example, may seem, in comparison with the class as a whole, to be advanced in such things as background of experience, ability to handle equipment, ability to follow directions, and mental age, but he may actually have trouble expressing himself. Perhaps he comes from a home where a foreign language is spoken. His linguistic patterns may be poor. The teacher, after weighing these facts, may plan to start book reading with him because he is nevertheless high in many other fundamental factors. The teacher recognizes, however, that instruction must go rather cautiously and that much attention must be given to the development of his oral language. Thus, for this child, instruction in book reading must proceed slowly. Many opportunities must be given him to talk about his reading experiences so that his linguistic capabilities may be improved. The reading experience provides excellent opportunities for the development in language to proceed rather rapidly. Consequently, this boy should receive oral-language instruction as reading instruction progresses.

Another child may be relatively low in many of the readiness factors. Although it is true that he can handle equipment fairly well, that physically he seems to be well developed and able, and that his mental ability is about average, he is low in background of experience and knowledge of vocabulary. He also has enunciation and pronunciation difficulties. The teacher, upon weighing these facts, decides that this child should be given more opportunity to build a general background and should be given further help in listening to and saying words. Therefore, he believes that it is wiser in the case of this pupil to continue the readiness program for a longer time rather than add the burden of beginning book reading to the tasks that already confront him.

Another boy in the class may measure high on the readiness and mental tests, and may be able to handle equipment well. Although he is hesitant about expressing himself, he uses especially good English when he ventures to make a contribution. In other ways, the teacher has sensed that this able child is very insecure; that is, he is unsure of himself and his abilities. He is immature socially and emotionally. He needs to learn many new skills so that he may gain confidence in himself. The teacher feels that the child will succeed in learning to read and thinks that success will do more for his personality adjustment than other therapeutic measures. So, after weighing the evidence carefully, the teacher decides that this child should begin book-reading instruction. If it were possible to teach the children, one at a time, taking into account each child's strengths and weaknesses, the task of starting instruction would be relatively easy. In the typical classroom situation, with some 30 children, all of whom have unique patterns of strengths and weaknesses, it is impossible to work with each child individually as much as is to be desired. The teacher, therefore, must form instructional groups, bringing together the children who need somewhat similar instruction. If these groups are relatively small, the teacher can make individual adjustments within the group as he carries forward the instruction. It must be recognized that merely forming groups does not meet the problem of adjusting instruction to individuals. It does, however, enable the teacher to work with a smaller number of individuals at any given time. The success of teaching is especially dependent upon the ability of the teacher to adapt instruction to the individuals within each group.

It is recommended that the teacher at the start divide the class into several flexible instructional groups. The number of groups will depend upon the kinds of instruction that the teacher feels the children need. However, many teachers find that three groups is a workable number to deal with. When the teacher divides the class into three groups, he appraises their instructional needs. He may find, for example, that five children fit into one instructional group, and 15 children should be placed in another, and the remaining ten or so should form a third group. When it is suggested that the teacher may find it expedient to divide his class into three groups, it does not, of course necessarily mean that he should divide the class into thirds.

The results of reading-readiness tests and teacher appraisals do not give anything like perfect prediction of a child's probable success in learning to read. Certain youngsters will be misjudged and misplaced. As reading instruction progresses, they will begin to show their abilities. Therefore, constant readjustment and realignment of the groups are inevitable. The groups are not to be thought of as fixed or permanent but are to be considered as a flexible class arrangement that enables the teacher to work with smaller numbers of children at any given time. Needless to say, the better the estimate of each child's capabilities arrived at during the prereading period and testing program, the more effective the outcome of group instruction.

A usable three-group organization is one that places the children in groups according to the likelihood of success in their learning to read. The first group under such an organization is made up of children who, like Sally, are likely to succeed readily in reading in the usual program. From the very beginning of the school year Sally showed leadership qualities. Quickly, other children sought her out to help them. Sally is a well-set-up girl physically. Apparently, her senses function normally. She is conscientious, attentive, and eager to do what is expected. Her language patterns are good. She seems fascinated by words and uses them well in conversations. The mental test results indicate superior mental ability. On the reading-readiness tests all her scores were in the upper fourth on national norms. She is able to read all the letters of the alphabet, can write her name, and can recognize many words. Her teacher judges that Sally will be able to read third-grade material fluently by the end of the year. The teacher estimates that Sally will do a large amount of individual personal reading. He realizes that before long he must add some additional, more mature books to the classroom collection of books to meet Sally's needs. Sally will work with the top reading group for skill development and on her own for personal reading growth. The teacher believes that this well-adjusted, capable girl will find school tasks interesting and vital; he knows that he must be sure she is challenged to learn in relation to her capabilities.

Helen is one of the more mature members of the class. Physically, she is attractive. She seems to hear and see normally. She makes overtures to other school children in an outgoing manner, but nonetheless is somewhat inept in adapting socially to them. Recently, her home situation has changed abruptly due to the separation and divorce of her parents. She has a fairly wide vocabulary and varied conceptual backgrounds. She is of high-average ability. Her scores on a readiness test were somewhat above average. She is able to name some of the letters of the alphabet. She is not able to read print, but has shown an interest in books and in reading. She is able to grasp and enjoy the substance of a story. One day while reading *Angus and the Duck* the teacher paused to ask the children, "What do you think happened next?" Immediately Helen gave an imaginative and good prediction. The teacher judges that Helen ought to be placed in the top group, at least temporarily.

The second group is comprised of children who will find book reading somewhat difficult and for whom minor adjustments must be made. This group can begin book reading soon after the first group starts and can be expected to come along nicely with but little continued readiness work.

Charles did reasonably well in the readiness tests. He shows no apparent sensory limitations. He is an energetic boy, of seemingly well-adjusted personality. He told of his experiences camping and fishing on a lake during the summer. He presented the ideas clearly and understandably, although with some linguistic immaturities. He gets along well with other children. He carries out instructions somewhat better than many of the children. He has shown an interest in books. He listens attentively to the teacher when she reads aloud. The teacher feels that Charles will be best assigned to group two and that he might be one of the leaders of that group.

The third group is made up of children, like Fred and Kathy, who in all probability will for one reason or another find book reading too difficult to be undertaken during the first month or months of the school year. Fred is one of the oldest and largest of the children. He is awkward and boisterous. He uses his superior size to bully other children, and he is not accepted by them. The mental test results indicate less-than-average mental ability. On the readiness tests Fred's scores were the lowest in the class. He failed to recognize any of the letters of the alphabet. He has shown no interest in books or reading. He is inattentive. Directions must be simplified and repeated for him. The teacher knows that Fred must be led gradually and skillfully through a reading-readiness program and preprimer and related activities. It would be disastrous to plunge him into primer work, chart work, and phonetic analysis. Kathy is pale, is easily fatigued, and tends to stay quietly alone much of the time. She seems socially immature. One day she brought a book to class to show her teacher, but she refused to share the book with another child. She is an only child, cared for by her grandmother while her mother works. Kathy cries easily when toys or playmates will not respond as she wishes them to. The teacher has requested a hearing test to determine whether or not there is an auditory deficiency, for Kathy often acts as though she has not heard him. Kathy is of average mental ability. On the readiness tests her scores were among the lowest in the class. In linguistic development Kathy is retarded. She rarely speaks and almost never listens. She seems unable to carry on a conversation with either a child or an adult. Clearly Kathy needs careful nurturing toward greater emotional maturity before beginning the complex task of formal reading. The children who will make up the third group have greatly varied needs, but none of them should begin reading until more readiness has been developed in background, perceptual skills, abilities, and knowledge.

It is sometimes wise to have the doubtfully classified children work with two groups. This avoids the danger of permanently retaining a child in a group not suitable for him. A child, for example, who seems to be almost ready to read in a preprimer can work both in the second and first groups. Or a youngster in the second group may get additional readiness instruction by working with the third group.

The following instructional pattern shows the way many successful teachers have organized the time allotted to systematic reading instruction.

GROUP ORGANIZATION

Group	First Time Segment	Second Time Segment	Third Time Segment
A	Work with teacher on basic instruction.	Independent of teacher work on material closely related to basic instruction.	Independent of teacher work on group or individual projects.
B	Independent of teacher work on group or individual projects.	Work with teacher on basic instruction.	Independent of teacher work on material closely related to basic instruction.
C	Independent of teacher work on material closely related to basic instruction.	Independent of teacher work on group or individual projects.	Work with teacher on basic instruction.

The actual amount of time devoted to the three parts of the program will vary from day to day and from group to group. Indeed it is often desirable to have no group work on a particular day. Rather, the teacher may work with the entire class upon a specific reading skill, or the class may share the independent reading that has been done. At another time the teacher may meet with the entire group to develop a chart about an experience in which the class as a whole participated. Nor is it necessary that he meet with each group each day. He might wish to give direct instruction in some interrelated reading skills to the children in the most advanced reading group, for example. In this case, the teacher might have the two other groups work independently during the entire time customarily devoted to reading. Comfortable routines should be set up that would enable a child, occupied with independent work, to come to the teacher to say, "I don't understand what I am doing!" In other words, even though the teacher may be giving direct instruction to the children in one group, it should be permissible occasionally for a child from either of the other groups to seek help from his teacher.

When the children have been divided into groups, it is necessary to train them so that they may work well by themselves, as a group, for longer periods of time and at more detailed work than has been demanded of them in the past. The teacher will probably find it expedient to start this training by working relatively independently of the most able group. This can be done in the later stages of the prereading period, somewhat as follows: The teacher may take aside the children who are to make up Group A. He should carefully set some goal for independent work. He must be sure that the purposes for the work are acceptable to the children, that the children understand how to arrive at the goal, and that they know that the goal can be achieved through their independent endeavors. Then he should leave the children to their own resources; but while he works with the remainder of the children, he should observe the work of the first group to see which ones of the children are in need of more careful directions the next time they are to work independently. In this way, by gradual steps, by increasing the difficulty of the task, and by increasing the length of the period of independent work, the teacher can train the first group to work without his close supervision.

The first independent group work might be the performance of some duty around the classroom, such as the building of a rabbit hutch, or putting the supply closet in order. Then the group might be allowed to go to The Reading Corner to "read" some picture books. Later they could be made responsible for preparing a chalkboard mural that might depict an experience they have had. Prereading books too provide excellent opportunities for developing habits of independent work. No matter what type of independent work is to be done by the children, the teacher needs to plan very carefully. He must be sure that the undertaking is well within their capabilities. He must be sure that the assignment given is well understood. Time taken to explain the project and to assure that each child knows what is expected of him is time very well spent. The suitability of the undertaking and the adequacy of the assignment determine in no small measure the effectiveness of group work. It is of especial importance that clear, concise, nonhurried, and complete directions be given to those pupils who are beginning to learn to work in groups.

When the more advanced group of children demonstrate that they can work well in a group without close supervision, systematic training in book reading may begin. Training the second group to work independently may proceed in much the same way. Such training may begin whenever the teacher feels the children are ready, but it should proceed somewhat more slowly.

As reading instruction progresses the teacher will need to work closely with each of the groups as the instruction demands. The teacher should be certain that independent work is planned for the two groups that are not under his immediate instructional care. The success of handling groups rests upon the adequacy of establishing purposes for the independent groups and upon the explicitness of the directions by which these goals can be reached. Success depends also on the suitability of the assignment in regard to length of time, difficulty of task, and availability of material that can be read independently by the pupils. Group work requires careful preparation and planning on the part of the teacher. It is the preparation for the independent work, as well as the efficiency in establishing the learning situation of the group with which the teacher is working, that insure success in group instruction. The adaptations of class organization to meet this problem will be further discussed in the section of this book devoted to adjusting to individual differences.

Introducing Book Reading

The prereading program developed a general background of understanding. In the beginning phase of book reading for any group it is necessary to build a larger background, one related to the selections to be read. Each child is given a book and is allowed to look at the pictures. Then the children are encouraged to talk about the pictures so that they can build an understanding of the happenings within them. The teacher gives the names of the main characters shown. In the discussion he repeatedly uses the words that are going to be introduced in the reading so that the children will be familiar with them in the sense in which they are going to be employed. The children should be familiar too with the specific concepts that are to be presented in the first story.

Sometimes as we work with these beginners we fail to recall their different and varied backgrounds of understanding. Let us suppose that the first story has to do with one or more activities of a boy named Jack and his dog. There is apt to be a child in the class who when he hears *Jack* thinks of the little baby who lives next door to him. *Baby* and *Jack* are for him almost synonymous. Here he is asked to change his understanding of Jack, for *Jack* is a big boy, dressed in boy's clothes, running and playing with a dog. For another child, *Jack* is an uncle, a grown man who lives in a big city. He has an adjustment to make if he is to understand the *Jack* in the first reading lesson. A third child's only contact with *Jack* is the word *jack,* when his father fixed a flat tire.

It will be important during the discussion of the pictures to make sure that faulty conceptions are corrected and that lack of understanding is eradicated. This type of preparatory activity should be continued for each new selection on up through the grades. Specific backgrounds of understanding must be developed. Knowledge of specific vocabulary must be built. The teachers' manuals usually give good suggestions on how to carry on the specific background development for the series of books being used by the group. It is worth the teacher's time to get hints and suggestions from such manuals.

The usual first selection of reading material is short and simple, rarely more than four or five pages in length, and introduces few new words. It is concerned with the common experiences of boys and girls of first-grade age, activities that are to be followed throughout the first year. Universality of experience, as well as reasonable variation in the activities of the youngsters about whom the children will read, have been considered in the choice of materials. Usually, the boy and girl are introduced, and some story or incident is told about them, mainly through the pictures but with some accompanying reading matter. The pictures in the initial selections carry much of the story, and the words are so closely allied to the picture story that they can usually be read by the children. The teacher's major tasks during this time are to introduce the words in a meaningful fashion so that the children have contextual clues to aid them in reading the words and then to repeat those words until they become the nucleus of a sight vocabulary. The words should be recognized as whole words. It is detrimental to future reading growth to have the children sound out words in the first lessons. After several pages have been read, initial lessons in phonic and other word-recognition techniques are started. When a line contains more than one word, the teacher should demonstrate the necessity for a left-to-right sequence in looking at the words. He should explain to the children, right at the start, that reading must be done in this fashion.

Each teacher's manual gives suggestions about how to introduce the first word and how to conduct the initial book-reading lesson. The teachers find these suggestions very helpful in formulating their own approach.

While the children are reading the material in the preprimers, a great deal of the work takes the form of discussion. There is much telling and talking about the stories. Backgrounds are always built before a new selection is introduced.

In addition to building backgrounds, word knowledge, and recognition skills for reading, the discussion enables the teacher to set real purposes for reading the material. In the early reading experiences of the children, the goals must be somewhat immediate so that the immature reader can see his way to each goal. The reason for reading may be "to see what the dog is going to do." Or "to see what Jack said while he was building the house." Or "to learn the name of the dog." The goals in the beginning lessons, thus, are immediate and real. The ability to read toward more remote goals is one of the capabilities that develops as the child increases in reading ability.

As the child progresses through beginning reading materials, he increases very rapidly in ability to read for more remote goals. Even at the end of the first year of reading instruction, the typical child is able to read upon a topic whose completion will take considerable time. The teacher, at every level, whether the child is able to read toward near or remote goals, must take time to make sure that the child does have a goal for reading and that the goal is acceptable and real to him.

After the background has been built for reading a unit and the purposes for reading a selection within the unit have been clearly defined, it is important that the child read material that is relatively free from word difficulties for him. Most modern readers have carefully worked out vocabulary controls so that the child will not encounter many new words in comparison to the number of words he actually reads [105]. In various ways, mentioned earlier, the child is prepared for reading those words. In fact, he has been either given the name of the word or has been led to recognize the word before he meets it in his purposeful reading activity. When, however, he does have trouble with a word, that difficulty should not be focused upon as a difficulty. At this stage the teacher should tell him the word or lead him to recognize it from the content or by comparing it with known words. He should imply through his actions that it is quite natural and perfectly understandable to forget a word now and then. It is well to allow the children to do much of the purposeful reading as silent reading. The silent-reading work should, of course, be accompanied by a large amount of oral discussion. The stories and incidents should be told and talked about. There should never be the tendency to hurry the child through the material in order to get on to the next lesson. The children should be allowed to think through and think about the story until they themselves are ready to go on to the next undertaking. Many listening, writing, and speaking experiences should accompany reading instruction at all levels. Unfortunately, these language experiences are sometimes neglected in beginning instruction.

In spite of the great care that is taken to make the basal reading program a consistent and carefully controlled development, in which words are introduced with extreme care, there is apt to be an unduly heavy vocabulary burden in the primary grades. It should be recognized that the seemingly oversimplified preprimer material, on the basis of unknown words per total number of words, is for the child reading it the most difficult material he will ever meet. For example, the following illustration of a simulated first story of a first preprimer will be seen to be difficult for the beginning reader, because the four different words of this six-word selection are all new to the reader. In addition, one of these words has a variant ending.

> Jack.
> Jack runs.
> See Jack run.

The child does not do all of his reading in the basal reader itself; in fact, the basal reading is a relatively small part of the total reading. There are many supplementary materials—science, social studies, number, children's story, and pamphlet materials—all with their own vocabulary burdens. Unfortunately, there frequently is not enough relationship between the nicely controlled vocabulary in the basal reading program and the heavy vocabulary burden in the rest of the child's reading. Great care should be taken during the primary years to limit as much as possible the tendency of the supplementary program to make reading development difficult, if not impossible, by the introduction of too many new and difficult words.

During the preprimer stage, the child's reading should be confined to preprimers, workbooks, or prepared material that uses the same or nearly the same vocabulary. Much of the topical-enrichment material and personal material should be read to the child by the teacher. There is a wealth of material written for, but not to be read by, children of these ages. The children in reality need many repetitions of a somewhat limited and controlled vocabulary if reading instruction is to be effective. This is especially true before independent word-recognition techniques are developed. Even though word-recognition techniques are introduced from the very beginning, sufficient development of these techniques for independence in recognizing new words takes place only after the children have had a considerable amount of experience with reading. Therefore, the early reading of lessons in science, social studies, and arithmetic should either be delayed, integrated with the basal reading program, or presented in picture form.

Selected References

Gunderson, Doris V. *Research in Reading at the Primary Level.* Washington, D.C.: Superintendent of Documents, Government Printing Office, Catalog No. 5.230:30008, 1963.

Harris, Albert J. *Effective Teaching of Reading.* New York: David McKay Company, Inc., 1962, Chap. 3.

Monroe, Marion, and Bernice Rogers. *Foundations for Reading.* Chicago: Scott, Foresman and Company, 1964.

Russell, David H. *Children Learn To Read,* second edition. Boston: Ginn and Company, 1961, Chap. 7.

Tinker, Miles A., and Constance M. McCullough. *Teaching Elementary Reading,* second edition. New York: Appleton-Century-Crofts, Inc., 1962, Chap. 20.

THE TEACHER USES
DIVERSIFIED METHODS
OF INSTRUCTION

Principles of
Reading Instruction

It is important that the program of instruction be carefully controlled, because both the attitudes toward reading and the habits formed persist. There are some principles of teaching, helpful in building favorable attitudes and proper habits, that should be adhered to regardless of what methods are used. These principles necessary in the proper teaching of reading constitute preventive measures against the development of seriously retarded readers. They will be discussed in the pages to follow.

THE CHILD SHOULD NOT EXPERIENCE
REPEATED FAILURE

Time should be taken to develop readiness for reading and to ascertain when instruction in actual book reading should be started for various children. Even more time and care should be taken to insure success in the initial phases of book reading. The teacher, for example, should exercise patience in giving his explanation on how to go about each of the tasks of learning to read. His manner should be calm, cool, and matter-of-fact. He should give careful attention to the organization of his explanations, so that they will be given in a way that the children will understand.

Extreme care should be taken to prevent failure in reading, with its resulting confusion and frustration in the school life of the child. The child who has gotten into difficulty with reading tends to avoid reading, and in that way he gets into more serious trouble unless classroom remediation is undertaken. Such failure has deleterious effects not only upon progress in reading but also upon the personal and social adjustment of the child. If he is allowed to get into difficulty, and if that difficulty is allowed to persist over a period of time, a reading disability of a serious nature may result. There is a good chance that such a poor reader may develop a serious psychological problem, which will be apt to become too difficult for a teacher to correct. It is important, then, for the teacher to take care to prevent any difficulties at the outset and to be sure that none persist.

THE PROGRAM MUST BE STIMULATING YET FREE FROM UNDUE PRESSURE

Usually, a desire to learn to read is present when the child enters the first grade. Even his young mind senses the worth of knowing how to read. Most children are eager to expend time, effort, and energy in gaining so worthwhile an ability. The desire to learn to read is often fostered in the readiness program and should continue to be fostered throughout the entire elementary school. A child may be expected to continue to work actively to learn to read only when what he is required to do seems to him useful and vital. If he loses his desire because the program is tedious, boring, disappointing, or actually distasteful to him, little progress can be expected. If the program is based upon material that is interesting in content and style, if the child gets along well in the program, and if he is aware of his progress, there will be little difficulty in making the reading situation pleasant for him. Reading itself seems intrinsically valuable and desirable to children. They like the materials, and they enjoy the sense of achievement that their growth in reading ability brings them. It is relatively infrequent that the teacher must resort to artificial incentives, for by and large a well-functioning reading program is in itself pleasant for the children. Any signs of distaste for reading usually indicate that something is fundamentally wrong with the reading program itself or with the child's progress in it.

A classroom environment that is rich and vital, one that uses reading in most of its enterprises, fosters growth in reading. Children are earnest learners; they react to a dynamic environment by attacking their reading tasks with energy and eagerness. Such an environment intrinsically gives the drive necessary for comfortable growth in reading.

There is a tendency on the part of some teachers to kill the very spontaneity the reading environment fosters by pressing the child too severely. The major objective in such cases seems to be to get through much material rather than to develop proficiency in reading. It is quite normal to expect children to develop in reading at different rates; no child should be unduly hurried or allowed to lag. The question is not how much material has a given child covered, but how soundly has he developed reading capabilities, attitudes, and interests and how adequately has he maintained the desire to learn.

METHODS SHOULD BE ADJUSTED TO INDIVIDUAL NEEDS AND CAPABILITIES

Even in the early lessons of reading there are wide differences among the pupils in ability to learn to read. Many of these differences should be isolated and made apparent in the readiness program. It is evident that the children cannot be expected to learn to read at a standard and uniform rate. Therefore, the method of instruction must be one that encourages individual rates of growth.

The adjustment of instruction to individual differences is much more than a method. It is an attitude [171], an attitude in which the teacher assumes that each child has the right to progress as rapidly as he is capable of doing, that each child can expect the school to provide for his rate of learning be it slow or fast, and that each child can expect the school to study him as an individual and to help him when he is in difficulty. Anyone with a belief in dealing with the children as individuals would have but little in common with the teacher who said that his greatest problem in teaching a class in reading was to keep the children on the same lesson in the same book; with the teacher who has the children read aloud in turn, paragraph after paragraph, page after page; or with the teacher who penalizes the good reader who reads ahead because he cannot wait for a slow reader to unfold the story for him; or with the teacher who assumes that there is one best method for teaching all children. The attitude of adjustment of instruction to individual differences can be accomplished only with methods and classroom procedures that are in keeping with and that make possible the full use of differences in ability to learn. It becomes the teacher's responsibility, then, to select and adjust his methods so that they make possible adaptations of instruction in reading to individual differences, which are so apparent among children.

Severely handicapped children learn to read and profit immeasurably therefrom when they are in programs that recognize their limitations and make adjustments to them. A child who is hard of hearing can be expected to learn to read equally well with other children if he is given a favorable seat in the classroom, if care is taken to be sure that he hears the explanations, and if the methods used in teaching him are those that make use of visual rather than auditory analyses of words. The child with poor vision may be expected to learn to read if he is placed where he can see the chalkboard and other visual aids, if he is seated where the light is good, and if suitable print is used. Periods of prolonged reading, resulting in possible fatigue, should be avoided. In word-analysis techniques, pupils with minor eye defects may profit from the usual approaches. Gates [102] suggests, however, that the larger elements, such as syllables and root words, rather than small details should be used to reduce the amount of eye work on each word as much as possible.

The physically handicapped child should not be held so long at a task as to fatigue him. Frequent short periods of instruction result in reading growth, keep interest kindled, and yet do not overtax the strength of the child.

Just as limitations should be recognized and provided for, so should strengths be recognized. If a child, for example, has unusual artistic ability, he should be encouraged to develop it not only for his own benefit but also for the enrichment it affords the class. Opportunities should be provided that enable the child of marked linguistic ability to grow even more facile in that respect. He may participate in writing dramatizations growing out of the reading and perhaps direct their production. The child with marked grace and agility may express what he is reading by dancing with creative rhythms. The child skilled in argumentation and debate or in oral presentation should reflect over and communicate in his own words what he reads. The reading program too, by wise choice of challenging materials and procedures, should enable the intellectually able child to grow in reading ability at a rate and in a way proportional to his intellectual superiority.

Adjustments of method of instruction, of lesson organization and class procedure, and of reading materials to their limitations and strengths enable all the children to learn to read.

INSTRUCTION IN READING SHOULD BE SEQUENTIALLY ORGANIZED

As mentioned throughout this presentation, growth in reading is developmental. The learning of each new skill and ability depends upon previous learning. Just as one does not attempt to teach a child to hit a baseball before he knows how to hold a bat, so one does not attempt to teach a child to read before the child knows how to hold a book right side up.

In order that smooth development in reading may be maintained, there must be a gradual, well-organized sequence. Organization is necessary to lessen the hazard of omitting essential skills and abilities on the one hand and of overemphasizing them on the other. The introduction of a new skill or ability is more likely to be preceded by requisite knowledge when instruction is organized.

In developing reading, the teacher should make every effort to introduce gradually new skills and abilities. Before the child can be effective in looking up words in the dictionary, he must know the alphabetical sequence. He must learn the processes of alphabetizing words, that words in the dictionary are arranged first by the first letter, then by the second letter within the words, then the third, and so on. At first, the child is taught how to alphabetize by putting him into situations in which successful accomplishment depends on alphabetizing only the first letter of each word. Then, in a later learning situation, he can be made to understand that a correct alphabetical sequence can be achieved by considering the order of the first and second letters of each word. Later still, the learning situation should require attending to, in addition to the first letter, two or more letters. At that time, the child can be led to formulate a generalization about alphabetizing. More permanent learning will result when the child is led to discover for himself the generalization than when he learns the generalization by rote memory. It is difficult for an adult who has led the child through such a sequential process to sense that learnings as mundane as alphabetizing may be exciting discoveries for the child and, at the same time, be fraught with hazard. All learning in a process as complex as reading has its own sequences that fit into the larger sequence. To order learning in haphazard or opportunistic fashion is to flirt with reading disability. By a gradual development with relatively slow and easy steps, the child learns a whole set of techniques that enable him to become somewhat independent in his reading. Obviously, the child should not be hurried through this development, or through any other development, for that matter. The child should be given time to assimilate the new learnings. Many experiences should be provided for using each new technique and for reviewing each previously taught technique.

The rate at which a given child progresses through the sequence depends to some extent upon his preparation, background, and capabilities. The sequence is important, but the rate at which a given child goes through it depends entirely upon the rapidity with which that child learns the skills and abilities the materials are designed to teach. There is not and never has been a teacher of any specific level of reading. The teacher is a teacher of children who have individual needs. He teaches each child at the point in the continuum of skill development where he is and helps him develop from that point on in accordance with his needs and capabilities.

In the discussion of teaching alphabetizing in its early aspects the processes were made meaningful to the child in order that he discover the generalization rather than learn it by rote memory. If learning of the processes of reading are to become permanent acquisitions, these processes too must be understood by the child. He should be led to see the place of a process in the sequence and its utility to him as a reader.

When the child discovers that the context can aid him in recognizing a new word, one word-recognition technique has been made meaningful for him. A discovery of that sort makes him a more productive pupil than he was before he sensed the utility of context clues. A generalization to be discovered from the preceding discussion is that learning is effective when the child is led to see the relationships of each new process to his total reading growth.

SYSTEMATIC AND CONTINUOUS APPRAISALS SHOULD BE PROVIDED

It is axiomatic that new learnings develop out of previous ones. Particularly is this true in the developmental learnings of reading, because each learning experience is rooted in previous ones and flourishes best when the previous ones are well established. Before beginning the development of new learning, it is necessary to evaluate achievement in those learnings upon which the new one is to be based. Appraisal of growth in technique, skill, or ability must be a daily part of instruction in reading. Many appraisals are informal in nature, made by teacher or child, in order to know what was accomplished during a period of reading. Before any reading is done, a reading purpose is formulated by child, group, or teacher. When the reading has been completed, the child, group, or teacher determines to what extent the purpose has been met. In that way an appraisal is made.

From time to time, appraisal, either teacher-made or standardized, is needed in order that a more formal evaluation may be made. It is necessary to supplement the daily appraisals with more systematic ones. The systematic ones may follow the development of a new technique, skill, or ability in order to ascertain gaps in the learning process so that corrective or reeducative procedures may be initiated before the child progresses to more advanced phases of reading. More systematic appraisals are necessary to measure growth in several techniques, skills, and abilities in terms of their interrelationships in order that one ability not be overemphasized at the expense of another. Such appraisals yield profiles of the reading abilities of each child. These profiles enable the teacher to plan instruction that will help the children to develop further in those several aspects of reading growth.

Both teacher and child profit from the results of measurement. Knowledge of development enables the teacher to proceed in a fashion more enlightened than he would be able to proceed without that knowledge and so makes for more progress. Awareness of progress brings reward to the child and motivates him to work more purposefully and energetically toward greater development.

Both teacher and child can have a better understanding of the reading accomplishments and of the areas of reading growth that need more concentrated attention as a result of systematic appraisals of reading growth.

There is nothing that stimulates success as much as awareness of success. Knowledge of accomplishment in previous learning enables work toward new learning to be wholehearted and enthusiastic. As children grow in reading ability, they should be acquainted with that growth in order that they may be encouraged toward more growth. The methods of instruction should be such that they make frequent appraisals possible. Then the child may follow his progress, and the teacher, as well, may know of the child's growth.

One device that enables the child to follow his progress is a dictionary in which the child writes words as he becomes able to read them. The child sees the words under each letter of the alphabet increase as the days pass, he feels he is learning many new words that will help him to read more easily and fluently.

Reading a sentence aloud to the teacher without error constitutes an appraisal and enables the child to realize that he is learning to read. Or the reading of a paragraph to answer questions about its contents may constitute an appraisal and furnish a means of acquainting the child with his progress. In other words, methods of instruction should include frequent informal appraisals of one sort or another, the results of which should be made known to the child.

The reading program constantly puts the child into more and more difficult situations. As he progresses through this sequence of development, he may lose sight of his growth because the new materials are making new demands on his reading. It is well occasionally to have the child read a selection that, earlier, he read with difficulty, so that he may demonstrate to himself his growth. The child reading a second reader, for example, may be surprised to find how easily he can read the primer that the year before he found difficult to read.

THE PURPOSES FOR READING
SHOULD BE ACCEPTED BY THE CHILD

The child should feel that there is a real reason for him to read the particular material at that particular time. The reason may be that it is going to answer a question that is important to him, or that his reading will enable him to make a contribution to his group, or that he is going to get enjoyment out of reading the particular selection.

Reading situations should be a natural outgrowth of the enterprises of the class. The pupils, for example, may have read in their readers an introductory story about bears. They may wish to explore the life and habits of bears somewhat more fully. One child may wish to find out where bears may be seen at the present time. This may lead the teacher to suggest that he can find out something about his question by reading a story about a bear in Yellowstone Park. That provides the child an acceptable purpose for reading. Other children may think that a certain story about a bear would be good to dramatize. They may read the story again to make a list of the characters that will be necessary for a dramatization. This purpose for rereading the material becomes real and acceptable to those children. Or again, the children may have to do some preparatory work for the reading of another story. They may need to work on some words that are difficult. The children know that in order to read the story with interest and without trouble they must be able to recognize the new words in it. So they approach this reading situation with the real and acceptable purpose of studying those new words.

As the child gets older, purposes may become more and more remote. The amount that can be read to reach the goal increases with growth in reading. In early reading instruction, the purpose for reading is often an immediate one, such as, "Read the next sentence to learn the surprise that father has." Later on, the child may read a page to find out how the mother robin builds a nest. Later on, he may read an entire presentation to find out how a rocket works. Still later, he may read an entire book to find out how to teach the child to read!

In any one unit, there are remote goals that result from pupil-teacher planning and more immediate ones that give purpose for reading a selection within the unit. Within the larger framework of reading about the westward movement, for example, a child may read the story of a family's trip by covered wagon to find out how a wagon train was formed. The overall purpose within the unit may have been to get an appreciation of the significance of the westward movement. There are certain children who could not sustain interest in the more remote purpose were it not for the more immediate day-by-day purposes. The adjustment of the remoteness of goal is one important means of adjusting reading demands to the varying maturities of the children. As the child matures in reading, the immediate purposes take a place of lesser importance, and the ultimate goal for reading assumes more importance.

CREATIVE USE SHOULD BE MADE OF THE RESULTS OF READING

The children should make active use of the results of their reading. The creative use may be of many sorts: it may be motor activity, linguistic or artistic creation, constructive work, or purely reflective evaluation. Whatever the use, it should be a natural outcome of the reading and compatible with pupil-teacher planning. Having the children write stories of their own is an illustration of using linguistic activities to further growth in reading. Children who have written stories enjoy reading them aloud. In that way they get experiences in writing and at the same time more experience in reading. Again, telling stories they have read in story hour helps develop their linguistic facility. This activity results in the careful reading of the stories that are to be told. Thus, linguistic activities may aid in the development of reading, and the reading program may have important linguistic outcomes.

The use of dramatic activities has proved to be an effective incentive for reading. For example, a television dramatization of material prepared from a story that has been read develops linguistic and dramatic abilities, and is at the same time an effective means of developing both oral- and silent-reading abilities. Listening comprehension is also an important outcome.

The children's art work is often used in conjunction with reading activities, with mutual benefit to both. Children may draw murals that depict the themes of a story they have read. Or the teacher may use drawing pictures as a means of appraising how carefully the children have read some material. The use of such picture work gives an incentive for reading. In turn, reading gives the children something to say through art. The artistic expression of what is read is a worthy outcome of the reading activities.

Construction work gives definite help in developing certain types of reading ability, namely, sensing a sequence, following directions, and reading to get a visual image of what is read. Construction activities give the children real purposes for reading material that tells of the activity and at the same time gives them experience in reading and in doing the construction activity itself.

It is possible for reading instruction to be so limited and circumscribed that no opportunity is given the child to develop initiative. Not only is it true that opportunities are lacking for developing initiative, but also the child is not permitted to use what initiative he does have. Such rigidity of instruction is to be deplored.

In most of the reading that children undertake, learning such things as factual knowledge, vocabulary, and concepts is constantly increased and developed. When the purposes for reading are real to the child, the reading program develops these broader educational aims as well as the ability to read.

PROCEDURES SHOULD FOSTER BOTH COOPERATIVE
AND INDIVIDUAL READING

Democratic living within the classroom implies that problems are solved cooperatively. Reading instruction is related to the cooperative solving of problems in two ways. First, it makes a contribution to this solution as does any other means of getting information. Reading is in this respect a fundamental tool in democratic procedure. It is good for the children to have these sorts of life-preparatory experiences. Second, the cooperative use of reading fosters growth in reading itself. The class, working on a unit cooperatively, determines purposes and outcomes expected from the study of the topic. Not only are purposes clarified and outcomes determined, but also the children, working together, clarify partially understood concepts and explore more material than is possible if each works alone. They also help each other with the reading of difficult passages, obtain accurate understandings, and reach their goals more adequately than could any one child working by himself. Two children, working as a team to clarify their understanding of a passage, are shown in the accompanying picture. Frequently, the individual working within a democratic framework assumes a higher degree of responsibility and becomes a more energetic reader than he would if he were reading for himself alone.

The individual needs reading experiences that are purely personal, such as searching out the answer to a specific question of interest to him. His interest may be in meteors, an interest perhaps not shared by others of the group. He should have opportunities to explore this area

through reading as well as opportunities to explore other interests that may or may not be shared by others.

READING INSTRUCTION SHOULD BUILD
INDEPENDENT READING HABITS

Reading instruction should be such that the children learn to be independent readers and workers. Methods of reading instruction should teach the child to be an independent learner even during the beginning days of learning to read. By learning to work individually and in small groups for longer and longer periods of time independent of the help of the teacher, the child begins to develop work habits that will be useful from the first grade throughout all his days of school and in his life beyond.

In the beginning, the child may follow through to completion some relatively easy tasks that require him to work independently of direction for only a short time. As the child gains in ability to work independently, the tasks may be made more difficult, so that their completion requires a longer period of work on his part. It is important for the teacher to be sure that the purpose for reading is so well defined that it does not have to be redefined. Let us assume that the child is working in a workbook upon exercises that require him to find the relationship between pictures and short sentences. The teacher must be sure that the child accepts and understands what he is to do. Then the teacher should see that he proceeds with the task without further help or guidance.

Growth in independence is developmental. Such growth should be started and fostered at the outset; then when the child becomes more mature in reading, he is prepared to do more difficult tasks with a minimum of direction on the part of the teacher. In the upper grades and the high school, the child's development should have proceeded to the point where he can work independently of the help of the teacher toward remote goals.

All too soon, too, the child who is now learning to read will later be away from the guidance and help of teachers. Before many years he will be dependent only upon himself in his reading activities. The instruction that fosters habits of independence from the outset is instruction that is preparing the child for life away from the school as well as more effective life within the school. It is to be desired that long before he leaves school the child will have learned habits that enable him to read independently, such as independence in locating information, in learning the meaning of words that are new to him, in applying the use of reading to his problems, and in sharing reading experiences.

READING INSTRUCTION SHOULD BE EFFICIENT INSTRUCTION

Reading methods should be used that make it possible for all the children to be growing in mastery of reading during the time devoted to learning to read. Round-the-room oral reading may be very wasteful of the time of both children and teacher. Likewise, a method of instruction that places too much dependence upon experience charts may be wasteful. Much time may be consumed in the preparation of reading material that, when it is prepared, is often of relatively little value for reading, because the children have long since memorized its content.

As an example of efficient instruction, let us look at a classroom in which each child has a real purpose for reading and is reading material suited to his level of reading growth. Such a classroom is a busy and efficient place. The teacher, freed of the task of keeping the children quiet and at work, is able to give individual instruction. Here, much growth in reading ability is taking place.

As an outgrowth of reading some interesting stories in their basal readers about early Americans, the children might be led into the desire to read about other great Americans. They might set up some definite objectives to be met in reading about these Americans, such as who each American was, the times in which he lived, what he did, and why he is considered a famous American. With these questions in mind the children might decide to study some famous Americans, grouped as follows: great musicians, great writers, great statesmen, great explorers, great pioneers, great inventors, and great scientists. The members of the class would be divided into working groups, each group being responsible to the class to get a list of men who could be called eminent contributors to the American scene. The members of each group, working together, could determine the answers to questions that had been formulated. In the culminating class discussions, each group could tell about the great men it had studied. Finally, the class could consider the more general question of how these great men had contributed to the enrichment of our lives.

At the outset, the teacher would have to know what topic was going to be handled and would have to have assembled considerable material. Such a unit in the fifth grade would make use of the wide range of reading abilities that are found within that class. The children, for example, who had seventh-grade reading ability could read biographies of seventh-grade difficulty about the great Americans with whom they were concerned. The children with second- or third-grade reading ability could read much simpler, but nevertheless interesting, materials about the lives of the men whom they were studying. Thus, the teacher not only would have assembled those books on great Americans that were definitely suited to children of fifth-grade ability, but he would also have selected books over a wide range from second- to ninth-grade reading levels. Through the proper allocation of these materials to the children equipped to read them, the teacher would not only have several times as many stories, discussions, and biographies about these great men, but he would also be enabled to make use of the reading abilities of the most able and the least able readers within the class. These children, reading at their respective levels, would profit markedly from this opportunity. The best reader in the class might find his material challenging and even somewhat difficult. The poorest reader in the class would find material that he could read. The reading ability of both of these children would be developed more than if each was attempting to read fifth-grade material. And, of course, the culminating discussion would be the richer, because in preparing for it the children would have consulted a wide range of material.

That method is effective, then, that employs the total range of reading ability within a class, that has the children reading toward real purposes, that makes them put forth their best effort, and that has a central theme so that all of the children profit in background and understanding from the reading of each member within the class.

AMPLE, WELL-GRADED MATERIALS OF MANY TYPES SHOULD BE USED

Whatever method of instruction is used, the materials should be carefully graded so that the vocabulary load and the concept load will not be too difficult for the child. Certain methods of instruction, such as too great dependence upon experience charts with uncontrolled vocabulary and an uncontrolled number of ideas and concepts entering into the material, are apt to cause reading disabilities that are unwarranted and unnecessary. Naturally, material produced slowly and carefully by an expert writer is better for the beginner than is material that is either dashed off each evening after school or hurriedly written during the pressure of the school day by an inexperienced writer. The experienced writer can give consideration to word difficulty, to the number and difficulty of concepts, to children's interests, to continuity and accuracy of thought, and to presenting sentences that are grammatically correct as well as being printed in easily read print. Material prepared by a primary teacher, or by the children and the teacher, has the merit of usually dealing with the activities and interests of the particular group of children who are to read it. And for that reason, such materials, on occasion, may be prepared and used in reading activities with profit. However, there should not be too great dependence placed upon the use of this type of material. Rather, the preferred material should be that which is expertly prepared.

The child should be furnished with ample material that is relatively easy for him to read in order that he may enjoy reading as the adult does. Although it is important for much of the material to be relatively easy, from time to time the child must have material with which he has to "tussle"; but there should always be a reasonable chance that he will win the tussle.

Not only should the material be in keeping with the child's reading development and his reading interests, but it should also give him many types of reading experiences. Reading is a complex process. Each type of reading makes its unique demands upon the individual. Each purpose for reading requires its particular combination of skills and abilities. Therefore, from the outset an increasing number of types of reading situations should be presented. At first, the reading will be centered around stories with simple plots. Gradually, as the child matures in reading, these stories will tend to deal with scientific, historical, or social subjects. Soon the materials of these fields will become factual in style.

Even in the early days of reading growth, the child reads for varied purposes. At one time, he reads to follow the exact directions in a workbook; at another, he reads to anticipate toward what a series of events is leading; at still another time, he reads to visualize a scene that he wants to draw; at another time, he reads to organize some factual material to present in class discussion. So from the earliest reading experiences the child encounters a variety of materials. As he progresses through the program, the materials do and should become more specific in nature. Even while the child is learning to read simple story types of materials, the teacher may prepare the child for other types by reading them to him and by showing him that factual information may be got from reading.

There has been a tendency to use story material to the exclusion of other types. This has been carried to the extreme in instances where the fourth-, fifth-, and sixth-grade basal reading programs contain only materials of the story type. The use of story materials has been emphasized to the point that it is possible, by means of reading tests given in the sixth grade, to predict ninth-grade achievement in English but not in any other discipline [20]. This is truly an unfortunate state of affairs.

THE READING PROGRAM AND THE CHILD'S PROGRESS SHOULD BE INTERPRETED TO HIS PARENTS

Aside from the child and the teacher, no one is more interested in the child's progress in learning to read than his parents. The parents all too often have no knowledge whatsoever of the child's progress in school. All too often too, the parents know little about the reading program. It is unfortunate that those who are so concerned about the child and his achievements should be so uninformed about them. There is great need for closer cooperation between parents and teacher, so that the former may know of the objectives, plans, and procedures of the latter.

The parent, in his attempt to understand the reading program, compares the way his child is now being taught with the way he thinks he was taught. Naturally and fortunately, methods of teaching reading have improved immeasurably since his day. The usual parent, knowing nothing of the need for readiness instruction, fails to understand why his first-grade child is not immediately plunged into the task of learning to read. The parent is frequently confused also when, for example, a neighbor child is singled out for individual testing and his son is not. Great progress has been made in dealing with individual differences since the parent attended school. Many parents have little or no conception of the fact that in the classrooms throughout the country today the child is often dealt with as an individual in contrast to the former practice of dealing with 40 children in a class as an entity. As a result, the parent feels that his child is at times neglected and at other times, perhaps, singled out for unusual attention.

Whatever the teacher does to enable the parent to learn of the activities of the reading program and of the progress of his child in developing reading capabilities should result in an enlightened cooperation between parent and teacher in carrying forward the program. Parent-teacher meetings provide one avenue for enlisting the aid of the parent. A visit to the home of a child is another way by which the teacher can acquaint the parent with the objectives of the reading program. The child may demonstrate to his parent his progress in reading by participating in a reading activity during a time set aside particularly for visit of parents to the school.

Informative materials about the school's program of reading may be prepared for distribution to parents and other members of the community. An attitude cordial to members of the community—to their questions and suggestions—should exist at all times. Such an attitude often clears up confusions, brings about closer cooperation, and enables children to progress in reading more normally than when pressures are exerted that run counter to objectives the school is attempting to achieve.

Selected References

McKim, Margaret G., and Helen Caskey. *Growth in Reading,* second edition. New York: The Macmillan Company, 1963, Chap. 2.

Russell, David H. *Children Learn To Read,* second edition. Boston: Ginn and Company, 1961, Chap. 17.

Smith, Henry P., and Emerald V. Dechant. *Psychology in Teaching Reading.* Englewood Cliffs, N.J.: Prentice-Hall, Inc., 1961, Chap. 3.

Strang, Ruth. *Helping Your Child Improve His Reading.* New York: E. P. Dutton & Co., Inc., 1962, Chaps. 1 and 3.

Whipple, G. "Characteristics of a Sound Reading Program," *Reading in the Elementary School,* The Forty-eighth Yearbook of the National Society for the Study of Education. Chicago: University of Chicago Press, 1949, Chap. 3.

CHAPTER 5

Current Approaches
to Reading Instruction

The teaching of reading has been studied by many people over a period of many years. The modern approaches to reading are the results of research in the field of reading, the science of linguistics, the psychology of learning, child development, and numerous other areas. Research has suggested modifications of method that have been given empirical tryout by teachers in classrooms throughout the nation. It has been found that no one specific method is suitable to all children, to all teachers, and in all reading situations. Probably in no case in practice is any method used in its pure form to the exclusion of others.

The discussion of current approaches to reading instruction will be organized as follows:

1. The phonic approach.
2. The linguistic approach.
3. The augmented Roman alphabet (initial teaching alphabet) approach.
4. The language experience approach.
5. The individualized reading approach.

81

6. The topical unit approach.
7. The combination approach.

THE PHONIC APPROACH

The phonic method teaches reading as primarily a matter of sounding out words; that is, it is a sounding-blending approach. Under this method of instruction, the child is usually given ear training to make sure that he attends to and learns that words are made up of individual sounds. He then is taught the most frequent beginning sounds of words, the most frequently used vowel and consonant sounds, and some of the more important phonic blends. In the strictest application of the method, initial instruction is limited to drill upon these elements. After the child has some familiarity with these elements, the elements are combined into words, and the child sounds out the words. The words are then combined into sentences. Theoretically, in reading the sentences, the child resorts to phonetic analysis only as needed [3, 56, 84, 104, 187, 211].

Some proponents of the phonic method emphasize the importance of starting with single-letter sounding [250]. Single-letter sounding could be called the *c-a-t* approach. Others teach the consonants unseparated from the vowel. This approach may be identified as *ca-t* [131]. Others teach the initial consonant sounds separate from the word families. [184, 234]. This approach may be identified as *c-at*. Which of the three approaches a given program uses can be ascertained by noting the way in which words are separated in the beginning lessons.

It is assumed in instruction under phonic methods that through the learning of sound elements the child develops a system of word recognition that makes him an independent recognizer of words. Modifications of these approaches are used extensively today. A phonic method is usually used in combination with other current methods [248]. As a sole method of reading instruction, it has limitations; but in combination with other methods it has much usefulness. It is not a question of whether phonetic analysis should be used; it is a question of when phonics should be introduced, how much phonics to use, and whether this aid to word recognition is taught so that it will be used effectively in real reading situations.

Another difference among the methods of developing phonic capabilities is concerned with how these capabilities should be taught. In strictly phonic programs the teacher presents the individual letters or other phonic elements and tells the children how they are sounded. The children by rote-memory drills learn to associate the sounds with the letters. The teacher also indicates the phonic rules, which the children again are expected to learn and apply. In the typical developmental program the children are led to discover the sound-symbol relationships within words and are then given sufficient drill on applications of their discovery of these relationships to enable the knowledge to become a permanent part of their reading equipment. In these programs the phonic generalizations as well as the sound-symbol relationships are learned through discovery coupled with practice on their applications.

THE LINGUISTIC APPROACH

In recent years materials developed by linguistics are appearing on the reading scene. Linguists, students of spoken language, have recently extended their observations to the visual representations of language. The linguists have brought some degree of order out of the diversification of the spelling representations of separate sounds present in spoken English language [66].

The approach to reading recommended by many linguists is one that progresses from regular spellings of sound elements through semiregular to irregular [16, 18, 160, 176, 275]. The initial stage is the transfer from auditory signs to visual signs. A suggested sequence entails the following: (1) learning to visually discriminate between letters of the alphabet and short groups of those letters (Fries [96] suggests that the letter shape should be limited to "unadorned capitals," pointing out that telegrams have been typed in this way for years); (2) learning spelling patterns, where print is used as the language "signals." In reality the child learns to change from auditory signs for his language signals to a set of visual signs for the same signals. An exercise, given by Fries [96] is:

AT—CAT
CAT—RAT
A CAT—A RAT
AT—CAT—RAT—PAT
PAT A CAT   PAT A RAT

The linguists contend that later on the child responds to the visual patterns so automatically he attends to the meaning and can read for comprehension and that still later he reads fluently and creatively.

The linguists are making a contribution to reading programs by indicating variations and irregularities in spelling patterns and by suggesting that regular patterns be used as much as possible in the early stages of teaching symbol-sound associations [236]. Another contribution of the linguists is in the area of the syntactical structure of language itself [66]. The structure of language used by elementary-school children and that used in basal materials has been compared to determine whether the language patterns that exist in each are similar. The findings [66] indicate that the spoken language patterns are considerably more advanced and diversified than the language used in the reading materials. More study is needed to determine whether or not a greater diversification of the syntactical structure of the language of basal and other reading materials would place too great a burden upon the children's immature reading capabilities [157].

THE AUGMENTED ROMAN ALPHABET (INITIAL TEACHING ALPHABET) APPROACH

An interesting innovation to teaching beginning reading instruction that is receiving much research attention is one that uses, in a two-stage approach, a modification of the orthography of the instructional material. The first stage is that of teaching reading by a newly designed adaptation of the augmented Roman alphabet, in which the attempt has been made to represent the basic sounds of the English language by 44 symbols. The basic consideration is to overcome the irregularities in traditional spelling of English. The fact that one letter in traditional orthography can stand for several sounds and that a sound can be represented by many spellings results in confusion in learning to read. The seeming irregularities make the possibility of discovering and using phonic generalizations difficult. These 44 symbols are designed not only to afford consistency in spelling words but also to approach as nearly as possible visual similarity to those words as they would be printed in traditional orthography. The child is introduced to reading in the initial period of a year or so using material printed in the expanded alphabet. When he has gained a degree of fluency and confidence in reading the modified alphabetic materials, the second stage, reading traditional orthography, is begun. From this point on the child progresses in reading through customary instructional materials.

The following illustration indicates that the goal of designing an alphabet that is both consistent in spelling and similar in visual word patterns to the traditional print forms has been largely achieved [260].

Research workers [77, 78, 180] report that children learn to read more rapidly and with fewer disabilities when using the modified alphabet. They report also that the transition from the augmented Roman alphabet to the traditional alphabet is made relatively easily. Indeed many children are reported to have read supplemental material in traditional orthography on their own with no apparent difficulty [79]. Much experimental work is being done at the present time to ascertain the efficiency, the

ted and maggi

ted and maggi wer at ʃhe beeɦ.

ʃhæ wer haviŋ a picnic at ʃhe beeɦ.

ʃhæ wer plæiŋ in ʃhe sand.

ted and maggi went cliemiŋ œver ʃhe rocks.

ʃhæ found a treʒuer ɦest.

ted and maggi wer very happy.

Reproduced by permission from Teachers Manual 1, *i/t/a Early-to-Read Series by Mazurkiewicz and Tanyzer, 1963, New York, Initial Teaching Alphabet Publications, Inc.*

problems, the long-range results, and the ways by which these materials may be used most effectively.

THE LANGUAGE EXPERIENCE APPROACH

Another approach to initial instruction in reading recognizes and capitalizes upon the interrelationship that exists between reading and the other language developments of the growing child. Under this approach reading is thoroughly integrated with the teaching of other language skills. In general, the sequence of development progresses from listening and speaking experiences to writing and reading experiences and then continues with total language development toward more mature capabilities.

The language experiences used are the outgrowth of a stimulating class environment where children have many opportunities to create and share ideas through the use of language. A child may explore a problem that interests him as an individual. The onset of reading instruction in this language matrix takes place when the children dictate accounts of their experiences, ideas, and interests that the teacher writes for them either as experience charts, chalkboard presentations, or personal charts. Under this approach the children soon discover that "reading is just talk written down."

Soon after shared writing is introduced, the teacher initiates instruction in vocabulary development, word recognition, and other reading skills. Lists of words, both group and individual, are accumulated. From these lists, exercises using words of high frequency and those illustrating word-recognition principles are prepared by the teacher. Doing class book exercises and reading dictated accounts offers sufficient repetition to develop a sight vocabulary without restricting the vocabulary to high-frequency words alone [174].

Concurrent with the development of word-recognition skills the children start independent writing. Soon they no longer need to rely upon dictating their stories to the teacher but can write about their experiences on their own. Before long children are able to read self-selected and teacher-guided book materials [174].

In using the language experience approach, the teacher, as he works "with individuals and groups in the extension of skills, must remember that steps where a measure of independence has been achieved need continuing exercise. *None is ever finished!*"[174]

Unquestionably, the language experience approach has contributions to make to reading growth. Most successful teachers of reading make daily use of listening, talking, writing, and reading about daily experiences, especially using this approach during the prereading and transitional phases of reading instruction. They also closely ally reading with the other language arts through the reading program. It would be unfortunate indeed to neglect the language development outcomes that result from interrelating the speaking, listening, writing, and reading phases of language growth.

Considerable research is being conducted on the steps involved in the transition from speaking and listening to writing and reading in order to investigate the degree to which a greater emphasis than usual would facilitate reading growth [4, 52, 122]. Modifications of this approach appear to be useful in teaching the reading of English to children for whom English at the start is a second language. In some instances the children are taught to read their first language and at the same time are given training in listening to and speaking English. Only after they gain stature in both aspects of spoken language and in reading their own language is reading and writing of English introduced by a modified language-experience approach. This approach is being used with culturally deprived children, apparently with some success. In this circumstance more attention is given to developing mature language patterns prior to and concurrent with the introduction of reading than is usually given. There is also apparently a greater need for instructional concern about associating the spoken and written language than is usually needed.

It appears that more attention to the relationships that exist between reading and other aspects of language is appropriate for all children. The language-experience approach, as a part of the diversified instructional procedures, has a useful role to play.

THE INDIVIDUALIZED READING APPROACH

Another method of reading instruction used enthusiastically both by teachers and pupils in some schools is a completely individual one in which each child selects his reading material, paces himself, and keeps records of his progress [92, 172, 186, 212, 226, 277]. Under this method, used even in grade one, each pupil reads widely materials of his own choice, even when his choice seems unsuitable to his teacher. The child is allowed to set his own pace even if it means he reads relatively little over a period of time. Once or twice a week the teacher meets with the child in a pupil-teacher conference for five or ten minutes. The teacher uses the conference time to find out what the child has read since the last conference, to evaluate by means of carefully thought out questions the degree of comprehension, to take note of special needs and difficulties and give specific help with these, and to keep a careful record of the child's reading capabilities and needs and his developmental progress. The teacher guides the child, to some extent, in future choice of material [278]. Occasionally, the teacher groups the children who have the same reading need into a temporary special group to teach them the required reading skill or to provide classroom remediation. Also, there are often small-group or whole-class sharing periods during which one or more children share with the other children material selected for that purpose [65].

Individualized reading is another of the attempts to adjust to the wide range of reading capabilities in any one class and to the differing rates at which children achieve in this complex learning. A large amount of reading material at many levels and on many subjects in the classroom collection of books is an essential feature of an individualized approach to reading. To satisfy the classroom demands for quantity and variety of reading matter, an excellent school library is essential also [98]. Children in first grade have read as many as several hundred books in their first year of school.

Some teachers use basal readers in an individualized program to provide for each child some skill-development materials that are presented in systematic progression. When this is done the child continues to work individually, to proceed at a pace comfortable to him, to explore a wide variety of additional material, and to select the material he will read.

In addition to need for many and varied classroom reading materials, other factors that determine the success of an individualized program include: (1) size of class—an individualized program is unwieldy if the class size is large; over 25 children in the primary grades has been found to be too large; (2) competency of the teacher—the teacher must know the sequences of skills in reading development and must be competent in providing systematic instruction in these developmental sequences. Further, the teacher must have a wide acquaintance with children's literature. A beginning teacher is apt to find himself deficient in this respect.

The teacher must be sensitive to the needs of each child. One value that accrues from an individualized program is that each child has the undivided attention of the teacher for at least five or ten minutes each week. The children gain comfort and pleasure from these conferences and are said to profit the more because of these feelings. Actually, a child in an individualized program may get more of the personal attention of the teacher than he would were he in a basal reading program even when the time allotted to each child is only ten minutes each week [118].

Good recordkeeping on the part of both the teacher and pupil is an essential part of this program. Enthusiasm and confidence in the teaching method on the part of the teacher is required. For children who cannot read well enough to work on their own, many activities of a nonreading variety, progressing toward reading, must be developed and provided.

Sartain [225] has come to the following conclusions in regard to the individualized method of teaching reading, as a result of his and other studies:

1. Under certain circumstances the individualized approach can produce adequate growth in general reading ability.
2. Especially competent teachers are needed to guarantee the success of the individualized reading.
3. Less capable pupils are less likely to achieve well in an individualized situation, because they are not able to work independently for long periods.
4. Children usually read more books in the individualized program.
5. The personal conference between the pupil and the teacher is especially productive of favorable reading attitudes.
6. Individualized reading frequently fails to provide a well-planned sequential skills program. As a result more extensive reading has not paid off in greater gains in reading abilities.
7. Totally individualized reading is extremely wasteful of teacher time.
8. The most defensible procedure is to incorporate the strengths of individualized reading into an excellent basic program.

THE TOPICAL UNIT APPROACH

The reading program may be organized into topical units. These units are carefully planned by the teacher so that materials at various reading levels can be assembled. Thus, each child can read material suited to him and can thereby make worthwhile contributions to the total class enterprise. The units are introduced in such a way that the purposes for reading are real to the children. With this approach, the entire class reads upon a given topic. First, background materials are read by all the pupils. Then, subtopics are selected to be studied further.

With the help of the teacher, who knows the available materials and the instructional needs of the pupils, groups are formed. Each group deals with a phase of the larger topic. For example, the topic in the second grade might be *Our City Helpers*. The children would talk about the work of such persons as the fireman, the policeman, the postman, and the paper boy. Then groups would be formed so that further reading about these community helpers could be done. Each group would consider the duties of one of the helpers and of his contribution to the community. One boy who could not read very well might get most of his information from pictures. An able reader might read material of third- or fourth-grade reading difficulty. But all the members of the class would be considering the same topic, *Our City Helpers*, and each would be able to make his contribution about the topic to the group thinking. Moreover, each child would be reading, at *his* reading level, materials that were suited to him and for purposes that were real to him.

The topical unit approach has much to recommend it. In the first place, it may be effective when it is well organized. The organization of the class and the organization of the material are logical and easily understood by the child. When such organization is accompanied by careful explanation as to how to go about the task at hand so that the whole process is meaningful to the child, learning is even more effective.

Another factor that makes this method a good one is that it is possible to adjust the materials to the various reading abilities within the class. When a topic such as *Our City Helpers* is under consideration, materials of several grade levels and materials that deal with many phases of the topic may be assembled for the children to read. Reading from many sources in varied materials by the members of the class enables the treatment of the topic to be far more interesting and meaningful than it would be if each child had to read precisely the same material as the others read. More than that, having available materials of various reading-difficulty levels makes it possible for all to read and to contribute.

Well-defined goals that are real and acceptable to the child may be formulated. Reading to find the duties of the postman is a real purpose. It is an acceptable purpose for most children of primary age, because they are fascinated by the life of the postman even to the point that they want to be a postman when they grow up.

The child can see his progress toward the achievement of a goal. He knows, for example, that his job is to find what the postman does for the community. As he lists the duties that he finds through reading, he can see the list grow larger as he discovers new facts. Reading is helping him find out something he wants very much to know.

Such a procedure necessarily stimulates thoughtful reading. The child reads to solve a problem. Therefore, he approaches that reading thoughtfully. And as he reads he thinks and later reflects about what he has learned.

Critical reading is likewise fostered. When the task of the child is that of listing the duties of a community helper, he reads materials and judges their worth in aiding him to arrive at his goal. The child may read in two sources and may say to his teacher, "I like this one page of reading better than everything else, for I found out more from it."

Such a purposeful method stimulates interest. The child learns of the duties of a postman. His reading may also include information about kinds of mail, which may lead him to enlarge his interests by reading stories that have to do with air mail and airplanes. He may read a passage that contrasts the trip of a letter across the country by jet plane with the trip of a letter by stagecoach. From here it will be difficult to say where his reading would take him, possibly into outer space. Especially would this be true when many materials are made available. Reading interests aroused in the primary grades may form the foundation upon which rather fundamental likes and dislikes in reading are built. When parents relive their early experiences in literature as they read a story again with their children, they sense the joy the story brought them the first time.

Especially does reading stimulate interest when care is taken to culminate the topics of reading in thinking and in other activities, and it fosters pupil planning and pupil participation in dramatic, linguistic, and other constructive activities. Dramatic activities grow quite naturally out of reading about subtopics within a larger topic. One group of children may culminate its reading by presenting a dramatization that will tell the other children the things they have learned. Another group may be interested in writing a story or poem about, for example, the city helper it read about. Or lively discussions may result in which one group debates with another the relative contributions of the various city helpers to the community.

The method develops a differentiated attack suited to the different types of materials and purposes the child has. If the purpose is to determine from a series of pictures some of the duties of a postman, the reading attack will, perforce, be different from the reading attack used to find the duties from a page of printed material. Or again, when the purpose is to read a specific passage to learn the duties of a postman, the reading attack would be different from that used when the passage is skimmed to locate a specific fact that is known to be in the passage. Under this method of instruction the topic used may stem from any field of human experience. One topic may consider personal health problems, another the scientific study of weather, a third may deal with outer space and the scientific considerations involved. Still another topic may deal with legendary characters in literature. The topics should be of many and various sorts. As the topics change and as the purposes for reading change with each new topic, the child will develop many of the study skills and comprehension abilities.

This method requires good teaching based upon careful planning, well-defined assignments, good guidance and direction, and the insight necessary to bring together the various phases of a unit into effective culminating generalizations. It also requires a wealth of well-graded materials dealing with the topics to be handled and covering the range of reading abilities of the members of the class. Most of all it demands a thorough understanding of reading growth and development on the part of the teacher.

THE COMBINATION APPROACH

A combination approach has as its core of reading instruction a basic reader with its related materials [2]. The basal reader will be discussed in the next chapter, which deals with materials. Within the larger and more fundamental instruction for purposeful, meaningful reading, a variety of approaches to word recognition, language experiences, individualized reading experiences, topical unit experiences, and many silent reading situations and workbook activities are used.

Accompanying the combination approach is the use of experiences emphasizing the other phases of the language arts, including listening, speaking, writing, and dramatic arts. Other creative arts are frequently coordinated with the reading experiences. The use of a combined method, centered around the reading of basal materials, is the most common approach to the teaching of reading [246].

Generally speaking, there is no one method that is best under all circumstances for all children. The teacher must select among the available approaches to reading that approach which is suitable to the task at hand and to the instructional outcomes that are desired. There seems to be rather universal belief among students of reading method that reading growth is fostered most effectively by a judicious combining of methods [10, 150, 185].

Selected References

Brogan, Peggy, and Lorene K. Fox. *Helping Children Read.* New York: Holt, Rinehart and Winston, Inc., 1961, Part Two.

Darrow, Helen Fisher, and Virgil Hawes. *Approaches to Individualized Reading.* New York: Appleton-Century-Crofts, 1960.

Durkin, Dolores. *Phonics and the Teaching of Reading.* New York: Bureau of Publications, Teachers College, 1962.

Fries, Charles C. *Linguistics and Reading.* New York: Holt, Rinehart and Winston, Inc., 1963.

Gans, Roma. *Common Sense in Teaching Reading.* New York: The Bobbs-Merrill Company, Inc., 1963, Chap. 6.

Harris, Albert J. *Readings on Reading Instruction.* New York: David McKay Company, Inc., 1963, Chap. 7.

Lee, Dorris M., and R. V. Allen. *Learning To Read Through Experience.* New York: Appleton-Century-Crofts, 1963.

McCracken, Glenn. *The Right To Learn.* Chicago: Henry Regnery Company, 1959, Chaps. 12–14.

Smith, Nila Banton. *Reading Instruction for Today's Children.* Englewood Cliffs, N.J.: Prentice-Hall, Inc., 1963, Chap. 7.

Spache, George D. *Toward Better Reading.* Champaign, Illinois: Garrard Publishing Company, 1963, Chaps. 2, 8.

Veatch, Jeannette. *Individualizing Your Reading Program.* New York: G. P. Putnam and Sons, 1959.

CHAPTER 6

Reading Program and
Materials of Instruction

The reading program designed to meet the broad objectives of reading instruction must itself be broad. Because of the developmental nature of reading and because of the difficulty inherent in learning to read, it is necessary that a well-rounded reading program give the children four fundamental types of reading experiences. *One,* those reading experiences designed to show the child how to read. This is frequently called the "basic reading program." *Two,* those reading activities designed to give the child wide experience in using his growing reading abilities in all types of materials. This is frequently called the "topical program." *Three,* those reading experiences designed to provide for personal growth and recreational appreciation. This is frequently called the "personal reading" or "children's literature program." And *four,* those reading activities designed to reeducate the child who has gotten into difficulty before that difficulty becomes involved with his personal adjustment and other types of problems. This is often called the "remedial program."

In so complex a learning as reading, the essential sequential organization of the learning experiences is provided by the basal program. Instruction in the basal program is concerned primarily with systematic development of reading abilities. The material is a set of reading experiences selected to teach the essential abilities, skills, and techniques of reading. In this phase of the program the child is shown how to read.

BASAL READING EXPERIENCES

The basal reading program is the one that is usually considered to be the reading program. It provides the framework through which the reading abilities, skills, and techniques are introduced and around which they are built. In the basal program, the child is shown how to work with words so that he becomes quick and accurate in recognizing them.

The basal program does much more than merely introduce the child to word-recognition techniques. It gives the initial experiences in such comprehension abilities as reading for factual information, reading to organize, reading to evaluate, reflective reading, and reading for appreciation. Many opportunities are provided for the development of these abilities from the very first lessons in reading. The teacher must be aware of the need to help the child adjust his reading to the various purposes in order that growth in these abilities may be fostered.

The basal reading program gives the child the background training in various reading skills. The following analogy is illustrative of how this works. A tennis coach might show a player how to "drive" and then watch him as he tries out the stroke in order to give him further help. The tennis player becomes accomplished in the skill by means of hours of practice that will enable him to apply the skill with certainty in many and varied situations. From time to time, the player may receive further suggestions from his coach and may act upon them in many hours of practice to still further refine the skill. With reading, the child may be shown, for example, that he need not read single words, but that he can read with greater meaning and more rapidly through grouping those words. The basal program gives him instruction and some experience under careful observation. He must, however, get the larger amount of his practice in using this new skill in the actual process of reading outside of the basal reading materials. The basal materials are prepared with the assumption that much reading is done outside of those materials. Therefore, they are designed to introduce a skill and later to appraise and refine it. There is provision made in basal reading materials for the immediate correction of possible errors in learning. This illustration shows that the basal program consists of carefully controlled instruction. The child is shown how an ability or skill may be learned. He is given sufficient experience so that the teacher can study the initial development of a skill. Then there is constant appraisal and additional instruction in order that further refinements may result.

BROAD TOPICAL READING EXPERIENCES

The child needs broad experiences in using the newly learned reading abilities, skills, and techniques in many different settings. Instruction in the topical unit program enables the child to have many reading experiences. These experiences are profitable to the degree that the reading material used is coordinated with the basal material. The interrelationship between the basic program and the topical unit program is shown in the following statements: (1) the experiences the youngsters undertake in the topical unit phase of the program are frequently an outgrowth of areas or topics introduced in the basic program; (2) frequently too the teacher anticipates the introduction of a unit in the basal reading program (highly charged with worthwhile experiences) by building readiness in the children to accept the topic as one around which to build an experience unit; (3) many times, in exploring within a topical unit, reading needs of the children are discovered that are thereafter provided for in the basal program or in the program of classroom remediation.

There should be under consideration at all times some important class enterprise in the form of a topical unit. This enterprise should be participated in by all the children in the class. Frequently, the topic will grow out of material introduced in the basal reading program. At times, it will stem from other class activities. For example, the unit introduced in the basal program of a second-grade class might be one concerned with "Everyday Workers." The children might read stories in their basal readers about the work of the storekeeper, the cobbler, the druggist, and the butcher. Such reading in their basal readers might stimulate a desire to find out more about "the everyday helpers who sell us the things we need." One group of children might be formed to study the work of "The People Who Supply Us with Our Food." Another group might deal with "The Workers Who Supply Us with the Things We Wear." Another group might deal with "The Workers Who Supply Us with Things for Our Homes." And still another group might deal with "The Workers Who Sell Us Gasoline and Other Things for Our Cars." In that way, a study of the selling of goods and services might be undertaken. In the collection of the data, the children, of course, would visit the various retail stores. They would talk to the storekeepers. In fact, all avenues for collecting information and for studying the problem might be used. Movies about the work of retail merchants might be shown. The children might attend to television and radio announcements relative to retail merchants. Such a unit would give many opportunities for the children to read with purposes that were real to them. The children would employ many reading skills and abilities to which they had been introduced in the basal reading program. Through comparing reading with other tools of collecting information, the children gain a functional understanding of the uses reading can and should serve.

The worthwhileness of such a unit depends in no small measure upon the availability of material. Only those units about which there are adequate materials for the children to read are suitable for topical study for a specific grade.

Much of the experience in the study types of reading is gained through those topical units, which are usually handled with a high degree of interest and enthusiasm. Abilities exercised in such group study include skimming, reading critically and reflectively, reading to remember factual details, reading to get various sensory impressions, reading to get the general significance, and reading to organize. It can be seen that through the use of units growing out of the basal program there is a systematic reinforcement of the skills and abilities that were introduced in that program.

The culmination of the unit wherein there is discussion and wherein the children do something with the material and ideas that they have collected creates an appreciation and understanding of the worthwhileness of reading. Moreover, it helps the child develop the habit of thinking carefully through his reading to see how he can apply the information that he is getting. Comprehension is kept at a high level. The child places demands on his reading that keep him from attempting to read too rapidly for adequate comprehension. The reading is important to the child and he is highly stimulated. The child is eager to arrive at the conclusion, so he does not dawdle or read more slowly than is compatible with meeting his purpose. The creative capabilities of the child are used in connection with the information he has gained. He will be using his creative, artistic, linguistic, and dramatic talents in the manner in which they will be used throughout his school and adult life. Such is reading experience in the highest sense.

PERSONAL READING EXPERIENCES

For well-rounded and satisfying growth, the child needs an opportunity to pursue his own interests independently. Such an opportunity is provided by the personal reading program. The basic program, with its emphasis upon sequential learning, and the topical unit program, with its emphasis upon "here and now" and upon problem solving, do not allow the child to stop to relax with reading, to explore the make-believe, to enjoy a plot, to get a truly esthetic experience, or to answer his personal problems and queries. To the extent that the personal reading program is a "pause in the day's occupation" it adds to well-rounded development. Of course, the interests a child pursues in his personal reading may have been awakened in other phases of the reading program. Certainly, there would be no purely personal reading were not the child taught to read in the basal program and were he not given experience in reading in the topical program. For reading, particularly in the early years, to be recreational, much of the material must be less difficult to read than that studied in the basal program.

Interests are aroused in reading in the basal and topical unit programs about which the child wishes to read more extensively. Reading interests are aroused too by classroom activities other than those directly growing out of the reading experience. Such activities as planting a garden, seeing a motion picture, or building an airplane may stimulate the desire to read. Activities outside school arouse interests. A television program, a trip to the park, or a community function may kindle a reading interest. About some, or all, of these the child may wish to read. He should be given an opportunity during some time in the total reading program to pursue his individual interests. The phase of the program in which he does this is called the personal reading program.

Smith [239] says: "A love of reading is one of the greatest gifts which school or home can give to children, and love of reading is achieved first of all through finding pleasure in books." Children find pleasure in books and gain satisfaction from reading when they are encouraged and enabled to pursue their interests by means of reading.

Although personal reading is guided reading, nonetheless, the child should have a great deal of freedom in the selection of the topics about which he reads and the types of materials he uses in exploring those topics. Because the teacher knows the availability and difficulty of the reading materials, he should from time to time make suggestions, based upon the child's interests and reading abilities, about materials he might find interesting.

The children's literature and personal development phases of the reading program should be based largely upon individual selection of books. This means that it is not necessary for any two children to be reading the same selection or even upon the same topic. In many cases, the children should have complete freedom of choice of material. The teacher, however, should be available to give help when requested and should also feel free to make suggestions as to books the children might enjoy or that might aid them in solving personal problems.

The recreational reading of the child should not be confined to reading during leisure time at home. Ample time should be set aside in school when the child is allowed to read just for the pleasure of reading. During that time he should read material because it satisfies a reading interest or because it answers a question. The question may have no relation to a reading project or to the content that is being learned in other subjects, although many times it is actually a direct outgrowth of class activities. In his personal reading, the child reads material that is not assigned. Probably the best way to encourage children to read during these times is to have many relatively simple and highly interesting materials available. The reading corner, filled with attractive and readable books, may function second only to the teacher in making the personal reading program successful. The teacher, of course, should be ever available to suggest pertinent and appropriate materials. If the child has liked one story by a given author, the teacher can suggest others by the same author. If the child has liked material on a given topic, the teacher can suggest other books and pamphlets on that or on a related topic by another author. The child should be allowed and encouraged to read freely and at will the materials in the classroom collection of books. He should be encouraged to take books home. Opportunities for discussion between the teacher and the child, and among the children, about their reading stimulates recreative reading. If the child finds a book interesting, he may desire to read part of it aloud so that his classmates may share the joy of it with him.

Often, such functions as story periods and book week can grow out of an active, personal reading program. Frequently, a good recreational reading program is exemplified simply by the fact that children read many stories. The recreational reading, however, should not be thought of solely as the reading of stories. When children are working on a unit in which they become absorbed, they read many kinds of material for many purposes as they learn about the topic. Some children will wish to explore the topic even more fully than they are able to do while the unit is being studied in school. Their personal reading may be a direct outgrowth of the topic being discussed. Such reading, nonetheless, is recreational, albeit informational. For some children it is as much a recreation to read a social science passage as it is to read a fairy story. A given child finds reading biographical material very interesting. At other times the same child may display a keen interest in a travel account. Personal reading is thus not limited to narrative material, but includes material from many subjects and of many types that the child actually prefers to read. It should be emphasized, however, that for the child to get an extended view of children's books the teacher should be ever alert to lead him from one interest to another and from one type of reading material to another, so that through an adequate sampling he can determine for himself what kinds of material make the greatest contribution to his interests and meet his personal needs most adequately.

Independent reading will be done with eager expectancy, because it satisfies personal needs. The child explores new avenues of reading and new interests to a greater extent than he is allowed in the regular curriculum. It is a time of leisure reading. When the materials are suited to the child's reading level and to his interests and tastes, they foster enthusiastic reading on the part of the child.

As he reads for recreation, the child develops his reading abilities and skills, builds backgrounds of meaning and vocabulary, extends and increases his reading interests, probably improves his reading tastes, and certainly learns much of the value that reading may be to him. Thus, it may be seen that the reading that the child does voluntarily in out-of-school hours and during school hours makes real and positive contributions to his reading development—contributions that often cannot be as well achieved in other phases of the reading program.

CLASSROOM REMEDIAL EXPERIENCES

From time to time, even in the best developmental program, children learn errors. If reeducative opportunities are immediately available, the difficulties need not persist nor become progressively worse. Every developmental reading program should provide day-by-day appraisal and corrective teaching. Corrective teaching at the onset of a difficulty should be done by the classroom teacher. When errors are allowed to persist, their effects radiate out and often become "stubborn" enough to require prolonged, extensive remedial treatment. As a matter of fact, the effects of prolonged disability may extend into the entire educational, personal, and social development of the child.

Every child who is capable of coming to school can be taught to read up to his capacity for such learning. Such an ideal will more nearly be met when all four classifications of reading experience are recognized as essential to reading growth and when no one phase of the program is overemphasized. Each phase has an important place in the total program, and the amount of emphasis given to each depends upon the level of maturity of the children. The basal program, quite obviously, plays a dominant place as the child becomes an independent extensive reader. The classroom remedial program prevents persistence and accumulation of errors because correction is undertaken immediately the need for it is discernible.

The good teacher constantly studies the reading growth of the individuals he is teaching. When he discovers that a child has made, for example, a faulty generalization, such as recognizing *look* from the double *oo*'s, which the child says are eyes, he institutes teaching designed to correct the faulty generalization. In such an instance, the reeducation may be a part of the regular instruction in word recognition. Remediation in other instances may require that the teacher work with an individual or a group for a period of time. Children whose difficulties have been allowed to persist and who have thereby become serious disability cases often need more specialized remedial instruction than the classroom teacher can give.

Materials for the Reading Curriculum

THE BASAL READING PROGRAM

A basal reading program is desirable for adequate reading development because it provides the teacher with a sequential organization, a gradual introduction, and a careful repetition of words and because it both minimizes the possibility of instructional gaps or overemphases and recognizes children's maturing reading proficiences. In considering basal reading material, it should be pointed out that the grade designation of a book indicates its place in the developmental sequence of reading instruction, its relative comparability in difficulty and sequence with other materials, and its suitability for the average youngster of the particular grade. The grade designation of a book does not indicate a standard that *all* the children are expected to achieve over a given period of time. Quite obviously, an able child should progress through the learning experiences provided by a basal reader as rapidly as he can acquire the skills and abilities that the book is designed to teach. The less able child should progress through those experiences at a slower rate, because he will require a longer time to acquire the skills and abilities. If the job were primarily one of getting through the basal reader as rapidly as possible, all the selections of the entire basal reader program of the first year could be read to the children in two days. The task is not to get through the materials quickly, but to provide instruction in reading. Basal readers are sets of reading experiences carefully prepared to encourage development of skills and abilities and to develop reading vocabulary without the unnecessary hazards an uncontrolled vocabulary carries. The writers of this book consider the basal reader to be of sufficient importance to constitute the core of the reading activities. Stewart [252] found indeed that the basal reader actually is the most used tool. All the schools in his sample were using one or more basic reading series. Stewart reports further that the basal series was the mainstay of the reading programs.

The materials of a basal reading program include the basal readers with accompanying work or skill-development book and teacher's manuals and a variety of other teaching aids. The additional aids may consist of big books, pocket charts with word and phrase cards, appraisal material, wall charts, and related supplementary books. In addition, some basic programs have film strips and recordings closely related to the instructional materials [182]. Some of the film strips are designed to give experience in word recognition, others to develop background. Recordings have been produced to give ear training in some of the important auditory discriminations. Recordings are sometimes used before a sound is associated with its printed symbol. In most programs, however, the teacher gives the necessary ear training.

The basal readers in a typical first-grade program consist of a readiness book with skill book and teacher's guide, four preprimers with skill books and guides, a primer with skill book and guide, and a first reader with skill book and teacher's guide. At least 15 books are organized systematically for the presentation of reading skills and abilities in the first grade! The preprimers are paperback, each one usually 64 pages in length. To illustrate the dramatic growth in reading capability that most children make during the first year, pages from a preprimer and part of a story near the end of a first reader, with abridged excerpts from the teacher's guide for each, are reproduced and discussed.

Fun with Us [25] is a third-level preprimer that consists of 64 pages, introduces 21 new words, has six units dealing with experiences about the home common to children of first-grade ages. Early in this preprimer is a unit called "At Work." The first selection in this unit is entitled "Daddy Can Work." The unit title page and three-page selection are reproduced in black and white on the next page.

The format of preprimers, as this selection illustrates, is made as simple as possible to lighten the reading task of the beginner. Nonetheless, the capability of the beginner is challenged. Sentences are short and restricted to one line of print. The amount of material presented on a page is limited enough to avoid confusion. The paragraphing is indicated by open spaces, as on the third and fourth page of the preprimer material above. The words are used in a meaningful context, and they are repeated often to aid in developing speed of recognition. The new word *work*, for example, is repeated 11 times in the 72-word story. To the adult this repetition may seem unnecessarily monotonous, but to the beginner there

At Work

16

Daddy Can Work

Billy said, "You work, Daddy.
I can work with you.
I like to work.
Look at me work, Daddy."

17

Ann saw Daddy work.
She ran to Daddy.

Ann said, "I can work.
I like to work.
Look at me."

18

Billy looked at Ann.
Billy said, "Look, Daddy.
Ann is at work."

Daddy said, "Come, Ann.
You can not work.
Play with Jane.
She likes to play with you."

19

From Guy L. Bond et al., Fun with Us, *Third Level Preprimer, The Developmental Reading Series (Chicago: Lyons & Carnahan, 1962). Reprinted in black and white by permission.*

is the satisfaction of reading *work* with greater and greater ease. Also there is the thrill of enjoying a story he himself can read.

Creating Interest

In teaching the day's lesson, the teacher might create interest first by encouraging the children to tell about various kinds of work done in the home, such as washing clothes, cooking, washing dishes, putting up screens or storm windows, mowing the lawn, clearing sidewalks of snow, and painting walls or woodwork. As interest in the story is created, opportunity is provided for linguistic development, clarification of concepts, sharing knowledges, and sensing personal responsibilities. Expert teachers use this part of a reading lesson to stimulate many forms of creative thinking and expression.

Presenting New Words

After interest is created, the teacher would introduce the new words. The teacher might ask, "Who is at work here?" When the response "Daddy" is given, the child should be asked to reply in a complete sentence to answer the question. The teacher then might show the sentence:

Daddy is at work.

The excerpt on page 104, dealing with procedures for presenting the new words in this selection, is from the teacher's manual [26].

Presenting new words is an important part of preparing for reading practically every lesson from grade one through high school. In presenting new words, the teacher builds both an understanding of the meaning of the words and gives experience in recognizing the symbols representing these words. Both presenting new words and creating interest help to establish readiness for the child to read the selection and the new words in it.

Purposes for Reading

Purposes for reading are set before reading is done. At this early stage of reading development teachers find it expedient to set purposes involving short segments of reading. These purposes may involve reading two or three lines, at the most a single page. This procedure may seem too simple to a mature reader, but it must be remembered that for the immature reader the task is not simple. As the children mature in their reading ability, purposes requiring a greater amount of reading will be established, often as a result of pupil-teacher planning. Even in the first grade, plans for reading an entire unit may be set.

Mention that the sentence has two new words in it. Have it read again and let the children find the words *is* and *work* in the content. Say, "Billy looks as if he is ready to help Daddy. I will write a question about him." Write:

Is Billy at work?

Have the sentence read and call attention to *Is* and *work*. Show them sentences in order to give experience with the new words, as:

> Jane is not at work.
> Mother said, "Work with me, Jane."
> Ann is with Rex.

Directing the Reading

A child may read the unit title on page 16. Then another child should read the story title on page 17.

Set purposes for the first reading of the story. After each question has been answered by a child in his own words, there should be oral reading of that segment of the story.

> Page 17   What did Billy say his daddy does and what can Billy do? (2 sentences)
> What does Billy like and what does he want Daddy to see? (2 sentences)

Let the children tell what is happening on page 18 and then set purposes for reading the rest of the story.

> Page 18   What did Ann do? (2 sentences)
> Why did she want Daddy and Billy to look? (3 sentences)

An oral reading of the sentences that answer a question may now be requested. Use the same procedure with page 19.

> Page 19   Who saw Ann? (1 sentence)
> What did he say Ann is doing? (2 sentences)
> What did Daddy want her to do, and why? (4 sentences)

Pages 16-19 should then be reread in sequence. One child might read the title and nonconversational parts; others might be Billy, Ann, and Daddy.

From Guy L. Bond et al., Teacher's Edition, Fun with Us, Preprimer, The Developmental Reading Series *(Chicago: Lyons & Carnahan, 1962). Reprinted by permission.*

From Guy L. Bond et al., Teacher's Edition, Fun with Us, Preprimer, The Developmental Reading Series (Chicago: Lyons & Carnahan, 1962). Reprinted by permission.

Developing Abilities and Skills

After the story has been read, comprehension abilities and skills are developed. The abridged reproduction of the teacher's guide, shown above, indicates the variety of reading skills and abilities that are being taught in connection with this story.

The comprehension ability suggested involves reflective thinking about the material read and projects the reasoning of the children far beyond the actual story. In this lesson a basic comprehension skill is practiced. An exercise on word meaning involving the selection of antonyms is given. In order to do this drill effectively the children must not only be able to recognize the words involved but they must also consider with precision the meaning of each.

As they work with the page of the *Fun To Do Book* [27] (skill-development workbook) directly related to the story just completed, during the independent seatwork period, the children will obtain additional needed drill on similar skills and abilities. The children will also have further experience with the reading vocabulary they are developing.

Happy Times [28] is a first reader, consisting of 205 pages, three of which are reproduced on the next page.

The format of the first reader is quite apparently more mature than is the format of the preprimer. The first-reader material will be more easily read by the typical child finishing the year's work than was the

The Rabbits Play a Trick

The little rabbits went away
from the window.

"Let us play a trick on him,"
said one of the rabbits.

"We can make Mr. Fox think
that a dog is coming.

He is afraid of dogs."

The rabbits went to the window.

"What was that noise, Mr. Fox?"
asked one of the rabbits.

"What noise?" asked Mr. Fox.

"We heard a very queer noise,"
said one small rabbit.

"We have long ears."

183

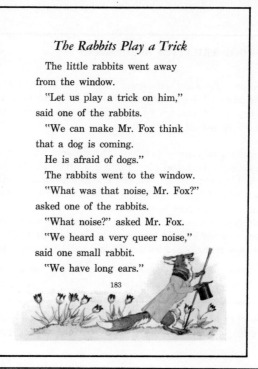

Mr. Fox did not feel happy.

"Is it your mother coming back?"
he asked.

"Oh, no," said the rabbits.

"It was not Mother.

Mother will not come back
before night.

It was something queer that
said bow wow, bow wow."

"If that is what you heard,
it must be a dog," said Mr. Fox.

184

"That is just what we heard,"
said the little rabbits.

"That must be a dog," said Mr. Fox.

"I do not want a dog to eat me.

If a dog is coming, I must
go away before I am seen.

I wish I had wings.

Good-by, my friends."

Mr. Fox ran away as fast as
he could go.

185

From Guy L. Bond, Marie C. Cuddy, and Kathleen Wise, Happy Times, *Regular First Reader, The Developmental Reading Series (Chicago: Lyons & Carnahan, 1962). Reprinted in black and white by permission.*

preprimer read by the beginner because of the many reading capabilities that have been learned during the year. Basic reading materials are designed to be attuned nicely to growth in the reading capabilities that are being developed.

The reproduced sections of the teacher's guide, shown below, illustrate some of the help a teacher can get from studying this aid to effective teaching.

Have the children locate the story and examine the pictures. Say, "On page 183, the fox seems to be talking politely to someone we cannot see." Page 184 shows the five rabbits at an open window; apparently, they did not open the door. Page 185 shows the fox going away.

Presenting the New Words

Write *light*. After it has been identified, use the substitution technique to change *light* to *night*. Have the new word identified and used in an oral sentence. Write *see*, have it identified, and then say, "I will add a letter to this word. Be ready to tell me what the new word is." Add *n* to make *seen*. After the word has been identified, say, "I want you to tell me something you have seen today." Write one of the sentences that are given, as:

I have *seen* my friends.

Have the sentence read and have *seen* underlined. Then say, "At times when we see something odd, we say that it is funny. What other word could we use instead of *odd* or *funny?*" If *queer* is not mentioned, add, "The word I am thinking of begins like *quart*." If *queer* still is not mentioned, tell the word as you write it on the chalkboard.

Say, "I am thinking of a word which means not ever. Who can tell me the word?" If *never* is not mentioned, say, "I am thinking of *never*. Who can use *never* in a sentence?" Ask the children, "After the hungry fox has found all the food he wants, where do you think he will go to rest? Will he go back to his home? Make a sentence that tells what he will do." When *The fox will go back to his home* is mentioned, write the sentence, have it read orally, and have a child frame *back*.

To give further experience with the new words, use them in phrases on the chalkboard or in the card holder. The phrases may be:

never saw him

a *queer* fox

will come *back*

not at *night*

had *seen* a rabbit

Directing the Reading

The general purpose may be to learn why the fox left the rabbits and what the rabbits thought of their trick. To stimulate silent reading of segments of the story, use questions, as:

Page 183   Of what is the fox afraid? (4 sentences)
           What did the fox and the rabbits say to each other?
           (5 sentences)

Page 184   What did the fox ask? (2 sentences)
           What did the rabbits answer? (4 sentences)
           Then what did the fox say? (1 sentence)

Page 185   What did the fox wish for and what did he do?
           (entire page)

Page 186   How did the rabbits feel about the success of their
           trick and what did they say? (entire page)

After a brief discussion of the story, parts should be assigned so that the story may be read orally in sequential order.

DEVELOPING ABILITIES AND SKILLS

Comprehension—Arranging a sequence: Write a few sentences on the chalkboard, but do not number them. The children are to number the sentences to show the order in which the events happened in the story.

(*3*) The fox runs away.

(*1*) The rabbits think how they can make the fox go away.

(*2*) The fox thinks that the rabbits heard a dog.

Word recognition—Phonic and meaning clues: On the chalkboard, write several words which have been presented in the unit. The teacher is to give phonic or meaning clues and have the children use their two index fingers to frame the words. Each word is to be used in an oral sentence. To facilitate the teacher's work, a clue is given here before each word, but the words should be written in a different order.

It means *not ever.* (never)
It has the word *see* in it. (seen)
It rhymes with *track.* (back)
It means *odd* or *funny.* (queer)
It rhymes with *bright.* (night)
It means *scared.* (afraid)
It begins like *was* but rhymes with *dish.* (wish)

Fun to Do Book, page 88, should now be used.

108

Language activity—Discussion and planning: There should be a discussion about dramatizing the story about the fox and the rabbits. The children may tell how the different parts should be acted out, in what section of the classroom the rabbits' home should be located, and how the fox and the rabbits should talk. Several actors may be given tryouts for the parts. Finally, those who are to dramatize the story may be selected. The story may be dramatized during the culminating phase of the unit.

From Guy L. Bond, Marie C. Cuddy, and Kathleen Wise, Teacher's Edition, Happy Times, Regular First Reader, the Developmental Reading Series (Chicago: Lyons & Carnahan, 1962). Reprinted by permission.

The section, "Introducing the Selection," shows the use of discussion of pictures as a means of building background and motivations without unfolding the plot of the story. "Presenting the New Words," of which there are five in these four pages of the first-reader material, illustrates the teaching of many word-recognition techniques, as well as the clarification of word meanings. Contextual clues, phonetic clues, structural clues and visual clues are among the skills used by the child as he works with the new words. The use of known words as a means of helping the child recognize unknown words is illustrated in the introduction of the new word *night* by showing its similarity to the known word *light*. *Seen* is taught as a modification of *see*. In "Directing the Reading" a general purpose for reading the entire passage is suggested. Immediate purposes are proposed for each page. The section "Developing Abilities and Skills" is devoted to drill exercises that call for reading to develop a sequence and the use of phonetic and meaning clues in recognizing words. Linguistic and dramatic capabilities are developed if the suggestion given in the "Related Experience" section is used.

The reading growth that takes place during this first year is apparent not only in the greater maturity of the stories themselves but also in the level of skill development shown in the sections of the two teacher's guides. The teacher of reading is helped to maintain a smooth sequence of reading development by the suggestions given in such teacher's guides. The teacher, of course, must study the growth of the children and adjust his lesson plans to their needs by reinforcing or extending the types of learning suggested in the guides or by modifying the suggestions in accordance with the local situation in which the reading is being taught.

Skill-Development Books

Among the most frequently used material directly related to the basal reading program is the skill-development book, made up of a series of exercises designed to be completed cotemporaneously with reading in the basal readers [74, 178, 261]. It belongs to the child, and he does the exercises in connection with the reading of each unit in the basal reader.

The skill-development book, often called workbook, has important contributions to make to the reading program in addition to being primarily a workbook in which the skills are developed and practiced. It affords a continuous diagnosis of the specific learning difficulties of each child. It has the educational advantage of building habits of accuracy through self-checking, and it gives the child experience in doing independent study.

The amount of time devoted to this type of material should depend upon the reading ability of the child. The child who is getting along well may profitably spend his time after completing the workbook material by reading other materials, such as supplementary stories and other material prepared for children from the reading corner. It is necessary from time to time to check the comprehension and word-recognition ability even of the best readers in the class. Such appraisals can be made either through using workbook materials or through using teacher-prepared tests. The advantage of the workbook material is that it is well prepared and fairly well standardized. If a child effectively does the exercises in a workbook of the degree of difficulty of the middle of the third reader, for example, it is possible to know that he is at least at that point in his skill development regardless of his level of general reading competency. A study by Woestehoff [282] shows that it is not unusual to find an able youngster's general reading ability considerably higher than his general skill development. Such a child, significantly above the general reading level for his grade placement, must often be given specific direct instruction in certain aspects of word-recognition techniques, complex comprehension abilities, and study skills, because these have not been brought to the level of his general reading competency. The implication of this study is that bright capable readers have not necessarily developed all the skills and abilities their general reading level would imply; rather these capable students are using the skills they have exceptionally well.

It should, of course, be recognized that skill-development books teach the sort of reading that the child is asked to do in the workbook. For example, if the workbook exercise is one wherein the child matches a series of words with a series of pictures, then it should be recognized that the child is getting isolated word drill. If the exercise requires that the child read a paragraph and then check among four or five sentences the one that makes the best title for the paragraph, he is learning to pick out the general theme of the passage.

One significant thing that is frequently overlooked when considering the value of workbooks is that the child likes to work in them. A child will work at a skill-development book with perhaps the same drive that an adult works with a crossword puzzle or a mathematical problem or a series of questions in a newspaper or magazine.

The skill-development books that are most helpful are those associated with the basal reader, because these books are correlated with any particular reader in such a way that they give added experience with the words and skills that need more repetition. When properly used, skill-development books contribute decidedly to the child's reading growth.

TEACHER-PREPARED MATERIAL

Recognizing the need for much material, the teachers prepare exercises. This is all to the good. Teacher-prepared material has many contributions to make to the reading program. The teacher can prepare material to meet specific deficiencies in the class. Such material may be prepared for the class as a whole or for an individual child. These materials may take the form of mimeographed or dittoed worksheets to go with a specific story or passage, or they may be typewritten. A primer type of typewriter is a very useful piece of equipment for a primary department. It is possible to so arrange the responses within the teacher-prepared work sheets that drill is provided on the specific words or on types of reading with which the members of the class need further experience. Many teachers find the worksheet type of material that grows out of the reading of definite stories or passages easy to construct and very effective.

Teacher-prepared material may take the form of teaching charts that are worked out for study by the class as a whole. Charts such as the one on which the plan of the day is recorded are effectively used in many classrooms. These may be either teacher- or teacher-pupil prepared.

EXPERIENCE CHARTS

A specialized type of chart prepared by the teacher and the pupils, or by the pupils, or the teacher, is the experience chart [127]. The experience chart is useful supplementary material in the introductory phases of reading instruction. These charts are related usually to classroom experiences rather than definitely tied up with the basal reading program. However, if experience charts are built upon the same vocabulary that is being learned by the class, they can contribute to extensive reading for building sight vocabulary, so necessary in the primary grades. The experience chart can perform a unique function if it is used as a means of introducing the child to the worthwhileness of being able to read print rather than just pictures. Through its use, the teacher can show that written material expresses actual happenings and important ideas. He can show also that when a person wants to share experiences with others he may write them for others to read. Reading and writing are seen to be interrelated aspects of written communication.

Experience charts have a place as material in the primary grades. Great care should be taken in their construction, however, to insure as nearly as possible reasonable vocabulary and linguistic loads. Slightly modified experience charts are used throughout the elementary school. For example, after a field trip the children may prepare a list of significant observations. The list might be recorded on the chalkboard by either the teacher or a child. In actuality, an experience chart has thus been prepared.

LIBRARY MATERIALS

An important type of material in any reading program is personal reading and independent study material. These materials should be attractively arranged in a reading corner. A corner of the room should include a spacious table, comfortable chairs, and attractive bookshelves. The shelves should be filled with children's literature, supplementary readers, reference materials, and other reading materials prepared for children. They should include fictional, factual, scientific and social studies materials—in fact materials of many sorts and from many fields. The materials in the classroom collection of books should vary in difficulty so that there are materials that will challenge the best readers in the room and so that there are materials that the poorest readers can read with satisfaction and profit.

When any given topic is being studied in the classroom, the teacher should replenish the classroom collection with materials from every available source on that topic. Available sources include the school library, the community library, the county library, the traveling state library, books brought by the children, other textbooks, newspapers, and pamphlet materials.

The reading corner should be a busy place. The children should be encouraged to go to the reading area when they have real purposes for using the material, whether the purpose is personal, recreational, or factfinding. The reading corner is a place where a child may go to read for the sole purpose of enjoying himself—to read just what he wants to read. When an individualized approach to reading instruction is being used, these materials become the major source of reading matter. The reading corner, with its books for children and other supplementary reading materials, should be one of the most attractive places in the room. It will be one of the best liked.

CHILD-PREPARED BOOKS AND MATERIALS

Many teachers find it effective to have children prepare books of their own, which they write and illustrate and which make up a section of the reading corner. The children enjoy reading their own materials to other children. The other children enjoy hearing material that has been prepared by one of their classmates. Unless the teacher typewrites stories from dictation, it will not be possible for the children to write books of their own until they have learned manuscript writing. Care must be taken that such dictated books are not so difficult that even the child who constructed the book cannot read it and can only recall the story from memory.

A more advanced illustration of pupil-prepared material is the creative magazine and class newspaper produced by children in higher grades. These semipublished materials are intensely interesting to children. Their preparation frequently entails a wide amount of reading by those who are compiling the product. Of course, the creative work of children even in the higher grades is not limited to published matter. In the active classroom, many written contributions of the children are to be found in the reading corner or in displays about the room.

Another type of child-prepared material found in the primary grades is the *picture dictionary* [195]. All that is needed is a notebook and some guidance on the part of the teacher to enable the child to make a picture dictionary. The child writes new words in the dictionary when he is learning them. He may illustrate the meaning of the word in any one of several ways. He may cut out a picture that tells the name of the word from a part of his workbook that he has used. He may himself draw an illustration or take illustrations from other sources. He may write the word in a sentence to give him a clue as to its meaning and name. Some words, like *up*, cannot be illustrated independently but have to be illustrated by the picture of a phrase or sentence. Commercially prepared dictionaries, which are helpful reference material for the classroom, are available. It is, however, worthwhile for each child to make his own picture dictionary of the words he is learning and wants to have in available reference form in case he gets into difficulty at any time.

The preparation of a picture dictionary by each child has two advantages. It liberates the youngster from having repeatedly to ask the teacher the name of a word. It also enables him to realize that his vocabulary is growing, for, as he sees his picture dictionary get fuller and fuller, he knows that he is learning many new words. Many of these words, of course, he soon learns, so that he does not have to refer to his dictionary.

It should be pointed out that the process of making a dictionary has reading outcomes. In the first place, the child learns the habit of looking words up in a dictionary, which is an excellent habit to establish at the outset of learning to read. Second, he learns the organization of dictionaries through his own experience of locating where words should go in his dictionary, so that he can readily find them when he desires. Third, writing the word in his dictionary in the right location forces the child to go through the word from left to right. Fourth, it teaches him the alphabet in probably the only functional way the alphabet is used, namely that of classification. There are other concomitant learnings. For example, pride in illustrating the words and in making a neat dictionary is fostered. Habits of independence are built as the responsibility for learning is put where it rightfully belongs—upon the child.

CONTENT-SUBJECT TEXTS

Throughout the elementary grades the children gain much practice as they read in the various subject-matter fields. From the very first, children study science textbooks, arithmetic textbooks, social studies texts, and other texts. They gain broad experience in applying their developing reading capabilities. During the past decade these textbooks have materially improved in reading demand, so that the reading load is commensurate with the general reading capabilities of the children for whom they are designed. To the extent that they are suited to the reading ability of the children, subject-matter texts are effective in encouraging reading growth as well as in enabling the children to gain knowledge in the content area involved. Teachers must exercise great care to insure that they do not assign textbooks too difficult in their reading demands. Textbooks too difficult are ineffective as tools to learn the subject-matter content and are apt to be detrimental to the reading growth and the personal development of the pupils.

Selected References

Harris, Albert J. *Readings on Reading Instruction.* New York: David McKay Company, Inc., 1963, Chap. 13.
Herrick, Virgil E. "Basal Instructional Materials in Reading," *Development In*

and Through Reading, The Sixtieth Yearbook of the National Society for the Study of Education. Chicago: The University of Chicago Press, 1961.

Lee, Dorris M. "Developing Experience Charts," *Instructor,* 71:85–86, March 1962.

Russell, David H. *Children Learn To Read,* second edition. Boston: Ginn and Company, 1961, Chap. 5.

Spache, George D. *Toward Better Reading. Champaign,* Illinois: Garrard Publishing Company, 1963, Chap. 2.

Tinker, Miles A., and Constance McCullough. *Teaching Elementary Reading,* second edition. New York: Appleton-Century-Crofts, Inc., 1962, Chap. 15.

Umans, Shelley. *New Trends in Reading Instruction.* New York: Bureau of Publications, Teachers College, 1963, Chap. 4.

CHAPTER 7

Teaching a Lesson
in a Unit

In basic instruction a lesson is usually a segment in a larger setting of unit organization. In the primary grades the part of the unit that makes up the content for one lesson is often a selection of from three to five pages. Later the segments are longer. The selection may be a complete story, or an incident from a larger story, or a factual presentation.

In this chapter the major emphasis will be placed upon teaching a lesson as a part of unit organization. The procedures followed in teaching a unit will be discussed briefly, using as an illustration a first-grade unit, "Animals of the Forest." The steps in teaching a lesson will be presented, followed by a discussion of teaching one selection from the unit "A Bear Plays a Trick."

Steps in Unit Organization

The steps of unit organization include:

1. Preparing for the unit.
2. Developing readiness for the unit.

3. Pupil-teacher planning.
4. Reading the basal reader material.
5. More pupil-teacher planning.
6. Cooperative and individual reading and discussing.
7. Culminating the experience.
8. Evaluating the reading experience.

PREPARING FOR THE UNIT

The teacher, Mrs. Lee, prepares before starting the new unit. She knows that the middle group of children will read about "Animals of the Forest" in their basal reader. Gradually, she accumulates materials to kindle interest, explores community resources that may be tapped, and investigates the amount and difficulty of available reading materials. After a thorough study of resources, she decides that a unit on "Animals of the Forest" will be a fortunate one to develop beyond the treatment of it in the basic text because it is rich in educational outcomes and conducive to growth in reading.

There are 31 children in Mrs. Lee's class. They are grouped for basal instruction in reading into three groups, with eight children in group one, 16 in group two, and seven in group three. For basic instruction in reading the middle group is using a basal reader of first-grade difficulty that includes the unit "Animals of the Forest." Mrs. Lee selected the content of that unit as a topic to be explored by the entire class.

The children in group one are able to read middle second-grade or higher material and have achieved a high level of independence in reading. They will read independently the unit from the basal reader of the middle group to gain a common background with them.

The children in group three are reading primer material. These children are not expected to read the unit "Animals of the Forest," as presented in the basal reader of the middle group, for they cannot as yet read material that difficult. Among the materials assembled for supplementary reading on the topic are some that are on a level appropriate to the children of group three.

All the children will participate in the phases of the unit except the day-by-day teaching of the lessons in the basal reader, which will be limited to the middle group. The materials assembled in the classroom collection on forest animals range from picture books to some that will challenge the most able readers. Mrs. Lee plans to display some of the more attractive books on the table in the reading corner. She has located in the audiovisual collection films and film strips useful in the first grade for building background, adding to vocabulary, and setting a forest atmosphere, including the films *How Animals Live in Winter* (Coronet Instructional Films), *Black Bear Twins* (Encyclopaedia Britannica Films), and *Learning About Bears* (Encyclopaedia Britannica Films), and the filmstrips *Common Animals of the Woods* (Encyclopaedia Britannica Films) and *Animals Get Ready for Winter* (The Jam Handy Organization). She has collected also a number of pictures of forest animals to display about the room. She has used her acquaintance with children's literature to choose stories and poems to read aloud as the unit progresses.

In preparation, Mrs. Lee has formulated plans for the treatment of the unit as a whole-class activity, in each of the groups, and especially in group two, where the children will use the basal reader materials of the topic as the basic material of reading instruction. She has made decisions on how to introduce the unit, on the activities to develop as the unit progresses, and on the creative way in which the knowledge and appreciation gained from reading about forest animals may contribute to the culminating activities. She knows she will have interesting and stimulating experiences with the children, ones that will contribute to reading growth and be educationally profitable in many other ways.

Developing Readiness for the Unit

The development of readiness is at least twofold in nature. Interest must be kindled and backgrounds of knowledge and vocabulary must be established. There are many ways of developing interest. The topic "Animals of the Forest" taps a natural interest of children—an interest in animals. Their interest may be directed primarily toward some specific animal, usually one of the larger variety, such as a bear. It is necessary to expand that interest to include a desire to find out about other animals of the forest. Without comment, Mrs. Lee posted on the bulletin board the pictures of forest animals, labeled by name. The children naturally became curious and asked questions. Some of the audiovisual materials she collected were used. One she used at the outset was a recording of the calls of the animals. The children enjoyed the recording. She planned to read aloud a story she felt would appeal to the children.

As interests were being aroused, backgrounds of concepts and vocabulary were built. The pictures were taken from the bulletin board and discussed. The children were encouraged to recall experiences they had had with animals. They talked about their pets, farm animals, animals they had seen at the zoo or circus, and animals they had seen in the forest. At this time, they started a list of animals they might see in a forest. The motion pictures and film strips were reshown to get understanding about homes or food habits of the animals. Care was taken in these activities to elicit the vocabulary that would be encountered in the basic reader and the supplementary materials and to clarify the word meanings.

Pupil-Teacher Planning

Pupil-teacher planning is an essential element in dealing with any fundamental topic. It is by means of such planning that long-range purposes are developed, problems are raised, and direction is charted. While background is being built, pupil-teacher planning is being initiated. Also, enough understanding of the topic is developed so that the general planning may proceed intelligently. A list was written on the chalkboard of the "Animals of the Forest We Wish To Know About." Another list included "What We Desire To Know About Each Animal." At this time, the activities that might be the outgrowth of the entire study of the topic were considered. "Shall we prepare a mural showing a forest scene of the animals we shall study?" "Shall we prepare a dramatic imaginative play of life in the forest?" "Shall we prepare a scientific television travelogue entitled 'A Trip Through the Forest'?" "Shall we prepare a chart showing facts about each animal, including size, what he eats, his enemies, how he protects himself, where his home is, how he lives during winter?"

Reading the Basal Reader Material

Inasmuch as most of the experience units evolve from topics treated in the basal material, reading this material constitutes the background reading for those who are dealing with the topic. It is in reading selections in the basal reader associated with topical units, such as the one under discussion, that the child is shown how to read and is given systematic instruction in the skills and abilities of reading. This is where reading is taught; the skills are practiced further in the reading connected with other phases of the unit. The unit within a basal reader is made up of selections that constitute the day-by-day teaching of the basal material. It is, therefore, important to discuss the fundamental steps involved in teaching a selection. These steps form the outline for the daily lesson plans of the teacher. A discussion of steps in teaching a selection will be given later, under the heading *Teaching a Lesson.*

More Pupil-Teacher Planning

Planning was continued as work in the unit progressed. Subgroups were formed under the guidance of the teacher. The unit "Animals of the Forest" can be subdivided in many ways. The children helped formulate a reasonable subdivision. They felt the most natural subdivision of this topic was in terms of individual animals or groups of animals. The children were then divided into committees. The responsibility of each committee was to collect information on a specific group of animals to be presented on the chart or in the television travelogue at the end of the unit.

Guidance by Mrs. Lee was necessary at this point to help determine which children would be on each committee. She considered the interests of each child, his reading ability, and the available material in terms of its amount and its level of difficulty. One of the best and one of the poorest readers were members of the same committee. Mrs. Lee suggested efficient ways of proceeding. She anticipated possible difficulties the children might encounter and gave direct instruction in how to meet them. A few youngsters in the upper group planned to consult reference materials for information. For these children, Mrs. Lee took time to show how to use the reference materials for their purposes. For all the children, she anticipated the need for instruction in isolating the major points of their findings.

Cooperative and Individual Reading and Discussing

Cooperative and individual reading and discussion was then systematically and intelligently pursued by the children. Their purposes were real and vital because interest had been aroused. They knew how to proceed. They understood the organization. They sensed their responsibility. They knew that what they read and produced was to be used in a cooperative venture.

Culminating the Experience

Culminating the experience of learning by making use of the results of his efforts is satisfying to any learner. It has special significance in reading experiences because it develops the essential habit of making a practical application of what has been read. It also has the advantage of producing accuracy in interpretation and of demonstrating the meaningfulness of the reading act. Discussions accompanying culminating experiences furnish opportunities for rereading in the case of inconsistencies or disagreements and thereby develop critical and reflective reading. Culminating experiences form a reasonable and sensible closure to a unit and develop habits of persistence by making it necessary for the children to hold to the task until the closure is formed. These final experiences, of course, should be a direct outgrowth of the suggestions introduced in the planning stage and should be compatible with the purposes for which the children are reading.

Mrs. Lee's class decided to have two culminating activities. One committee planned to prepare the chart *Our Animal Chart,* the other committee a television travelogue. Mrs. Lee thought that a chart constituted a profitable culminating experience. It would introduce the children to the basic study skill, reading to organize, in a form that is suitable for retention and generalization. She considered a scientific television travelogue another good culminating experience.

The chart developed by the first committee follows. As they used the findings from their reading creatively to produce the chart, the children gained experience in planning, organizing, reflecting, and discussing.

OUR ANIMAL CHART

Animal	Summer Home	Winter Home	Food	Protects Self	Size
Bears	Roams about the forest.	Sleeps all winter in logs or cave.	Fish, berries, honey, ants.	Big and has sharp claws.	Very large.
Rabbits	In the bushes or in a hole.	In a hole. Comes out sometimes.	Leaves, clover.	Runs very fast. Can hide in bushes.	Small.
Squirrels	In a bunch of leaves in the top of trees.	In holes in tree trunks.	Nuts, seeds.	Jumps from tree to tree. Can climb trees very fast.	Smaller than the rabbit.
Robins	Builds a nest in a tree.	Goes South for winter.	Worms, insects.	Can fly away.	Very small.

The second committee prepared the television travelogue. One of the slower readers, who had helped make the illustrations, placed the pictures into the mock television set, and four children read aloud to the class facts about other forest animals.

Evaluating the Reading Experience

Evaluating the reading experience was done by both pupils and teacher. Evaluation was made throughout the course of the experience as well as after its termination. The children considered what they had learned about reading as well as what they had learned about the topic. The evaluations also appraised the creativity displayed in culminating the unit.

Mrs. Lee evaluated the worthwhileness of the unit in terms of its educational achievement. She evaluated the participation of each child, the independence with which each child worked, and the growth in reading that took place. At the end of the unit, a comprehensive test was given to the group that read the basic reader to measure how much was retained of the information presented. The ability to recognize and understand the meanings of the words introduced in the unit was also tested at this time. Whenever a child failed to recognize the words presented, some review was given. Whenever a misunderstanding of any given concept was revealed, the part of the book presenting the concept was reread by the child or children who displayed the ineffective reading.

Teaching a Selection

The steps involved in teaching a selection make up the daily lesson plans of the teacher, whereas those involved in teaching the unit make up the long-range plans. The fundamental steps in teaching a lesson include:

1. Building readiness.
2. Introducing new vocabulary.
3. Setting purposes for reading the selection.
4. Guiding the silent reading.
5. Discussing the content read.
6. Rereading.
7. Developing specific skills and abilities.
8. Extending the reading into supplementary materials.
9. Relating the selection to the unit.

Building Readiness

As in the unit, building readiness for a specific selection includes stimulating interest in the selection and developing a background for it. If a unit organization is being used, the building of interest and background for a given selection is relatively easy and requires a minimum of time. It is important, however, to direct the children's interest and thinking toward the content of the specific selection or portion of the unit that they are to study. The concepts necessary for reading the selection with understanding should be built.

The teacher can develop readiness by doing one or more of the following: (1) have the pupils tell of their own experiences related to the selection or tell of related material viewed on television or seen in motion pictures; (2) the teacher may tell some of his own experiences, both actual and vicarious; (3) discuss current happenings related to the selection; (4) refer to selections previously read in the unit; (5) present visual aids, such as pictures, motion pictures, bulletin board displays, clippings, models, dioramas, slides, and tabular and graphic material; (6) oral reading of related material by the teacher to the class; (7) talks by visitors; (8) have the children estimate the content by means of the title and the illustrations of the selection, or by what would logically follow what has previously been presented.

Introducing New Vocabulary

The task of introducing the new vocabulary is made natural and effective if in the readiness discussions the teacher has been careful to call attention to the meanings and pronunciations of new words and if he has had the children use the new words in their discussions. As the words are used, they should be presented on the chalkboard in phrases or in sentences that convey their meaning in the selection. These sentences and phrases should be left on the chalkboard so that the children may refer to them as needed. In this presentation, the teacher should also teach the children suitable means of identifying the new words by the appropriate word-recognition techniques. In presenting the words the teacher will use this opportunity to insure that children needing a given technique are called upon to participate in the recognition of the words in which that technique is used. Other children will get experience with words that utilize other techniques of word recognition, each according to his needs. Inasmuch as the children will not only recognize the printed symbol but also associate the appropriate meaning with the printed symbol, the words should always be introduced in context.

Setting Purposes for Reading the Selection

During the pupil-teacher planning for the unit, long-range purposes were established. Specific purposes for reading the selection grow out of the long-range purposes and are related to them. These purposes also grow out of the content of the selection itself and are compatible with the reasons for which the selection should be studied. It is important that these purposes be set prior to reading the selection, because it is by means of such purposes that the comprehension abilities are taught. Some illustrations of suitable purposes are to do the following: (1) locate definite information; (2) answer specific questions; (3) verify ideas; (4) determine sequence of events; (5) understand character presentations; (6) appreciate the plot of a story; (7) enjoy the humor of a situation; (8) understand directions; (9) appreciate the esthetic values of the selection; (10) critically evaluate the content; (11) judge the relevancy, reasonableness, or intent of the content; and (12) organize the facts in relationship to other information that has been obtained on the topic.

Guiding the Silent Reading

Now the children should read independently the selection for the purposes that have been established. If adequate preparation for reading the selection has been made, the children will be able to read with comfort and in a way to fulfill the established purposes. Under certain classroom organizations, the teacher may work with another group of children at this time. Any child who gets into difficulty should be allowed to ask the teacher for help so that he may proceed. In the earliest stages of reading development, in first and second grades, it is advisable for the teacher to work directly with the children reading the selection, because it is often necessary for him to set purposes for reading shorter segments of the selection.

Discussing the Content Read

The discussion of the material read should be an informal one, not a testing device. The discussion should be related to the purposes for which the reading was done. The pupils should express the ideas they have gotten from the reading. The teacher should raise questions, if necessary, to stimulate the discussion or to direct it into more appropriate channels. The teacher should act much in the manner of the chairman of an adult discussion group. If a child demonstrates a faulty understanding of the material, the teacher should use this misconception as an instructional opportunity. The instruction might entail working momentarily with the child who expressed the faulty concept or working for a longer time with the entire group when the misconception is somewhat general. Quite frequently, the teacher will find it profitable to have an immediate rereading of the part of the selection in which the faulty idea arose in order to clarify the point in question.

Rereading

Whenever the teacher deems it worth while, he should suggest rereading the selection for a new purpose. The purpose might be specifically applicable to the long-range plans for the unit, designed to further a developmental learning in reading growth, or it may be reread simply because the children failed to read the selection with sufficient comprehension the first time. Quite often it is necessary to reread a selection to locate ideas pertinent to the creative activity that is progressing in connection with the total unit. At other times rereading might be done to locate a section of the material to be read orally later, in which case, the primary purpose might be to further the development of ability to read orally. Rereading, on the other hand, might have as its purpose selecting parts for dramatization, contrasting the point of view in this selection with that given in material previously read, or locating words that give sensory impressions, especially in the case of specific children who need vocabulary development.

Developing Specific Skills and Abilities

Skills and abilities are developed in two ways. One is by having the children reread a selection, silently or orally, for new purposes, ones that emphasize a specific skill or ability. The other is by assigning tasks especially designed to aid in the development of particular skills and abilities in the areas of word recognition, basic study skills, comprehension, and adjustment to specific types of materials. These tasks include work on teacher-prepared exercises the teacher uses while working directly with the children. The teacher uses chalkboard work following the reading of the selection; exercises involving rereading of the textbook where the purpose is to develop a specific skill or ability; pocket chart exercises; flannel board exercises; and all exercises wherein the teacher is working directly with the children. It is in this type of work that the teacher can make some of the greatest adaptations to the individual needs of children within a group or to the instructional needs of the group as a whole. Other tasks include materials designed for the children to use independently at their seats, both special exercises prepared by the teacher and the workbook activities that accompany the readers being used. The advantage of using the exercises suggested in teachers' manuals and those given in workbooks is that they are related directly to the vocabulary and skills being developed by a selection and to the overall skill-development program to which the specific exercises contribute. Exercises prepared by the teacher enjoy the first advantage and, in addition, are directed toward correcting a known limitation in the reading development of a specific child or group of children.

As far as growth in reading is concerned this phase of the lesson plan, developing skills and abilities, is of paramount importance. Having the children merely read and discuss a selection will not in and of itself develop the skills and abilities necessary for orderly growth in reading capability. The most important phases of instruction take place in the preparatory activities, where new vocabulary is introduced and purposes are set, and in these follow-up skill and ability exercises. Too often the teacher neglects the preparatory and follow-up phases. Skill of teaching is demonstrated when the teacher shows the children how to go about reading and when he provides them with the experiences and the drills necessary to establish the specific skills and abilities that make up the act of reading.

Extending the Reading into Supplementary Materials

In amount of time, this phase of the program constitutes approximately one third of that which is allotted to basic instruction in reading. During this time the child reads, independent of the teacher's help, materials directly related to the unit for the purpose of expanding his knowledge about the unit. Reading supplementary materials closely related to the long-range goals and to the creative activity is highly motivated, providing the child with the opportunity to gain fluency in the use of his developing skills and abilities. The importance of being able to read and its usefulness in solving problems and gaining knowledge is demonstrated to him as he reads to fulfill various purposes. This purposeful type of reading provides practice in a wide variety of comprehension abilities. As the units themselves in a basic program are diversified, so are the comprehension abilities being practiced in the supplementary reading. The supplementary reading material should be well adjusted to the reading capabilities of the children and of a difficulty that can be read without teacher help.

Relating the Selection to the Unit

The ideas gained from the study of a selection should be used by the children in creative ways. It is not essential that all children engage in the same creative enterprise. These creative enterprises should as often as possible be related to the ongoing activities of the unit, of which the selection under study is a part, and they should contribute to the activities planned for culminating the unit. The creative work for the selection, as for the unit itself, should emphasize other language activities, including discussing, speaking, listening, writing. There should also be other creative enterprises, such as drawing, construction, demonstration and display, and physical and musical activities. The nature of the experiences will vary with the type of selection that has been studied and with creative activities that have previously been engaged in, and also with the general purposes of the unit.

As an illustration, let us consider the creative work of a committee of fifth-graders who had read a selection about the forty-niners in a unit connected with the Westward Movement. The children decided to dramatize a day in the life of the forty-niners. These children lined three chairs in a row. The seats of the first two chairs faced forward, and the last chair faced backward. The backs of the chairs were then covered with a blanket. Two youngsters sat on the seat of the first chair and drove imaginary oxen, and two children rode on the tail gate of the improvised covered wagon. The children discussed the events of the day of travel as they rode. Then they made camp for the night. The children made an imaginary campfire consisting of four twigs, set up in a pyramid fashion, around which they cooked an imaginary dinner and sat and discussed plans for the next day. Setting the stage and carrying out the activity took less than 15 minutes, but as a culminating product of reading, it was immensely satisfying and profitable.

Creative work aids in clarifying meanings, stimulates critical and reflective thinking, develops initiative, and gives experience in working with others. Work of a creative sort is one of the best means by which the appreciative comprehension abilities, such as forming sensory impressions, understanding plot, action, or characterization, and enjoying humor, can be developed. This work also stimulates imaginative thinking on the part of the children. Any creative work related to the unit or to a selection within the unit should be the children's own and should not be carried to extremes of refinement nor be too time-consuming.

An Illustration of Teaching a First-Grade Lesson

The selection shown below was one read by Mrs. Lee's first-grade class as a part of the unit "Animals of the Forest." This selection of four pages is from the first-grade basal reader [28] that was used by the middle group.

The following description of the way Mrs. Lee taught the selection "A Bear Plays a Trick" illustrates the steps involved in teaching a selection.

Building Readiness

After finishing the assignment with the other two groups, Mrs. Lee had the 16 children of the middle group join her in the reading circle. Alice, the chairman this week, passed a book to each child. Mrs. Lee had the children locate the previous story, one about the black cub's adventure in getting honey out of a tree, in the list of stories at the front of the book. She had the children recall the characteristics of the black cub and the brown cub. They recalled that the brown cub is somewhat smaller and more timid than the black cub and that the black cub is

A Bear Plays a Trick

One summer day the bears went
down to the water.

The mother bear was looking
for some fish.

She wanted to catch fish
for the little bears.

Soon the mother bear got a fish.

She gave it to the brown bear.

He sat down to eat it.

147

The black bear saw the fish.

He wanted to get that fish
before the brown bear could eat it.

He tried to take the fish away
from the brown bear.

The bears pushed and pulled.

Over and over they went.

The fish got away from them.

The bears heard the splash.

The black bear ran to the water.

He looked and looked, but
he could not find the fish.

148

The brown bear was behind
the black bear.

The black bear did not turn around.

Splash! Splash!

The black bear was in the water.

The brown bear had pushed him in.

The mother bear heard the splash.

It made her turn around.

She saw the black bear
under the water.

Into the water she went
after the little bear.

149

The mother bear put out her paw.

She put it under the little bear.

Up came the little bear.

Soon he was on the ground.

He shook the water
from his black coat.

He looked for the brown bear.

The little brown bear was
under some bushes.

He did not want the other bear
to find him.

He did not want to be pushed
into the water.

150

From Guy L. Bond, Marie C. Cuddy, and Kathleen Wise, Happy Times, *First Reader, The Developmental Reading Series (Chicago: Lyons & Carnahan, 1962). Reprinted in black and white by permission.*

lively and daring. The children then turned to the new story to examine the pictures. In the first picture they see that the brown bear is holding a *fish* in his paw, and the black bear is looking at him. Did the brown bear *catch* the *fish?* Referring to the final picture, Mrs. Lee asks: "Is the mother bear giving the black cub a bath? Why is the brown bear hiding in the bushes?" She draws the attention of the children to the *splash* of the water and to the fact that the little bear is partly *under* the water. Thus, she builds background and arouses interest in the day's lesson.

Introducing New Vocabulary

The new words are *fish, catch, splash,* and *under.* After the new words were used in the introduction, Mrs. Lee presented them to the children by writing them in meaningful sentences on the chalkboard.

> Bears like to eat *fish.*
> The mother bear can *catch* fish.
> The little bear made the water *splash.*
> He was *under* the water.

Mrs. Lee was careful in the sentences to use no words unknown to the children other than the new ones of the lesson. As she prepared the children to read the sentences on the chalkboard, she called attention to the fact that *fish* begins like the word *fun* and ends like *dish,* both familiar to the children, and pointed to what the bear was holding in his hands. All the children read the sentences silently. Then Mrs. Lee called upon a volunteer to read the first sentence aloud. Then she had a child find the new word and underline it in the sentence on the chalkboard. In a like manner the other words were introduced. She called attention to the similarity of ending of the words *fish* and *splash.* She left the sentences on the chalkboard so that any child who had difficulty while reading the selection could refer to them in the context with which he was familiar. Reference could be made easily inasmuch as the new words had been underlined in the presentation. With regard to the word *splash,* Mrs. Lee emphasized its meaning and that a splash can be heard as well as seen. She wrote the phrase *heard a splash* on the chalkboard to enrich its meaning further.

Setting Purposes for Reading the Selection

Mrs. Lee had the title of the story read. Then she suggested that the children read to find the answer to "Which bear played a trick?" and "What was the trick it played?" and "What was the mother bear doing to the black cub?"

Guiding the Silent Reading

To stimulate the silent reading of segments of the story, Mrs. Lee guided the reading by setting purposes as follows. She had the children read the first three sentences to find out why the bears went to the water and what the mother bear wanted to catch for the little bears. After a sufficient time had elapsed for most of the children to complete reading the three lines, Mrs. Lee asked one of them to read the sentences aloud. Then she had them read the next three sentences to find out whether the mother bear got a fish and, if so, to whom she gave it. After the silent reading she had a volunteer read the sentence that told to whom the mother bear gave the fish. The silent reading was guided similarly throughout the rest of the story.

Discussing the Content Read

After the reading was completed, the story was discussed. First, the children told what the trick was, who played it, and how the story ended. During the discussion one of the children told about the time he was pushed in the water and how he got out. Then followed a short discussion on water safety.

Rereading

Mrs. Lee had the children reread to locate the parts in the story that they thought were funny. And then she had the children volunteer to read the humorous parts orally.

Developing Specific Skills and Abilities

1. *Comprehension.* Mrs. Lee had first one child, then another, tell what he thought the black cub would do when he found the brown cub. This oral activity gave the children experience in predicting the outcome of a series of events.

Mrs. Lee had them recall specific items of information with the following questions: To whom did the mother give the fish? How did the fish get away? Which bear looked in the water for the fish? How did the black cub get into the water? What did the black cub do as soon as he got out of the water?

2. *Word Meaning: Opposites.* Mrs. Lee wrote the words *under, catch,* and *find* on the chalkboard. She asked the children to think of words that mean the opposite by saying, "Little is the opposite of big." "Inside is the opposite of outside." As the children gave the opposites, Mrs. Lee wrote them on the board and had them used orally in sentences.

3. *Word Recognition.* Mrs. Lee then worked on the teaching of variant endings. She had the children recognize and read aloud as she added various variant endings to some of the new words and to words recently studied. The following words were used:

fish	fished	fishing
splash	splashed	splashing
catch		catching
walk	walked	walking
talk	talked	talking

An assignment was made in the skill-development book for the independent work at their seats. All of the children were to do one page in the workbook; a second page was to be done by John, Sally, and Kenneth only, for they were the children Mrs. Lee felt most needed the additional experience provided by that workbook page.

Extending the Reading into Supplementary Materials

Mrs. Lee indicated that when the children were finished with their workbook pages they could do further reading in the books they had selected from the classroom collection. In their extended reading Mrs. Lee suggested that they look for facts to record on the chart or for the travelogue they were preparing about "Animals of the Forest."

Relating the Selection to the Unit

Mrs. Lee suggested that the Committee on Bears look through the selection just read to find out whether the story contained any information they wished to include in the chart of facts they were making.

After the children of the middle group returned to their seats, Mrs. Lee went about the room to see how the work of the children of the other groups was progressing. Then she called a new group to work with her.

Selected References

Any two recently published basal readers with their accompanying teachers' manuals. Compare these materials to see the ways by which basal readers and manuals provide for the systematic introduction, practice, and review of reading skills and abilities.

Bond, Guy L. "Teaching Selections in Reading," *The Road to Better Reading.* Albany, New York: The State Education Department, 1953, pp. 30–41.

Causey, O. S. *The Reading Teacher's Reader*. New York: The Ronald Press Company, 1958, Parts II and III.

Hunnicutt, C. W., and W. J. Iverson, editors. *Research in the Three R's*. New York: Harper & Brothers, 1958, Chap. 4.

Purcell, Barbara A. "Methods of Teaching Reading—A Report on a Tri-State Survey," *Elementary School Journal*, LVIII:449–53, May 1958.

III

THE TEACHER
FOSTERS GROWTH

Developing Word
Recognition

In order to become independent as a reader, the child must build certain skills and techniques of word recognition. Effective word recognition depends upon adequate development of knowledge of word meanings and the ability to recognize these words in their printed form [194, 215].

At the start the child must have at his command the meaning of the word he is recognizing. His listening and speaking vocabularies must be large enough so that they encompass all the words he will be learning to recognize. Research [67, 75, 164, 229] indicates that these vocabularies are very large indeed. Nonetheless, the teacher aids in meeting this demand by means of readiness instruction.

When the child becomes a more mature reader, he begins the process of advancing his reading vocabulary ahead of his listening and speaking vocabularies by deriving the meaning of a word from the context of the passage and from explanations by the author of the passage. He derives an understanding of new words from the meanings of enough other words of the passage to make the meanings of the new words clear.

A knowledge of the meaning of a word, be it ever so broad and ever so clear, will not ensure the recognition of the word from the printed symbol. There is, in addition to understanding the word, the need for a systematic attack upon the printed counterpart of the word. In order to be efficient in interpreting the printed symbol, the child must be able to do three things: first, he must be able to recognize well-known words at a glance with a minimum of analysis or inspection; just as he might at a glance recognize a car of the same type, model, and make as the car owned by his family and that he has seen many times. Second, he must be able to recognize rapidly with but little analysis or inspection less well-known words but words that have been previously encountered; just as he might rather quickly recognize an automobile that he has had some experience with but would have to look to see if it had the proper type grill, the correct-shaped body, and the proper-shaped trunk. Third, he must be able to work out and recognize words that have not been encountered before, just as he might recognize a car, through very close inspection, that he had never seen before but that he knew a very great deal about. After he has recognized the word, it is necessary for the child to select among many the appropriate meanings for the word in the setting in which he finds it. This process represents a skill that requires a complex set of techniques that may be employed or discarded rapidly and effectively at will.

In considering word-recognition techniques, it must be realized that some techniques are not effective—for example, the spelling attack. Other techniques, although effective for the most part, can be overemphasized to the point that they become detrimental rather than helpful to rapid word recognition—for example, the letter-by-letter sounding attack, the phonetic attack, or an attack that depends largely upon the striking characteristics of words. There are techniques that are useful in combination with the proper selection of other techniques—for example, combining the general characteristics of words with the use of context clues.

The recognition techniques that are most effective for associating the printed symbol with meaning, and therefore the techniques that should be taught, are the following:

Meaning clues to words
    Pictorial clues.
    Context clues.
    Expectancy clues.
Visual perception techniques
    General shape of words.

Distinguishing characteristics of words.
Large known parts within words.
Systematic visual study.
Analytical techniques
  Phonics.
  Syllabication and accent.
  Structural analysis.
  Word synthesis.

Meaning Clues to Words

A quick and efficient technique used in recognizing an unfamiliar or partially familiar word is anticipating the word from the meaning of the phrase, sentence, or passage [237], of which the word is a part. Before school entrance, the child has added many words to his speaking vocabulary by using the meaning of a sentence as a clue to the meaning of a word. With expert help, this technique of word building could transfer from the spoken language to the reading setting. The reader, as he gains in reading comprehension ability, depends more and more upon context to help him recognize a word or infer the correct meaning of words in passages he is reading. Although the context clue is the most used meaning clue in word recognition, pictorial and expectancy clues also contribute to recognizing words quickly and accurately.

Pictorial Clues

Probably the greatest use of picture clues is found in the early reading experiences of the child. Often teaching procedures lead the child to inspect the pictures prior to reading the selection. The child soon forms the habit of glancing at the pictures on a page to give him a clue to the words that will make up the reading matter. Often, in the prestudy of the pictures of a selection, the names of the characters are given and the actions are interpreted. In this way the child knows he is going to read about certain people, animals, or objects, and he also has a good basis for anticipating the action words. The use of picture clues at these early stages of reading development are certainly an aid to word recognition in that they allow the child to anticipate the words to be met in the passage. At the onset of reading instruction, when a sight vocabulary is being developed, prior to the introduction of the more analytical approach to word recognition, picture aids are indispensable.

Picture aids have another role to play in word recognition in that they help the child evaluate the accuracy of other word-recognition techniques he uses. For example, should a child faultily recognize the word *house* as *horse* in the sentence *See the big house,* the picture will set him straight. At higher levels many of the pictorial presentations are not only aids to meaning, they are also aids to word recognition by means of helping the reader anticipate and therefore more quickly recognize words during the reading act. For example, the reader who recognizes that the picture or slide is a representation of *stegosaurus* is apt to recognize that word at sight as he reads. Certainly, if not at sight, the inspection he will need to make will be less detailed.

Context Clues

The use of context clues is one of the most important, if not the most important, means of recognition. The effective adult reader probably uses this method every time he employs any of the others except when recognizing words in isolated lists of unrelated words. It is a rapid sort of recognition technique in which the meaning of the word is sometimes derived completely from its setting. For example, in the sentence

Tom climbed to the ———— of the tree.

it is not difficult for the child to get from the context that the word he does not recognize is *top.* Of the more than 600,000 English words, less than ten might reasonably fit the context in this sentence. The task is thereby made easier.

The use of context clues has another and equally, or more, important contribution to make to word recognition. Its use checks on the accuracy of all of the other techniques that are used. In the example given in the paragraph above, if the word *top* were reversed and recognized as *pot,* the child would reject this recognition and reinspect the word to arrive at a recognition that would fit the context.

Context clues are practically always used in combination with other methods of word recognition, for example:

The man got in his ———— and drove to town.

It would take only a rapid glance at the word to tell whether it was a car, a helicopter, or wagon in which the man had journeyed to town. In this case the context, supplemented by the rapid glance at the general shape of the word, enables the child to recognize it. If the word were either *helicopter* or *wagon,* the child would likely make a closer inspection than he would if the word were *car.*

In all probability, context clues should be used in the recognition of every word that is in a meaningful setting. Instead of having to recognize the word from the total of words in the English language, the use of context clues limits the choice of words to the few that would fit the meaning of the passage being read. Context enables the reader to use only those techniques that are necessary to distinguish rapidly this word from other reasonable words. In addition the use of context clues materially affects the accuracy of recognition, because these clues allow immediate detection of errors by the reader. As the reader becomes more and more proficient, he makes an increasing use of context clues.

The effective use of context clues is developed, in the first place, through having the child read meaningful material from the start. There was a time when beginning reading materials for children consisted of isolated letters of the alphabet and isolated words. Some largely phonic or phonemic methods make little or no use of meaning in beginning lessons. In most reading programs today children work with meaningful materials from the outset. It is recommended that work with new words be done in meaningful content. In other words, the child should recognize words in the actual process of reading meaningful materials.

The effectiveness of using meanings to find out what a word is should be pointed out to the child, and he should be shown how meanings help him to recognize words. The teacher frequently may ask, when the child is in difficulty, "What word do you think would fit into the meaning of the sentence?" When there is an erroneous answer, the teacher might say, "Yes, that word fits the meaning, but does it start with the same sound as the word in the sentence?" This forces the child to use the context clue in association with another recognition technique.

There are specific exercises too that are helpful in teaching the child to use the context to give him a clue as to what a new or partially familiar word is. Completion exercises—a key word of a sentence is left out; the word is supplied by the child—give experience in using the context to recognize an unknown word. In such exercises, the child need not write down the word but merely read the sentences, filling in the words mentally as he goes along. An illustration of such an exercise is:

> Jim caught the ball.
> He _____ the ball to father.
> _____ caught the ball.
> Then father let the dog _____ with it.

Multiple-choice exercises provide experience with this technique too. In such exercises the child selects from a group of words the one that gives meaning to a sentence.

Underline the word that best fits in the blank space.
Jim caught the _____.   ball   auto   sound   tree
He _____ it to father.   jumped   threw   which

Multiple-choice exercises using context plus the initial element of the word are helpful, as:

Underline the word that best fits in the blank space.
He will go to the beach for a sw_____.   swift   farm   swim
The girl thr_____ the ball.   threw   jumped   thrill

Expectancy Clues

In approaching any reading situation, the more mature the reader is, the more he anticipates the words and concepts he meets in a particular passage on a specific subject. It is evident that when a person is reading in a field in which he is very familiar with the terminology, he recognizes the words and concepts much more rapidly and accurately than he does in a field he knows less well, not only because of familiarity with the words and concepts, but also because he expects to meet the words and concepts in the discussion of topics. It is equally evident that a person who is at home in several reading situations anticipates the words and concepts that he will meet in any of those fields and is enabled, thereby, to recognize the words more automatically.

Many a person has encountered a similar experience when he has met an old acquaintance in a city far removed from the one in which his friend lives. Upon seeing the acquaintance down the block, the person might think, "That looks like Mary, but really it cannot be. Mary is back home. Therefore, I shall have to look more closely." If the person were back in the town where he knew Mary lived, there would be no question in his mind; he would not have to wait until his friend came nearer; he would not have to inspect more closely. He would merely think, "Here comes Mary." Upon recognizing his old acquaintance Mary on the street in the different city, the person might think, "Had I known she was in town, I would have recognized her instantly."

So it is with words. A person reading in a given field, or on a given topic, anticipates to some extent the words he meets. He is prepared to meet them, and therefore he is the more able to recognize them instantaneously. Such anticipation is a great aid to the rapid recognition of words.

Not only does the general subject-matter area within which the person is reading enable him to anticipate and thereby quickly recognize words that are likely to be encountered, but the general subject-matter area also enables him to anticipate the correct meaning to attach to the word that is quickly recognized. Suppose the reader is reading about a biology experiment with bacteria. Within the material is the word *culture*. The reader immediately recognizes *culture* and knows that it means a cultivation of bacteria in prepared-nutrient media. On the other hand, the same person, reading about primitive people in the field of the social studies would anticipate meeting *culture* and would think of *culture* as meaning a particular stage of advancement in civilization as *primitive culture* or *Roman culture*.

The ability to anticipate words from the general subject matter in which the reading is done, and thereby be the more able to recognize them, may be developed by purposeful reading. In purposeful reading, the area of study is well defined and is based on some introductory general reading that tends to clarify the concepts and give the child an idea of what is to be discussed.

Another method of enabling children to learn to anticipate words while reading within a given subject-matter area or about a specific situation is to have them name beforehand the words that they might expect to read in a specific passage. This is one of the ways by which good teachers build the background for reading a passage. Suppose the children are to read of a trip to a flour-milling plant. The teacher might be apt to say, "What do you think will be seen at this plant where flour is made?" Or take the example of a child who is reading about the adventures of a boy at a zoo. He is likely to anticipate the words that will be introduced, and he will thereby be prepared to recognize them within the context of the material. Such complex word configurations as *kangaroo, giraffe, elephant, monkey, baboon, camel,* and *hippopotamus* will be easily recognized, because the child expects to read about these animals in an account of a "Trip to a Zoo." The teacher might ask, "What animals do you expect to read about in the story 'Trip to a Zoo'?" and thus build a background of word knowledge, and at the same time prepare the children to anticipate the vocabulary they will meet.

The teacher might wish to prepare exercises specifically designed to develop the use of expectancy clues, as the following, for example:

Mark in the spaces provided the animals you expect to read about in a story about a Farm F *and those you would find only in material about a Zoo* Z.

_____ cow	_____ goat	_____ fox	_____ geranium
_____ hen	_____ deer	_____ spruce	_____ table
_____ kangaroo	_____ elephant	_____ horse	_____ pig
_____ giraffe	_____ camel	_____ catalog	_____ duck

Mark with an S the phrases you would expect to find in material dealing with making maple sugar.

_____ the snow-covered ground
_____ tapping the tree
_____ cutting the tree

_____ a hot summer day
_____ frying the eggs
_____ boiling the sap

The meaning clues to word recognition work as a team. The picture aids are effective only to the extent that the child is familiar with the concepts depicted. Even the value of context clues is related to the background the reader brings to the printed page. The expectancy clues are associated also with the knowledge of the field possessed by the reader. The teacher, being aware of these relationships all along the way, helps the children build backgrounds. In preparation for reading a selection, he builds the background specifically to the selection, so that these meaning aids may be more effectively used by the children. There is great variability in children in respect to the background with which they approach a given reading situation. The teacher of children of limited experience must give added attention to the development of backgrounds specific to reading a selection as well as to enriching concepts in general. Especially does the culturally deprived child need enriching experiences.

Visual Perception Techniques

Visual perception techniques consist of skills that enable the reader to recognize words with a rapid visual inspection and include use of general shape of words, use of distinguishing characteristics of words, use of large known parts within words, and systematic visual study of words. These rapid techniques often suffice in recognizing words at a glance or in recognizing them with a minimum of inspection. They are effective especially when used with context and other meaning clues.

From the very start of learning to read the child begins to build a sight vocabulary. His sight vocabulary increases until when the child is college age it consists of many thousand words. A sight word is a word a reader can recognize in a fraction of a second. Indeed, a mature reader can recognize approximately four such words in one one-hundredth of a second. This speed of recognition does not employ the detailed analysis that is often necessary in recognizing a word never before met in its printed form.

The reader may wish to try the following experiment with a fellow student. Print on a piece of paper a word, such as *structural* or *synthesis*, without allowing the other student to observe it. Then flash it before him as rapidly as possible. Then have the classmate describe how he recognized the word. Reverse the process, with you as subject. Have the fellow student flash a similar word for you. Then analyze the visual perceptual techniques you used to recognize the word. Did the large-part *thesis* help in recognizing *synthesis?* Were not the general shape and the distinguishing physical characteristics what enabled you to recognize *structural* at a glance? There were no meaning clues to help.

You may wish to expand the instantaneous presentation by flashing such phrases as *the larger elements* or *used in recognizing words* to see whether several words may be recognized at a glance. In the instantaneous recognition of the thought units, meaning clues are largely inoperative.

If you and your coworker were successful in these experiments, you used the rapid perceptual techniques that are necessary in developing a sight vocabulary, which is required for reading thought units and which, in turn, is essential to rapid, meaningful reading.

General Shape of Words

Quite frequently, a person recognizes a word from its general shape. As he becomes more familiar with the word and as it becomes more quickly recognized at sight, the general shape often suffices to cause its recognition. Some words that do not lend themselves to easy analysis tend to be learned as sight words more naturally than words that tend to fall normally into usable parts. The words that will be recognized as sight words solely from their general shape depend, of course, upon the person who is recognizing them and upon his familiarity with them. Such words as *taught, ability,* and *through* are more frequently recognized from their general shape than is such a word as *therefore,* which readily falls into effective usable parts. The child is apt to see *therefore* as *there fore.*

As the child becomes more familiar with words, he normally builds up a repertory of words that are recognized at sight by their general shapes. This ability is often accompanied by dependence upon the meaning of the phrase or sentence as an aid in recognizing the word. Nevertheless, in lists of isolated words many are recognized, without the aid of context, from the shape and other rapid perceptual techniques and need not be broken down visually or sounded out phonetically. Obviously, the use of the general shape of the word is a very rapid sort of recognition and is one to be encouraged, especially when combined with the use of meaning. Gates [102] has pointed out that in typical reading situations, prompt and accurate recognition of a word and an understanding of its meaning is best insured by using context clues and word-form clues simultaneously.

Dependence upon the use of the general shapes of words will not suffice in all instances. This technique makes its major contributions in recognizing well-known words at a glance and in rapidly recognizing words previously encountered but not yet thoroughly known. The development of this quick perception technique is encouraged by rapid reading of material free from word difficulties, while reading for such purposes as getting the general significance, the import, the action or plot, or the humor.

Distinguishing Characteristics of Words

Another rapid visual technique is the use of distinguishing characteristics of words as a means of instantly recognizing them. A word that is recognized by one person because of certain characteristics may not be so easily recognized by another. However, every effective reader uses to some extent the visual word-recognition technique of noting distinguishing characteristics.

Try another experiment. Present as rapidly as you can the word *disappeared* as

d–s–pp—r–d

Then present

–i–a—ea–e–

The first will be easily recognized, whereas the second will not. Usually, the consonants form the distinguishing features of words for quick and accurate perceptual recognition. Systems of shorthand are based upon this perceptual knowledge.

Perhaps your fellow student recognized d–s–pp—r–d not as *disappeared* but rather as *disapproved*. Were the word embedded in continuous matter, the meaning would signal that he was in error, and a second instantaneous glance would suffice to correct the error.

Now present the following contrasts:

teaching of reading

ιƺαϲɦιɳɡ σι ɾϲαɑιɳɡ

The upper half of the phrase is far more easily read than the lower half. These experiments should illustrate facts of visual perception to you and your fellow experimenter.

Many children in the early stages of developing a sight vocabulary learn a word because of a striking characteristic, and this is effective until other words having the same characteristic are introduced. At that time, because the method of attack is not sufficient to meet the new situation, these children may encounter difficulty and confusion unless the technique is supported by other methods [191]. For example, it has been found that a child may recognize the word *donkey* from the tail at the end of the word, and he is effective in his use of this technique until the word *monkey*, which also has a tail, is introduced. Then he is no longer able to tell whether it is a *monkey* or a *donkey* he is reading about. When he finds that the donkey climbs a tree and throws down coconuts he is in confusion indeed. When distinguishing characteristics of words are used, this method must be supported by other word-recognition techniques, although it is a very good aid to rapid recognition of well-known words.

In the early stages of learning to read the child may use striking characteristics to remember words. For example, the letter *o* may enable him to recognize the word *on*. He has learned to say *on* when he sees the letter *o*, and when other words with *o* are encountered he is apt to make an error and consistently call words with *o* in them *on*. Such a procedure would soon cause a great amount of confusion. Unless the child resorted to other means of recognition to supplement the use of the distinguishing characteristic of a word, he would be in very grave difficulty. Nevertheless, the use of striking characteristics, if properly employed, is an aid to rapid word recognition. By itself, however, it is not an adequate word-recognition technique.

As reading ability develops, various incentives for rapid reading make the child utilize both the general characteristics and distinguishing features of words. If the child is to read rapidly, he must depend more and more upon these rapid means of recognizing familiar words. A program of extensive reading under the motivation of purposeful goals causes the child to tend to read more rapidly and more understandingly and thereby encourages dependence upon these two almost instantaneous visual perception techniques. It should be pointed out that in employing these techniques the child should be taught to accompany them with the use of context clues to enable him to anticipate words and to tell when to look more sharply at them or to study them in more detail because he is in error.

A nice control of vocabulary in the early grades, which gives many repetitions of words, enables the child to become so familiar with many words that he can effectively depend upon the working together of these two techniques. If the child attempts to recognize a word from its distinguishing characteristics alone, before he has become familiar with that word, he may fall into error.

Large Known Parts Within Words

The use of large known parts within words is helpful in recognizing them, as is also the use of small words in compound or affixed words. Although this technique tends to be more rapid than having to analyze the word in greater detail, it is not as rapid a technique as the use of the distinguishing characteristics of a word or its general shape.

Illustrative of the more familiar large known parts upon which a reader depends are *ight, tion,* and *tech.* The use of large known parts within words can be taught by comparing words that employ the large sight unit that is being emphasized. For example, the child can be shown that the center part of the word *frighten* is well known to him from his experience with it in the words *light, night,* and *right.* In this way the teacher encourages the child to build up a large repertory of sight elements that can be recognized at a glance and that become an effective aid to word recognition. This technique, of course, is useful in working out words that have not been seen before, as well as in the rapid recognition of words that are familiar.

Another use of large known parts within words is the identification of words within compound or affixed words. There are many words in the English language that contain smaller words that can be used effectively in the recognition of these larger words. The use of the smaller word within the larger word is a recognition technique that is commonly used by able readers. However, it is not in and of itself enough. It cannot be depended upon at all times to be an effective means of recognition. In the case of compound words, such as *sometimes, within,* and *therefore,* it is always effective if the correct smaller words are selected as cues. There are many compound words in the English language, and to have a means of breaking down compound words into their smaller component words is very useful. The fact is that when a person reads most compound words he really sees both parts and recognizes them almost simultaneously and therefore has a very rapid means of recognition. The location of root words within affixed words is also a use of smaller words within larger words and is a consistent aid to word recognition. *Rebuilding,* for example, is quickly recognized as a variation of the word *build.*

In the case of using small words that are neither parts of compound words nor root words, such as *candy, caboose, skill,* and s*tair,* the use of the small word is frequently helpful in recognizing the larger words. Just as a person who is working a crossword puzzle finds having some of the letters of the word filled in is an aid to him in finishing the word, so also does the child find it helpful in recognizing a word to have a part of it immediately recognizable because of a known small word within it. And it is especially helpful if the small word comes at the beginning of the larger word, just as in working a crossword puzzle it is more helpful to know the first letters of a word than to know ones in the middle or at the end.

Too much dependence upon searching within a word for smaller known words in order to recognize the larger word may get the child into rather serious difficulty. With some words it is far more helpful not to attempt to break them into smaller words. The child would be in difficulty in recognizing such a word as *shave* if he tried to separate out the word *have.* The child would be in difficulty in attempting to blend *s-have.* Equally difficult would be the task of recognizing the word *making* from *ma king.* Again, the child may select the wrong small word within a larger word; for example, such a word as *really* might become for him *re all y* or *re ally* rather than *real ly.* This would result in considerable confusion on the part of the youngster, and unless he was able to discard the small words he found within the larger one, when that system failed to function, he would continue to be puzzled by the word being studied.

Again, a child might attempt to analyze those words that should be recognized as wholes by breaking them down into smaller component words; for example, *rather* might be broken into *rat her* or *ra the r, great* into *gr eat, same* into *sa me.* Unless his approach to recognizing such words is altered, he will be in trouble.

In spite of what probably represents an overemphasis on the difficulties inherent in the use of breaking a word into smaller known words, or one smaller known word, it is felt that this technique has a positive application in the process of word recognition. One advantage in using this technique is that it, unlike the rapid visual methods mentioned above, is an excellent one for recognizing words that are only vaguely familiar or that are new words to the child. Finding a smaller word or words within a larger one often gives the child the clue that enables him to figure out the unknown word. In particular, much experience should be given to the child in locating and using root words in word derivatives and words within compound words. It is in these two applications that the technique really establishes its usefulness.

A good way of teaching the child this technique is for the teacher to use it in helping him recognize words. The illustrations should be limited to root words and to compound words, because with them the usefulness of the technique has no exceptions. Suppose the word to be recognized is *growing*. Calling the child's attention to only the first four letters will aid him in recognizing the entire word. Another way in which training may be given is by having the child make up a list of compound words from a list of appropriate words. The reader might ask, "What big words can you make out of these little words?" Actually this word-recognition technique is best taught in the process of analyzing words in contextual reading. When a child identifies the root word within the word, he likely will have arrived at an understanding of the word without help.

Systematic Visual Study

From time to time, it is necessary that even a known word or a partially familiar word be given systematic visual study. Such careful visual study does not necessarily imply that the word be sounded out, although it is always essential that the sounding be preceded by a careful and effective visual analysis of that word, at which time the elements that can be effectively sounded are isolated.

In the usual reading of a good silent reader, not subject to vocalization (that is, the habit of excessive use of the vocal mechanisms in silent reading situations), many words are recognized purely by visual study, and the sounding technique that might have followed proves to be unnecessary and is therefore not undertaken. Although visual study is a slow technique as compared with more rapid visual appraisals, it is much more rapid than sounding out the parts in order to recognize a word. It should not be necessary for the child to resort to careful systematic visual study of words that have been encountered many times previously.

Systematic visual study of words is developed in the actual process of silent reading by a child who has considerable ability in using other visual perceptual techniques. The teacher can help to develop this skill by encouraging the child to look carefully and sharply at the word he is trying to recognize.

At times, a child makes mistakes that fall into a pattern that indicate faulty visual study of words. For example, a child may consistently make his errors in the initial parts of words. In such a case, the teacher should train him to look more sharply at the beginnings of words. The teacher may even set up exercises in which the words to be distinguished are the same in all parts except the beginnings, as for example:

The girl wore her new _____.
mouse   house   blouse

Or again, he may have the child locate within a list of words those that begin with the same visual characteristic, such as:

street   change   string   strange   sheet

The teacher should have the child identify, in the above words, which one a person would use to fly a kite. In this way the matter of meaning is not neglected. Included in the list are other words that are somewhat similar, compelling the child to observe closely the initial parts of the words in order to locate those beginning with the same visual element. Another method of overcoming this type of faulty visual study is to have the child locate words in a dictionary. Obviously, he must inspect the beginnings of the words in order to find them in the dictionary. Any method that causes a child to look more closely at the beginnings of words teaches him to pay special attention to the beginning elements and thereby helps him correct his faulty visual study of words.

Another child might be looking at the beginnings of words closely enough, but he might be neglecting the middle parts of words, attempting to recognize them somewhat too hurriedly through a sharp inspection of the beginnings and the endings of words and skipping rapidly over the center section. Such a child might easily mistake such words as *falter* and *faster*. To overcome such a tendency the teacher might prepare exercises much like the ones indicated above, but in such a way that the child is required to look more closely at the middle parts of words. He should be told that he is not looking carefully enough at the middle of the word. It is effective for the teacher to show the child his actual error by placing the correct word on the chalkboard and putting directly underneath it the word for which he mistook it. Much of the job of correcting faults in systematic visual study is in showing the child what is expected of him and indicating to him wherein he is in error. Clearing up one or two persistent types of error often results in removing major confusion difficulties. In preparing exercises designed to increase flexibility and rapidity in the visual study of words, the teacher should use words that are known to the child. Exercises should include the association of the meaning of the word with its printed symbol.

A third child might use the beginnings and the middle parts of words as his cues and somewhat neglect the careful study of the endings of words. This is not as serious a fault in visual study as the two preceding types of errors. Usually, when a child uses context and other effective methods of word recognition the mere fact that he neglects the endings of words will not be so detrimental. As a matter of fact, in attempting to correct this difficulty the teacher should proceed cautiously in order not to overemphasize the endings of words. Certain current methods of having the child select families of words, and the like, tend to place too much emphasis on the final visual elements of words and thereby actually get the child into new difficulties even though they may help him avoid ending-errors. From time to time, however, it is advisable to direct the attention of the child who neglects the final characteristics of words to word endings. He might be asked to find the members of the *ight* family, the *ell* family, the *eep* family, and the like, within a group of words. In all cases these exercises must include stating the meaning of the words, so that each will have to be read in its entirety. A meaning association is easily made if the child not only finds the members of such a given word family but also identifies the one in that family that fulfills another criterion, as here:

> *Find all the words that end in* eep, *and identify the one in the* eep *family that names an animal,*
> deep   ship   sheep   sling   peep   song   sleep

However, the teacher should again be cautioned that overemphasis on word endings is a dangerous practice and is often detrimental to effective reading, because it tends to break up the left-to-right sequences, and that, obviously, must be maintained.

In all recognition techniques, beginnings of words should be emphasized. Reading proceeds from left to right; an emphasis on endings may make reversal errors (*tar* read as *rat*)more likely to persist. The ability to recognize unfamiliar words, in its early stages, may be likened to the ability to work a crossword puzzle. First it is necessary to know the meaning of the word. The content is the aid in reading; in the crossword puzzle, meaning is given by definition. The length of the word is given by the general configuration of the printed symbol in reading and by the number of blank spaces in the puzzle. Soon after the first letter or so of the word is filled in, the task of completing the word is easier. As suggested earlier, in working a crossword puzzle, it is far more informative to know the first two letters than to know the last two. So it is with reading. In all recognition techniques beginnings of words should be emphasized, because they constitute the most useful cue to be found within the word itself.

Analytical Techniques

In addition to the rapid visual techniques for independence in word recognition, the child must develop more analytical ones. These include phonetic and structural analyses, syllabication and accent, and word synthesis. Phonetic analysis deals with sound-print relationships. Structural analysis is concerned with structural modification of root words and the changes in meaning involved. Ability to distinguish the syllables of words and to determine accent aid in recognizing polysyllabic words. Once a word is broken into visual or structural elements or syllables, the child needs to fluently fuse (synthesize) these parts into the whole word.

Phonics

Phonics is an important part of teaching word recognition [7, 187, 247]. Phonics is the training designed to give the child a means of sounding out a word so that he may recognize it as a word he knows when he hears it spoken. Words are made up of single sound units called *phonemes*. Consonant sounds, vowel sounds, and accent make up the three main types of phonemes. Letters or letter combinations that represent phonemes are called *phonograms*. Phonetic analysis, as used here, means the skills involved in associating the letters and letter combinations with sounds. Phonics involves the development of the associations between phonograms and the phonemes they represent. The teaching often includes also the development of generalizations dealing with the relationships between the printed and spoken language. In reading, the child must be able to recognize the phonograms within a word, recall the phonemes they represent, and combine them into the word. In spelling, on the other hand, the child must think of the spoken word, separate it into phonemes, and recall the phonograms used to represent the phonemes in the word. Obviously, this process means that the child also must recall the visual patterns of the word, because a given phoneme may be represented in written form in several ways. For example, the *oo* in *too* is represented in written language in at least 17 ways [79].

At the start children are able to recognize more spoken words than printed ones. The purpose of sounding words, as a word-recognition technique, is to relate the printed word to the child's extensive knowledge of spoken language. As a result of training in phonic analysis, the child is enabled to work out the pronunciation of many words that then become familiar to him in print.

Phonetic analysis depends on a knowledge of the phonemic accompaniments of individual letters and groups of letters. Through this knowledge the reader identifies the sounds represented by the printed elements in the proper order and then recombines them through blending into the complete sounding of the words. In this way he works out the pronunciation of the word. Then he recognizes the word as one familiar to him in his spoken language and is thereby able to associate meaning with it.

The phonic method of recognizing words is slow but often helpful. In addition to being slow, dependence solely upon phonetic analysis may result in disability in reading. The child may learn to depend so much upon phonetic skill that he neglects to develop a sight vocabulary or the more rapid recognition techniques. He may therefore develop into a slow word-by-word or even part-by-part reader who cannot group words into thought units. Reading for him becomes a slow and meaningless task, one he seeks to avoid.

Although the child may be familiar with many sounds, he may not be familiar with the phonograms used to depict these sounds. To learn the latter is difficult indeed. The phonemes are spelled in many different ways. Many letters of the alphabet represent more than one sound. The letter *a*, for example, represents eight very common sounds (common enough to be in the pronunciation key of simplified dictionaries). To be completely effective in phonetic analysis the child would have to learn the sounds depicted by each letter and basic letter combination and would have to be skillful enough to select the correct one to use in sounding out a given word. Fortunately, each letter and letter combination, as most frequently used, has a limited number of sounds. Indeed, most of the consonants represent only one sound. The child, recognizing a word through a sounding procedure, must select for each printed element the correct sound and then combine the sounds into the word. Nevertheless, phonics has a contribution to make to the total hierarchy of word-recognition skills. This method is simply one means that may be used, but unassisted it cannot meet all the problems of word recognition.

In developing phonetic ability the teacher should be concerned with the most frequent and regular phonograms. A phonic sequence is difficult to list, because the presentation is more a matter of emphasis than a discrete series of independent learnings. The most acceptable approach in phonics is to teach the elements inductively and analytically. The child is led to associate the printed representation of a sound with its spoken counterpart in known sight words, to formulate a general principle, and then to use the knowledge gained thereby in recognizing new words. This procedure, of course, involves the study of the entire printed word. When emphasis is placed on the initial consonant sound and meaning of the word, the child, by the very nature of instruction, must systematically observe the whole word from start to finish and associate the printed forms with the sounds they represent.

In the description below, the sequence represents points of emphasis. It should be recognized that there is much overlapping among the items of the sequence. For example, a great deal of ear training is given to the child in kindergarten and in prereading experiences, and this training is continued as a preparation for all the new elements to be presented. In the second and third grades, for example, prior to teaching the recognition of syllables, ear training is given to sharpen the child's ability to hear the syllables.

Although the grade designations vary in basal reading materials, the usual order of emphases presented in teacher's manuals and skill-development books is as follows:

1. Ear training is emphasized in the prereading experiences of the child and is continued throughout the elementary-school years. Before the introduction of the printed representation of a phoneme, practice in hearing the speech sound is given.

2. Consonant sounds in initial positions in words are given early emphasis. The consonants that have only one sound are learned most easily and therefore introduced first: *b d f k l m n p t v j r q.* Five consonant letters, *h w y s z,* when they are in the initial position of words, also represent single phonemes. The letters *c* and *g* have two sounds in the initial position. At the first, the most common sound is presented: the *k* sound of *c,* as in *cat* rather than the soft sound of *c* as in *city;* the hard sound of *g,* as in *get,* rather than the alternate sound of *g,* as in *gem.* The letter *x* is practically always sounded *ks,* as in *fox. x* rarely appears in the initial position. When it does, it has the *z* sound. (This fact suggests that some phonetic principles are so rare that it is not worth teaching them, either inductively or deductively.)

3. After the consonant sounds have been learned as beginning elements in words, the child should be led to discover that these sounds are also found in other positions, at which time alternate sounds of *c, g,* and *s* might be introduced.

4. Soon in the progression, the most often-used word-variant sounds, such as *s, ing, ed,* and *es* should be taught. These elements, although representing sounds, also represent structural changes of base words. Structural analysis of words as well as other word-recognition techniques are being developed concurrently with phonics.

5. Common consonant blends are presented in the initial position and later in other positions. Blends consist of combinations of two or three consonants that are blended into a unit, with each letter representing its own sound. For example, *st* in *stock* or *post* and *str* in *strong* are con-

sonant blends. The usual practice is to start with two-letter blends and progress to common three-letter blends.

6. Common consonant digraphs (combinations of consonants that represent single phonemes, not their independent sounds), such as *sh, th, ch,* and *wh,* are taught. It must be recognized that these digraphs change their sounds in different words, as for example: *ch* in *churn, character,* and *machine* and *th* in *this* and *think.* An illustration of a digraph-consonant blend is *thr* in *three;* an illustration of a consonant-digraph blend *tch* in *patch.*

7. Vowels are presented, beginning with the short sound, because the short sound occurs more frequently. Long vowels, sounds where the vowel precedes the consonants *r, w,* and *l;* vowel digraphs, such as *ee, oo,* and *ai;* and diphthongs, such as *ow* and *oi,* are presented, using the words the children read in basal and other materials.

8. Silent letters are presented next. The child should be made aware of the fact that letters occasionally are silent. Three generalizations dealing with silent letters, as commonly taught, are these: (1) When there are two vowels side by side, usually the long sound of the first one is heard and the second is silent. Even though this generalization is accurate less than half the time in primary-grade basal reader words [56], it is the best generalization that can be made for this circumstance and is therefore worth teaching. *bead goat;* (2) when there are two vowels in a one-syllable word or the final syllable of a word, one of which is final *e,* the first vowel is usually long, and the *e* is silent. This generalization works in about two out of three words [56]. *rate lime telephone;* (3) when a word begins with either *kn* or *wr,* the first letter is silent. This rule works in every word situation in which these combinations occur. *knife write.*

Other phonetic generalizations that seem helpful are these: (4) a single vowel in a syllable is usually short unless it is the final letter in a syllable. *mat run pupil;* (5) an *r* usually modifies the immediately preceding vowel sound. *horn arm;* (6) when *c* or *g* appears before *e, i,* or *y,* the sound is usually the soft one. *cent gymn circle.*

There are many opportunities for the teacher to give the child the experience necessary for developing knowledge of phonetic parts. The most effective way to teach word elements is in connection with the other aspects of reading instruction in the basal readers. Such training as finding similarities in known words, as *talk, chalk, stalk,* gives the child experience with the word ending *alk* common to these words. When presenting a new word, the teacher is supposed not only to clarify the meaning of the word but also to show the child the most efficient way of analyzing the word, by comparing it with known words containing the element likely to cause difficulty. In this way the child gets experience in phonics that enables phonetic analysis to become a permanent part of his reading equipment.

The teacher can find in workbooks and manuals of basic readers, samples of exercises suitable for direct instruction in developing phonetic knowledge of word parts. Exercises that accompany the basal reader have a distinct advantage over exercises not so closely related to the text-book. These materials are written by authors who know the words that have been previously taught; therefore, they are aware of the words that are familiar to the children. Authors use these known words in preparing material to teach the phonetic elements needed for the recognition of new words. The known words are also the ones included in the drill exercises. These words constitute the vocabulary that is used many times on succeeding pages of the basal reader, thereby affording the child further experience with the words and the phonetic elements within those words.

The teacher, however, may find it necessary to prepare additional exercises emphasizing the phonetic parts that are causing the children within his class difficulty. In making such exercises, the teacher should be sure to use words that are familiar to the children and then to have them use the element introduced in the familiar word in the recognition of new words. As nearly as possible, all exercises designed to develop knowledge of phonetic elements of words should be taught in context rather than in isolation. To insure it will be learned, it is important that a phonetic element get frequent, spaced repetition once it has been introduced in the reading program. In the accompanying picture several children are shown working together to gain experience with the initial digraph found in such words as *where* and *why*.

It is probable that in the learning of a repertory of phonetic elements, the need for systematic, organized instruction is greater than it is in any other phase of the reading program. Phonetic elements must be introduced gradually, they must be introduced in a reasonable sequence, the learning must be carefully controlled to avoid confusion, and there must be assurance of adequate experience with the elements to afford a reasonable chance they will become permanent acquisitions. Inasmuch as some children have greater capability than others in establishing phonetic knowledge, the teacher must constantly appraise the learning taking place. It will be necessary for the teacher to supplement for some children the experiences that are sufficient for other children.

COURTESY DOUGLAS W. TATTON

The following exercises are illustrative of those that have proven helpful in teaching important phonetic knowledges.

1. Exercises emphasizing initial consonant sounds.
    a. *Say* come *and* can. *Draw a line around all the words that both start with the same sound as* come *and* can *and that name animals.*

catch	camel	chicken
cow	candy	horse
cub	cat	canary

b. *Put the first letter of the words on the left in all the correct blank spaces that make words which name things that grow.*

doll	_____ig	_____uck	_____ays
come	_____ake	_____umpkin	_____alf
pull	_____og	_____orn	_____ish

c. *Put a line under the right word.*

                    run
(1) See the dog   fun
                    sun

                                  ride
(2) The horse gave the boy a   hide
                                  side

d. *Draw a line from each picture to all the words that start with the same sound as the sound with which the name of the picture begins.*

                            monkey
                            pony
                            make
(picture of a pig)   many   (picture of a man)
                            pie
                            pay
                            mat

e. *Make a word naming an animal by putting the first letter of one of the words on the left in the blank space at the right. The first one is done for you.*

come	__h__orse	cake	_____ig
hand	_____eer	put	_____onkey
door	_____ow	did	_____amel

2. Exercises emphasizing initial blend sounds.

a. *Draw a line under the word that finishes the sentence and starts like the key word.*
stick

                      stand
The toy dog could   run
                      story

b. *Finish the word by adding the ending of one of the words below the sentence.*
The boy was str_____.
sweet long cap

c. *Draw a line from each picture to all the words that start with the same sounds as the sounds with which the name of the picture begins.*

                            train
                            strong
(picture of a tree)   straw   (picture of a street)
                            true
                            truck
                            string

   d. *Say the key word after the number. Then read the first part of the sentence and draw a line under the right word to finish it. The word must start with the same sound as the key word.*

     (1) trick

                             true
           The monkey is in the   water
                             tree

     (2) fruit

                         frog
           We found a little   from
                         kitten

     (3) branch

                 bring
         The bat   broke
                 hit

     (4) straw

                   string
        The man was   tall
                   strong

3. Exercises emphasizing consonant digraph sounds.

   a. *Write in the blank space the word that begins with the same sound as the part that is underlined.*

     Why is the paper _____?

     where   dry   white

   b. *Finish the word. It should start like one of the words below the sentence.*

     1. See _____at dog jump!

       this   cow   hat

     2. We make butter in a _____urn.

       take   chair   face

     3. _____en will he come?

       Where   Here   Town

     4. The girl has some new _____oes.

       doll   goat   shall

   c. *Say the key word after the number. Then read the sentence and draw a line under the right word to finish it. The word must start with the same sound as the key word.*

     (1) shop

                         shall
        We will sail on a   plane
                         ship

     (2) chair

                         chimney
       Smoke came out of the   fire
                         chicken

     (3) thin

                 there
        It is a new   home
                 thing

(4) the

          this

We like think

          cake

(5) white

          whose

I see a big whale

          tree

4. Exercises emphasizing vowel sounds.

   a. *Find the right word. It must have a long vowel sound.*

      (1) We will soon be _____.

         there   home   take

      (2) I like to eat _____.

         candy   hose   cake

      (3) We went in a _____.

         wagon   car   boat

   b. *Find the right word. It must have a short vowel sound.*

      (1) See the horse _____.

         run   rope   hot

      (2) That is a large _____.

         goat   cat   warm

   c. *Find all the words that name animals. If the word has a long vowel sound, put l after it. If the word has a short vowel sound, put s after it. Remember, the words must name animals.*

home	_____	pig	_____	sheep	_____
goat	_____	coat	_____	lamb	_____
cat	_____	duck	_____	trick	_____

Syllabication and Accent

Another word-recognition technique is syllabication. Many word problems, met in basal readers and other materials in the third grade and beyond, entail words with two or more syllables. At these levels the child should be taught to break down words into their large usable parts, for the larger the elements that can be isolated and recognized, the more effective the study of the words will be. With words of two or more syllables, degrees of accent are involved. It is necessary for the child to learn how to accent and how to interpret accent marks as presented in dictionaries.

One advantage of syllabication over other of the more detailed methods is that it breaks the word into relatively large elements. For example, the word *immense* is broken into only two parts *im mense*. A second advantage is that often these parts are well-known smaller words. When this is the case, syllabication tends to reinforce the dependence upon the technique of known words within larger words. For example, *dam age* is separated into two usable words. A third advantage is that syllabication teaches the system that is employed in the most usable book of all for word recognition and word pronunciation, the dictionary.

The teacher can help the children learn to analyze words by syllables by knowing or looking up the syllables in the dictionary and then demonstrating them to the children. When the teacher and the children are working with a word at the chalkboard, the teacher may separate the word into syllables, thereby focusing attention upon the usefulness of syllabication. Or again, he may cover the later syllables and show the children the first syllable of the word. He may give the children lists of words, for each of which they might indicate the number of syllables. Or the children may mark off the syllables in a list of words.

The teacher may prepare material in which difficult words are broken into their syllables, as they are in the dictionary. The difficulty with this last method is that the child who could otherwise recognize a specific word at sight has it separated to the point where rapid recognition is difficult; thus, the method tends to overemphasize syllabication at the expense of whole-word recognition. However, such a method will prove effective for the child who needs drill in syllables. When the dictionary is used, working with it materially helps in developing the ability to locate syllables within words.

Syllabication is used in both visual recognition and the sounding of words. And as an analytical technique, it is more desirable in most cases than strictly phonetic or letter-by-letter sounding, because it uses larger elements. Syllabication also lessens the necessity for blending ability and offers less chance for confusion than does more piecemeal observation. Many words that cannot be recognized through the visual approach alone can be recognized through using a sounding-of-the-syllables approach. Syllabication is usually used as either a visual or a sounding technique. The person who is able to isolate these elements within a word employs syllabication in either his visual or sounding study. Care should be taken in teaching syllabication to insure that the child goes systematically through the word from left to right, because any method that breaks words into segments may bring about confusion as to the order of the segments.

Breaking words into their syllables is started usually by ear training during the latter part of the second grade. This ear training is designed to help the child hear the syllables within the word and is confined to having the child tell the number of syllables a spoken word contains. Thereafter, the child is asked to read words to indicate the number of syllables each contains. Sometime during the third grade the child is expected to show the actual separation of syllables in multisyllable words.

This sort of training is continued during grades four, five, and six. Generalizations concerning syllables and their accents are formulated inductively; that is, a number of words are studied, and by discovery, a general principle is formulated. Rules for syllabication and accent that may be helpful to the child include:

a. Every syllable has one vowel sound. *u nite   tel e gram*
b. When the initial vowel in a word is followed by two consonants, not digraphs or blends (*fa ther*), the consonants are usually divided. *lit tle   car pet*
c. In most two-syllable words the first syllable is accented. *tá ble*
d. Words that contain affixes are usually divided between the affix and the root word. *un like ly*

Exercises that emphasize syllabication follow.

1. *Complete the following sentences by drawing a line under the right two-syllable word. Remember, the word must have only two syllables.*
   a. The witch made the children _____.
      run   afraid   unhappy
   b. They went swimming in the _____.
      lake   stream   river
2. *Read the word and write the number of syllables you hear after each.*

question	____	permanent	____	adventure	____
moment	____	porcupine	____	button	____
baboon	____	village	____	banana	____

3. *Mark the syllables in these words, as for example:*   im | por | tant

alone	enemy	adventure
rather	tomorrow	interested
nodded	beautiful	forgotten

Structural Analysis

Structural analysis is a word-recognition procedure that deals with root words and their inflected and derived forms, including variant endings, compound words, prefixes, suffixes, contractions, and syllabication. This visual analytical approach not only aids in recognizing words but also in understanding their meanings. Each unit in structural analysis is meaningful. For example, the prefix *re* added to the root *live* makes a new word that means "to live again." The root word retains its meaning; the prefix has its meaning; when combined, a third meaning emerges.

In studying words that lend themselves to structural analysis, the reader analyzes the word into meaningful units and from them derives a recognition and understanding of the word. As Thorndike [262] has indicated, correct responses to affixes are not a luxury in the comprehension and use of English but a necessity. A similar comment could be made of all the elements in structural analysis.

Variant Endings. Variant endings include endings affixed to words to form plurals, possessives, comparatives, and verb changes. The teacher should, in the presentation of new words, use every opportunity to indicate root words and variant changes. When introducing the word *looking,* the teacher should lead the children to identify the word *look,* a known word, and to note that *look* has been changed slightly. The children should use both *look* and *looking* in sentences to note the change in usage. Shortly after this, in words like *running,* the teacher should lead the children to note the root word change that took place when the variant ending was added. Next, the word *liking* may be used to show another type of change that takes place in root words when variant endings are added.

Exercises designed to give the pupil experience with variant endings are found in teacher's guides and skill books of basic readers. The teacher may wish to prepare exercises similar to the following:

For verb forms:
  Write on the chalkboard the words

look	looks	looking	looked
like	likes	liking	liked
play	plays	playing	played

  Have each word used in oral sentences. Then let the children select the right words to complete the sentences.

  The boy is _____ with the train.
  The girl _____ the doll she lost.
  See the man. He _____ tall.

For possessives:
  This is the _____ train.
    boy   boy's
  This is the _____ ball.
    baby   baby's

For plurals:
  Here are two beautiful _____.
    doll   dolls
  See all the _____.
    dish   dishes

Comparatives:
  He is the _____ dog I ever saw.
    strong   stronger   strongest
  John is as _____ as Jim.
    brave   braver   bravest
  John is _____ than Sally.
    big   bigger   biggest

Compound Words. Compound words are words made up of the root words, such as *railroad.* The two root words retain their meaning sufficiently to afford an understanding of the compound word. Sometimes the meaning of the compound word is somewhat removed from the meaning of the two words from which it was derived. *Sweetheart* is a good example of that kind.

Each day, in the course of teaching a selection, the teacher will find opportunities to give the children experience in recognizing compound words and in recognizing how the two root words are used to understand the meaning of the compound word. Specific exercises like the two given below are helpful:

> *Make a new compound word to fill the blank from one little word in each of the two compound words.*
> The _____ came to the burning house.
>   fisherman   fireplace
>
> *Find the two words in each compound word and state how they tell what the compound word means.*
>   steamboat   fireplace   mailman   doghouse

> *Prefix and Suffix Exercises:*
> *Draw a line around the prefix in the following words, and put the right number after each word to show what the prefix means:*
>   1. again   2. not   3. before
> unhappy _____   replay _____   forehead _____
> disappear _____   forenoon _____   foreground _____
> dislike _____   unkind _____   retell _____
>
> *Draw a line around the suffix in the following words, and put the right number after each word to show what the suffix means:*
>   1. without   2. in that way   3. full of
> boldly _____   trustful _____   thoughtless _____
> coatless _____   thankful _____   thoughtful _____
> gladly _____   honestly _____   helpless _____
>
> *Draw a line around the correct word to complete the following sentences:*
> They must _____ the rope to set the horse free.
>   tie   untie   retie
>   helpfulness
> The boys were   help
>   helpful

Additional training should be given during the introduction of words in the preparatory phases of reading a selection. Probably the best way to develop an understanding of prefixes and suffixes is to have a child draw a line around the affix and tell how it changed the meaning of the root word. It is good occasionally to use words that have both prefixes and suffixes for this training. For example, *disagreeable, unkindness,* and *unworkable.*

Children enjoy making up and comparing sentences in which words are used in their root form and various affixed forms. This type of work is emphasized in the intermediate grades and is sometimes given in more advanced grades.

Contractions. The children have been using contractions in spoken language for some time. Before they have read for long they will have met contractions in printed form in conversational material. Teach the recognition of a printed contraction by comparing the contraction with the words from which it is made, indicating that the apostrophe takes the place of the missing letter or letters and that the contraction is a shorter way of saying the two words. Teaching of contractions should be started in words in which single letters are left out—*do not, don't*—and then extended to words in which two or more letters are missing—*he would, he'd.*

Exercises that emphasize contractions, such as the following, are helpful:

1. *Match each of the contractions with the word it represents by writing the correct number before it.*

_____ don't	(1) he would
_____ can't	(2) will not
_____ won't	(3) I will
_____ I'll	(4) I have
_____ it's	(5) can not
_____ she'll	(6) do not
_____ didn't	(7) let us
_____ I've	(8) it is
_____ let's	(9) she will
_____ he'd	(10) did not

2. *Write after each sentence the two words the underlined contraction represents,*
   (1) I <u>can't</u> go with you.   _____ _____
   (2) <u>He'd</u> like to go.   _____ _____
   (3) <u>She'll</u> be there.   _____ _____
   (4) <u>I've</u> a new car.   _____ _____
   (5) <u>Let's</u> walk faster.   _____ _____

Word Synthesis

The previous sections on word recognition have indicated that in order to be independent in word recognition the child must make efficient use of meaning clues; he must be able to visually locate within words those elements that are usable in word recognition, and he must have developed a knowledge of these visual, structural, and phonetic parts of words. The child must also be able to synthesize rapidly the word parts into whole words if identification and recognition are to be accomplished. The development of the ability to synthesize words progresses along with the establishment of other word-recognition skills. Most children at the start resort to auditory blending or fusion; that is, they say the parts of the words somewhat separately and then try to say the whole word as an unbroken entity.

As the child matures in reading, he finds it less frequently necessary to sound out the parts and then reassemble them through pronunciation. An increasing percentage of times, he looks at the parts, identifies them, and visually synthesizes the words as he attaches the appropriate meanings to them. As his silent reading becomes faster than his oral reading, he resorts considerably less often to auditory blending techniques. No doubt, part of the reading development that enables a child to read faster silently than orally is the transition from auditory blending to visual synthesis of words.

Many children find this progression difficult to establish. In fact, some children find it difficult to blend words auditorily that they have previously separated into sound components. These difficulties are frequently caused by somewhat faulty approaches to word recognition in general. If, for example, a word is broken into too many parts, entailing piecemeal observation of the word, the problem of blending becomes difficult. In fact, many children will have forgotten the initial sounds they have pronounced before they come to the end of some of the larger words. Such overanalytical characteristics make even the auditory blending of words difficult and of course make visual synthesis impossible. Another type of instruction that causes difficulty in word synthesis is too extreme a separation of the word parts while they are pronounced, or even while they are studied visually. If the child, for example, says a word with prolonged gaps between each part, he may find it difficult to reassemble the spoken pattern of the word for continuous pronunciation. If the child must make too detailed a visual study of a part of a word, he may find it difficult to recognize the word in its entirety. It therefore becomes apparent that some difficulties in synthesis are caused by insufficient knowledge of the word parts. If, due to lack of sufficient knowledge, the child has to reflect for a considerable amount of time in order to recognize the word elements, he may have difficulty in synthesizing the word.

Many times, the teacher, in pronouncing words, makes an exaggerated separation of the word parts. For some children, this practice tends to cause difficulty in auditory blending and may even carry over into difficulties in visual synthesis.

Another cause of trouble in synthesizing words is the use of exercises that teach the word parts as isolated drill. Under such circumstances, the child does not learn the word elements in connection with real words and does not gain the needed practice in synthesizing the parts into word wholes. One of the main reasons that children develop difficulties in word synthesis is that too much emphasis has been placed on isolated drill. To avoid these pitfalls, all of the skills in word recognition should be taught in words rather than in isolation. Failure to use meaning clues in word recognition is another cause of difficulty in synthesis. If the child anticipates a word in his contextual reading, the task of synthesizing the word is so greatly lessened that the child either auditorily or visually synthesizes it with little difficulty. This fact gives another reason for teaching all of the word-recognition techniques in meaningful content rather than by isolated drill procedures.

There is still another cause for difficulty in this area of word recognition. Some children seem to lack capacity in blending ability. Such children find it difficult to recognize spoken words if the words are separated into parts. For example, there are children who cannot recognize the oral presentation of the word *paper* if it is separated into the sound elements *p a p e r*. The fact is that after the word has been so separated these children lack the ability to synthesize or fuse to such an extent that they will be unable to tell what word the teacher is saying if he again pronounces the word *paper* unbrokenly. In the case of such unusual children, more dependence should be placed on visual recognition of words and use of context clues and large sight elements than upon any method of detailed study of the words. Such a modification in method often helps these children establish reading capability in spite of a physiological limitation. Bond [22] has pointed out that lack in this auditory ability predisposes the child to get into severe trouble if the method used is primarily an oral-phonetic approach to word recognition.

There are certain suggestions that will encourage the children to make the transfer from dependence upon auditory blending to the more rapid visual synthesis. The following principles indicate the nature of training needed:

1. Any sounding of word parts by the teacher should be done in a smooth unemphasized way.

2. While studying a word, the children should be encouraged to use the word in a sentence immediately.
3. The children should not be allowed to sound out a word until they have visually studied it sufficiently to recognize the parts.
4. If the child gets into difficulty with any word part, he should immediately stop pronouncing the word and begin again at the beginning, after the part that caused him difficulty has been recalled to him by his familiarity with it in a known word.
5. The child should be encouraged to separate the words into the largest recognition elements that he knows.
6. Exercises can be developed in which there is contextual reading with hyphenated words at the ends of the lines. The child should be encouraged to read this material silently, visually synthesizing the words.
7. If the child has difficulty in this area, reading relatively simple material with few word difficulties will encourage rapid visual synthesis of any unknown words he encounters.
8. The teacher can give some specific ear training to aid auditory blending. In such training the teacher would start with two-syllable words, saying the parts of each word in an unbroken way, and then have the child repeat the whole word.
9. To aid in visual synthesis of words, a set of cards with words correctly broken into syllables might be shown to the child one at a time and he should tell some fact about the word that would indicate he had recognized it without synthesizing it through pronunciation. For example, the following words could be used in such an exercise, the child saying whether the word on each card names an animal or a plant:

don key	rob in
pump kin	chip munk
li on	clo ver
dog wood	gi raffe
cam el	kan ga roo
on ion	to ma to
ze bra	hip po pot a mus
let tuce	chrys an the mum

Again, the teacher could give a list, such as the one below, in which the words are divided into sound elements and then have the children study them and be prepared to use each in a sentence.

r at	w alk	g ame	st ick
str ing	thr ough	str ong ly	ex am i na tion

Adaptability of Attack

As can be inferred from this discussion of word recognition, the child must have at his command many techniques in order to recognize words independently. In addition, he must have the ability to adapt his repertory of techniques to the word being recognized. The technique or techniques to be employed depend upon the characteristics of the word being studied. In the case of a given word, some of the techniques that are frequently effective may be unsuitable for it. Therefore, the child must discard the good but unsuited techniques in favor of those that apply to the word being studied. The word being recognized might be *thermometer*. To select the beginning known word, *the*, would be a hindrance in recognizing this word. Therefore, that technique must be discarded in favor of a more usable one. Probably one of the better means of recognizing this word is to use its larger elements, *therm o meter*.

The ability to change or to modify the attack to suit the recognition of different words is the crux of effective and rapid word recognition, and hence this ability must be developed. By showing the child how to attack words he does not recognize readily, the teacher is using the best means of teaching adaptability in word recognition. In doing this, the child is shown how to employ the techniques that are most effective for the particular word considered. Many combinations of techniques may be used. At one time, the child may be able to recognize and get the meaning of the word from the content. At another time, it may take the content plus a large known word. At still another time, it may be necessary to analyze the word visually, sound it out element by element, and synthesize it, the more rapid techniques having been discarded because they did not prove sufficiently effective for recognizing the word in question.

General Principles for Teaching Word Recognition

There are certain suggestions for teaching word recognition that aid materially in developing word-recognition techniques in a manner that will make for flexibility of application. These suggestions follow:

1. *Adjust instruction in word-recognition techniques to the individual.* In developing word-recognition techniques it should be recognized that the children of a group will be ready for the more analytical approaches

at different times, and they will develop the abilities at different speeds. In order to avoid overemphasis or inaccurate generalizations, instruction must be adapted to the individual.

In a given group with whom the teacher is developing a special technique, such as locating specific phonetic elements within *known* words, one child may learn the technique rapidly, and any further instruction might cause the child to see elements within words, not the words themselves. At the same time, another child may fail to make the generalizations and may need continued experience with those elements. If, for the latter child, the instruction proceeds to the next step, that of using phonetic elements in recognizing *new* words before he knows the elements sufficiently well, he could easily become confused.

In addition to differences in rate of learning, there are individual children who fail to profit from certain types of instruction. For example, in the case of a youngster with an auditory deficiency, it is usually unfortunate to emphasize phonic approaches. For many such children, this group of word-recognition techniques may have to be omitted entirely. In developing independence in word recognition for a child with faulty vision, more dependence should be placed on large word elements, such as syllables, than would be necessary for the child with more normal vision.

2. *Undertake the more analytical types of word-recognition techniques only after the child is aware of the meaningful nature of reading, has established the habit of recognizing words as whole words, and has built a small sight vocabulary.* This makes it possible for the child to use meaning clues, and it also creates a tendency on his part to employ more rapid recognition techniques. On the other hand, if the child is started to read by methods that use analytical techniques, such as word sounding, he tends to use these techniques at the expense of more rapid methods of word recognition.

3. *Teach the ability to locate a new word-recognition element in known words before applying the use of that element in identifying new words.* The child is led to discover, for example, the initial letter-sound in the known words *run, ride,* and *rat* before he uses this knowledge in identifying the new word *rabbit.*

4. *Always teach word recognition in meaningful material.* Because the ultimate objective of all word-recognition techniques is to recognize words in meaningful material, it is better to develop the techniques in the situation in which they are going to be used, namely, meaningful content. This allows the child to use not only the analytical techniques but also the various meaning clues. It teaches him to interpret a word in

the light of the situation in which he finds it. Word recognition is not word calling but is the recognition of the correct meaning of a word for a given situation. Teaching word recognition in meaningful content fosters the correct balance between the development of meaning vocabulary and the word-recognition techniques.

5. *Teach word recognition in situations where it is important to the child to recognize the word.* If the purpose for reading is real to the child, and if he has accepted that purpose, he will make a more vigorous attack on word difficulties that get in the way of arriving at his goal. This will make him tend to persist in his efforts to recognize the words even though that recognition entails careful analysis, as will be necessary in some cases. So in purposeful reading no matter how detailed the analysis may become, the child is likely to work out the word rather than skip it. If he can recognize a word immediately through relatively rapid techniques, of course, he will not study that word further, because he has met the demand. But when a word requires detailed study, he will make the careful inspection needed rather than allow an error or an omission to occur. If the material in which the child is getting practice in word recognition is meaningful and if he has a real purpose for reading it, he will have a means of appraising for himself whether he has correctly recognized the word. In such cases, the responsibility for accurate, though rapid, reading rests with the child, as it should.

6. *Be sure that the child knows the meaning of the words he is trying to identify or has the background necessary to derive their meaning.* It is obvious that the child, in the primary grades at least, should have, or be able to secure, the meaning of the word he is attempting to recognize. It is difficult enough for him to use the appropriate recognition clues when meaning is present. But if meaning is absent, the child may not realize whether he has studied the word adequately or even that he has the correct pronunciation when he has never heard or encountered the word previously.

Frequently, the word a child is trying to identify may be introduced in content that not only enables him to recognize it but enables him to derive its meaning as well. For instance, the child might be reading a story about Mexico. The story is written in relatively simple language. However, the word *tamale* is introduced. The child knows from his first contact with it that a tamale is something to eat. The next sentence may say that a tamale is very hot. After reading the second sentence the child knows a little more about the food that the boy in Mexico is eating. The child may go on reading the passage without having worked out the pronunciation of *tamale,* simply recognizing each time that this word is the name of the food being eaten by the boy in the story. The child may retain a visual impression of that word, so that the next time he encounters it in a story he will again recognize it as a food and recall some of its characteristics. In his total life the child may never pronounce that word or find need to. He will have derived his recognition of the word and its meaning from the printed page. Nevertheless, it is important to note that he must have either a knowledge of the word or the requisite background to understand the description of that word in order to recognize it meaningfully. His recognition would have been much more rapid and effective if he had known the word itself as a spoken word, before he saw it for the first time on the printed page. It is the usual practice for teachers through conversation, pictures, and the like, to build an understanding and the correct pronunciation of such words before they are first encountered on the printed page.

7. *Avoid isolated drill and artificial teaching devices.* Whenever possible, the child should recognize and remember words as sight words. Drill upon isolated elements tends to cause the child to analyze words that he might otherwise have recognized quite easily at sight. Isolated drill on word elements, such as *tion* and *tr*, is a relatively easy teaching technique and is therefore frequently employed. Such drill, however, hinders rapid word recognition. When it transfers into the actual reading situation, it may slow up the child's reading and interfere with meaning. For this reason it is unwise, as a general rule, to use isolated drills upon discrete word endings and upon discrete phonetic and visual elements.

A cardinal principle in all teaching is to teach material as it will be used. It is unwise to create a dependence upon artificial devices in teaching word-recognition techniques inasmuch as the child must learn to recognize words in reading situations where he has no artificial device to aid him.

8. *Build the habit of inspecting words rapidly, thoroughly, and systematically from left to right.* Many of the difficulties in word recognition result from failure to attend to whole words systematically, starting at the left and looking completely through the word from left to right. Reading seems to be the only task in which recognition must be systematically carried on in one direction. Children who fail to make this left-to-right inspection may recognize a word like *stop* as *pots* at one time and *tops* at another. Although the parts are recognized adequately, the order of those parts is confused, and the child is therefore in difficulty. Many reversal cases are caused by failure to establish a systematic left-to-right inspection of words. The neglect of any part of the word in that inspection may also cause difficulty, as has been previously indicated. Therefore, in

the teaching of word-recognition techniques, the teacher should always start at the beginning of the word, work through it systematically, and refer to the characteristics he wishes to call attention to in left-to-right order. For instance, if the word being recognized is *right*, in the sentence *"Turn right at the next corner,"* the teacher might wish to focus attention upon the sight element *ight* within the word, but it would be necessary for him first to establish the initial sound *r* before he brought in a comparison with the word *sight* to get the final element. It should proceed in this fashion:

> "You know the word *ran*. With what sound does *ran* start?
> "You know the word *sight*. How does *sight* end?
> "Now put the two sounds together."

Of course, the recognition of *right* is of little use unless the child knows that in the particular case *right* means the opposite of *left* in direction, rather than "correct."

9. *Teach the child to analyze the word visually before he attempts to sound it.* Visual analysis must always precede sounding, because it is through visual analysis that the child isolates usable word elements to be sounded. A large proportion of the ability to analyze words effectively is the ability to locate usable elements. Frequently, through isolated drill, certain of the word elements are taught to children who find this learning of little use, because they cannot locate elements within large word patterns fast enough. How much better it would be to proceed from location of the elements within a word through rapid visual study, to sounding, and then to recognition, rather than attempting faulty and unwarranted sounding and blending because the proper elements have not been located through such a visual inspection. Flexibility in the study of words is essential, because a faulty start will have to be quickly rejected if words are to be recognized by analytical means.

10. *Develop the habit of noticing similarities and differences among words.* Through many comparisons, most of which he himself will make, the child can establish this habit—one that encourages careful and rapid inspection of words and helps to develop many of the word recognition techniques. The child can through this procedure, for instance, build his own families of words, and can notice similarities in meaning and configurations of words that have the same roots. This habit encourages building large sight-recognition vocabularies and discourages overanalysis. However, as in the case of most good things, it can be carried to an extreme. The child may be halted in his reading for meaning by noticing that a particular word is similar to another that he knows and

making a mental comparison that would have nothing to do with getting the meaning of the printed page.

11. *Teach word recognition in material that is at the child's reading level.* Any material that is usable for reading is useful for teaching word recognition. There are certain precautions that must be observed however. The material should not have too many new words. Obviously, if the child is to use the meaning of the printed page and context clues to aid him in word recognition, he must know a sufficient number of words, so that the meaning will not become lost. In the initial lessons, it is especially important that new words should not only not be too numerous but that they should not be too difficult or too abstract. They should be words that are readily analyzed and ones that do not cause undue confusion. Such words as *which, what, where,* and *when* should not be introduced until after the child has a certain proficiency in various word-recognition techniques. In the first place, such words make it difficult for meaning to become an aid in word recognition. They are too abstract. In the second place, too much similarity in the initial part tends to force the child to place too much dependence on the latter part of the word for its recognition. In the preparation of basic reading materials there is a tendency to use words that do not mean anything directly but can be applied to any object, as *something, this, that,* or *some.* These words are unsatisfactory for developing the use of the meaning clues.

Selected References

Bond, Guy, and Miles A. Tinker. *Reading Difficulties: Their Diagnosis and Correction.* New York: Appleton-Century-Crofts, Inc., 1957, Chaps. 11 and 12.

DeBoer, John J., and Martha Dallmann. *The Teaching of Reading,* revised edition. New York: Holt, Rinehart and Winston, Inc., 1964, Chaps. 6A and 6B.

Dechant, Emerald V. *Improving the Teaching of Reading.* Englewood Cliffs, N.J. Prentice-Hall, Inc., 1964, Chaps. 10, 11, and 12.

Durrell, Donald D. *Improving Reading Instruction.* Yonkers, New York: World Book Company, 1956, Chaps. 10–12.

Feldmann, Shirley C., and Kathleen K. Merrill. *Ways To Read Words* and *More Ways to Read Words.* New York: Bureau of Publications, Teachers College, 1959.

Gray, W. S. *On Their Own in Reading,* revised edition. Chicago: Scott, Foresman and Company, 1960.

Heilman, Arthur W. *Teaching Reading.* Columbus, Ohio: Charles E. Merrill Books, Inc., 1961, Chaps. 6 and 7.

Smith, Nila Banton. *Reading for Today's Children.* Englewood Cliffs, N.J.: Prentice-Hall, Inc., 1963, Chap. 8.

CHAPTER 9

Basic Comprehension Abilities

The writer, visiting a second-grade in Scotland, found the teacher, Miss MacDonald, worried about the range of reading capability in her class and her attempts to adjust instruction to the varied reading needs of the children. She wished to show the visitor just how large the variations were so that later she might discuss the question with him. She had three children—a poor reader, an average reader, and a good reader— read aloud in a conference room to the visitor.

The able reader, Bonnie, brought in a selection about cowboys in Texas. The story, which Bonnie read well, sounded orally very different from the way it would have sounded had it been read by a child in second grade in Minnesota. For the Minnesota child to read aloud as the Scotch girl did, the entire selection would have had to be printed differently. Every time an *r* appeared, she read it as though it was spelled *r-r-r*, for Bonnie had a marked Scottish burr. Print, it appears, does not present uniform sounds. The reader says the words in the way he has heard them with the pronunciation he has learned. The sound elements used in interpreting print orally depend upon the nature of the linguistic patterns of the individual doing the oral reading.

While discussing this story with Bonnie the visitor soon found that her cowboys were not riding over the Texas prairies nor were they watering their horses at a Texas waterhole. Bonnie's cowboys were riding through the heather of a Scottish moor and were watering their horses on the shores of Loch Lomond.

Comprehension depends upon the background the reader brings to reading, his vocabulary development, and his ability to interpret the author's words into concepts. Bonnie's meaning and vocabulary backgrounds were not sufficient to enable her to communicate accurately with the author of the selection about cowboys. She interpreted the words of the author into somewhat faulty concepts and reorganized the concepts in her effort to gain the ideas, new to her, that the author endeavored to communicate. Nonetheless, no doubt Bonnie added to her understanding of the life of a cowboy in America.

Fortunately for the teacher of reading, the children of today come to the classroom with wide and varied experiences and with relatively rich vocabularies and concepts. From the start the child is concerned with establishing meanings and associating the meanings with spoken symbols. Preschool children build a wealth of understanding without which it would be impossible to develop reading comprehension. The Literature Committee of the Association of Childhood Education, discussing vocabulary and concept development, wrote:*

> Inquiring eyes and eager hands aid them in the discovery of a wealth of meanings. The fitting of names to things becomes an intellectual adventure. Sensitive ears delight in sounds which invite repetition and encourage free experimentation with language as a medium. Out of their world of familiar sights, sounds, smells, and objects large and small, children establish a variety of relationships through enumeration of sounds, objects, names of persons and repetition of rhythmic phrases.

Through constant attention to words and their use the child builds a meaning vocabulary that symbolizes his concepts. He attends to words because he finds them useful in getting along with his environment. There is a wide variety in the extent of vocabulary that children are able to assimilate and the concepts they are able to develop prior to entering school. There is also a wide variation in the components of those vocabularies, because there is a difference in the specific learning situations that the children have experienced.

One child who has in his spoken and hearing vocabularies the same

* Association for Childhood Education International, *Told Under the Blue Umbrella* (New York: The Macmillan Company, 1945).

number of words as does another child may have an entirely different appreciation of any one word from the appreciation the other child has. Bonnie, when compared with a child who has grown up on an open Texas prairie, has a very different appreciation of the words *cowboy, waterhole,* and *prairie.* Contrariwise, a Texas child's understanding of *heather* and *moor* would likely be less good than Bonnie's.

A child from a disadvantaged environment also has been using his "inquiring eyes," "sensitive ears," and "eager hands." He may not have developed fewer concepts and smaller vocabularies. His concepts and vocabularies may merely differ from those assumed by the authors of the materials prepared for his use, limiting his ability to communicate effectively with those authors. It is not safe to assume that a child living in a city, located in the center of an agricultural area, has ever seen a farm or that he has developed sufficiently clear concepts to read about a farm. Nor is it safe to assume that a child who lives in a transportation center has been on a train, on a bus, or has even been to the airport. It is a wise teacher who appraises the concepts and language the child brings to the reading situation in order to fill in gaps and who encourages continued development of meaning vocabulary.

From the first reading lesson, the emphasis of instruction should be placed upon deriving meaning from the printed page [205, 222]. The word-recognition techniques, for example, have been considered as helpful tools in recognizing words for the purpose of being able to arrive at their meaning; and in the development of the techniques, contextual reading has always been considered of great importance. At first, of course, the comprehension is of short, simple sentences. Even in reading these short sentences, the child is led to see the relationships between the words and thereby to understand the thought; and he is expected to see the relationships between the sentences so that he can follow the action. Later, the child is taught to give different weightings to the words, the thought units, and the sentences within a passage so that he is able to arrive at a logical meaning.

An Overview of Comprehension

Comprehension is made up of a number of basic abilities, including skill in recognizing words and their meanings, in grouping words into thought units, and in giving the proper emphasis to the thought units so that the sentences may be understood. Moreover, it is the ability to ascertain the relationship between the sentences that enables the reader to understand the paragraph. When the relationship between paragraphs is understood, the reader arrives at the meaning of the total passage and its relationship to the understanding that he brings to his reading.

Although these basic comprehension abilities underlie the communicative act of reading, they are not sufficient. The reader needs a group of diversified comprehension abilities with flexibility in their use. Unfortunately, there are many adults for whom the elementary program did not develop flexibility in the use of specific comprehension abilities. Some people read all material as though each detail were to be retained forever. They have not developed such higher-order comprehension abilities as the ability to organize facts so that generalizations can be made, the ability to evaluate, or the ability to reflect. Other people read primarily for appreciation, and they retain but little material that should be read for more specific purposes.

There is a distinct need for improving the ability to comprehend a wide variety of materials for a great number of purposes. If an analysis were made of the purposes for which people read, and if the types of reading abilities employed in meeting these purposes were listed, it would be found that certain abilities, in varying combinations, were used to meet certain reading purposes and that other combinations of abilities were used to meet other reading purposes. If the purpose of the reader, for example, were *to choose between two courses of action,* he would be likely to use the following types of reading: skimming to get the general impression, reading to draw inferences, and reading to predict outcomes. Or again, if the purpose of the reader were *to estimate the worthwhileness of some material,* his types of reading might be: skimming material for the general impression, reading for appreciation, and reading to note details of organization, quality, interest value, and factual content for the purpose of drawing inferences. Finally, if his purpose were *to read for enjoyment,* his types of reading might be to sense the main idea and form sensory impressions.

Instruction in Basic Comprehension Abilities

The diversified comprehension abilities will be discussed in the next chapter. This chapter will be devoted to a discussion of the basic comprehension abilities. The discussion of teaching the basic comprehension abilities will be presented under the following headings:

Word meanings
Thought units
Sentence sense
Paragraph organization
Total selection organization

WORD MEANINGS

Probably the most basic of all comprehension abilities is associating the correct meaning of a word with its printed symbol. If the reader is to communicate truly with an author, he must not only recognize the printed symbol but he must also select from many possible meanings the meaning the author had in mind. When the child first comes to school, he is given material in which the words are introduced with only a single meaning. After he has become efficient to some degree in associating meanings with printed symbols, semantic variations are introduced. The introduction of new vocabulary entails both recognition of the printed symbol and association of meaning with it. The teacher must help the child relate meanings to printed symbols through introducing vocabulary in meaningful, contextual situations.

At the start, the child reads material that is highly related to experiences rather common among children in the United States. All children run; all children play; all children know something about cats, dogs, and other pets; all children have birthdays; all children devise playthings; all children imitate their elders; all children eat and sleep; all children see the sky with its sun, moon, and stars. Before long, however, the child reads about places that he could not have seen, experiences he could not have had, and concepts he could not have formed. He is expected, through reading, to develop new concepts, new understanding, new experiences. He can develop this understanding and these concepts and share experiences with authors only to the extent that he brings knowledge to his reading. It is certainly true that the reader gets from the printed page in proportion to the understanding he brings to it. It is also true that he comprehends the printed page only to the degree that he understands the specific meaning of each essential word used by the author.

When he enters school, the child's listening vocabulary is his largest vocabulary. The estimates of size of listening vocabulary of the child entering first grade vary greatly, depending upon how the estimate is determined. These estimates vary from 3,000 to 4,000 words [116] up to about 24,000 words [240]. Whatever the actual number, authorities are agreed that the listening vocabularies of first-grade children are extensive indeed and have increased in recent years because of broadened horizons brought about through television, motion pictures, extensive travel, plentiful and available materials, and increased oral reading to children by parents [242].

There is as well the child's speaking vocabulary, made up of the words that he uses in his own oral language. The child's speaking vocabulary, at the time of entering the first grade, is his second largest one. Then there is his reading vocabulary, made up of the words that he can recognize and understand from printed symbols. The reading vocabulary of the child entering school is indeed small—frequently not more than the child's own name. Soon he will begin the establishment of an ever-increasing number of words he can recognize instantly at sight from their printed symbols. There is his writing vocabulary, made up of the words he uses in his written expression. At the time of school entrance, in the case of most children, the writing vocabulary is limited to writing their names. The development of all these vocabularies is, of course, important to the education of children.

Within a few years after he starts to school, the reading vocabulary exceeds the child's speaking vocabulary, and for truly good readers, the reading vocabulary even surpasses the listening vocabulary. To promote such growth in reading vocabulary for all children, special attention must be paid to this phase of the reading program.

Need for Controlling Reading Vocabulary

The child has been developing his listening vocabulary for six years prior to entering the first grade. It is no small wonder that at the start his listening vocabulary is so much larger than his reading vocabulary. It is fortunate that the child comes to reading instruction with a multitude of word meanings. Frequently, the erroneous assumption is made that a child can read in an uncontrolled vocabulary situation simply because he has a large meaning vocabulary when he enters school.

In most of the child's early listening experiences, any lack of understanding is accompanied by immediate remediation (explaining, rephrasing, simplifying). Such remediation could be duplicated in reading development only if it were possible to change the print on the page (to explain, rephrase, or simplify) every time the child lacked understanding or did not recognize a word. Individualization in a reading program of this sort would be wonderful, but it has never even been approximated. The teachers of reading have had to depend for the most part on the controlled introduction and repetition of words and concepts that their basal reading materials provide. In his early reading experiences the child learns to use a new set of visual symbols in order to recognize these words in their printed form. Thus, he must be in controlled-vocabulary materials when new word-recognition instruction is given.

It is apparent that the control and simplification of language, so necessary for introducing the child to printed symbols, makes the expression of the printed material somewhat immature. The immaturity of language used in early reading materials is regrettable but necessary because it is prepared for children with almost nonexistent reading ability. In order to overcome any detrimental influence on the development of the speaking and listening vocabularies of the child, the teacher should read extensively to the children and provide for discussion of what he has read to them and also encourage discussion of the child's personal day-by-day experiences, both in and out of school. The listening and speaking vocabulary development of the children will progress nicely if provision is made for discussion of daily experiences and for oral experiences in connection with the oral reading done by the teacher. It is far better to have extensive reading done by the teacher than to force the children to attempt to read material that is more difficult than what they meet in the controlled basal-reader material. As has been pointed out earlier, the basal material, which to the adult seems immature, is the most difficult that the child will ever be called upon to read throughout his entire life. In every 20 running words, on the average, the child reading a pre-primer meets a new word he has never before seen in print. Even the most technical materials met by the mature reader are for him vastly easier in vocabulary load. And the mature reader has a wide repertory of proficiencies and skills to aid him as he reads technical materials.

In the initial phases of reading instruction, the child has become accustomed to handling materials. He has learned to work somewhat independently with reading materials for which he has been so well prepared prior to reading them that they now contain few difficulties. He has read materials in which the teacher either carefully led him to the correct recognition of the word or in which he was told the word outright. He has been building requisite habits and attitudes. He has been building a reading vocabulary that he can recognize with a minimum of study.

The child has not as yet acquired methods of independently recognizing new words. However, he has become fairly adept at noticing similarities and differences among words. In fact, he may have been heard to say to his teacher, "These two words look like they start the same." Or "These two words sound like they start with the same sound." These facts indicate that the child is now getting ready to recognize new words independently. At this stage of his reading development, the child should be taught with materials that are designed carefully to give him a vocabulary load of new words that he can be expected to identify and still be able to understand the thought, no matter how simple these materials may appear to adults.

Three Phases of Word Meanings

The knowledge of the meaning of words is basic to reading. Let us examine the background of understanding of a particular child who was reading a passage in which he met for the first time the word *blizzard*.

Brad, a fourth-grade child, lives on a ranch in Montana. Each winter there have been times when he has been unable to get to school because of blizzard conditions. He has heard his father, a cattle man, speak of the severity of winter storms and the measures taken to protect the herd. He has heard his mother lament that no mail came for several days at a time because of blizzard conditions. One day last year the school bus took the children home early, before a storm became severe. Even so, Brad had to run rapidly up the pathway into the house to get out of icy winds and blowing snow. Because of the context in which he met it, this boy easily recognizes the word *blizzard* the first time he meets it in print. He recognizes it as a word he knows well in his speaking and listening vocabularies. It is probable that one exposure of the printed form will forever suffice Brad in his ability to interpret the printed symbol instantly at sight. The appreciation of meaning of *blizzard* for a child born and raised in Florida would be meager contrasted to its meaning for Brad. When the Florida boy meets *blizzard* he may understand that it refers to a storm and may bring a degree of understanding to the reading through his knowledge of *hurricane*. However, he has never seen a *blizzard*, nor has he felt the sting of wind-blown snow. Adding *blizzard* to his sight vocabulary might constitute a complicated learning task. He might have to meet the word several times before it becomes a part of his sight vocabulary. The different meanings he brings to the printed symbol *blizzard* may always be more immature than Brad's was on the first occasion he met it. Even though the Florida boy knows what the word means, his understanding would lack depth and vividness.

There are three phases of word-meaning that have an influence both upon an individual's effectiveness as a recognizer of words and as a reader and upon the interpretations and inferences he makes while reading. These are simple meaning association, extensiveness of meaning, and depth or vividness of meaning.

In order to understand simple meaning association, it might be helpful to observe the efforts of three first-grade pupils who are learning to read the word *cat*. A meaning must be associated with this word if the reading is to be more than mere verbalization. It is interesting to note that on hearing the word *cat* each child will get a different picture. One child's *cat* might be a gray house cat; another's might be yellow; a third *cat* might be a black-and-white gingham cat with red bow, tinkling bell, and button eyes. Any of these various associations of meaning would probably suffice for the mere recognition of the printed word. Each child associated his own meaning with the word *cat*.

Extensiveness of meaning for an individual is the number of connotations a word has for him. In order to get a more generalized concept of the word *cat*, the child will have to establish a background of many meanings. This process of learning the word continues throughout the life of the individual. *Cat* has many meanings. To the hunter or naturalist, it means a family of animals, including the domesticated cat, tiger, lion, leopard, puma, cheetah, lynx, to say nothing of the lowly bobcat. To the sailor, *cat* might give the added meanings of a type of sailboat and a strong tackle used to hoist an anchor to the cathead of a ship. To the sportsman, *cat* may, in addition, imply a type of baseball and other games and equipment used in playing them. To the historian, *cat* has an added meaning—a whip made of rope or leather.

It can be seen from this incomplete list that even the simplest words have many distinct meanings. Part of the development of word meanings is, therefore, acquiring extensiveness of meanings.

The third phase of word meaning is depth or vividness of understanding and appreciation. Although two individuals may recognize that the word *cat* can mean lion, the hunter who has bearded a lion in his den will be likely to bring to the meaning of *cat* a more vivid impression than will the individual who has had no such experience. It is possible that the hunter who has actually been confronted by a lion will think *lion* when he reads *cat* because of the vividness of the experience.

The young child who has had many experiences with house cats will bring a deeper and different understanding to the learning of *cat* than will the child whose experience has been limited to a toy cat. Of course, the child whose only experience with *cat* has been that of playing with a toy cat will be better prepared for the reading than will a child whose experience is even more limited.

Furthermore, there are different types of appreciation. The child who has had and loved a toy cat may have a different sort of appreciation of *cat* from that of the child who has had the experience of pulling a live cat by the tail and has suffered the consequences. It is difficult to say which would have the deeper and more lasting impression. These two children are apt to bring to the reading of the word *cat* quite different generalized backgrounds. One child might infer that all cats are objects that he can play with in any fashion without any reaction on the part of the cat; the other might bring the generalized inference that it is hazardous to play with all cats [29].

It must be recognized that these three phases of word-meaning development are not discrete but overlap, both in their importance and development. The teaching of vocabulary entails more than merely teaching the child to recognize words. It comprises, in addition to recognition, enriching new words and extending their meanings. Strang, McCullough, and Traxler [256] say that the further the sense of a word is from its usual meaning, the more difficult it is to understand.

The nature and accuracy of the meaning depends upon several factors:

1. The extensiveness of meaning depends upon the number and kinds of situations in which the word is met.
2. The accuracy depends upon the skill by which the reader relates the new understanding to previous backgrounds.
3. The vividness depends upon the emotion, interest, acceptance, and purposefulness of the reader.
4. Retention depends upon the usefulness of the word to the reader.

General Ways of Enriching Word Meaning
1. Firsthand experiences

All of a child's firsthand experiences offer many opportunities for building backgrounds for the understanding of words. Such firsthand experiences include all those that the child has both in and out of school. He takes trips—he goes to the zoo, on a picnic, to a farm—and he learns the meanings of new words. He participates in games and in sports; he constructs things; and as he performs these activities, he learns new words. The child helps paint a mural or helps plant a flower or a vegetable garden; and as he does so he builds backgrounds of understanding that enable him to learn new words. He goes swimming at a lake or at the seashore; he goes to Sunday school; and he adds to his vocabulary.

The elementary-school teacher should encourage, establish, and cooperate with enterprises that provide firsthand experiences for the children in his class. He should use the wide variety of experiences the children have outside the school. Children are in school only five or six hours a day. In the hours outside school, they have countless experiences that result in vocabulary growth. The teacher who is inclined to disregard the educational significance of the experiences the children have outside the classroom is making a mistake. He should also take into consideration the resources of the homes and the community to capitalize upon the many learning opportunities related directly or indirectly to the work of the class.

It is often erroneously assumed that firsthand experiences will guarantee the development of understanding the meanings of words. Just as reading is meaningful to the extent that the child has developed readiness, so firsthand experiences have meaning to the extent that the child is ready for them; that is, to the extent that he has requisite backgrounds to benefit from the experiences. In addition, the child must be an energetic agent in the enterprise, which he will be if the enterprise is important to him. Word meanings must be identified with the actions, objects, and concepts of the experiences and must be actively used in discussion. It is through pooling concepts and word meanings in discussion that firsthand experiences may have their greatest fruitfulness as a vocabulary-building medium.

Opportunities should be made for the children to have many experiences. For that matter, discussion, in which the children have many chances to use the new words, should follow and precede firsthand experiences. In such ways new words and new meanings of words may easily be gained by the child.

2. Wide reading

Another way in which word meanings may be built is through wide reading. In the preprimer and primer days of a controlled reading vocabulary of approximately 200 words,* there is little opportunity for the child to develop a meaning vocabulary through his own reading. The teacher helps to overcome this limitation by reading orally to the children. He reads aloud not only the stories and factual materials related to the topics of the basal readers but also many of the fine stories that are known to be of interest to children. Through discussion of the pictures and talking about the stories, the children are led to make the new words part of their oral vocabularies.

It is not long before the primary child can begin to do what is for him wide reading. He can read in material at his reading level. Thus, he can precede and follow up a firsthand experience with reading that gives more meaning to the experience. In this way, too, vocabulary may be built. But

---

* In four widely used series of readers, for example, the number of words introduced in preprimer and primer material is 158, 189, 219, and 229.

in the primary grades, and, in fact, even beyond those grades, much of the enrichment of vocabularies will continue to come from selections read to the children by the teacher. In the intermediate grades, as the children become more mature readers, an ever-increasing amount of meaning vocabulary is developed by the reading that the children themselves do.

Exercises such as the following, associated with wide reading and given informally, are helpful:

1. Why did the author choose a given word rather than another word he might have used?
   "The water *gushed* down the hillside." Rather than,
   "The water *flowed* down the hillside."
2. Finding picturesque statements, such as "The lowing herd winds slowly o'er the lea." Rather than, *"The cows came home."*
3. Finding descriptive words, such as "The *murmuring* pines."
4. Identifying the sense aroused by the word.
   the *tinkling* of the bell
   the *penetrating mist*
   the *sparkling* light
   the *tang* of the lemon
5. Figures of speech.
   "He *threw the saddle over his shoulder* and walked out of the corral."
   "The *strip of golden sand.*"
6. Determining why a given word is more accurate than another that might have been used.

3. Audiovisual aids

Clear, precise, and extensive meanings of words can be built by the use of audiovisual aids. Experiences such as listening to the radio, watching television, seeing motion pictures, filmstrips, models, and the like, help build a background of word meanings. In using these vicarious aids to building word meanings, the teacher should recognize that vocabularies are built to the extent that these aids are used properly. It is inefficient merely to present such experiences without first preparing the children for them and without following the presentation with discussion. The preparatory work should set purposes for viewing or listening. These purposes should include the concept that vocabulary growth is one of the outcomes of the experience. The preparatory work should indicate the way in which the audiovisual material may best be studied. During the discussion that follows the presentation, the children should be encouraged to use the new vocabulary and even to explain the meanings of the terms used.

In fact, the fundamental steps in teaching a reading selection could well be used in teaching audiovisual material. It is obvious that whenever possible the teacher should preview the material in order to prepare for its use in the classroom.

Formal Ways of Enriching Word Meaning

The meaning vocabulary of children is so important that it is essential to include a systematic study of words in the reading program in addition to the more general teaching. Such systematic teaching is designed to develop the habit of attending to words and to teach the children techniques that will enable them to derive more precise meanings of the words they encounter in their reading. The techniques to be taught include the use of context clues to meaning, authors' definitions, structural aids to meaning, and the dictionary, as well as exercises designed to encourage the child to sense meaning relationships through noting synonyms and antonyms, descriptive words, figures of speech, and symbolic expression.

1. Context clues to meaning

The overall sense of a sentence conveys the precise meanings of the words that make up the sentence. Continued growth in meaning vocabulary is encouraged by giving instruction in using context as a way of deriving more exact and precise word meanings.

Exercises such as the following, in which the meaning of each of the italicized words can be derived from the context in which it occurs, illustrate materials helpful in giving instruction in the use of context clues to meaning.

1. The train made so much *noise* that the boy did not hear his mother call.
2. When John heard the band and saw the elephants, he knew the *parade* had started.
3. The river was *diverted* from its main channel and flowed instead through the new canal.

Multiple-choice exercises, such as the following, teach the child to use context as an aid to word meaning.

> *Underline the word that best completes the sentence:*
> The boy heard the lion _____.
> bray   roar   chirp

The following exercise, using context to develop word meaning, emphasizes extensiveness of meaning. Here the child is expected to choose the appropriate word to satisfy the two completion sentences:

Underline the one word that best completes both of the sentences:
The elephant had a long _____.
The tree had a thick _____.
bark   trunk   tail

Many similar exercises can be found in workbooks. The teacher can lead the children to locate sentences in the material they are reading that give them meanings to a specific word or a new meaning of a known word. The purpose of these exercises is to teach the child the habit of noting cues to meaning.

2. Authors' definitions

Another aid to giving specific training in word meanings is to encourage the child to note the definitions of words furnished by authors. The author has the responsibility for indicating the meanings of those new words he uses that he assumes will be unfamiliar to his readers. As a result, written material abounds in authors' definitions. The first two sentences of this paragraph indicate the meaning of the phrase *authors' definitions.* The teacher can locate definitions in the materials the children are reading, and he can have the children find the sentence or sentences that tell them what specific words mean. For example, the teacher might have the child find in a selection the following two sentences, which define the meaning of *a half-face camp.*

The front of the shelter was left open. That was why it was called a half-face camp.

The teacher can develop exercises in which a sentence defines a word. Sentences such as the following are illustrative of this kind of exercise.

1. After several hours of fierce *combat,* the fighting suddenly stopped.
2. The *monoplane,* an airplane with a single wing, can fly at great speed.
3. Venus, a *planet,* was seen in the early morning.

3. Structural aids to meaning

There are structural aids to meaning. The children should be systematically taught to recognize them and to use them in understanding words. Among the more common, for which exercises are provided in workbooks, are: prefixes, suffixes, variant endings changing the meanings of root words, and known words in compound words. As the children encounter affixed words in their readers, the teacher, in presenting these words, should indicate how the added prefix, suffix, or variant ending alters the meaning of the root word.

Training in structural aids to meaning should be given in contextual situations, such as are illustrated in the following exercises:

> *The prefix* un *can mean* (a) *not,* (b) *opposite action, or* (c) *something was removed. Show which meaning is implied by putting the appropriate letter before each sentence.*
> _____ 1. The boy *untied* the horse.
> _____ 2. The man was *unkind* to the horse.
> _____ 3. The rider was *unhorsed.*
>
> *Complete the following sentences:*
> 1. A snowball is a ball made of _____.
> 2. A steamboat is a boat run by _____.
> 3. A flowerpot is a pot for _____.
> 4. A fireplace is a place to have a _____.

4. Dictionary aids to meaning

Even in early reading lessons children may be taught to use dictionaries and other like reference aids to word meaning. In the primary grades this instruction is usually limited to the use of picture dictionaries. In the intermediate grades, systematic instruction is given in the use of dictionary work as a basic study skill. Only the word-meaning use of the dictionary will be discussed at this time.

An effective exercise to develop extensiveness of meaning is to have the children determine which of several dictionary definitions given for a word applies to the use of that word found within a particular sentence. This can be done either in connection with regular reading material or in exercises similar to the ones given below:

> *Read the definitions at the left. Then number the sentences at the right to show which definitions they fit. The sentence that fits definition 1, for* lace, *for example, will be numbered 1.*
>
> lace (lās) 1. an open weaving or net of fine thread. 2. a cord or string for pulling or holding together. 3. put laces through.
>
> ____ He had to *lace* his shoe again.
> ____ The lady had a *lace* shawl.
> ____ The *lace* on his shoe was broken.
>
> *Using your dictionary (picture or word), decide which meaning fits the underlined word in the sentences. Write the number of the meaning, as given in the dictionary, on the line in front of each sentence.*

_____ The fly in the house was big.
_____ I saw the airplane fly out of sight.
_____ The girl acted in a play.
_____ We will play a new game.
_____ The boy made a run in the ballgame.
_____ Let us run home before it rains.

5. Noting meaning relationships

There are many types of exercises available to the teacher to enable instruction to be given in noting such meaning relationships as antonyms and synonyms, figures of speech, symbolic expression, and descriptive words. The teacher will find that those exercises that use previously studied selections are effective in developing these abilities. Illustrative are the following.

If the words mean the same thing or nearly the same thing, put an S in front of them. If they mean opposite things, put O.

__ rear-front	__ thick-thin
__ tugged-hauled	__ shallow-deep
__ ranch-farm	__ fast-rapid

Have the children skim through a selection to find descriptive words or phrases that caused them to see, hear, taste, smell, or feel, such as:
the *shivering* aspen
the *roaring* river
the *sweet-scented* pines
the *luscious* berries
the *soft* moss

Have the children select the word that gives the most vivid picture in multiple-choice and completion exercises, such as:

      flowing
The moving tide carried the log away.
      surging

The spring gushed over the rock in _____.
   torrents haste volume

Find the word from the list below to complete each of the following sentences:

The water made a _____ sound.
The breaking branch made a _____ sound.
The bells made a _____ sound.
The train whistle made a _____ sound.
   cracking gurgling shrill musical

Have the children tell the meaning of words in the following figures of speech:
school of fish
weight on the hoof
go ahead and buck

Have the children explain the author's intended meaning of words in these phrases:
as straight as a pine
as cold as ice
sweating with concentration
a great appetite for life

The above examples of systematic ways in which to develop the habit of attending to words and techniques for deriving word meanings are by no means inclusive. They are intended to illustrate the fact that all exercises designed to develop word meanings must be in contextual situations. They also indicate that there is a place for the concentrated study of words and their meanings from the very first days of reading instruction on up through the reading program.

It must be remembered that activities involving the preparation of illustrations, friezes, or other displays, and those involving dramatizing or writing, encourage the systematic inspection of word meanings, especially in their sensory and descriptive aspects.

THOUGHT UNITS

The crux of efficient meaningful reading is having sufficiently rapid word-recognition techniques to enable the reader to assemble words into thought units, coupled with skill in locating and using those units in rapid, thoughtful reading. When the child is being taught to become effective in the word-recognition techniques, he should also be taught to locate and recognize thought units. Much of the difficulty in establishing thought-unit reading is caused by the lack of ability to analyze the printed line into usable thought units. This is accomplished by anticipating the thought units that are to come through the more or less automatic use of the peripheral or marginal vision. When the child is reading for purposes that are real and when he is employing contextual clues effectively, he tends to develop the skill of reading by thought units rather than by isolated words. However, some direct instruction is advisable. The instruction is given in several ways. The material may be so printed as to emphasize thought units. In the materials used in early instruction, for example, the thought units are not broken; rather a complete sentence is printed on one line. A little later, when sentences extend to the second line, the thought unit is not broken at the end of the first line; rather it is used to start the second line of print. Certain multiple-choice exercises in the workbooks and in teacher-made materials require the child to mark thought units rather than isolated words. Thought-unit phrases on flash cards, games requiring the child to respond in thought units, and devices that force reading by thought units provide additional experience. Certain punctuation marks aid in reading by thought units, and their help should be pointed out to the child. In materials for the early grades, punctuation marks are used effectively to emphasize thought units. The thought units are made apparent in the following sentence:

He said, "Look! There is a boat."

In addition, the teacher can demonstrate, on the chalkboard, breaking sentences into thought units in much the same way in which he demonstrates breaking words into their syllables or other usable units. Stories that follow a pattern of repetition may be read by children who need special emphasis on reading in thought units. Such stories contain repeating phrases, such as these:

"Not I," quacked the Duck.
"Not I," said the Mouse.
"Then I will," said the Little Red Hen.
And she did.

Interpretive oral reading helps in developing the ability to read in thought units if the interpretation is emphasized and if the child is given ample opportunity to prepare before he reads the material aloud. Under such conditions the child senses that the use of thought units is a usable skill. It is the job of the basic program to show the child various ways of grouping words into usable thought units and to induce him to do such grouping in all of his reading. If the materials in other fields are selected on the level of the reading ability of the child, as they should be, he will get experience in locating thought units throughout all his reading. If the material is too difficult, however, it will force him away from thought-unit groupings into word-by-word reading. Reading by thought units is encouraged when the material contains few, if any, word difficulties. It should be stressed that not only does the development of reading by thought units increase the speed of reading, it also produces more adequate comprehension of the material read.

```
                        over the fence
   The horse jumped   over the moon
                        under the swing
                  ran fast
   The little boy   sang sweetly   in the race
                  said quietly
   The big dog   ran rapidly   down the street   to get a bone.
   He saw a cat   and barked loudly   at it. The little cat   quickly climbed
   to the top   of a tree.
```

After reading a selection about flood control, an exercise such as the following could be given:

Write C in front of each phrase that deals with flood control.

_____ made a levee
_____ on the ocean liner
_____ straightened the channel
_____ the raging river
_____ jumped over the icy crevasse
_____ protected the lowlands
_____ mixed the waffle batter
_____ carried bags of sand

As you read the phrases below decide whether the author is trying to make you (1) see, (2) hear, (3) taste, (4) smell, or (5) feel something. Write the correct number before each phrase. Some phrases need more than one number.

_____ roar of the incoming tide
_____ cinnamon penetrated the air
_____ lemon made his lips pucker
_____ hit by the icy blast
_____ the lowing herd

_____ delicacy of the lace
_____ smooth as velvet
_____ sampled the hot roll
_____ the yellowness of the roses
_____ through the bumpy air

SENTENCE SENSE

Sentence sense is another component of basic comprehension, and it should therefore be taught. The child must appreciate the unity of a sentence. He must be taught to sense the relationship between its parts. He should be taught to sense even those parts in sentences of unusual order. Of course, the instruction should start with the direct sentence, in which the parts are located easily, and progress to sentences that utilize inverted orders of one sort or another. The child should be introduced gradually to sentences in which connectives change the anticipated ending of the sentence, as here:

We were going to town, but our car wouldn't start, so we stayed at home.

After the sentence is presented, the children can be asked whether the people went to town, what words show that they did not get there, and which words tell why they did not get there.

Another form of exercise that proves useful is to have the child locate, in sentences in material he is reading, those parts that tell who, (did) what, when, why, and so forth. An aid to the development of sentence sense is to have the child locate the antecedents of pronouns. The child will develop an understanding not only of pronouns but also of sentence sense by indicating who is referred to in such a sentence, as this one:

John sat watching *his* wife work at *her* sewing machine.

Interpreting punctuation marks as an aid to meaning also develops sentence sense. At the start, this may be no more than teaching that a sentence begins with a capital and ends with a mark of punctuation. Relatively soon, the children learn some of the common uses of the comma: separating words in a series; setting off parenthetical expressions; setting off words in apposition; and the like. At more advanced levels, the use of punctuation marks in more complex situations should be taught. The children may be expected to show how punctuation marks help them to understand the meaning of sentences, as these, for example:

1. Birds, too, were in the forest.
2. By paddling hard, they went swiftly through the water.
3. The fawns have very little scent, and if they lie still, they are safe.
4. Deer, bear, rabbits, and many other animals—several hundred in all— ran from the fire.

Other complexities of sentence structure in relation to understanding reading should be developed through drill and example:

1. *Read each sentence. Put a c in front of the answer that you believe gives the best meaning.*
   With hesitant steps we entered the haunted house.
   _____ a. The porch floor was uneven.
   _____ b. We were fearful of the adventure to come.
   _____ c. We were tired after the long walk.
   _____ d. We expected a gay party.
2. *Draw one line under the phrase that tells* where *and two lines under the one that tells* when:

   The engineers started building the Coulee Dam in the state of Washington soon after the plans were completed.
   Just as the guests arrived, the hostess put the meat on the grill.
   Other exercises may be prepared using phrases to answer *who, what, why, how,* and so on.

PARAGRAPH ORGANIZATION

Understanding a paragraph depends, to a great extent, upon an appreciation of the interrelationships among its sentences. This basic element of comprehension is taught by giving specific attention to the meaning and organization of paragraphs. Exercises requiring the child to find the best of several statements of the general meaning of a given paragraph are helpful. It is even more helpful to direct attention to various types of paragraph organization. Such instruction should be started by using the simplest type, that in which the topic sentence comes early in the paragraph, and supporting evidence follows. This instruction can be followed by introducing a second type of paragraph, one in which the fundamental information is given and then the topic sentence used to summarize the information. Finally, the child should study paragraphs in which initial introductory facts are presented, these summarized by a topic sentence and then supported by additional evidence.

Such learnings should be introduced gradually and might well proceed as follows:

1. Have the child find which of three statements best summarizes the main idea of a paragraph.
2. Have the child write headlines or general statements of the central meaning of a paragraph.
3. Introduce the child to the three types of paragraphs described above.
4. Have the child detect extraneous parts, ones that do not rightly belong within paragraphs.
5. Have the child write paragraphs of the three types described above, underlining the topic sentence of each.

The teacher can also have the child identify various types of paragraphs in materials he is reading. In all of these activities, the child should identify the topic sentences. He should tell how the topic sentence helps him understand the meaning of the paragraph and in what way the other sentences are related to the topic sentence. To illustrate, look at the first paragraph in this section and answer the following questions:

1. Which sentence is the topic sentence?
2. Which type of paragraph is this?
3. Does the paragraph develop the meaning of the heading of the section?
4. Do all the sentences support the topic sentence? If not, which sentence is extraneous?

THE ORGANIZATION OF A TOTAL SELECTION

Sensing the meaning of a total selection is a basic comprehension ability and one that depends upon discerning the interrelationships among the paragraphs and also the interrelationships among the various sections of the larger presentation. In a short story, for example, or in an even larger selection of narrative material, there is usually a "story" organization. Often, the writer, at the start, sets the stage, then introduces the plot, then unfolds the plot, and finally completes it. The writer follows an established sequence that the reader should sense as he reads.

The child can be helped to understand interrelationships among the paragraphs by having him recognize that narrative material has organized segments. Naturally, all the segments are not always apparent in any given story, and plots are frequently somewhat more complex than has been indicated here. Nonetheless, the child can often detect various segments in narrative writing.

Factual material also has organization. It frequently follows a sequential pattern: the topic is introduced, facts are accumulated and studied, conclusions or generalizations are made, and in some instances, exceptions are noted and discussed.

An understanding of the total selection may be developed in many ways. The children, for example, may be expected to list the main ideas of the paragraphs and then separate the ideas into sections, indicating for each section the purpose of the author. Or, using a familiar story, they can indicate where segments, such as those described above, start and end. Factual selections also can be analyzed. Of course, the children should recognize, in analyzing written material, that segments vary and not all segments are necessarily included. Children are led to an understanding of the organization of long selections when they locate transitional sentences and paragraphs—sentences or paragraphs used to make smooth and logical the transition from one part to another of the presentation. Detecting the difference between well-organized and poorly organized factual or narrative presentations teaches understanding of the total selection.

Selected References

Harris, A. J., *How To Increase Reading Ability,* fourth edition. New York: Longmans Green Company, 1961, Chaps. 15 and 16.

Hester, Kathleen B. *Teaching Every Child To Read,* second edition. New York: Harper & Row, 1964, Chap. 12.

Spache, George D. *Toward Better Reading.* Champaign, Illinois: Garrard Publishing Company, 1963, Chap. 4.

Tinker, Miles A., and Constance M. McCullough. *Teaching Elementary Reading,* second edition. New York: Appleton-Century-Crofts, Inc., 1962, Chap. 8.

CHAPTER 10

Diversified Comprehension Abilities

People read for many purposes, requiring diversified comprehension abilities. At certain times, the reader reads to locate or retain factual information. At other times, he reads to sense the relationships among the facts presented in order to organize them to suit his purposes. Many times the reader is involved in creative thinking as he reads. He may read to evaluate information given. In this case, he reads between the lines of print. He may reflect upon the ideas presented and, thus, read beyond the lines of print. Or finally, he may read to appreciate the content. In this reading his imagination may take him far beyond the line of print.

The more important diversified comprehension abilities are listed below and will be discussed each in turn.

1. Reading to retain information.
2. Reading to establish relationships.
3. Reading to evaluate.
4. Reading to reflect.
5. Reading to appreciate.

Reading to Retain Information

There are many times when the primary concern of the reader is to get specific or detailed information. When, for example, a trip is planned, he reads travel materials to find places of interest he might enjoy visiting. Under such a circumstance, the reader wishes to find out enough about the place he plans to visit to recall, at a future date, specific items of information. This is a careful sort of reading that necessitates attention to specific details within the discourse rather than a general impression of it. Such reading may employ skimming the material to isolate an important detail and then noting that important detail closely enough to recall it later. It may also entail attending not only to detail but also to some fundamental concepts. In the illustration above, the reader would attend to detailed information and also to fundamental concepts about the information of the scenic points. These fundamental concepts should be read to be retained. Reading for specific information is, in general, reading to remember somewhat isolated facts and concepts.

Reading to recall specific items of information is a factual type of reading comprehension in which the reader is directly concerned with remembering the items within a passage. This relatively slow and exacting type of reading enables the child to isolate and remember important details. This ability is the reading ability that is used, for example, in reading to list the types of products found in a given state or in reading any other collection of factual data. Wherever possible, when reading to recall specific items of information is employed, the purpose for collecting those facts should be real to the child. In other words, the collection of facts should serve some purpose immediately useful to him.

Although this is a much-practiced ability, there are children who cannot hold themselves to the degree of accuracy and careful reading necessary for remembering significant details within a selection. It is sometimes necessary to give direct drill in this ability. One such drill might be to have the child read a selection, then lay it aside and see how many facts he remembers after one reading. Then he should refer again to the selection to find those facts he failed to note or remember from his first reading. He might keep a record of the number of details he missed in order to see whether he could improve his score.

If the child has a reason for reading that makes it intrinsically worthwhile to him to note factual detail, reading to recall specific information is apt to be more careful and accurate, and consequently, it will result in growth in this ability. For example, a boy who has recently become interested in constructing model airplanes would read descriptive accounts to note the materials he needs to construct such a model or to check the accuracy of the construction he is undertaking. With a reading purpose that is so intrinsically important to him, he would be likely to note the details carefully as he reads and thereby get exceptionally good experience in this type of reading comprehension.

Reading to retain fundamental concepts is a factual ability very similar to reading to recall specific items of information. It differs in that the information to be remembered is of another kind. Actually, in most reading situations, reading to retain fundamental concepts is a higher order of reading and is of greater value in the total scheme than is reading to recall specific items of information. The fundamental concepts to be retained are frequently broad generalizations of specific facts. The similarity is that in both instances the major consideration in reading is to retain somewhat discrete entities—in the former, specific details, and in the latter, broader concepts.

Training in reading for retention of fundamental concepts is given by having the learner list the most important concepts included in a selection he has read. Because this is a very valuable study aid, once the child comprehends the usefulness of it, he will himself utilize this method and thereby establish the ability. As in all reading situations, the more real the need is, the greater the resultant learning. In this instance, the more the child feels the need to retain concepts, the greater will be the development of this comprehension ability. If the child is given opportunities to make use of the concepts he has retained, the independent use of this reading ability will more likely result.

Teachers tend to emphasize the recall of factual detail more often than the retention of fundamental concepts. This emphasis is unfortunate, for in most adult reading one wishes to remember fundamental concepts, of which facts are but supporting evidence.

In addition to developing the ability to read for factual information as an outgrowth of establishing purposes that demand this type of reading, there are specific exercises that may be used to get additional growth, such as these, for example:

Turn to page 178 of this book. Read the final paragraph to recall the information given. Now answer the following multiple-choice questions.

_____ 1. Some people estimate the listening vocabulary of entering first-grade children to be as few as (1) 24,000 words; (2) 10,000 words; (3) 4,000 words; (4) 1,000 words.

——— 2. The vocabularies of school children of today in comparison
with the vocabularies of school children of two decades ago
are (1) smaller; (2) about equal; (3) slightly larger; (4)
larger.

Reading to Establish Relationships

Many purposes for reading emphasize the need for establishing relationships. In certain cases, the purpose may be to classify factual material into
several categories. Again, the purpose may be to follow the chronology
of a series of historical events. Or it may be to follow specific directions,
such as those for making a puppet or for assembling a train printed on
a cereal box or for making a pudding out of the cereal. Possibly the reading is being done to follow the steps involved in preparing the cereal. The
purpose may be to combine information that has come from several
sources. In all of these illustrations there is a need to sense the relationships of concepts and facts so that an order among them may be established.

Establishing a sequence is the comprehension ability in which the
reader assembles the ideas or happenings in a logical arrangement. The
children in the top picture on page 201 are discussing the steps leading to
vulcanization, a process about which they have been reading. This logical
arrangement may be of several sorts, depending upon the material being
organized. It may be organized from the standpoint of the *sequence of
happenings*—a chronology. The child who wishes to tell the story "The
Three Bears" to the class gets experience in reading to organize, because
he must notice the events in the order of their occurence. In telling the
story he follows a chronological arrangement of the interrelated ideas. He
first has Goldilocks taste the various porridges in order and has her eat
the last one; he has her sit in the three chairs in order and has her break
the last one; he has her go upstairs and has her sleep in the last bed. Then,
he remembers that the three bears come home and that each inspects his
porridge, chair, and bed in order. Next the child has Goldilocks awaken
and run home. The child does not reverse the order in telling the story.
In the higher grades he might use the same chronological arrangement in
telling a story, although the time sequence of events might not be as
clearly defined for him as in the story "The Three Bears."

The items within the material may be arranged in sequence according
to *importance*. For example, the children of a class might want to organize
the background of material read in such a way as to ascertain the areas
they were going to study further. They might want to list these areas in

COURTESY DIANA KNIGHT

COURTESY ROBERT G. PAYTON

order of importance for an understanding of the larger topic, because they were aware that they could not deal with all aspects of the topic but only with the more important ones. Then the subordinate ideas might be listed as subtopics. The children in the class might want to know which phases of each topic they wished to include. Such an ordering of interrelationships would enable them to see the total subject.

Frequently, readers find it expedient to classify factual information in order to achieve their reading purpose. For example, before the housewife prepares a meal she thinks about what she is going to serve; second, she reads the recipes to list what she will acquire from the canned goods section, the meat counter, the bakery section, and the fruit and vegetable section of the supermarket. In this instance, she classifies ideas into categories. She knows she will wish to retain these ideas only long enough to do the marketing; her list is primarily a result of classifying related factual items to avoid darting back and forth around the supermarket.

The classification of the information may be for more effective retention. This ability in the first place is dependent upon the ability to note specific items of information, but in addition to pure recall, relationships between specific bits of information are perceived. Whenever such relationships can be established, classification should be made to encourage retention. This is a higher order of reading than is recalling discrete items of information. In studying the industries of a country, for example, classification may be used effectively by arranging industries into such categories as agriculture, manufacture, and use of natural resources.

In the intermediate grades, the child learns to outline in the more formal sense. Of course, before this time he has organized material for discussion, for storytelling, and for other purposes. He has organized, from his reading, topical papers to be presented. However, outlining per se is a part of the curriculum of the intermediate grades. Reading to establish relationships is frequently more than merely outlining. When the child sets down under major topics the subtopics in the order given in the passage, he may be said to be outlining that passage. But when he rearranges the topics and subtopics of a passage in their order of importance to him, or when he changes the author's organization in any way, he is doing more than merely outlining. He is establishing the relationships between ideas to fit his purpose rather than to follow the author's purpose. The ability to establish relationships and to order them grows out of the need to assemble material read to meet a real purpose. For example, the child who wishes to understand occupations or customs of people in foreign lands might arrange his material in various fashions and collect it from many sources. In his organization he is primarily concerned about the occupations and customs and only secondarily about the countries. On the other hand, in order to understand a foreign land in comparison with other foreign lands, the child is primarily interested in each of the foreign lands and only secondarily in their occupations and customs. He might read the same material on the two occasions, yet his arrangement, because of his different purposes, would be different and his learnings would be different.

Even a third-grade pupil can organize into a systematic whole material he has obtained from several references. The practice of having children give reports on material derived from several sources provides experience in this difficult form of establishing relationships. Outlining the passages and studying the author's organization gives the child an understanding of the interrelationships of information that exist in the material he is combining. Under such circumstances the child will find it expedient to read through to get the general significance of the passage, noting any headings or subheadings that the author has in the material that will later prove useful to him as he outlines it. Needless to say, the child does not have to write an outline in order to prove that he has been able to combine the ideas from several sources, but outlining gives experience in establishing a logical arrangement. In selecting material to be organized, the teacher should be sure that the context has been organized in a sequential way.

The sequence in developing the ability to combine ideas from several sources might be somewhat as follows. First, the child reads a selection and writes short statements that enable him to tell the sequence of the ideas the passage contains. After the child has had considerable experience in doing this type of exercise and has demonstrated ability in doing it, he might try to arrange the statements under major and subordinate headings of an outline. Next, the child might read another reference and attempt to expand the items of his outline to include those from a second source. Then he may attempt a relatively simple reorganization of a selection to meet a somewhat different purpose from the one the author had in mind when he wrote the selection. When the child becomes adept at this type of organization of material, he should be encouraged to read several references to get a general background within a field and to make a detailed and careful organization of a topic. This latter type of reading to establish relationships should, of course, be recognized as a difficult task of reading comprehension.

Reading to follow directions is a specialized sort of organized reading that requires care in following the step-by-step sequence to learn what the directions are and how to proceed with them. The reader must be able to understand each step in the sequence and to keep the steps in the correct order. This type of reading ability is used in reading recipes in a cookbook, in reading directions for assembling a toy, in reading a science experiment, and in reading from the chalkboard the directions for the day's work.

Frequently, in reading to follow directions, the child reads a step and then does it; he reads the next step, then executes it; and so on until the task is completed. Such might be the case in constructing a model. At other times, he may have to read the entire directions before he can start to follow them to completion; in this case, he reads to remember each item and the order of using them. Of the two types of directions just mentioned, the latter is usually the more difficult. At another time, the child may have to read a description of how something is made in order to write his own step-by-step sequence in making it. Reading to formulate a sequence of directions is still more difficult, but even this is within the capabilities of children in the intermediate grades. For example, a child might read two or three references about how candles are made, and from this reading he might formulate a step-by-step description of how to mold candles. Training in ability to follow directions is usually best given when children carry forward an activity. As such activities are brought to completion, the child who gets into difficulty because he did not understand the directions can at that time reread them in order to set himself straight. In this way, under the guidance of the teacher, the child can be expected to develop the ability to follow printed directions in his construction activities. He can also be led to appreciate the importance of each step in the process.

The activities found in workbooks are frequently helpful in developing the ability to follow directions. In these instructional materials, the child is asked to color according to specified directions, or he is told how to make certain things with paper, scissors, and paste. All such activities aid materially in developing the ability to follow directions.

The teacher will find performing experiments in science unusually useful in giving experience in following directions. He will also find useful following the printed or written directions in cooking, sewing, and industrial and fine arts. There is a wealth of opportunity in the elementary school to develop the ability to follow directions, and fortunately too, any confusion is immediately apparent. When, for example, the girl reads and follows the directions of a pattern in sewing, it is evident to both her and the teacher whether her reading has been accurate. It then becomes dramatically apparent to her, if a mistake has been made, that she needs to read more accurately. This kind of reading should be done at a relatively slow rate in order that the significant details and the sequential order of operation may be noted. The child should understand that he must read slowly, that he must understand each step in the sequence, and that if he fails to understand a step he should reread it.

Experience in reading to establish relationships is developed throughout the school day. The teacher should use the many opportunities afforded by reading in science and social studies to give practice in this type of comprehension. Additional practice exercises, in connection with material the child is reading, similar to those that follow, may be prepared.

1. *Establishing a sequence*

After the expiration of a time interval since reading a sequence of events the child should list the items in sequential order and then check his list against the passage.

You might wish to test your capability at sensing a sequence of events by listing the sequential order of emphasis on phonetic instruction, as given in this book. Then test your accuracy by referring to pages 153–54.

2. *Classifying information*

Write the following headings: (1) intellectual; (2) physical; (3) social; (4) emotional; (5) educational. Turn to pages 23–24. Classify the questions by placing the number and letter of each under the appropriate headings. Decide whether you think a question could be classified under more than one heading.

3. *Combining ideas from several sources*

Recall the four fundamental types of reading experience essential to growth in reading (given on page 93). Refer to Chapter 5. Think of the contribution each of the current approaches would make to each of the types of reading experience.

4. *Following directions*

You could, if you wished, make a wheel to teach variant endings. First, you must cut a circle three inches in diameter from a manila folder. Next, cut a circle two inches in diameter. Punch a small hole in the center of each. Now clip the two circular wheels together with a brass staple by putting the prongs through the holes. Then bend the prongs outward. Around the edge of the large wheel print various variant endings, such as *s, ed, ing*. On the smaller wheel, near its edge, print verbs, such as *walk, print, talk, end,* and so on. If you actually made the wheel, you would have read the above passage to follow directions and would have sensed the relationships between the steps.

Reading to Evaluate

Reading to evaluate is a type of comprehension in which the reader appraises the worthwhileness, the relevancy, or the accuracy of one or more passages. Gans [97] has shown that general capability in reading does not insure the ability of the pupils to locate authentic relative material.

During the primary-grade years, children have had experience in appraising the worthwhileness of stories. They have estimated whether the story would make a good play; whether it would be suitable to read before a group; whether it, in comparison with another, was the more pertinent to a specific discussion; and whether a given selection of material would be helpful in the study of a topic.

An example of a critical appraisal, to determine relevancy of material, took place in a class of second-grade pupils who were working on a story to be dramatized. The pupils read the story carefully and found it somewhat long. They decided that they should delete a part of the story, so they reread it carefully to decide what part they could best omit. Later, as they discussed the outcome of their critical appraisal, two of the children held different points of view. One defended his desire to omit a certain section of the story because it did not really contribute to the total unfolding of the plot, and its omission would not detract from the theme. In fact, he thought the story would have moved a little faster if the author left out this part. The other child, although agreeing with the first that the story was too long, desired to omit the end of the story and to change it because he felt that the author's ending was not in accord with the facts. Both of these children had made evaluations. Their purpose for reading had led them to do effective creative reading. The second child's criticism was actually somewhat erroneous, because his background of understanding was not rich enough to enable him to see the author's implications. Nevertheless, for him the story did not end right. As a result of the group discussion, the second child conceded that the story could have ended in the fashion in which it did, and so the suggestions of the first child were followed.

Another example of reading to determine relevancy took place in a group studying the growth of transportation in America. One of the children brought to class a description of the development in England of steam-driven engines. The children discussed the relevancy of the treatment to the growth of transportation in the United States. They decided that the material was relevant because of the contribution made to American railway transportation by inventions and refinements done in England. The purposeful activity of children, working within the unit framework, gave the teacher ample opportunity to develop the ability to determine relevancy of content. The children themselves soon held individual readers to a good level of performance, and thus they gained proficiency. When children are actively engaged in finding information about concepts important to them, they will not tolerate the loose thinking that permits unrelated material to enter a discussion.

In the upper grades of the elementary school, it is necessary to expand the analysis of the material read. Dewey [72] indicated the need to teach children to judge material when he said: "He who has learned as we call it to read without having learned to judge, discriminate, and choose has given hostages of dependence to powers beyond his control. He has prepared for himself a readiness to undergo new modes of intellectual servitude."

The children should judge the material for the adequacy of its treatment, the appropriateness of its content, and its accuracy and freedom from prejudice. This knowledge is difficult to acquire. In the study of a topic, for example, the children can readily be shown that some material treats the topic more fully and more adequately than does other materials. They can be shown that the mere length of a treatment does not necessarily indicate the adequacy of the treatment. They can also be shown that extraneous content is often included in a discussion that contributes little or nothing to it; sometimes the extraneous content actually biases the presentation. The child should establish early the habit of weighing the reasonableness and adequacy of an author's presentation. He can do this by constantly relating what he reads to the background of understanding he has already developed. The child should learn to think of the reasonableness of a presentation in the light of his understanding of the topic being presented. As far as reading instruction is concerned, the ability to judge the reasonableness and accuracy of an account is as much a habit as an ability. It is the habit of appraising the validity of statements; it is the ability to make those appraisals [117]. The ability depends to a considerable extent upon the background the child brings to the reading situation. Nevertheless, he can be taught to detect inconsistencies among authors' presentations, to judge authenticity in light of his background, and to judge the authoritativeness of authors. All of these appraisals are important in judging the reasonableness and adequacy of a treatment.

One fourth-grade class, for example, was reading about the animals of the arctic region when a controversy ensued. One child insisted that arctic wolves are brave, and another considered them cowardly. Both children brought stories to support their points of view. The first child gave evidence that arctic wolves attack polar bears, which seemed to him to be brave indeed. The other child brought evidence that showed that an arctic wolf will not approach a home if a husky dog is there. This behavior appeared cowardly to the second child. The teacher suggested that the children read other authors from reference material to resolve the controversy. Upon further study, the children found that there were no inconsistencies in the passage from which the difference of opinion started. They found that a wolf supported by other wolves is very brave, but by himself a wolf is not as bold. The children also noted that the intent and purpose of each of the authors was different, but that both authors were writing authoritatively and accurately. Such experiences develop a high order of critical evaluation.

In the early grades when the teacher asks "Do you think this could really have happened?" he is giving instruction designed to encourage the ability to evaluate the material read. When the children read that father "thinks the lost dog is over at a neighbor's home," the teacher may question whether father's statement is one of fact or one of opinion. In such instances, the child reads further in order to evaluate. Later on in the story the child may discover that the opinion was not verified by subsequent findings. The lost dog was shut up in a room within the family's own home.

A very good means of developing the ability to evaluate is to have the children tell how they know a certain fanciful story could not be true. At such times, the children may point out that the animals talk and that this is not in accordance with their own experience with animals, or that the fairy turned the pumpkin into a coach and that such a happening is not likely to be real. On the other hand, the children may read of an incident that all would agree was quite likely to happen. They might conclude, however, that the incident had little application to the topic under consideration.

In the later grades, the children can be shown that in regard to some controversial issues, different authors have arrived at different conclusions. Perhaps they may even be able to see why it is that the authors have arrived at different conclusions. Certainly, when they read material wherein there are apparent differences in points of view, the children can be led to see the differences and to account for them.

In reading about Switzerland, a child may find the statement that the scenery of Switzerland is the most beautiful in the world. He may, the next week, read a passage saying that the scenery of Alaska is the most beautiful in the world. Because these two statements are incompatible, he would like to reconcile them in some way. Opposition in point of view comes up again and again in reading the material of the upper grades. When differences in points of view are found, the teacher has an excellent opportunity to teach the child to appraise materials. In the above illustration, for example, the teacher could show the children each author was simply indicating that to him the scenery he was speaking of was the most beautiful, whereas, of course, the child himself knows that Iowa to him, if he lives there, has the most beautiful scenery in the world! And the same might be said of any other state or country.

The evaluation of material obviously depends upon the background of the person doing the evaluating. We enter the reading of materials with certain backgrounds and certain prejudices, which in themselves influence our ability to evaluate it.

McKillop [189], working with eleventh-grade pupils, found that attitudes and values had become important factors in determining evaluative responses. She reported "a disconcerting characteristic of the responses of the students was their tendency to label as false or stupid a passage which did not fit in with their attitudes." She made the plea for providing experiences in evaluation from the primary grades up. The child, as he develops in reading maturity meets countless emotionally charged articles (in current materials, in historical and other social studies material especially), which he must learn to evaluate. He must learn, too, the psychological fact that his own attitudes and values influence his perceptions, in order that he may allow for his own attitudinal biases when making his judgments. These learnings should be initiated in the first days of reading and continued throughout the years of instruction in reading.

The broader and richer the background, the freer from prejudice will be the reader, and the more adequate will be his judgments. In order to enable the children to read critically, the teacher should be concerned with building backgrounds and with eliminating prejudices. There is more to the development of reading to evaluate than having the background necessary to do that reading. The child must be taught continuously to appraise the statements in light of his understanding and his understanding in the light of the statements. It should be pointed out, however, that the child should recognize the need for reading with a certain amount of tolerance, because he is apt to be biased if he possesses an insufficient background.

To develop evaluative reading, the teacher may wish to prepare exercises similar to the following, which are based upon the material you have just read.

1. In the following statements, judge which are based upon fact and which are opinions.
   a. Switzerland is the most beautiful country in the world.
   b. The child read a passage that said Alaska is the most beautiful country in the world.
   c. McKillop reported that students in her study had a tendency to label as false a passage that did not fit their attitudes.
   d. Arctic wolves were found by the children to be both brave and cowardly.
2. Judge which of the following statements are reasonable and which are unreasonable.
   a. Primary children can judge whether or not a story will make a good play to be presented.
   b. The development of steam engines in England had little relationship to the growth of transportation in the United States.
   c. Dewey thinks that the ability to evaluate in reading is of little consequence.
   d. The adequacy of the evaluation of material depends upon the background of the person doing the evaluating.

Reading to Reflect

Reading to reflect involves a high order of reasoning with the material read and includes those reading comprehension abilities the reader uses to restructure the information presented so that he can understand its implications. This type of reading makes a heavy intellectual demand upon the reader. He must consider what he has read in the light of his knowledge and project his reasoning beyond the actual statements within the printed matter in order to come to conclusions, to sense new ideas, or to predict something that may come about as a result of the trend of the information given. He may from such reading form or change opinions. This reasoning is really an extrapolation of the information from which the reader forms an insight that for him is new.

When a child in the first grade says, "I think Epaminondas was foolish," he has considered the evidence and has gone beyond the stated information. He has formed an opinion. In this case the opinion was a highly accurate one. (Frequently, opinions are gained from reading about controversial issues, where the truth is unknown.) The soundness of the opinion will be determined by the amount and accuracy of information available to the reader, the accuracy with which he incorporates the material into his thinking, his freedom from prejudice, and his ability to suspend judgment until he has looked at the controversy from several points of view. Inasmuch as people continually form opinions about what they read, the instructional task is one of teaching the child to form sensible opinions—ones based upon carefully weighed evidence.

The reader often forms an opinion by reading the works of an author in whom he has confidence. He believes that the author has studied the issue carefully, and is, by and large, fairly accurate in his information. The assumption is that the author has spent more time on the issue and has a broader basis for judgment than the reader. At other times, the reader consults several authors, reflects upon the arguments of each, and then forms his own opinion [251].

In teaching the child to form opinions, the teacher should encourage him to appraise the importance of the opinion to him, the amount of time and effort he should devote to the question, and whether he will be satisfied with seeking aid from one or many authorities. The teacher should use many "What do you think about this?" questions to encourage the child to reflect upon the ideas presented. The teacher should note the reasonableness of the response and, in cases of obvious faulty opinion, indicate to the child that perhaps he failed to consider all the evidence before he formed a final opinion and show him how the inclusion of additional evidence might alter his judgment. As the child develops, the more difficult situations he meets will demand more extended reading before opinions are formulated. As he develops and as he reads more widely about questions, he will often refine opinions that he formulated earlier.

Often the reader may wish to form a single impression about the general point of view or the main sense of the selection. This takes only an easygoing kind of reading. Reading to note the general significance of a passage is the reading ability usually employed by adults in their leisure or recreational reading.

After reading a story about pioneer life, a child might say, "The life of the pioneers was one of many hardships," which, let us say, was in truth the principal import of the story. If the child were to be asked to tell upon what facts he based this generalized statement, he might say, "This story tells of the hardships of the life of the pioneers." If he were to be pressed further for more specific details, he might well be unable to give them, or at best be able to give only a few of them. He might open the book in an attempt to locate specific details that created in him the impression that pioneer life was full of hardships.

Much of the time it is neither necessary nor wise for the reader to remember the details upon which impressions are based. He frequently reads solely to get the chief sense of the article or passage. In fact, the person who becomes unduly concerned with details may entirely miss the feeling that the author is trying to portray or the underlying concepts he is trying to develop.

Most reading of newspapers is for the purpose of getting a general impression of the events recorded. In reading the society page, for example, the reader usually skims until he comes to an item of interest to him. Then he reads that item somewhat more carefully to get a general idea of its contents. Other newspaper reading, of course, is done for the purpose of getting details, or to verify an impression of a happening, or to attempt to foretell what is going to happen next. But much newspaper reading is for the sole purpose of getting an idea of the main import of the discussions of what has happened or is happening, so that the ideas gained may be reflected upon.

The ability to get the significance of a passage may be developed in the early grades by having the children formulate in one sentence what a given passage is about. Or again, have the children choose among a group of generalized statements the one that would be the most appropriate title. Or, when a child is reading a story that he will tell the other members of his class, caution him to tell about the most significant happenings.

Within the classwork there are many opportunities for developing this ability. In the personal reading program, the teacher could have each child keep a list of stories and other materials he has read, each annotated by a single statement. From time to time, the teacher might suggest that a child give other children an idea, in a short summary, of why he wishes to recommend a story to them. Inducing the children to write suitable headlines for news items provides other opportunities for building the ability to get the main idea of an item. A news summary for a television or radio program gives experience in reading to get the general significance.

The materials used for developing the ability to sense the main idea of a passage should be relatively easy and of a type that is easily summarized. They should not contain too many factual or detailed statements. From the very first days of reading, the teacher has been accustomed to ask, "What is this story about?" or "What is this passage about?" Thus, he gives the child experience in formulating a statement of his general impression of what he has read. It is often expedient to prepare the children for this purpose by saying, "This story is to be read to see what happens and what the significance of it is for you." As the child progresses through the grades of the elementary school, ability to read to sense the significance of a selection is refined to include reading larger and more difficult passages, from which clear interpretations involving reflective thinking are expected.

Frequently the reader is expected to generalize from factual information, another example of reading that requires reflective thinking. Generalizing aids in establishing relationships among seemingly discrete concepts. Reading to generalize is a type of comprehension in which the important elements within a passage are related one to another so that they can be combined into a principle, inference, or generalization. It includes the ability to see the connections among germane facts, to reflect upon them and to formulate tentative or final generalizations. The reasonableness of the generalization should be checked by relating it to backgrounds of knowledge that have been gained through firsthand experience, previous reading, and other sources. Such a generalization, for example, might be that the reason that certain foods cost more in the winter than in the summer is that they must be shipped from great distances in the winter; in the summer they are home-grown. Or again, the child may read that the baby grouse lay quietly against a leaf while his mother led an enemy away. The child may read a little later that a worm, green like the leaf, could not be seen. Later he may read of a rabbit, brown in the summer and white in winter. From these readings, and his thinking about them, the child is expected to make a generalization concerning protective coloration of animals. This is a high order of reading. It is the ability to interrelate fairly discrete information into a logical generalization.

The reader of this material should generalize at this point that reading is an art involving reflective reasoning and that the comprehension abilities are ways of thinking that use printed material. These ways of thinking can be taught. Such high-order mental activity is possible because with the printed page the reader can stop to reflect, he can turn back to reconsider, and he can progress at his own rate.

At the beginning, the generalizations should be between two closely related bits of information—information within the firsthand experience of the child. The child creatively restructures his thinking into new relationships. A child reads, for example, that a piece of wood stays on top of the water and that a penny sinks. He comprehends that objects large and light float, whereas objects small and heavy sink. He sees the relationship between the size and weight of an object and the likelihood of its floating in the water.

One child in a third-grade class, in answer to the question, "Why is Yellowstone Park called Yellowstone?" generalized from reading the map in his book that it is called "Yellowstone" because it is shown in yellow on the map. This child had generalized, but he had generalized upon insufficient data. Mark Twain recognized the possibility of such a faulty generalization when he had Huckleberry Finn think he was flying over Illinois, for the land was still green and his map showed Indiana as pink. Children naturally attempt to generalize in their reading. They must be taught, however, to withhold judgment until sufficient evidence has been collected to warrant a generalization. They must be taught too that they must test the reasonableness of their generalizations.

The teacher should encourage the children to formulate generalizations. Discussions of the merit and possible weaknesses of the generalization help the children establish this difficult reading-comprehension ability. When the teacher finds that a generalization has been made too quickly, he can encourage the children to read additional material that will enable them to clarify their generalization. In the above illustration of the faulty generalization about Yellowstone Park, the teacher might have had the child locate his own state on the map and find to his surprise that his state was colored yellow, too. The teacher should be careful not to discourage the child from generalizing. He should encourage the child to suspend his judgment, reflect more carefully, and then verify his conclusion.

Many generalizations derived from reading should be tried out experimentally to emphasize for the child the usefulness of reading to generalize. Reading to generalize is so frequently required of the child in science, arithmetic, and social studies that there are many opportunities for the teacher to lead the children to discover the usefulness of this ability and to enable the children to become proficient in generalizing from their reading. It should be noted that this high order of reading is often inversely related to speed. Here, speed of comprehension is frequently slow of necessity and often entails considerable rereading and always pauses to reflect.

Another type of reading in which reflective thinking is required is reading to extrapolate the information given to make an estimate of possible outcomes of a series of events or of stated points of view. In reading to predict outcomes, the elements within a passage must be seen in relation to one another in order that the most likely result can be estimated. This type of reading requires the ability to reflect upon the relationships between the items and to foretell the possible outcomes. When, for example, a person reads the story "The Lady or the Tiger," he is forced by the author to make his own choice as to the most likely outcome. Frequently, as an individual reads fictional material, he asks himself, "What is going to happen next?" Magazines make great use of the fact that people read in this fashion, and by printing stories in installments, they encourage the reader to buy subsequent issues.

Much of a child's interest in the plot of a story is derived from his ability to make estimates of what might happen and then to continue reading to see what did happen. In reading current events, this type of reading is frequently employed, because the ultimate outcome is in the future, and the reader must therefore make his estimate. In studying current trends of most sorts, the pupil is required to make predictions from his reading. The accuracy of his predictions depends in some measure upon his ability to read to appraise and to estimate the trends. In reading arithmetic problems, the effective reader makes an estimate of the correct answer. This is a specialized type of reading to predict outcomes. The child's life is full of situations in which he reads to make estimates of the consequences of given situations.

In a democracy, where people have a voice in the operation of their government, reading to predict outcomes needs especially to be developed. The adult reads of happenings in the newspaper; he makes an appraisal of what will happen if one course of action is followed and what will happen if an alternative course is followed—how it is likely to affect his life and the lives of his family and his friends. Then he wires his senator. The degree of wisdom found within his wire depends in no small measure upon his accuracy in predicting the outcomes of the different courses.

The development of reading to predict outcomes was begun in the prereading period, when the teacher, after reading halfway through a story, asked the children, "And what do you suppose is going to happen to the little gray rabbit?" This question, in somewhat more difficult form as the child progresses, will continue to be asked throughout the elementary school.

More direct experience may be given by selecting or preparing paragraphs that contain some related happenings from which the child may choose the one that tells the most likely consequence. Debates on social problems develop the ability to read for the purpose of estimating what will happen under various alternative conditions. It can be seen that reading to predict outcomes is a specialized way of thinking reflectively about reading material; so also are many types of reading comprehension. The best way of getting children to think in this fashion about a sequence of facts is to place them in reading situations that demand this sort of thinking. Any situation that requires an estimation beyond the data presented gives experience in this type of comprehending.

Exercises such as the following, which are drawn from the material you have been reading, are useful to give additional experience with these comprehension abilities.

> From reading this chapter on diversified comprehension abilities, which of the following generalizations seems most inclusive?
> 1. There is so much interrelationship among the comprehension abilities that there is little use in concerning oneself with diversified learning.
> 2. Refining of comprehension abilities to meet a variety of reading purposes should be taught to the mature reader only.
> 3. Reading is reasoning.
>
> From reading this chapter, which of the following would you predict to be the outcome of failure to teach diversified comprehension abilities?
> 1. Many children would be limited in one or more comprehension abilities.
> 2. Many children would develop a well-balanced comprehension repertory in general development of comprehension ability.

Reading to Appreciate

Reading to appreciate is creative reading. The reader forms mental images with the author's words as stimulus. It is impressionistic reading; it carries the reader somewhat beyond the stated elements of the discourse. The reader forms sensory impressions, he follows the change of events of unusual circumstances that makes for humor, he senses the logical construction of plot, he understands a character accurately portrayed. The reader appreciates the ways by which the writer conveys impressions. In discussing questions of providing esthetic experience, Smith [239] says: "Enjoyment of beauty, delight of an idea well expressed, joy in symmetry of form, in lilt of line, in suggestiveness of phrase, or in the pictorial power of words, all increase not only the reader's joy in reading but his joy in life." The individual reads to visualize and to enjoy the word pictures the author has painted; he reads to smell the odors that are described; he reads to feel temperatures or textures; he reads to hear the sounds described; and he reads to taste foods.

Materials that are written to be read to young children, or for children to read, have many appeals to the senses. Interested as they are in the world about them, young children especially enjoy reading materials that tell them about sights, sounds, feelings, tastes, and smells.

When a child reads such a book as *Little Eagle*, he should read it appreciating the sights, sounds, feelings, smells, and tastes depicted by the author, some of which are illustrated by the following excerpts: *

> Little Eagle was tall for his fourteen years. His skin was as coppery-red as the cliffs of Arizona's Canyon de Chelly, where he lived. His cheekbones were high and flat, his body lean and whip-strong. His long hair was looped into a knot at the back of his head and kept out of his eyes by a band of bright silk.
>
> The boy sniffed at the boiling meat, and a grin lighted his face. M-m-m-m-m! but that smelled good! The twins smelled it, too, for they began to squirm on the baby-boards where they had been tied securely all night long. Soon they set up a loud howl for their breakfast.

After the child has finished reading the selection he might be encouraged to point out the sensory appeals that were made and realize the pleasure he got from them as he read.

Literary materials are not the only ones that appeal to the senses. Many other materials also appeal to the senses. While the child learns science, he "feels" the wind, "sees" the moon and the stars in the sky, and "hears" the roar of the ravaging river at flood time.

The ability to read to form sensory impressions may be encouraged in ways such as the following: (1) comparing words, such as *walking* with *waddling* or *trudging; flowing* with *trickling* or *gushing,* to determine which gives the more vivid impression in sentences; (2) finding an illustration that goes with a descriptive passage; (3) creating illustrations designed to convey the mood of a passage or the picture of a passage; (4) describing the feeling-tone of a passage; (5) constructing murals—impressionistic or realistic—depicting a series of scenes in material read; (6) developing stage settings compatible with the action and times of a play; (7) selecting music to suggest the feeling-tone for a dramatization; (8) choosing from two passages the one that best conveys a sensory impression.

Humor brings enjoyment and offers release from tensions. The capacity to enjoy humor is developmental. Children should be taught to expand their way of living to include sensing humor in situations. A great part of the opportunity for enjoying humor comes from the printed page.

* From Armstrong Sperry, *Little Eagle* (Philadelphia: John C. Winston Company, 1938). Reprinted by permission of Holt, Rinehart and Winston, Inc., Publishers.

Teachers have made good use of published cartoon and comic material to stimulate ability in reading to appreciate the ridiculous or funny. Children eagerly cooperate in the enterprise of collecting cartoons to share during a current events or like period. Teachers keep files of humorous pictorial materials to be read by the children. These materials are useful for both silent and oral reading. In oral reading settings, the child must be taught how to read in order to communicate appreciatively with others as well as with the author of the material. When the children and teacher meet humor in their reading, time should be allowed for its appreciation. There is a contagion about humor that helps the teacher establish this learning.

The unfolding of stories such as *Treasure Island* is an experience that every child should enjoy. Identifying the cause-and-effect relationship of plot brings to the reader a high degree of satisfaction and understanding. The ability to follow a plot gets its start early in the reading experience of children. They learn to appreciate the plot of a series of pictures in the readiness program, and from the first days of reading, they read many stories with excellent plots. The plots at first, of course, are relatively simple where the cause-and-effect relationship is not made complex by digressions into characterizations or multiple actions.

After the child has learned to appreciate the plots of stories, he should be taught to unravel the central theme and subthemes in more and more complex presentations of series of related happenings. The teacher can aid children materially by having them show that subsequent events were the natural outgrowth of earlier ones.

To the child, the characters in books are practically as real as the child, the man, the woman, or the dog next door. In fact, the characters in books are often almost as alive and as much his friends as the living, breathing people with whom he associates. This is as it should be, for great is the pleasure that may be gotten from reading the doings of storybook folk. Great, too, is the understanding of behavior that may be gained from knowing book people. Many a child enlarges his understanding of loyalty as he travels with the deaf-mute in *King of the Wind*—a character who portrays boundless loyalty between man and beast.

Instruction in reading should provide for developing an appreciation of characterization in children's literature. Opportunity should be provided to enable the child to have as friends such characters as Lassie, Black Beauty, Heidi, and the many others. First acquaintance with famous storybook creatures and folk may come as the teacher reads to the child. Later, the child may become acquainted with the characters of children's literature through his own reading, chiefly in connection with personal reading and with experience-unit reading. Here the task of the teacher is one of introducing the child to the interesting people and other characters within books in order that the child may, through his own efforts, get to know them well.

Let us choose *Cinderella,* a story we all know, and assume that the children in a class have just finished reading and enjoying it. Exercises such as the following would develop capabilities needed for reading to appreciate.

1. Have the children draw the pumpkin coach.
2. Have them describe orally the ballroom.
3. Have them discuss the sounds they might hear.
4. Have them contrast Cinderella as a person with her sisters as persons.
5. Have the main actions of the plot enumerated in single sentences.
6. Have the children draw a humorous picture of the attempts of the two sisters to put on the glass slipper.

Diversified comprehension abilities develop as the child has day-by-day experience in their use. In the basal reading program the child is shown how to employ these comprehension abilities in situations of gradually increasing complexity. The child is also given experience in their application. In other phases of the program—the topical reading, the reading in the subject-matter areas, the personal reading—the child gets added practice in using these abilities in varied materials when reading for many purposes. It is not a matter of teaching one type of ability and then getting on to the next but of developing them side by side. Just as in the case of word-recognition techniques, it is versatility of attack, with understanding always emphasized, that is desired. The child should have a degree of proficiency in each of these abilities; moreover, he should be able to adjust the ability or abilities used to meet the purpose for which he is reading. For example, when a child reads a storybook for appreciation, it would not only be a waste of time, it would also spoil the recreatory aspects of the story to employ a detailed or highly organized reading ability in that reading. On the other hand, if he is reading a passage for the purpose of finding out how to construct something, merely getting a general impression of what the passage was about would not enable him to meet his purpose. He must have the abilities at his command and use them when and if applicable.

It is important to emphasize again that starting from the first lesson in reading the child develops the many comprehension abilities and versatility in their use. These achievements he must make if he is to meet the reading requirements of even the first grade. The child reads directions from the bulletin board about the day's activities. He has other experiences in reading to follow directions. He reads "Things To Do" in his workbook. He reads many stories to get the general significance or purport. He reads to organize in helping his committee prepare its report. He reads to evaluate, as when he asks about an experience chart that has been prepared, "Does this really tell what we did?" He reads critically in science, as when he looks up from his book and says, "This sounds the way winter really is." The materials of the first grade are filled with opportunities for gaining sensory impressions of what is read. What first-grade child has not heard the little goat go tripping across the bridge in the story "Billy Goat Gruff"? Or has not seen the vision of the wolf in grandmother's bed in the story "Little Red Ridinghood"? So it is with other comprehension abilities. This diversification begins at the first lesson and becomes more and more specific as the child progresses through the primary grades into the upper grades of the elementary school, high school, and college.

Adjusting the Rate of Comprehension

During recent years there has been some emphasis and a great deal of public interest on increasing the rate of reading as though it were a general attribute equally efficient in all situations. It has been believed by many that the person who reads rapidly in one situation tends to read rapidly in all situations, whereas the person who reads slowly in one situation tends to read slowly at all times. Customarily, in measuring the rate of reading, the number of words of simple material that a child reads within a given time has been carefully determined [235].

Rate of reading should not be thought of as the number of words per minute nor the number of eye fixations at which a child can read relatively simple materials. Carlson [49] has shown that the more important consideration should be the speed with which he can accomplish the *purpose* for which he is reading and the speed at which he can read material of different degrees of *difficulty*.

There are certain fundamental reading skills related to rate of comprehension that are characteristic of good readers. Among these is skill in progressing systematically across the line of print. Fluency in reading is characterized by effective eye movements. In reading, the eyes perceive the line of print through a series of pauses and forward jumps from left to right. Then the eyes make a *return sweep* to the beginning of the next line. It is during the pause, or *fixation*, that the actual recognition of the word or group of words takes place. Now and then the reader may lose the meaning, forget what he has read, or have difficulty in recognizing a word or phrase. Then he may find it necessary to jump back along the line of print with his eyes in order to reestablish his thinking. Such return jumps are known as *regressions*. The amount of the line of print that can be recognized at one glance is called the *span of recognition*. It should be noted, however, that this span of recognition for any one individual varies with the reading situation and with the difficulty of the materials. The larger the eye span, the fewer will be the fixations along the line of print. The fewer the regressions needed, the fewer the fixations, and therefore the more rapid the reading [110].

The role of eye movements in reading has been studied perhaps as much as any other reading skill associated with effective reading ability. There is much evidence to support the contention that the more rapid and effective the reading is the fewer will be the fixations. Good readers of any given material have effective eye movements for reading that material [49, 50, 111, 264, 265]. Poor readers of any material have faulty eye movements while reading that material. The question is: Do the good eye movements of the rapid reader cause his rapid reading? Or are the good eye movements simply another demonstration of the fact that he is a good reader—a reader with sufficient sight vocabulary, with adequate recognition techniques, with the ability to group words into thought units, and with similar abilities? Or again, do the poor eye movements of the poor reader cause his poor reading? Or are the poor eye movements the result of the fact that the poor reader was not familiar with the material he was reading—that he had to puzzle over the recognition of certain words, that he lost the meaning and had to regress to reestablish himself in the content, and that he was so concerned with individual words that it was impossible for him to group those words effectively? The answers to these questions determine whether the teacher should give training in the skill of effectively moving the eyes across the printed page, or whether he should devote instructional time to improving such skills as word recognition, thought-unit reading, and rapid comprehension [245].

The authors feel that time devoted to the training of eye movements would be better used in improving such skills as word recognition, thought-unit reading, and rapid comprehension. The major problem is not training eye movements; rather it is the improvement of reading.

There are mechanical devices designed to increase rate of reading. These devices have no usefulness in the primary grades, where the rate of oral reading is as fast or faster than the rate of silent reading and where instruction should rarely, if ever, be focused on rate of reading. The use of mechanical devices is questionable even in the intermediate grades. For the child who in all reading situations is a slow but accurate reader, specific help by an enthusiastic teacher can be given to increase his fluency. Highly interesting short-story material is the most suitable to use. The purposes for reading should be to enjoy the plot, to understand the main idea, or to read to predict what might happen next. These materials may be read as timed exercises, either by having the child determine how many pages he can read in ten minutes or how fast he can read a story of a given number of pages. The child may wish to keep a line chart indicating his rate of reading by placing the number of words per minute along the left-hand margin of the chart and the trial periods along the bottom. In this way he can watch his rate of reading improve from day to day. If there is a leveling off in the increase in rate, the teacher can insure a more adequate performance by devoting more attention to preparing the child for the reading, by setting slightly less exacting purposes, or by lowering the difficulty of the material until the child's upward progress is reestablished. Soon the broad reading of interesting material of appropriate difficulty will suffice for increasing the rate of reading unless a specific remedial problem has developed, such as excessive vocalization, overanalytical study of words, or lip reading.

The major problem of speed of reading is a problem of adjusting the rate of comprehension to the reading situation. The child should be taught that there is no one rate at which all materials should and can be read, but that the rate of comprehension should be in keeping with the purpose for reading and the difficulty of the material. What is wanted is that the child be able to read as rapidly as is compatible with his purpose and with the difficulty and type of the material. Certainly the child who is reading a story for purely recreational purposes can afford to read it more rapidly than he could the same story if he were preparing to tell it to his class. Certainly, too, the child who is reading a description of the making of butter just to get an impression of how butter is made would read much more rapidly than he would if he were intending to sense the step-by-step sequence in order to make butter.

Purpose is a factor in determining the rate at which a passage is read. It is important for the student to develop the technique of adjusting his speed of comprehension to the specific purpose at hand. Certain purposes require a careful analytical sort of reading. Other purposes lend themselves to more rapid and hurried perusal of material. If the child is reading to formulate a generalization, it is necessary for him to read carefully, to note all of the important concepts, even at times to reread and pause to reflect upon the relationships in order that he may arrive at an adequate generalization. Such reading takes time. After an hypothesis has been formulated, the reader must test it as he continues his slow, careful, and analytical reading. If, however, the purpose for reading the same material is to see whether it contains a discussion of a given topic, the passage can be covered in a short time. The task in this second case is not to think carefully through the material but merely to skim through it to determine what topics are discussed.

The rate of comprehension must also be adjusted to the difficulty of the material. Easy material with few, if any, vocabulary and concept difficulties can and should be read at a relatively fast rate, because the reader is not obliged to read slowly in order to recognize words or to think through abstract concepts. He can, therefore, read such material rapidly. For efficiency in reading easy material the child should not dawdle over what he reads. The question is not how rapidly he can read the material. The question is how rapidly he can comprehend the materials of various types and difficulties while reading for various purposes.

Material with many new and unfamiliar words or with many and difficult concepts must be read slowly if it is to be understood. In the first place, the child will have to take time to work out the recognition of the unfamiliar words, and he will have to think through the difficult concepts by recalling the meaning background needed for their interpretation. If he attempts to read such material rapidly, the child will be forced to skip some important key words or to neglect some of the major concepts. Unless he reads such material more slowly, he will have failed to comprehend it fully and will get an incomplete and erroneous idea of the passage or else no meaning at all. Unfortunately, moreover, the child will not only fail to understand the meaning of that passage, but he will also develop habits of inaccurate reading, habits he can ill afford to establish. He should learn to read material of varying difficulty as rapidly as he can with the type of understanding his purpose requires.

When the teacher finds that the child is attempting to read difficult material too rapidly, he should give the child comprehension exercises that require him to slacken his speed or which show him his inaccuracies. When he possesses knowledge of his inaccuracies, the pupil can be encouraged to read more slowly when he is reading difficult material. Some children, on the other hand, develop the habit of reading all material slowly. Although the slow speed is appropriate to some of the material, it is inappropriate to a great deal of it. The slow-reading child should be given practice in reading relatively easy and highly interesting material for less exacting purposes so that he may be encouraged to read rapidly. He might keep a record of his rate of reading so that he can observe his increase in rate of comprehension over a period of a month or so.

The child who is skilled in adjusting his reading rate soon learns that certain content-subjects frequently require slow reading, whereas the materials of other subjects can usually be read more rapidly; for example, the child knows that a mathematical problem cannot be read at the same rate as a story. Scientific material must be read much more slowly than is often suitable for reading social-studies materials. Within a subject-matter area, the child must learn to adjust his reading; a poem is read at quite a different rate than a short story.

Selected References

Cutts, Warren G. *Research in Reading for the Middle Grades.* Washington, D.C.: Superintendent of Documents, Government Printing Office, Catalog No. FS 5.230:30009, 1963.

Gans, Roma. *Common Sense in Teaching Reading.* Indianapolis: The Bobbs-Merrill Company, Inc., 1963, Chaps. 10, 11, and 19.

Harris, Albert J. *Effective Teaching of Reading.* New York: David McKay, Inc., 1962, Chap. 11.

Heilman, Arthur W. *Teaching Reading.* Columbus, Ohio: Charles E. Merrill Books, Inc., 1961, Chap. 9.

Smith, Nila Banton. *Reading Instruction for Today's Children.* Englewood Cliffs, N.J.: Prentice-Hall, Inc., 1963, Chap. 11.

CHAPTER 11

Basic Study Skills

Proficiency in the basic study skills is needed for successfully using reading in today's world. Many maps, graphs, and charts are to be found in daily papers, informational magazines, as well as in other types of printed materials. Everyone needs to be able to locate material to answer his daily problems. He needs to know how to use effectively a variety of reference materials, even if these are limited to a telephone book, time-table, book of maps, or catalogue. Everyone also needs the ability to organize information in logical order. These proficiencies constitute basic study skills and must be taught. They cannot be classified as comprehension abilities, but are closely allied to comprehension abilities and word-recognition skills.

The skills often thought of as basic study skills are those included in locating information through the use of library aids, tables of contents, the indexes within a book, and the like; the use of basic reference material, such as the dictionary, encyclopedia, atlas, almanac, telephone book, city directory, *Who's Who*, and newspaper and magazine files; the reading and effective use of tabular and pictorial material, such as maps, graphs, charts, tables, and schematic drawings; systems of organizing material, such as outlines, classification charts, time lines, and taking notes of material read; and reading special notations, such as formulas, abbreviations, and symbols. All of these are skills much needed in locating material that must be read with comprehension and in aiding study of the printed page. Mechanical aspects of handling reading equipment are included in the basic study skills. For example, in using an encyclopedia, effectiveness in the basic study skills implies that the child knows (1) what information for his purpose is most adequately discussed in the encyclopedia; (2) under what heading it can be found; (3) within what volume the treatment occurs; and (4) how to locate the discussion within the volume. The actual reading and comprehension of the material may be studying, but it is not one of the basic study skills.

Instruction in basic study skills is given in the basal reading program of the intermediate grades. Many experiences for using the newly learned skills are provided in the other phases of the reading program. Much readiness preparation for the basic instruction takes place as a part of the day-by-day reading in the primary grades. However, before concentrated learning of the study skills may be pursued the child must have achieved some measure of maturity in a number of reading techniques and abilities.

Locating Information

Effectiveness in locating information results from the application of many skills and abilities. If a child wishes to find material on a given topic, he must be able to appraise the subject and to make an estimate of the source that will most likely prove fruitful in his search. Then he must be able to use the library aids to locate that source. After he has located the likely source, he must locate the selection within the source. If the source is a textbook, for example, the child must be able to use the table of contents or the index in order to find the actual discussion of the topic. In the use of these two aids, the child's skill will, in a great measure, be determined by his knowledge of the appropriate key words or key topics under which the information desired is apt to be classified.

The child, in his first reading book, learns to read the numbers at the bottom of the page. The teacher, at that time, acts as the table of contents, and as he writes 9 on the chalkboard, he tells him, "Our new story will be found on page nine." The child soon develops skill in finding page numbers within the book. Next, a simple table of contents takes the place of the teacher in acquainting the child with the number of the page to which he should turn for the beginning of a specific story. At the start, this table of contents must be introduced carefully. Building upon previous learning, the teacher shows the child that the table of contents gives a listing of the selections of the book and that directly to the right of the title of each selection is the number of the page upon which it begins. So the child starts developing one of the skills that make up the complicated overall task of locating information.

As new and more mature aids to locating information are included in the books the child uses in his daily reading, the teacher has the responsibility of showing the child how to use them effectively. By careful teaching, the step-by-step sequence of locating information within a book is thus developed. These skills must be developed gradually to prevent the child from forming habits detrimental to establishing later learnings.

Before the child finishes the third reader he should have become acquainted with a city or school library. He should have obtained his own library card and been shown how to withdraw books of his own choosing. Then he should be introduced to the arrangement of the materials within the children's room of the library where he observes the librarian's use of the card catalogue and senses that therein is contained a record of each book in the library, with an indication of its location. The librarian or teacher tells him that he will find books in a certain section. Soon he learns the system of arrangement of books in the library and thereby gets an appreciation of the orderly placement of books.

The instruction given in the primary grades, although useful to the child at the time, takes the form of readiness for the more systematic instruction in skills involved in locating information that is a part of the intermediate-grade work in the basic study skills. The child in the primary grades has not as yet developed the reading capabilities nor the informational backgrounds necessary for effective systematic instruction in locating information.

Skill in locating information is dependent upon the child's ability to appraise his problem, estimate the likely source, locate that source within the library, use the index and table of contents, and skim to locate the exact discussion. Also there is a need for knowing enough about the problem so that he will make a fair estimate of where a discussion can be located and so that he can select the most likely key words in using an index. The skill in locating information can break down at any of these points. Therefore, each step must be taught.

The child should be taught to use the card catalogue and other aids within the library. The most fruitful means of teaching the child to use the library is to set the educational scene so that it is necessary for him to use the library to reach his goal.

In addition to making use of the library aids necessary for the child to meet his purposes, the teacher should give direct instruction in how to use them: show the child the card catalogue and how to use it; indicate how to write the slips when several references are to be located; teach him the use of indexes, such as *Readers' Guide to Periodical Literature;* give him help and experience in selection of key words; and in other ways teach him how to locate material in a library.

Skimming is one of the skills involved in locating information. Skimming is a rapid sort of reading in which the reader attempts to find out only what the passage is about or in which he undertakes to locate specific items of information. Skimming does not demand a careful weighing of the elements within the passage but simply requires a rapid inspection of those elements. Skimming is the most rapid sort of reading, and it is due to its rapidity that skimming gains much of its usefulness.

The reader may skim for the purpose of getting a general impression about a topic. Or he may skim in order to find out what is dealt with in some particular material that he has no intention of reading with more exactness. He may be reading to find out what is usually discussed under a given heading. Or at times he skims to refresh his memory concerning facts contained in material he previously has read with more exactness. He is not at such a time locating material to be read more carefully, but is achieving his purpose by means of skimming. The children, in one class, for example, might be interested in the topic of pioneer life, a topic they are to deal with for a month or so; they wish to isolate subtopics in order to plan group work that is important and relevant to the topic. They might skim through much material to find suitable segments of the larger topic. Skimming a great deal of material would help them list subtopics of greater breadth more rapidly than if skimming were not used. In this illustration, another useful outcome of employing the ability to skim might result, namely that of locating material containing worthwhile discussions of the topic under study. Then the children would know where material, that merited more careful reading, could be found. They might also have discovered the location of some of the best discussions of the subtopics to be treated.

Skimming is often used to locate a statement known to be within a given passage. A child, with this purpose, would skim the passage until he located such a statement. Then he would note the factual detail in which he was interested. In this way, he would achieve his purpose without having to resort to a careful and detailed reading of the entire passage. He might wish to know, for example, the exact date on which gold was discovered in California. He might recall, as a result of previous reading, that the date was given in a story about Sutter's Mill. Because he wanted to know the date, he might glance rapidly through that story until he found it. His skimming here might consist of looking only for numbers. At another time the child might want to know how the discovery of gold at Sutter's Mill came about. Such a reading purpose would require a more careful type of skimming. As he went through the story, the child would estimate the place wherein the discovery was actually recorded, and as he approached that place in the book he would read somewhat more carefully in order not to miss what he was looking for. Skimming requires different amounts of care, depending upon the type of information to be located. Children frequently apply skimming for the purpose of verifying a statement they have made.

At another time, a child might need to locate a given fact, but he would not know the exact discussion within which it was located. In such a case he probably would have to skim several discussions in which it might be reasonable to assume that the fact is treated before he found the one in which it actually was treated. In this sort of procedure the child must know enough about the subject to estimate with a fair degree of accuracy the sort of presentation in which the fact would likely be treated. The child, for instance, might wish to know whether Buffalo Bill had ever been a pony express rider. Normally, the child would assume that he would have to read material about Buffalo Bill. However, if he knew something about the westward movement, he might be able to estimate the part of Buffalo Bill's life that would be most fruitful to search. He might reason that if Buffalo Bill had been a pony express rider at any time, it would have been early in his life. He would therefore skim through enough presentations of Buffalo Bill's life to locate the bit of information that he wanted.

It can be seen from the above illustrations, which are by no means all-inclusive, that skimming is a highly useful skill and therefore one that should be encouraged. The practice of having children locate evidence in their basal reader to prove a point or to clarify a misconception is one method of developing ability to skim. Much of the ability to skim will be gained through the program of reading upon topical units, where there are many opportunities to skim. The teacher should show the children how to go about finding information quickly and how to make a rapid appraisal of its relevancy. It may be necessary too, from time to time, to give specific drill on skimming. At the start, exercises may be prepared that require the child to select an important fact within a single paragraph. The child, in doing such exercises, quickly locates and reads the sentence that gives the bit of information desired. Speed may be increased by having small groups of children of about equal reading ability compete with each other to see who can find the fact most quickly. As skill in skimming increases, the size of the selection may be lengthened, and the item of information to be located may be more obscure. The greater part of growth in this skill, however, should result from the reading the child does while he is actively engaged in locating material on a given topic, in locating important subtopics from those materials, and in employing this rapid skill to find specific items to verify facts and to clarify discussions.

The best time to teach the location of information is in the actual process of doing the extended reading in connection with a topical unit. Such instruction should be done in close relationship to the basal reading program, because it is here that the pupils and teacher are focusing their attention upon developing skills that make for sequential growth in using printed material. Then too there are opportunities for the youngsters to practice these skills in relationship to the reading done in the content fields.

Formal exercises on locating information are useful. The following exercises are based on the reading you have done in this book.

1. Look at the table of contents. Determine in what chapter you might expect to find a discussion of word synthesis.
2. Under which of the following words in the index would you look for a discussion of the relationship between hearing and first-grade reading ability: (a) auditory aids; (b) auditory readiness; (c) hard-of-hearing child; (d) ear training.
3. In what type of book would you look to find suggestions for overcoming reversal problems in reading? (a) a developmental reading book; (b) a teacher's manual; (c) a book on remedial reading; (d) a book on children's literature.
4. There is a quotation from John Dewey in the previous chapter. Skim to find it for a page reference.

General Reference Materials

There are many books that are not to be read from cover to cover but are merely to be referred to when the need arises. There are about 5,500 standard reference titles. It would be impossible to know all of them well. These reference books cover many fields and are of many types. One interesting reference book for an elementary-school child in relation to his personal reading is *The Junior Book of Authors*. This reference book contains photographs of authors of children's literature and brief biographical or autobiographical sketches, and is written "for boys and girls from seven to seventeen" years of age. The child interested in places will find atlases very informative. Dictionaries and encyclopedias are, of course, necessities in modern education. Among the better encyclopedias suitable to the elementary-school grades are *Britannica Junior, Book of Knowledge, Childcraft, Colliers Encyclopedia, Compton's Pictured Encyclopedia, The Golden Encyclopedia, Our Wonderful World,* and the *World Book Encyclopedia.* Most encyclopedias are difficult reading for most elementary-school children [88].

For the most part, growth in the use of general reference materials during the primary reading experiences takes the form of building a background for the more systematic presentations later. This learning is not incidental or haphazard but planned by the alert teacher who recognizes the reading problems the child will meet as he becomes more mature. The teacher plans activities similar in nature to the use of the encyclopedia. His file of pictures is arranged similar to the arrangement of an encyclopedia. He has large tabs indicating ANIMAL, CITY, FARM, TRANSPORTATION, WEATHER, and the like. Behind the ANIMAL tab he places pictures of animals arranged by name in alphabetical order. The children go to this file of reference material to illustrate activities. The readiness for the use of such an alphabetical listing may have been established through the picture dictionary the child used while he was reading his first reader.

The teacher develops awareness and understanding of the uses of reference material by planning activities that require that he use such material as a source for answers to questions that have been raised during class discussion. At such times he demonstrates how he goes about locating the material and reads pertinent information aloud to the children, naming as he does so the general reference aid to which he first turned in order to get the information. When he or a child uses an unusual word, one that excites the curiosity of the children, he refers to the dictionary, demonstrates how he finds the word, and reads aloud the definitions, having the children select the most suitable to the context in which it was used.

In many activities, the children get experience in arranging words in rough alphabetical order. Mention has already been made of the child's own picture dictionary. Sometimes, too, it may be worthwhile to have the children, as a group project, develop a more complete dictionary for the use of the class. Further experience in alphabetizing can be built by grouping by initial letters words derived from social studies, health, or science as a spelling aid. Activities such as these are to be encouraged, for they provide essential prerequisites to the much more detailed instruction in the use of general reference aids given in the intermediate grades.

Probably the most useful single reference book is the dictionary. Because there are few elementary-school children who sense the many functions of the dictionary, instruction should be so directed as to acquaint them with the variety of information to be found within a dictionary. The value of the dictionary should be recognized by all the children, and the habit of using it should be established. Use of the dictionary should not be limited to finding word meanings but should include other important functions. Mott and Baisden [199] list at least 28 distinct and helpful uses of the dictionary, which include various aids to the pronunciation, interpretation, and spelling of words, aids to understanding word relationships, and such facts as names of places and people, flags of various countries, and common signs that appear in print.

The children should learn many of these functions of a dictionary. By and large, the instruction should be a direct outgrowth of need—recourse to the dictionary in the regular classroom activities. If an attitude of studious attention to words, word meanings, and similar matters is developed, the children will find many intrinsic opportunities to refer to the dictionary for a variety of purposes. However, the instruction in the usefulness of the dictionary and the development of efficiency in the use of the dictionary cannot be left to an opportunistic method. The teacher should create situations wherein the dictionary must be used for various purposes. He should then show the children how to meet these situations, when necessary, through direct instruction in the use of the dictionary. As instruction goes forward, the teacher can appraise the effectiveness of the individual pupil's use of these skills through the use of teacher-made tests.

In a like manner, direct instruction should be given in using other important reference materials. Time used for such instruction will be time profitably used. The child must develop the habit of going to and using reference materials if he is to use reading effectively to aid him in solving his problems. The successful student is frequently distinguished from the unsuccessful one by his skill in the use of reference materials.

Formal exercises on general reference materials are useful. The following exercise is based on your knowledge of reference books.

Exercise:

Write the number of the appropriate reference tool in the space provided before the statement of information wanted.

1. Encyclopedia	_____ Date of birth of the President of the United States
2, Dictionary	_____ A word derivation
3. World Almanac	_____ The location of a college
4. Telephone Book	_____ Treatment on monsoons
5. Who's Who	_____ Type of architecture used in the cathedral of Rheims
6. Card Catalog	_____ Location of the shop of a TV repairman
7. History of European Art	_____ Who wrote *Silas Marner?*

Graphic and Tabular Materials

The use of graphic and tabular aids in communication is increasing daily. These aids to understanding a large body of information in a relatively short time constitute a difficult learning that needs to be taught. Included in compact informational aids are such graphic materials as maps, charts, schematic pictures, diagrams, and tables. Inasmuch as informative presentations of such aids have become a part of printed material in many fields, it is important that all children be instructed in their interpretation in the reading program.

Opportunities for gaining experience in reading pictorial and tabular materials of many sorts abound in the day-by-day living even in a first grade. Such materials must, of necessity, be simple, often depicting a single concept at the outset. Later, several concepts may be included in the presentation. For example, a simple map is prepared showing the location of the school on the street. Then it is expanded to include the adjoining streets. Later the homes of the children may be recorded. Still later, this map may be used to illustrate to the children safe and direct routes to school. By fifth grade a vast number of concepts may be included on a single map.

Experiences enjoyed by children may provide opportunities for teaching map reading. "A Treasure Hunt" is one such. Many good teachers have globes in their rooms and point out where a current event took place in relation to the location of their town. This procedure provides another opportunity for teaching map reading.

The discussion that follows will consider, as an example, some of the problems the child faces in learning to read maps in the intermediate grades [57]. It is not possible for a map to include all the mass of information about the area being pictured, nor is it possible for it to show accurately all the information that it includes. The map must focus upon one type of information. In doing so, other information will be distorted to some extent. In other words, it is not possible to have truth of area, angle, scale, and shape on one flat map. One truth only may be emphasized, sacrificing other truths. The inexperienced map reader has not learned to make allowances for the distortions. Consequently, he gets erroneous ideas— erroneous ideas that may persist for many years. Children, for example, brought up in sparsely settled areas, in which the vast distances they know are depicted on a rather compact map, transfer the scale to maps of more thickly populated areas based upon a larger scale. They therefore are surprised to find that distances in these other areas are not nearly so great as the distances in the areas they know well. Again, in looking at the typical map of the United States, the child finds it difficult to reconcile the fact that Maine is actually farther south than the northern border. of the western states, because through distortion Maine usually appears considerably closer to the top of the map.

In order to avoid one type of distortion, it is recommended that globes be referred to frequently and that comparisons be made between areas on the globe and the flat-map representations of the same area. [274]. It is recommended also that map segments be located on the globe in order that the child may get a more generalized picture of the location of the segment under consideration as well as its relation to other segments.

Another problem in reading maps arises from variation in types of maps. Many types of maps, illustrating specific kinds of information, must be read by the reader of geographical materials. In discussing the use of maps in historical reading, Johnson [153] says: "Maps are representations of the whole or of parts of the earth's surface. They indicate location, direction, distance, extent, area, land and water forms. They may indicate innumerable other conditions: elevation, air or ocean currents, routes of travel, areas of political or other control, the quantity and distribution of rainfall, of agricultural and mineral productions and of manufactures, the volume and movement of trade, the number and distribution of communicants of churches, of members of political parties, of votes in an election, of native and foreign-born persons, of illiterates, of schools and colleges, of readers of good books, of frequenters of art museums, of the number or quantity, and distribution, of phenomena of any kind that can be counted or measured, and located." A child may be able to read one type of map and yet be totally unable to get meaning from another type. Consequently, experience should be given in reading many types of maps. For example, pictographic maps (maps on which important concepts are superimposed by means of pictures) lead to distortions of distance. Faulty generalizations should be corrected immediately. One boy faultily generalized when he remarked, "I do not know how large the United States is, but I think it is about as large as our cow pasture." This faulty generalization resulted from examining a map upon which was a picture of a covered wagon plodding along the Old Oregon Trail. Schematic presentations must be supplemented by direct explanation.

Some difficulties in reading maps are due to their compactness. Compactness makes it difficult to locate information. Key letters and numbers constitute excellent aids. The child should be taught early to use key letters and numbers in locating items on a map, and he should be given much experience in using these key letters and numbers so that he may become an effective reader of compact maps. Michaelis [192] discusses the symbolic nature of maps as follows: "Because maps are symbolic representations, attention must be given to the gradual development of map language. First of all, simple maps with very little detail should be selected for use. . . . The map-reading skills require specific instruction in the symbols, colors, scale, and network of lines used to represent specific information. Such instruction should be related to specific needs for the use of maps so that children can make immediate application of what they learn. . . . It should never be assumed that children can read maps simply because maps are in their books and on the walls of their classrooms."

Because of the vast number of items included on compact maps, there is overcrowding, and as a result small print is used, which makes maps hard to read. The written material does not always appear in left-to-right order. Words and phrases are lettered in every direction—uphill, downhill, in circular fashion—and this practice complicates the reading somewhat. In locating a city, for example, the dot that indicates the city may be either at the beginning, the middle, or the end of the name of the city; sometimes there are two or more dots, any one of which could be the one that shows the location of a specific city. A careful visual scrutiny, or a concentrated study, must be made if the map is to be read accurately. Many of the uncertainties in reading compact maps found in textbooks can be overcome to some extent by referring to larger wall maps when there is doubt. Many times too the teacher may help the children read the map accurately by supplementing, from his knowledge, the facts shown on the map itself.

Some confusion in reading maps is due to the fact that most map study is done on a wall map, where north is at the top of the map. Children in the Northern Hemisphere get the notion that the Mississippi River flows south, because it goes "downhill" on the map hanging on the wall. They find it difficult to understand that the Red River, which flows north into Hudson Bay, also flows downhill. This confusion can be overcome by having the children make relief maps of an area and compare the relief map with the wall map. Another example of this misinterpretation occurs when a person who lives in Colorado says, "I'm going *up* north to Idaho." Maps should occasionally be put on the floor and studied to correct this misconception that has become a part of the American culture.

In teaching map reading it is well to go from known localities to unknown localities, from simple presentations to more complex ones. Picturing an air view of a locality, along with a map representation of the same scene, is an excellent way of enabling maps to tell their story to children. From these simple learnings, the steps of learning to read shaded maps, dotted maps, and cross-hatched maps (which are often tables in the form of maps) constitute a gradual developmental process.

Tables, charts, and other representations of comparative data are read with understanding only when the child comprehends quantity, and only when the child has had direct instruction in getting meaning from them. The child must learn to read all explanatory material, such as title, key, scales, headings and subheadings, and so on. Graphs used in the elementary school should be simple in design, and at the outset, a graph should present only one concept. Then too, uniformity in presentation is necessary.

Most of the initial instruction in reading graphic material should be an outgrowth of regular activities in the reading class or in the topical-unit work related to the reading program. When a child has some quantitative information to communicate to the class, he may prepare a graphic representation of it, or he may find a graphic representation to show to the class.

Teaching the use of graphic materials is started early in the child's educational experience. The developmental sequence of learning may be shown by the following illustration. On a calendar, the child may keep a record of the days of sunshine and rain for a month by darkening in the rainy days and painting in the face of the sun on the sunny days. This is graphic representation in its early stages. Later, the children of a group, studying a weather unit, may keep a month's line graph, indicating the temperature at noon each day. Still later, they may prepare a more complicated line graph of the high and low barometer readings of representative cities in the United States—one in the South, one in the East, one in the North, one in the West—to compare climatic conditions over a period of time. So it is that an understanding of graphic material is gradually developed.

Formulas, Abbreviations, and Symbols

Formulas, abbreviations, and symbols are compact ways of representing ideas. They are used in all types of reading material and in all subject-matter areas. Alphabetical abbreviations are overworked in United States. Learning to read them quickly and with understanding is a basic study skill. Abbreviations and symbolism have become a part of everyday reading. Newspapers, for example, are replete with abbreviations and symbols. The textbooks and other materials the children read from the first grade on contain them.

Instruction in reading these forms of expression is provided in the basic reading program as well as reading in those content fields where they actually get their major emphasis. The responsibility of the basal program is to provide enough experience with these shorthand means of expression to establish the habit of attending to them and demanding understanding of them when they are found in print. The child should be taught to recognize that interpreting them is necessary for understanding, and he therefore should not skip them when he meets them.

Systems of Organizing Material

Skill in using systems of organizing material consists of arranging basic concepts in an orderly manner and putting down the arrangement on paper in systematic form. The preparation of classification tables depicting informational concepts, outlining, and preparing time lines are representative of this organizational skill, which is dependent upon comprehension abilities that emphasize orderly relationships. The skill is different from reading to comprehend orderly relationships in that it consists of tabulating in an organized system the concepts or facts gleaned from reading one source or several.

Very early in their reading program, the children start to develop the ability to formulate a simple organization of material read and the ability to integrate facts from two or more sources. In the readiness program, the children frequently classify pictures of things into a twofold classification. They might be asked, for example, to sort a group of pictures into two piles, one consisting of pictures of objects that would be found in a house, the other of objects found in a garage. They might further sort the pictures of household items into those used in the kitchen and those used elsewhere in the house. And they might sort the pictures of garage objects into those used for the car and those used for the care of the lawn.

They have had experience in listing sequences of ideas and have used this ability in composing experience charts. In connection with the development of the comprehension ability of sensing a sequence, they have been given experience in systems of organization. After having read a selection, the children have placed sentences stating the important elements of the material in numbered arrangement to show the proper sequence. Later, they may have written and arranged their own generalized statements of the significant features of a selection and may even have used that organization in telling about it. They have listed major headings and classified related facts under those major headings. Usually, however, they have not, by the end of their primary reading experiences, been taught the outline form and structure per se. When the first experiences in outlining are given, these outlines should be simple ones. The children have, however, had a great deal of experience of the kind that prepares them to make more extended outlines later. One such experience may have been in connection with planning a topical unit. The subtopics are listed upon the chalkboard; under each is noted the chief points to be considered and the names of the children who are to constitute each reading-study group. More mature aspects entail both outlining the material and reading the outline after it has been written. The child must learn the form for indicating the major topics and the subtopics.

A topical unit frequently used in the reading experiences of third-grade children is one on Indians. Several tribes of Indians showing widely different cultural patterns are studied. The information about each tribe may be organized under such subheadings as "Food" "Shelter," "Clothing," "Occupations." Then, by inspecting this information, interrelationships between the way of life and the means of getting a livelihood may be developed. The organizational study skill involved is making a two-way table. Along the left-hand margin of the table the names of the tribes are listed. Along the top are the subheadings "Food," "Shelter," "Clothing," "Occupations," "Customs." In the boxes so formed the statements of fact about each tribe and each characteristic are tabulated. Generalizations are made by comparing the interrelationships. By such an arrangement the children, by looking down the column "Food," can readily see that the food of various tribes differed. By looking across the row for a given tribe, other relationships come into focus. In this way, more complex relationships can be detected than the children would otherwise have been able to see. Generalizations are made by comparing the interrelationships. It may have been that one tribe was highly migratory, because of the necessity of following migrating animals, and that another tribe built permanent homes, because it depended chiefly upon agriculture for food. From these generalizations a summarizing generalization might be made, that the means of obtaining a livelihood had a marked influence upon the customs and the home life of the tribes of Indians. By such experiences, even in the early years of reading instruction, the child develops skill in organizing material in logical arrangements.

The basic study skill of organizing is the method of tabulating the findings. Among the comprehension abilities involved are those of locating in the running content, or in the pictorial and tabular material, the concepts to be placed in the system of organizing and sensing the relationships among the concepts to formulate generalizations. The child with a repertory of systems of organization can become skillful in selecting the one most appropriate to the findings he is interested in putting down on paper.

Selected References

DeBoer, John., and Martha Dallmann. *The Teaching of Reading*, revised edition. New York: Holt, Rinehart and Winston, 1964, Chap. 9.

Durrell, Donald D. *Improving Reading Instruction*. New York: Harcourt, Brace and World, Inc., 1956, Chap. 13.

Harris, Albert J. *How To Increase Reading Ability*, fourth edition. New York: Longmans Green & Company, 1961, Chap. 16.

Hildreth, Gertrude. *Teaching Reading*. New York: Holt, Rinehart and Winston, 1958, Chaps. 14 and 19.

Russell, David H. *Children Learn To Read*, second edition. Boston: Ginn and Company, 1961, Chap. 11.

CHAPTER 12

Oral Reading

Oral reading is the oral presentation of printed or written material. Although it is true that only a small portion of the reading of a person is done orally, it is usually done in a situation that is highly important to the reader. Studies showing the frequency of the use of oral reading as compared with that of silent reading tend to deny the value of oral-reading instruction, because oral reading is used so relatively infrequently. This, however, does not mean that it merits little of our attention [64]. If a person reads to a large group just once in his entire life, school time spent in learning effective oral reading will not have been wasted.

It could be hypothesized that if oral reading had in the past been better developed throughout the reading program, much greater use would be made of it now. One has only to listen to the efforts of the usual oral reader at a parent-teacher meeting, at a church meeting, or at a service club to recognize that the school has failed to develop excellence in this phase of instruction. When we remember that many adults of today were taught by oral-sight methods, we wonder why such methods are still tolerated.

There are occasions, both in school and out, where it is necessary for an individual to read aloud in order to communicate ideas he has found or to share ideas he anticipates he will find. The communicative worth of oral reading is dependent upon the excellence of that reading. For that reason, one who does oral reading (and practically everyone does) wants to do it well. Not only does a poor presentation waste both the reader's and listener's time, but it also loses much of the communicative possibilities.

Relationship Between Oral Reading and Silent Reading

Interpretative oral reading depends upon the same techniques and skills that are used in silent reading. As the child develops silent-reading abilities, he prepares himself to read orally as well. There are, however, certain fundamental differences between oral and silent reading. Oral reading is usually a much slower process than silent reading, because there is a greater use of speech mechanisms. Oral reading is usually done in a situation where more than one individual is present. Consequently, the reader is concerned not only about getting the meaning from the printed page but also about imparting that meaning to others. He wishes his listeners to understand and enjoy what he is reading. As he reads, he puts special emphasis upon interpreting meaning, so that what he is reading may be understood by the others. In certain situations he is attentive to his appearance, to his manner of presentation, and to his enunciation and pronunciation. At other times, he is so concerned with sharing an idea related to the group discussion that he loses himself in his reading.

Spontaneous activities in reading orally should be encouraged. There will be many of them. But there is a need for specific instruction in oral reading in order that the child may be able to communicate the ideas of authors' meanings, and his interpretations of them, to others as well as to himself. Very rarely does the poor reader get so enthusiastic about his oral presentation as to forget himself and his reading difficulty.

It is common practice for the beginning teacher to use oral sight-reading as a device for initial instruction in silent reading. The contention is made that oral sight-reading benefits the teacher, because it enables him to detect errors quickly annd diagnose the youngster's instructional needs. It is true that the teacher can gain diagnostic insight by listening to a child read a passage at sight. However, this technique for noting the types of errors the child is making should be done individually, with teacher and child working together, not in a group setting. A diagnosis of errors can be made in other ways; for example, by checking the errors made in workbook activities, or by ferreting out the reasons for mis-understandings displayed during discussion periods. Nonetheless, the teacher will find it profitable to have oral reading sessions with each pupil to make informal appraisals of his instructional needs. The teacher can observe any indications of word-by-word reading, failure to read in thought units, specific types of word-recognition difficulties, lack of sentence sense, and any other symptom of poor comprehension ability.

Oral reading sessions, during which the child reads aloud material he has previously read silently, afford the possibility of diagnosing a child's reading difficulties. Only persistent errors will be made in such situations. Careless or random errors will tend to have been eliminated during the silent reading. Therefore, the teacher should be on the alert to detect the errors in prepared oral reading sessions, because they more truly indicate the kinds of errors that are causing confusion in the silent read-ing of the child. In all reading activities, the teacher continually studies the child's reading needs, diagnoses his problems, and gives remediation.

There is little justification for oral sight-reading round-a-group, one child reading after another. Silent reading can be taught more effectively by methods that do not use oral word-calling by the children [276]. And more importantly, the emotional reaction of many children to such misuse of oral reading is detrimental both to the child's adjustment to school and to the establishment of desirable skill in silent and oral reading.

Unfortunately, the sight-round-a-group (sometimes called the barber shop method, "Next, please") is used often in primary grades, especially in the first grade, where children are poorly equipped to do oral sight-reading. Teachers using this method wonder why children become word-by-word readers. The child can do nothing else, because he has not developed an adequate sight vocabulary to read in thought units. If he has not preread the material silently, he is able only to pronounce the word he is viewing at the time [158].

Only after a child has acquired considerable skill at reading prepared materials is he ready to do oral sight-reading. The teacher should realize that sight-reading is much more difficult than either reading prepared material or relating an experience that he has had. There are many factors that enter into oral sight-reading that make it difficult. Only a mature reader has sufficient reading ability to keep far enough ahead of his reading to anticipate what is coming next, and to interpret immediately the meaning of the passage by his voice. The mature reader has well over a five-word eye-voice span: that is, the mature reader is looking at least five words ahead of the word he is actually pronouncing. When a mature reader is reading aloud, it is possible to cover the print and have him continue voicing five to eight words. This eye-voice span enables him to overcome word difficulties, using rapid recognition techniques. He can also sense the meaning of the selection before he actually has to say it orally. The eye-voice span of the first or second grader is limited to one or two words. So he can do little other than oral word-calling, and he is forced to pause to work out word difficulties as he meets them. He not only loses his audience in the process, but he also frequently becomes blocked, making more and more errors. He becomes so intent with the problem of recognizing individual words that he is likely to forget what has been previously read, and he will therefore have difficulty in giving an adequate interpretation. He will long since have lost his listeners.

Oral Reading and Emotion

In his whole school life there is probably no educational experience so highly charged with detrimental emotional reactions as that of forcing a child who has little reading ability to stumble through an oral presentation. Such an emotional situation is very much augmented by the practice of having the other members of the group follow the passage in their own books. Experiences of this kind tend to cause feelings of confusion and frustration, which in turn make for inadequate reading and personal adjustment, as well as lay the foundation for insecurity in future oral-reading experiences.

If the teaching of oral reading is handled carefully, it can become an effective means of aiding in the development of more adequate oral-language patterns and also in the development of effective silent reading. If handled incorrectly, emotional results may occur that will seriously limit the growth of oral language, ease of expression, and the development of poise before groups. In fact, emotional reactions may be so severe that they result in a rejection of both oral and silent reading. All too frequently, serious reading-disability cases have been started through emotional reactions to being placed again and again in impossible oral-reading situations.

In group work, where the children are reading under the immediate direction of the teacher, it is wise to have a child read aloud the answer to a specific question, such as, "Read the next four sentences to find the answer to the question 'Of what is the fox afraid?'" After the children have read the four sentences silently, the teacher may call for a volunteer, or he may call upon a specific child to read out the answer, "He is afraid of dogs." The children are then asked to read the next five lines silently to answer the question "What did the fox and rabbits say to each other?" The teacher may wish to have the children answer this question by taking parts, one the part of the fox and two others the parts of the rabbits, or the teacher may wish to have one child read aloud the entire answer. You may wish to turn to Chapter 6, page 104 of this book, under "Directing the Reading," to read the series of questions given in the teacher's manual for this first-grade story material.

Such oral reading is in a sense prepared oral reading, because the child has read the material silently before he reads it to the group. It might reasonably be said that no material should be read orally during the primary years without giving the child the opportunity to read that material silently before reading it aloud, except in those instances when the child is reading individually to the teacher for diagnostic purposes.

Types of Oral-Reading Instruction

There are many situations within the classroom in which oral reading instruction may be given. In the early grades, as has been previously discussed, oral reading is closely related to guided silent reading. In the first part of grade one, during group work, the segments that are read silently and then orally are relatively short, involving four or five lines of print. As the child gains stature in reading, the amount of silent reading encompasses a page or even more. The child locates to read orally only the part of the total silent reading that answers a specific question. Later on, an entire passage may be read silently and the oral reading confined to rereading a relatively small part of it that answers the specific question. A variation of this procedure is one in which an entire selection may be reread orally, with individual children reading the conversational part, with one child as the narrator. Extensive use should be made of oral-reading activities that are directly related to the silent reading.

Another type of oral reading grows out of sharing the independent reading the children have done. Time should be set aside for a child to share with others books he has enjoyed. In sharing, at least part of the presentation should be in the form of oral reading. This oral reading enables the child to give the other children a sample of the quality of expression used by the author. Children enter into this type of oral reading with a high degree of enthusiasm. Not only does the reader enjoy presenting a well-liked passage, but his audience listens. The material is fresh and new and appeals to the listeners, who want to hear what their classmate has to say about the material he has chosen to share with them. This procedure is lifelike, somewhat akin to what many children have experienced in their homes.

Another type of oral-reading experience useful after children have gained stature in both oral and silent reading (end-of-third-grade or higher ability) is sharing a book by reading it aloud in somewhat the old New England fireside way. For those children who have the reading stature to profit, this reading provides experience in oral *sight*-reading. In some classrooms the teacher and some of the more able readers take turns. This type of reading may even be started toward the end of the second grade because some children in second grade read above third-grade levels. The best reader in a second-grade class may well have a reading proficiency above fifth grade and certainly can profit from experience in sight oral reading. These enjoyable and profitable class experiences are looked forward to with eager anticipation by all the children.

Choral reading is a type of reading experience used effectively by many teachers. The children enjoy reading aloud together poetry or other rhythmic material. This type of reading experience is especially useful for the child who is a slow, hesitant reader, because he can pick up cues from the more able without having his reading mistakes focused upon. Nor do his mistakes accumulate. Choral reading is profitable also in audience reading, where a choral group offers background reading in a dramatization. In preparation for the interpretative presentation, all the children gain good experience in oral reading. Another advantage of choral reading is that it enables the less mature readers to participate on an even basis in the class project. These children demonstrate to themselves that they *can* read, and they gain poise and confidence. They also gain added motivation to continue tussling with the task of learning to read, because they see they have a reasonable chance of winning the tussle.

Another type of instruction involves interpretative audience reading. Audience reading should be taught in those situations where oral interpretation of material is natural and realistic. The situation should be such that a purpose for silent reading is to prepare for audience presentation. The entire group is involved in this kind of activity. The audience may be the other reading groups, another class, the principal, or parents or other visitors.

The teacher can use various opportunities where audience reading is the product sought in the learning situation, such as dramatizing stories the children have found interesting and feel are suitable. Frequently at the close of reading a unit within their basal reader, the children are given the opportunity to choose a selection within the unit that they feel is appropriate to oral presentation. Types of activities in which oral reading is a natural part are the development of a radio program or the development of a series of pictures to be used as a television presentation, in which the selection is read as the pictures are shown. At times, the children may wish to prepare a tape recording of their oral presentations so that they too may hear their own audio interpretations as they watch the pictures. If these experiences are to be shared with other groups, the sense of social responsibility will stimulate a high quality of oral reading. The desire to improve in oral reading will also be encouraged.

When the children recognize that they want to improve their oral reading in an audience situation, they and the teacher may find it helpful to formulate objectives for improving oral reading. Questions such as the following may be prepared:

1. Was the selected material interesting?
2. Did the child know which parts he was to read?
3. Was he well prepared?
4. Did he read loudly enough for all to hear?
5. Did he read as though he were talking?
6. Did he keep sufficient eye contact with his audience?
7. Did he read at an appropriate rate?
8. Did he use pauses well?
9. Did he use his voice well to let the listeners know what was happening?
10. Did he face his audience in a relaxed, comfortable position?

One child in the class might try to improve his oral reading by taking heed of only certain of these objectives; other children might concentrate upon others. The class as a group might judge whether the oral reading being done and being heard is becoming better. Their immediate goal is to improve the oral presentation of the material they plan to share with others. The listeners should tell what they liked in the oral interpretation and how they think the oral presentation could be improved. The suggested improvements will be natural and welcome.

Possibly as important a question as any other in the above list for improving oral reading is the one that has to do with pacing and timing the reading. The child can be helped if he understands that he must take time to pause frequently as he proceeds in order that both he and his listeners may better understand his presentation. Many children who have difficulty in reading orally attempt to read too rapidly. Proper pauses will help overcome this tendency .

The Introduction of
Interpretative Oral Reading

Oral reading should not be a device for teaching silent reading; rather, oral reading should be taught because it is in and of itself important. At the beginning of reading instruction the foundation for good oral reading is laid by encouraging the children to talk without embarrassment to a group. This ability can be developed by motivating a child to relate experiences, tell stories, and plan activities in a conversational fashion before or during the initial stages of the reading program. After the child has acquired a certain degree of ease in such activities and has some skill in silent reading, he is ready to undertake the initial practice of interpretative oral reading.

The child's first practice in oral reading should be an outgrowth of his oral experiences. While relating a story, for example, the child should be encouraged to read a small section of the story, which he has previously prepared himself to read orally. The initial oral-reading experiences should be enjoyable to the child and to the group and should be free from word-recognition problems. In order to ensure success at this stage, the child should read aloud to the teacher the selection he has prepared so that he can be helped with any difficult words before he reads aloud. He should approach this introduction to oral reading with confidence of success. If he gets into any reading difficulty, the teacher should immediately and unobtrusively supply the word that is causing trouble.

After the child has demonstrated poise and confidence in reading short passages in conversational situations, he is ready to read relatively easy and well-prepared material in the audience situation. As has been indicated above, the child should be made to feel his responsibility to his audience and should be helped in securing reading material that will be of real interest to the class. He should have material that the class has not read. The listeners should also realize their responsibility as an audience. They should not have books or other materials about that will interfere with their listening. It should be stressed again that the teacher should help the child immediately if he gets into any difficulty. If he gets emotionally tense, if he reads in a high and strained voice, it is well to let him finish the presentation by simply telling in his own words the rest of the passage. Or the teacher may decide it is wise to help the child finish the presentation. Teachers at more advanced levels should also be aware of symptoms of emotional tension in oral reading situations. These symptoms include an increase in rate of oral reading, high and strained voice, hiding behind the book, lowering voice volume, slurring words, fidgeting, flushing. In extreme instances the child loses control of his voice. He may be seen to have tears in his eyes.

The materials for oral sight-reading should be relatively easy, with few, if any, word difficulties. If the child shows signs of emotional tension and embarrassment, it is likely that the task set for him is too difficult and should be set at a lower level. In all the oral activities at the early stages, a skillful rendition is neither necessary nor to be expected. If, however, the child is allowed to progress by easy and interesting steps, skillful interpretation will be developed. Not until after the techniques of oral reading are established should the refinement of expression be undertaken.

There are many opportunities to use oral reading in the primary and the upper grades of the elementary school. In the basal reading program the child is shown how to read orally. It is in the basal program that the objectives of oral reading are formulated. However, much oral reading may be done in connection with reading in the content fields and in reading topical units. Some of the oral reading grows out of the personal reading of the child. When he finds a story, a passage, a poem, or a clipping that he wishes to share with others, he may be encouraged to do so by means of an oral-reading presentation of it. Any material in which the child has an interest, or in which he has ideas to share, is suitable for oral reading. The child should learn to read well orally a wide variety of material. Systematic instruction in oral reading, however, is given most effectively in connection with sharing materials of a literary type. Among the better materials for developing oral reading are those that contain passages with conversations in them, because the child is aware that by means of reading his part he is expressing how the person he is representing would say them.

Selected References

DeBoer, John J., and Martha Dallmann. *The Teaching of Reading*, revised edition. New York: Holt, Rinehart and Winston, Inc., 1964, Chap. 10.
Harris, Albert J. *How To Increase Reading Ability*, fourth edition. New York: Longmans, Green & Company, Inc., 1961, Chap. 8.

Spache, George D. *Toward Better Reading*. Champaign, Illinois: Garrard Publishing Company, 1963, Chap. 11.

Tinker, Miles A., and Constance M. McCullough. *Teaching Elementary Reading*, second edition. New York: Appleton-Century-Crofts, Inc., 1962, Chap. 10.

Worthington, Louise Willson. "Oral Reading? Certainly!" *Contributions to Reading*, No. 19. Boston: Ginn and Company.

IV

THE TEACHER
ENCOURAGES
THE USE OF READING

Reading Content-Subject Materials

Each of the various fields of human experience has developed its own unique way of recording its organized content. The task of communicating to a reader the realities of geography is a quite different one from that of communicating "a touch of magic even greater than the wonder of reality," as Smith [239] expresses a function of poetry. It was necessary for each field of human experience to develop a way of writing that was compatible with the ideas it handled. Also it was necessary for each field to develop its own specialized vocabulary to describe its phenomena. For example, *photosynthesis* identifies in one word the process whereby plants manufacture food by means of the energy of the sun. It takes several pages to elucidate this process, but the person to whom it has been explained requires only the one word, *photosynthesis,* to communicate the phenomenon.

The materials of the school subjects read by a child of fifth-grade reading proficiency, for example, demand many abilities. Even a cursory inspection of the materials of the various subjects shows that there are important differences among them. The materials are different in difficulty, in compactness of ideas, in continuity of presentation, in vocabulary used, and in many other respects. The child approaches the reading of the materials of each field with purposes specific to that field.

DIFFERENCES IN READING MATERIALS

To illustrate the startling variety of reading material to which a fifth-grade child must adjust, excerpts from some of the basic textbooks used by the typical child in the fifth grade are presented herewith. In addition to reading these books, the child reads other textbooks, reference books, and a wide variety of trade books. To read these different kinds of materials, marked reading adjustments are required.

Basal Reader

The first sample is a page reproduced from an imaginative story about Paul Bunyan, entitled "The Greatest Lumberjack," in *Days of Adventure* [24], a fifth-grade basal reader used by a middle reading group. This book was used systematically to teach reading skills and abilities. The lessons were taught specifically to develop skills and abilities, as discussed in Chapter 7, on teaching a lesson.

Mathematics Textbook

The second samples (reproduced on page 256) are excerpts from a fifth-grade mathematics textbook, *Seeing Through Arithmetic* [130]. This book was studied in a systematic fashion. The directions for each new arithmetical operation were considered with care. Then the children read and solved the problems to gain experience in the newly established mathematical concepts.

It can readily be seen that this reading task is entirely different from that of reading the basal reading text. There is no running context in the problems that the child can use for help in recognizing words. The book contains a technical vocabulary that must be learned. The reading material calls for careful and exact reading, which must be done at a relatively slow rate. Each step in the process must be fully understood before the next step is taken. Much more time is used in reflecting upon the material presented than in recognizing the words within it. When the child attempts to read this material with the reading techniques that are suitable and effective in reading the basal reading material, illustrated above, he is in difficulty almost immediately. In reading the materials of mathematics, even the habit of continuous reading must be laid aside, for much of the time the child reads a short problem, thinks about it, goes back to reread, and then takes pencil in hand and works for a time. He may then

"Feeding so many men was quite a problem. For breakfast the loggers liked pancakes, which they called flapjacks. Paul got an immense griddle so that a large number of flapjacks could be made at one time. Right beside the griddle there were tall buildings that looked like grain elevators. Those elevators were filled with tons of flour. But mixing so much pancake batter was a problem, also. Paul invented a huge machine for mixing batter. Since that time people have made smaller machines like it to use for concrete mixers. Of course, in Paul Bunyan's day, there wasn't any concrete to be mixed.

"Well, Sir, when the griddle and batter mixer were ready, another problem came up. How could the cooks grease such an immense griddle? First they tried fastening large bunches of empty flour sacks to the ends of telephone poles. Then they dipped the sacks in grease and rubbed the grease on the griddle. That took too much time.

"Paul chose several cooks' helpers and had them fasten fat hams on their feet, with the fattest side of the ham down. Then he had them get up on the hot griddle. As the fat on the hams melted, the helpers began to slide around on the griddle. In just no time at all the greasing job was done.

From Guy L. Bond, Marie C. Cuddy, and Leo C. Fay, Days of Adventure, *Fifth-Grade Reader, The Developmental Reading Series (Chicago: Lyons & Carnahan, 1962). Reprinted by permission.*

be ready to go to the next problem. The nature of the material and the purpose for reading cause marked adjustment of reading abilities, habits, and attitudes.

Science Textbook

The third sample is a page from a fifth-grade science textbook, *Science in Our World* [227]. (See page 257.)

Much of the work in science consists in performing experiments. To perform an experiment the individual reads about other experiments and

G Before you try to say how much less $\frac{3}{5}$ is than $\frac{2}{3}$, you change both fraction numerals to other fraction numerals with the denominator ■. 15 is the common denominator because $\frac{3}{5}$ and $\frac{2}{3}$ can each be expressed as a number of fifteenths.

H Rectangles D, E, F, and G are all the same size. $\frac{■}{4}$ of Rectangle D is red. $\frac{■}{6}$ of Rectangle E is red.

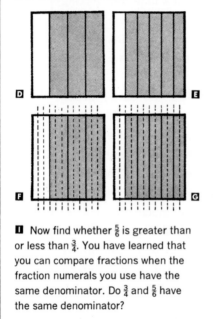

I Now find whether $\frac{5}{6}$ is greater than or less than $\frac{3}{4}$. You have learned that you can compare fractions when the fraction numerals you use have the same denominator. Do $\frac{3}{4}$ and $\frac{5}{6}$ have the same denominator?

J You should find a common denominator for $\frac{3}{4}$ and $\frac{5}{6}$. $\frac{5}{6}$ has the larger denominator. Can you express $\frac{3}{4}$ as a number of sixths? 6 is not a common denominator for $\frac{3}{4}$ and $\frac{5}{6}$.

K Pictures F and G show Rectangles D and E marked off in twelfths. Can you tell how many twelfths there are in $\frac{3}{4}$? In $\frac{5}{6}$? 12 is a common denominator for $\frac{3}{4}$ and $\frac{5}{6}$.

L $\frac{5}{6} = \frac{■}{12}$. $\frac{3}{4} = \frac{■}{12}$. Is $\frac{5}{6}$ greater than or less than $\frac{3}{4}$?

B One morning Jim rode $3\frac{9}{10}$ mi. on his bicycle. In the afternoon he rode $2\frac{1}{2}$ mi. How far did he ride that day?

C Nancy grew $1\frac{3}{4}$ in. during the first six months of the year. During the last six months she grew $1\frac{5}{8}$ in. How much did she grow in all that year?

D After a grocer had sold $10\frac{1}{2}$ lb. of fresh green beans, he had $26\frac{1}{2}$ lb. left. How many pounds of fresh green beans did he have to begin with?

E Sally bought a $3\frac{1}{4}$ lb. chicken and $\frac{1}{2}$ lb. of bacon. How many pounds of meat did she buy?

their results, the step-by-step sequence in the experiment itself, and he reads and reflects to generalize from the results. Also he builds a science vocabulary as he reads. To read the above page of material, the child must read the pictures as well as the running content. Often in science the diagrammatic, tabular, and pictorial material must be read carefully and with thorough understanding if the content is to be mastered.

Social-Studies Textbook

The next sample is a history selection from a social-studies book, *Your Country and Mine* [40].

Inclined Planes

You can't possibly find a machine that is any simpler than this one. It's just a plank with one end higher than the other. You have seen such sloping planks used for many jobs where heavy things have to be lifted. A sloping plank used in this way is called an **inclined plane.** Inclined means sloping. A plane is a flat surface. Any flat surface with one end higher than the other is an inclined plane.

How does an inclined plane work as a machine? You can find out by doing the simple experiment shown in the picture.

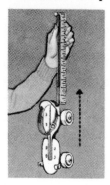

EXPERIMENT

You will need a medium-thick rubber band, a skate, a wooden ruler, a thumbtack, a foot of twine, several books, and a board.

With the thumbtack, attach the rubber band to the "zero" end of the ruler. Tie the twine to the other end of the rubber band and to the skate. The amount of stretch of the rubber band can now be measured on the ruler. The stretch indicates the amount of force you are using.

Lift the skate as in the picture. How much does the rubber band stretch? Does the skate feel heavy?

Now make an inclined plane with the board and the books. Pull the skate up the inclined plane. How much does the rubber band stretch? Does the skate feel as heavy as it did before?

With an inclined plane do you need to use more or less force than when lifting straight up?

From Herman and Nina Schneider, Science in Our World, *1961. Reprinted by permission of D. C. Heath and Company, Boston.*

From Gertrude Stephens Brown with Ernest W. Tiegs and Fay Adams, Your Country and Mine, *Grade Five, rev. ed. (Boston: Ginn and Company, 1960), p. 57. Reprinted by permission.*

This book was also studied systematically with the various units expanded through supplementary reading from other texts and reference materials. This reading more nearly approximates that of the basal reading, inasmuch as there is a degree of continuity of presentation. Here the reading purposes are to get an understanding of the historical period and a logical organization of the material presented. There are differences, however. The names of people and places must be recognized and many of them remembered. There is a need to relate the various episodes to the chronology of history, so the ability of reading to organize is important. Included are dates that must be noted and some remembered. Some specific difficulties in reading the passage can be seen in relationship to the concepts involved. For example, what is the difference between the former 13 colonies and the 13 independent states? What is the difference between a nation and a united nation? As far as that goes, what is the difference between a state and a nation? What is the difference between state and a territory? How long did the writing of the peace treaty take? What difference might there be between this account and an account of the happenings in a French or English textbook? Historical reading involves historical interpretations.

Geography Textbook

The next sample is a geography book from the same fifth-grade social-studies textbook, *Your Country and Mine* [40].

Some Important Cities in the Middle Atlantic States

The Middle Atlantic States have many cities. The larger ones are named on the political map on page 209. The map key will give you a general idea of their size. Let's make use of this key.

Locate Washington, D.C., on the map. Is it about the size of New York City or about the size of Baltimore? Look at the key and decide. What other cities seem to have a population about the size of Washington, D.C.?

Of course, the size of the print used for each city name gives us only a general idea of its population. We can get more exact information on each city's population by using Table 5 in the Tables for Reference. Turn to this table and find Washington's population.

On the map, find Albany, the capital of New York. What does the map tell you about its size? How many cities in the Middle Atlantic States have a population of more than 100,000? You can count them if you use Table 5 in the Tables for Reference.

Most cities of the Middle Atlantic States are manufacturing centers. Buffalo is noted for its flour mills and factories making iron-and-steel products. The wheat and iron ore are brought from farther west by boats. Much iron ore is mined around Lake Superior. Schenectady makes railroad locomotives, washing machines, refrigerators, and many other kinds of electrical goods. Rochester is famous for its cameras and film. Troy

From Gertrude Stephens Brown with Ernest W. Tiegs and Fay Adams, Your Country and Mine, *Grade Five, rev. ed. (Boston: Ginn and Company, 1960), p. 212. Reprinted by permission.*

Here again it is apparent that the reading abilities required for effective work within this selection are different from those required in the other materials that have been presented. The actual habits probably approximate more closely those used in reading arithmetic than they do the basal reader, for the child is expected to read, then to lay aside his contextual reading and refer to a map three pages removed and to a table at the back of the book to answer specific questions. It is, however, different from the mathematical material in that there is a running content, even though it is an interrupted one. Reading the geography material is complicated by reference to facts previously studied. For example, the children have to recall the names of the Middle Atlantic states in order to answer one of the questions. Therefore, the child who is in difficulty or has forgotten previously learned facts is at a handicap in continuing the reading. References to material previously read are not so often made in the basal reader. In reading geography it is essential that the child remember many facts. In mathematics, much of the content of the problems is to be forgotten; the content is usually a means to an end, namely to get the child to work the problem. In social studies, facts are to be remembered, and remembering them is one of the major goals of instruction.

DIFFERENCES IN PURPOSE

The child reading fifth-grade materials may encounter the following problems:

> In his arithmetic book is the problem: Barbara weighed 80 lbs. two months ago. Now she weighs 77½ lbs. How many pounds has she lost?
>
> In his social studies book is the following problem: The land in this locality produced 80 bushels of corn per acre ten years ago. Now it produces 77½. How much has it lost in productivity?

These two problems appear to be fundamentally quite similar, but the comprehension expected is very different. In the arithmetic problem, the reader is expected to answer that Barbara lost 2½ pounds. Any attempt to retain the specific information of the day's arithmetic problem is not expected. It would be inefficient, too, to analyze the problem to consider such questions as these: Should Barbara lose weight? Was the loss due to illness? If so, how can she stop losing weight and regain the weight she has lost? Or perhaps the loss of weight was due to dieting. If so, where did Barbara obtain the diet she was following? To analyze each problem of the arithmetic lesson after this fashion would consume more time than the child has available and would not contribute to achievement in arithmetic.

In the social-studies section, however, it is demanded that the child comprehend the significance of the loss of productivity of 2½ bushels per acre, and he is expected to retain specific information gained from this and other materials of the day's reading. He must reflect upon such questions as these: What does the loss of productivity mean to the national economy? Is it good or bad? What brought about the loss? Was it due to erosion? If so, how can the depletion be corrected? Reflection upon such questions contributes to achievement in the social studies.

In addition to the different demands made upon the reader by the nature of the reading material, there are variations in demands made upon the reader by the nature of the subjects themselves and by the ways in which they are taught. The teacher of arithmetic expects the child to read only a page or so every day. The child is not expected to do extensive reading in many arithmetic books. He is supposed to read carefully and accurately, and he must give great attention to detail. In the field of social studies, on the other hand, the child reads many pages during any one day of school. He reads from many sources, and often he reads merely to get the gist of the material; at other times, he reads intently an important section to organize its details.

Although there is the need for adjustment in reading to the specific ways of writing within each field of human experience [241], there is more that is common among those fields than there is that is unique to a single field. All of the reading proficiencies that the child has at his command are useful in making the adaptations. Recognition of the problems inherent within a field by the teacher and the pupil will in and of itself aid materially in establishing the flexibility in the use of general reading capacities necessary to be successful readers within that field. There is, then, a problem of isolating characteristic demands of a specific subject, recognizing them, and using the most effective ways of reading to meet them. By and large, the solution is simply employing adequate word-recognition techniques, comprehension abilities, study skills, and speed appropriate to the situation at hand.

Reading in Science

The children of today live in a world of great scientific discovery and achievement. It is imperative that an early start be made in developing interests and capabilities in science. The modern elementary and secondary schools have given the field of science as important a role as have been given to the fields of social studies, English literature, and mathematics. This added emphasis on science results from the recognition of the fact that the applications of science are all about us. That child may understand the world in which he lives—his world—and prepare for the demands that will be placed upon him as an adult, he must be helped to interpret that part of his environment that science explains. In order to aid him in developing an understanding of the scientific concepts that are important to everyday living, books in science have become a necessary part of school equipment. These books make specific demands upon the child's reading ability.

There is no doubt that much scientific information and much of the method of science can be and is arrived at by experimentation and observation. The young child, for example, before he can read, studies things about him and formulates and tests hypotheses. He is an intense student of the phenomena about him and is a keen questioner concerning scientific facts. He cannot read, so he uses the spoken language as his source of information by asking many questions of others who have traversed the ground before him. He has searched, through query, into the knowledge of his experts (usually his mother or father), and he is often seen to test his conclusions. He tries to verify, by experimentation, the knowledge learned from answers to the questions he has raised. The more mature young scientist refers to the printed page for answers to his queries. He is not limited in his quest for information to asking questions of adults. He studies also the world about him, makes tentative hypotheses, seeks more information by means of the printed page and other sources, and then tests his conclusions.

There is little wisdom in having the child use any means of getting information inefficiently if he can easily be taught to get it more efficiently. It is therefore necessary for the school to systematically develop effective means of communicating with authors of scientific materials. Reading science materials confronts the child with some rather unique problems to adjust to [14, 218, 231, 232].

AN ILLUSTRATION OF READING
RELATED TO A SCIENCE LESSON

There are many types of science lessons. The selection below is presented as an illustration of one type: the interrelationships between reading, observation, and experimentation. The discussion will show that teaching a science lesson in which the children read involves steps similar to those used in teaching a reading lesson. The teacher of science is, in fact, also a teacher of reading. One of the goals of science instruction is to develop capability and interest in reading the materials of science.

The following selection, from a unit on weather in a first-grade science textbook, *Looking at Science* [19], is likely to be studied about the middle of the first grade. By that time, in basal reading, many of the children in a typical first-grade class would have read several preprimers and a primer and would be reading somewhere in a first reader. They would have developed some skill in several word-recognition techniques and would be able to read, reflect, and generalize as they read. They would bring to reading science the needed skills and abilities to study this lesson. In connection with this reading the teacher would have the opportunity to teach the children words and concepts as he helps them learn to read science materials. The reading phases of studying this science lesson will be discussed.

Introducing the Selection

The teacher might have the children recall that there are various types of weather—sunny days, rainy days, snowy days, and days during which hail falls. The teacher might then ask for a description of hail. A child's answer might be, "Hail is like little pieces of ice." After a brief discussion

Experiments with Snow and Ice

Get some snow.
Is it cold?
Warm the snow.
Where does the snow go?

Get some ice.
Is the ice cold?
Warm the ice.
Where does the ice go?

What is snow?
What is ice?

53

From Austin D. Bond, Guy L. Bond, Theodore Clymer, and Kate Bell, Looking at Science, *Grade One (Chicago: Lyons & Carnahan, 1963). Reprinted in black and white by permission.*

of weather, the pictures on the page might be discussed. The children should be led to observe that an experiment is described.

Introducing New Vocabulary

Words that would be somewhat difficult for the children to recognize in their printed form would be presented while the selection was being introduced. When the children mention the words *snow* and *ice,* the words should be written in sentences on the chalkboard.

On some days there is snow.
We have ice at home.

The word *experiment,* previously introduced, should be reviewed by writing it on the chalkboard in a sentence.

We are going to do an experiment.

Setting the Purpose

Through a study of the pictures, the children note that they will perform an experiment and that the material on the page gives them directions for conducting it. At this time the teacher may wish to set the problem in the form of a null hypothesis. "Ice and snow do not turn into the same thing when they are warmed." If the hypothesis is stated in this way, the teacher will be introducing the children to one form of scientific proof. They will learn through experimental observation that information can be gained that enables them to accept or reject the null hypothesis.

Performing the Experiments and Discussing Them

First the children should read the title. Then they should read the page to find out the equipment needed to perform the experiments. The children now collect the materials and perform the experiments. After the experiments have been performed the children should answer the questions in the science text. Then, through inductive reasoning, they should decide what snow and ice really are and whether their hypothesis should be accepted or rejected. In this case, of course, the hypothesis is rejected inasmuch as both snow and ice turned into the same thing, water.

Related Experiences

The following excerpts from the *Teacher's Guide* suggests additional experiences: "After the snow or ice has melted in the container, it can be heated further until the water evaporates, thereby showing that the water can change into water vapor. A piece of wax may be placed in the container and heated until it melts, showing that other substances change from the solid to the liquid state when heat is applied. A freezer tray may be filled with water and placed in a refrigerator. After a time, the children will see that water has been changed to ice."

It should be noted that the children have been led to understand several generalizations: many substances change from solid to liquid states when heat is applied; when cold-enough, many substances change back into a solid state; when water is heated it turns into a gas—water vapor.

The *Teacher's Guide* suggests further that the children may wish to relate this day's work to the unit on weather by drawing pictures of the same scene on a snowy day, a rainy day, and a sunny day. Or, some children may wish to draw a series of pictures showing ice, water, a kettle with boiling water in it, with condensed water vapor showing a little above the spout.

The interrelationship between firsthand and reading experiences is shown by this day's work. First, the children read to find out what equipment is needed for the experiment and how to conduct the experiment. After performing the experiment, the questions contained in the reading matter lead them inductively to generalize. This is a specialized type of reading. It is impossible to conceive of a capable scientist who has not developed a high order of proficiency in the reading skills the children have used.

Most of the children learning to read science in the first grade and throughout their school years will not become scientific specialists. They will keep abreast of future developments largely to the extent that they are able to read reports of those developments. Frequently, scientists bemoan the fact that it is difficult to communicate scientific understandings to the lay public. This is due partly to the fact that the opportunity of developing reading skills and abilities necessary for interpreting science writing itself has not been used fully. The child cannot be trained to read factual scientific presentations through the reading of stories or fanciful materials. He can be taught scientific reading only in scientific content and only with the problems of science and the purposes for reading science confronting him. It is to these materials and purposes that he must adjust. The discussion of reading in science will treat further adjustments of vocabulary, basic study skills, and comprehension abilities.

ADJUSTMENTS OF VOCABULARY

As is true of other fields, science has a language of its own. The child must learn the language of science as he develops proficiency in reading in the field. The language is made up of words that have been developed to express scientific concepts and are therefore encountered much more frequently in reading in science than in reading in other subject fields. For example, a short selection dealing with electricity from a fifth-grade science textbook contained such words as *experiment, electrons, magnetism, charges, conductor,* and *electricity.* These are specialized scientific words, the meaning and recognition of which must be learned by the child. In order to develop the concepts of science through the use of language, it is necessary to use the exact language of science. Consequently, a science book must contain, in addition to general vocabulary, a considerable number of scientific words. These words obviously have to be taught and understood. And that is one of the major difficulties of reading in science, whether it be in the primary grades, the upper elementary grades, high school, or college. It is essential for the teacher at any level to anticipate vocabulary difficulties and to aid the child in building the understanding necessary for an effective use of the terminology.

As is to be expected, the language of science contains specialized meanings. Learning the scientific meaning of a special word is often more troublesome than learning an entirely new word. Within the passage dealing with electricity, mentioned above, the word *charges* has a rather distinctive meaning in the sentence "There were more negative *charges* than positive *charges* on each ball." In the same selection the word *conductor* has a new meaning for many children.

The avoidance of technical vocabulary is not only unwise, it is impossible. Those who prepare science material and those who select material for a child to read should question themselves rather carefully about how much technical vocabulary the child at his level of advancement in scientific learning can reasonably be expected to assimilate. Probably there should be no more technical or specialized words introduced than the number that can become a part of his permanent learning and no fewer words than are needed to identify the basic concepts with exactness. Only the concepts that are of sufficient importance to warrant careful study should be identified with a technical term.

Frequently, it is believed that material will be understood with clarity just because it is stated in exact terms. It should be remembered that the word conveys exactness only to the extent that it has full and precise meaning to the reader. If the child does not have exact understanding of the word, the word itself gives no clarity or precision. In the elementary school, it is the reader, not the writer, who usually determines the scientific exactness of what he reads. For the most part, the writer has a clearer understanding of the technical vocabulary than does the immature reader. It is therefore necessary for the teacher to inspect the material and develop for the child clarity of understanding of unusual words. However, whenever the author of the material is aware that a new word is one the reader is unlikely to know, it is his responsibility to define that word in the content of the print. When words are so defined they should be left for the child to interpret. He may, thereby, gain experience in a valuable means of vocabulary development, namely, by reading authors' definitions.

In no other place is the relationship between firsthand experience and reading so apparent as it is in science. The teacher, while teaching science reading, has a fine opportunity for developing clear and vivid meanings of words. There is no other field that can bring the printed page and firsthand experience so closely together. The child can experiment, observe, read, and test in a way that makes the page live for him. Firsthand experiences directly related to the science material are abundant. The child performs an experiment as background for reading within a field of science. In this case, his reading may be done solely to verify his own observations and results. Or conversely, he experiments and then reads further to test the validity of what he has read. The interrelationship between experimentation, observation, and reading is indeed close! This interrelationship aids materially in developing technical vocabulary.

Readiness for the firsthand experience must first be built. Words that identify the concepts must be used in discussion with the children both prior to the experience and in talking about it afterward. Interest in the technical words and in their exact meanings must be kindled. All of these essential acts involve careful, systematic planning on the part of both teacher and children.

Extensive reading is an effective means of developing meanings. The child who reads widely in science encounters new words in many and varied situations. He continually meets with new examples of the use of a word. All such reading extends and refines the understanding of concepts and the words that represent them. Extensiveness of meanings depends upon the number and kinds of situations in which the word is met. Accuracy depends upon the skill with which the reader relates the new understanding to previous backgrounds. Vividness depends upon the interest, emotional acceptance, and purposefulness of the reader. Retention depends upon the usefulness of the word to the reader. The child then has a much greater chance of building the vocabulary of science, if his reading is much broader than that of a single text. He should get information from many sources about the scientific ideas considered. Care must be taken, however, to insure that the child does not meet too heavy a vocabulary burden when reading related materials.

BASIC STUDY SKILLS IN SCIENCE

Basic study skills have been taught in connection with the social studies far more than with science materials. Krantz [167] has shown that standardized tests of basic study skills are confined to those frequently encountered in social-studies reading and are unrelated to success in science. In order to study the physical and natural sciences, even in the lower elementary school grades, the child must be equipped with specialized basic study skills appropriate to science materials and scientific reading.

Among the more important basic study skills used in science is the ability to interpret symbolic language and scientific abbreviations. The symbol Zn, for example, is more than an abbreviation for zinc. It implies that the child knows the atomic weight, the valence, and so forth, and that he is able to use the symbol effectively in chemical formulas.

Another basic study skill in science is the ability to read a formula. If an arrow points one way—in a formula, for example—it means that the reaction will go in that one way; if the arrow points in two directions, it means that the reaction is reversible; and so on. It is not only in the field of chemistry that we have scientific formulas and symbolic expressions. The writings in health, biology, botany, and physics also are heavily laden with symbolic language and expressions in formulas.

All fields of science make extensive use of graphs and diagrams. These graphs and diagrams are frequently schematic in organization and differ from those in other fields. The teacher is so familiar with the field of science that he often overlooks the unique characteristics of scientific graphs and diagrams. The child, however, confused by the uniqueness of these graphs and diagrams, is likely to develop the habit of skipping the pictorial presentations. The teacher who explains these graphic representations and encourages their use in class discussions will do much to eliminate the tendency on the part of the child to avoid the graphically presented data and will make them meaningful to him.

Locating information in scientific works is another of the basic study skills oriented to the field of science. The bare knowledge of the mechanics of using dictionaries, encyclopedias, indexes, and so on, although essential, is not sufficient to enable the child to locate scientific information rapidly and efficiently. He needs an understanding of the sorts of materials that are most reliable for science. He must know the key words under which scientific information is likely to be classified. He must be shown the sources most helpful in locating scientific information to help him solve his own problems and help him pursue topics of study. There is a place in science for the systematic presentation of material, but it is unfortunate if a child's understanding of the topic being considered is limited to the treatment in any single textbook. The child must learn how to supplement the concepts therein discussed with treatments from a number of sources.

COMPREHENSION ABILITIES IN SCIENCE

Comprehension abilities must be reorganized to meet the specific demands of scientific reading. There are few fields that demand as frequent or as careful following of directions as the field of science. The description of an experiment must be read slowly and thoughtfully so that the sequential order of the steps described may be followed. The construction of laboratory equipment depends upon careful reading to follow directions. In botany the location of the name of a plant requires much reading. Although all of these are reading to follow directions, the specific way to go about the reading is different in each case. The child must be taught to meet these different situations adequately.

Facts must be accumulated and retained because each fact becomes part of the working capital of the scientific thinker. There is need, however, for the selection of important concepts and facts and the rejection of illustrative data. Frequently, the immature scientific reader becomes overwhelmed by the illustrative material and fails to grasp the important facts and concepts being developed. At higher levels in a treatment on the expansion of metal, for example, the important consideration may be that metal expands in a uniform manner when heated and that each metal has a specific coefficient of expansion. The author may use the expansion of various metals and cite their coefficients and have the youngster test these coefficients of expansion in the laboratory. It is not important that the student remember all of the coefficients for all the metals, because they are readily available in tabular form. There are, however, many students studying science who attempt such feats of memory and are unable to differentiate between the examples and the generalizations to be learned. From the start, the child should be taught to isolate the important facts for retention. As he matures, he may be able to assimilate more of the specific illustrative details, when such an assimilation is appropriate to his reading purpose.

In order to retain the great number of concepts and facts that are developed in science, the child must be able to organize factual information. Such organization usually takes quite different forms than the organization that is useful in other subject-matter disciplines. Often an outline form will not suffice for organized thinking in science. Nor will a time line be of much benefit in many scientific considerations. A child should be taught specific ways of organizing scientific information, such as, sorting concepts into major categories to prepare classification tables, listing major concepts and then summarizing them in a generalization, and step-by-step planning of research.

Reading in science, then, is more than remembering facts related to a given topic, because it comprises the ability to determine relationships among pertinent facts. The student of science is often required to formulate a statement of these relationships. In fact, the reader of science is continually formulating and clarifying generalized concepts. In this way, he builds a background of knowledge in science that aids him in retaining and understanding the facts so that he may better interpret the world about him. Also he brings to his future reading of science a broader background than if he attempted to remember an unrelated body of factual knowledge.

The child may get into difficulty in several ways in trying to see relationships. In the first place, he may not have formed the habit of attempting to see relationships and may try to learn science by rote memory. He will soon be in trouble if he does so. Such a child would not make a generalization when a generalization was warranted. A second source of difficulty is the tendency to overgeneralize. Children are apt to generalize upon insufficient evidence. The child who does not suspend his judgment until a sufficient number of facts are given may arrive at a conclusion to which he tenaciously holds even in the face of further evidence opposed to his conclusion. A third difficulty is that of failure to test the generalization in the light of previous reading and of known experience. The child should be taught to reflect as he reads.

Often, the best way to comprehend a scientific treatment is to read, reflect, reread, pause to restructure or to assimilate the concept being discussed. Thus, science materials must usually be read slowly in order that comprehension may take place. Materials from other fields may frequently be read more rapidly. It is true certainly that in the fields of science and mathematics rate of reading must be slower to fit the reading purposes and the compactness of ideas.

Often the materials of science are cumulative and not repetitive. To understand a given paragraph, the previous paragraph must have been understood thoroughly. Understanding the paragraph to follow requires the understanding of all that has preceded. For example, there is often marked difference between a scientific statement of fact and a literary piece in which an author is building the understanding of a character. The literary writer reveals the character's reactions in a number of situations in which the character displays a consistent performance and thus gives the reader many opportunities to form a generalized impression. The scientific writer develops an understanding by means of one presentation and assumes that thereafter the reader has learned the generalization. Therefore, scientific material, in general, must be read more slowly than most literary material.

Reading in Mathematics

Reading the materials of mathematics in any one year of the elementary-school grades, although not extensive, is so specialized that the child must be taught how to do the reading. The child must note details and weigh them. He must judge the relevancy of the information to the problem to be solved. He must be able to follow directions. And he must be able to organize the facts of a problem and to relate one to another. In reading the problems in mathematics great care must be taken for exactness, for understanding each item within the problem, and for adjusting to the compact nature of problems. The reading is so highly specialized that the usual measures of reading competency will not distinguish between good and poor readers of mathematics. Fay [94] found no difference in arithmetic achievement between good and poor readers as measured by standardized reading tests (when intelligence was held constant). Hanson [124], in studying problem solving in arithmetic, found that there was no significant difference between good and poor students of arithmetic in comprehension abilities; he found that the poor achievers in arithmetic were the faster readers on the average, thus indicating lack of ability to differentiate speed. Koenker [163] found no difference in reading comprehension ability between good and poor computers of long-division problems at the sixth grade level. All of these studies used tests designed to measure general reading capabilities, not arithmetic reading capabilities.

ADJUSTMENT TO VOCABULARY

There is a relatively large vocabulary of words that are specific to mathematics [161]. Such words as *invert, multiply, quotient, numerator, subtrahend, perimeter, rectangle,* and many others, are rarely met (with the same meanings) in reading outside the field. Then too, there are words that are more frequently encountered in mathematics than anywhere else, as, for example, the terms of linear, dry, and liquid measurement, including such words as *yard, foot, inch, pound, ton, peck, gross,* and *quart.* There are combinations of words such as *partial product, common denominator,* and *decimal point,* that are, for the elementary-school child, unique to mathematics. These words are part of the reading equipment necessary to read the descriptions of processes and problems within the usual mathematics book. Therefore, if the child is to understand the explanations given in the book, he must learn this language of mathematics. Sometimes the language may seem somewhat abstract to the child, and in such instances backgrounds of understanding must be carefully laid so that the explanations will not be given back as mere verbalisms, but will be understood. Perhaps the best way to teach such specialized terms is through their informal use. The teacher calls the concept by its specific name as he goes about his instructing.

Another vocabulary problem is that of specialized meanings of words— words that have a meaning in arithmetic that is unique to arithmetic and different from the more common one with which the child is familiar. The child must learn such meanings as *mixed* in mixed numbers, *improper* in improper fractions, *times* in two times four, and *carry* in multiplication. Such specialized meanings add to the vocabulary difficulties of mathematics and are often sources of confusion. The teacher should anticipate the difficulties and give the child the specialized interpretation, inasmuch as in the majority of cases the child cannot derive the meaning of the word from the context of the reading material.

BASIC STUDY SKILLS IN MATHEMATICS

Frequently, in reading the materials of mathematics the child meets abbreviation and symbolization, for mathematics has its shorthand, which must be learned. The child has to know the meaning of such symbols as these: $+$, $-$, $\times$, $>$, $<$, $\div$, $=$. In addition to learning the symbols, he must learn the many abbreviations, such as *lb., hr., mi., ans., qt., ea.,* and *add.* In order to read the following problem, the child must know many abbreviations:

> If it costs 95¢ for the first 3 min. and 30¢ for ea. add. min., how much must Jane pay to talk over the telephone to her mother for 5 min.?

One page in a sixth-grade book had the following abbreviations:

a.	ft.	hr.	min.	qt.	wk.
cwt.	gal.	in.	mo.	rd.	yd.
da.	gi.	lb.	pk.	sq.	yr.
doz.	gr.	mi.	pt.	t.	

Needless to say, these abbreviations make the reading of that page difficult for the sixth-grader.

It is necessary for the child to learn these symbols and abbreviations. They therefore constitute a reading task. Care should be taken when the child is experiencing trouble to ascertain whether it is because he does not know how to do the mathematical operation or whether it is because he does not know the symbolism of mathematics. The basic study skills of reading formulas, symbols, and abbreviations must be taught and much experience given in reading them in mathematics.

Mathematics material, too, is replete with graphic and tabular presentations and so provides an opportunity to develop these study skills.

COMPREHENSION ABILITIES IN MATHEMATICS

Mathematical reading material used in the elementary school lacks the continuity the child has become accustomed to in other reading experiences. One paragraph of material often bears little or no relationship to the paragraph immediately preceding or following it. Arithmetic problems are generally short and compact statements with very little descriptive material. Often, there is no contextual relationship between the problems on a page. Even the names of the people of the problems are not the same from problem to problem. In most other fields where reading is employed, the child is taught to continue the meaning from paragraph to paragraph. To transfer a generalized attack to reading mathematics is confusing. Many of the newer textbooks attempt to overcome this difficulty by presenting a series of problems on a theme common to all.

The introduction of numbers into the reading matter makes a break in continuity. Although numbers are not unique to mathematics, they are much more frequently a part of the materials in this subject than in any other. In reading material that is broken up by numbers, the child must pause in the natural process of reading and attend to those numbers, because he is aware that the numbers are to be his tools of operation after the problem has been read. The introduction of numbers frequently breaks the thought units and thereby tends to disrupt the habits of reading that the child has established in other fields. The introduction of numbers cannot be avoided, so the child must be taught to read material laden with numbers. He must be cautioned to read problems relatively slowly and with care and exactness. It is recommended, too, that the child read through a problem before he attempts to organize its content in preparation for working it. Thus, much of the material of mathematics must be reread reflectively several times. The child rarely reads more than two pages of arithmetical material per day, as contrasted with reading many pages per day in the social studies. All mathematical material must be read slowly, and most of the facts in the material should be forgotten quickly, because the facts will never be referred to again.

Reading to form a visual impression is a comprehension ability important in mathematics. Many problems in modern textbooks are related to construction activities or to measurement activities of one sort or another. In problems, for example, dealing with the construction of a playhouse, the child may be told that the house is 8 feet long, 6 feet wide, and 6 feet high at the eaves and 8 feet high at its peak. The description will be of little value to the child who has not developed the ability to visualize as he reads. The child who is unable to read to get the sensory impression may experience difficulty in working out such problems, not because he is unable to do the mathematical operations, but because he cannot visualize the problem he is working with. The ability to visualize the problem—that is, to see the field that is being measured, to see the wall that is being papered—is an aid to its solution. Similar problems are frequently met in life situations, so the child must be prepared to read them understandingly. The ability to visualize abstract problems can be increased by using many concrete experiences related to verbal descriptions. In connection with problems dealing with building a playhouse, it will be helpful for the children to lay out in the corner of the classroom the floor space of the playhouse, and up the side wall of the classroom indicate the height of the eaves and the peak in order to give experiences in visualizing the abstract.

Often, the data given in the initial description of a series of problems includes much numerical information that is irrelevant to many of the problems within that series. In solving such a series of problems, the child must refer to the original description and reject those items that have no bearing upon the problem that he is solving. Many children find this difficult. They feel it is necessary to use the distance between the two cities to solve the following problem:

> The distance from Glen Valley to Kings Cliff is 20 miles. It takes one half hour to travel between the two cities by bus. Bob can ride his bicycle from one to the other in 3½ hours. How much time can Bob save by taking the bus rather than riding his bicycle?

The answers many children obtain in solving this problem indicate that they fail to realize the irrelevancy of the distance between the cities. The children should be shown how to read such problems so that the facts are seen in the proper relationships. A good procedure might be to have them first rapidly read the problem through to get a general impression and to ascertain what they are to find out; then to reread the problem, isolating those facts that are pertinent to its solution and to formulate in their minds how those facts should be used; then to do the necessary numerical computations. After the problem has been solved, the child should read it again in order to see whether his solution is a tenable one.

Failure to solve a problem correctly is often due to failure to know how to do the mathematical processes involved. At other times, failure may be due to inadequate or faulty reading of the problem. It may be that some necessary steps are frequently omitted because the child has given the problem too rapid or too cursory an inspection. In many problems, the steps involved in the solution are not clearly defined in the order in which the operations must be performed. Thus, reading in mathematics presents questions of reorganization of ideas presented in the material [220].

These problems of reorganization are somewhat unique to mathematics. As he studies the problem, the child who has a tendency to omit necessary steps will be helped by asking himself the following questions: (1) What am I asked to find out? (2) What facts do I need for the solution? (3) What is the first step in the solution? (4) What are the subsequent steps? (5) What is the probable answer? After solving the problem it is profitable to reread it to see whether the solution is complete and the answer reasonable.

Reading in the Social Studies

Successful achievement in the social studies depends upon ability to read. In discussing the significance of reading ability upon achievement in the subject-matter areas, Fay [93] says: "The evidence is clear, both from research and from the experience of countless teachers, that after the primary grades it becomes increasingly more difficult to be 'poor' in reading and 'good' in the content fields." Wesley [273] emphasizes the importance of reading ability more specifically in relation to the social studies, as follows: "Success in the social studies depends to a large extent upon the ability to read. The range of direct experience is sharply limited. The pupil cannot go to Norway, visit Congress, travel in a prairie schooner, cut wheat on the plains, interview Lincoln, follow the course of the Mississippi, or experience directly any one of a thousand ideas which can contribute to his development. While reading is important in all subjects, it is peculiarly so in the social studies, for an understanding of historical, geographic, civic, and economic realities can scarcely be gained in any other way."

The role of reading in making social studies concepts more meaningful and, conversely, the role of the social studies in contributing to reading development are discussed by Michaelis [192] as follows: "Reading materials can be used to open the gateway to many vital learnings in the social studies. Family and community living, places near and far, great men and women, children of other times and places, stories of people in other cultures, life in America today and early times, the story of industries, and a host of other topics are included in social studies material. As a result of reading experiences, the child can identify himself with others, gain new concepts and understandings, and develop positive attitudes toward others and richer appreciations of their ways of life. Reading ability and study skills can be strengthened as the child engages in functional reading to solve problems in units of work. The many new concepts developed in the social studies promote the child's growth in developmental reading. Many opportunities also exist for recreational reading as stories, novels, and biographies are made available to children in connection with units of work." The variety of vocabulary and concept, the need for critical evaluation, the demands of organization and of wide reading, and other typical requirements of reading in the social studies make adjustments inevitable. Reading adjustments to enable the child to read effectively within the social studies will be discussed under the headings of vocabulary, study skills, and comprehension abilities.

ADJUSTMENT TO VOCABULARY

In reading social-studies material, adjustments to the language of social science must be made. Klausmeier and collaborators [162] discuss as follows the vocabulary problems faced by the elementary-school child as he reads textbooks prepared for him: "Although authors of textbooks in arithmetic, social studies, language, science, and other subject areas generally attempt to base their choice of words on reading difficulty, new words are frequently used which are extremely difficult for children. Children need preparation for this kind of reading. Each new key word should be presented in a concrete, meaningful way so that the children can gain the meaning intended by the authors. Unless attention is given to vocabulary load and unless they have assistance with difficult words and ideas, many children do not obtain maximum profit from reading. Some say the new words without understanding their meaning, others "skip" any new words they cannot identify, and still others come to dislike reading because they do not understand what they read."

In social studies reading, for example, some of the words with which a fifth-grade child comes in contact for the first time and that can cause him difficulty in reading are: *monastery, hemisphere, invincible, cuneiform, armada, patrician, plebeian,* and *mosaic.* The child might be able to pronounce the words, but he would not be likely to arrive unaided at their meanings. Without help with these words, the child would be facing an almost impossible task in attempting to get meaning from reading the passages in which they appear. New words should be related to past experiences, used in discussion and in group planning, used in reporting and in other linguistic-sharing activities, as well as in reading, in order that they may become familiar to the child.

In addition to many, many words, such as those included in the above list, the materials of the social studies are filled with names of people, civilizations, places, and other proper names. These proper names invariably present reading problems to the child. He must learn to recognize, identify, and understand them, as well as to ascertain their significance and decide which are worth remembering.

There are also problems of learning the specialized meanings of words. In the social studies, words sometimes have meanings other than the more common and possibly more familiar ones to the child; for example, for such words as *settlement, ford, judgment,* and *culture,* new meanings must be learned.

Another type of problem to which the child must adjust and which is more often encountered in the social studies than in other fields is learning the meaning of words for which there is no clearly defined meaning —words whose meanings are gradually learned through meeting them in many situations. The meanings of such abstract words as *democracy, civilization, community, ancient* and *toleration* can be learned only gradually.

The teacher, whenever he can, should anticipate vocabulary difficulties, or possible misconceptions and, through discussion, clarify and expand word meanings for the children. Naturally, as is the case in all understanding of vocabulary, the child who has had firsthand experiences is at an advantage, as Jarolimek [148] points out in the following statement: "The child who has visited Yellowstone National Park will find reading material concerning Yellowstone much more meaningful than the child who has not had such an experience. He reads meaning into such words as 'geyser,' 'mud-pots,' and 'canyon' which the next child cannot possibly obtain." The teacher should capitalize upon the firsthand experiences of the one to make more accurate the understanding of all.

Much of the development of vocabulary in the social studies will come through extensive reading of materials that are rich enough in verbal illustrations to build the needed background. Materials in which the vocabulary burden is relatively light and in which new or unusual words are explained through the content are good for this purpose. The child should approach such reading with an awareness that one of the important aims of studying the social studies is to build a useful vocabulary of terms frequently used in the social studies. He should approach that reading with a desire to find the meanings of the words and with the demand upon himself that he understand their use.

BASIC STUDY SKILLS

Reading in the social studies depends upon the use of a large amount of supplementary materials. Therefore, the ability to locate materials is an extremely important one in social-studies reading. Inasmuch as the concepts of the social studies are somewhat abstract and are often written in a contracted fashion, their expansion and further explanation are frequently necessary. Supplementary materials provide one means of finding out more about a topic. The child who wishes to explore a topic more completely may be frustrated by his inability to locate other material pertinent to that topic. He may have the desire to read further, but he may be unable to do so because materials that he can read are not readily available. He may also be frustrated by lack of knowledge about how to use libraries, indexes, and similar aids and sources. Such an inability would constitute a difficulty in reading in the social studies as well as, of course, in other fields.

The social studies have their own special reference materials, and they should be used extensively. The atlas, the *World Almanac*, encyclopedias, dictionaries, biographical and other reference materials, city, state, and national directories, government bulletins, newspapers, and magazines and their microfilms are reference materials in whose use the child must develop skill if he is to be a successful student of the social studies. He develops basic study skills in the reading program where he is also taught adjustments he must make to meet the requirements of the social studies.

The materials of history, geography, and the other social studies are organized, and each has its own system or systems of organization. Jarolimek [148] expresses this point as follows: "History may be organized around movements, periods, trends, chronology, or topics. Geography may be studied according to regions, physical features, economic factors, or by areas. When elements are selected from the social sciences and fused into a single study for elementary school children, as is done in the social studies, problems of organization become complex indeed." The child must, as he is reading, be able to sense the organization of the presentation. He must be able to use the headings, italicizations, and other special markings as an aid to sensing the organization. He must, moreover, be able to reorganize the material, when necessary, in light of his purposes. He must be able to relate his reading to the theory that he is exploring, to the trends that he is investigating, and to the generalizations that to him are important. Likewise, he must be able to relate incidents to the chronology of facts and episodes he has assembled. It is in no small measure through this organization that the results of reading become a part of his working capital for further study.

A mature type of reading is required to sense organization. The ability to do this type of reading must be built in a developmental fashion. When the teacher in the primary grades says, "Tell us in your own words what you have been reading about," he is starting the youngster on the long road to independent thinking about material he is reading and has read. The social studies lend themselves admirably to giving experience in the ability to reorganize and to apply learnings derived from reading.

There are many instructional opportunities for teaching organization. The making of a *time line* by the class is one such opportunity. To understand the development of our nation, for example, it is helpful to locate events in terms of the passage of time. A line representing time in terms of decades may forever establish a sense of the chronology of events and also the lapse of time between events. The child will be surprised to see that the lapse between the discovery of America and the writing of the Declaration of Independence was longer than the elapsed time from the writing of the Declaration of Independence to the present. Even adults have a feeling that Washington pressed hard on the heels of Columbus in the march of time. The children, as they read, may locate on their time line other important happenings in the story of the development of our nation. There are many types of time lines. The one described above may be expanded to include parallel world happenings. The development of our nation may be traced by recordings on one side of the line and those of the world in general on the other.

In geography, to cite another example, a fourth-grade child who has dealt with story material for most of his three years of reading experience is suddenly confronted with a geography book for the first time. Such a child will find many new reading problems. He has always read a story from the top of the first page, down the page, and on through several pages uninterruptedly. In the geography book, he starts at the top of the page in the customary manner. He reads about ten lines and is then told to look at Figure 1 on page 12. He looks at Figure 1 on page 12, and returning to the page he had just left, he starts at the top of the page again. He has always done this. He reads ten lines, which seem familiar, and is asked to look at Figure 1 on page 12. He says to himself that he has already looked at Figure 1, so he goes on reading down the page. It says later, "You noticed on Figure 1 that—." He had noticed no such thing. No one had told him to, and he was unfamiliar with the ways of the geographer [33]. These are, of course, minor misunderstandings, but it should be pointed out that there are reading disability cases that were originally caused by an accumulation of such minor misunderstandings and faulty learnings. How much easier and how much more profitable the experience would have been had these problems of organization been anticipated and a readiness for reading geography material been developed in the basic reading program.

It is not possible for a child in his study of the relationship between man and his physical environment to travel the world over. He cannot live in each part of the world in order to experience its year-round climatic conditions. He cannot visit the industries of each given locality, climb the mountains, and swim in the rivers and the lakes. He cannot follow the iron ore that is dug from the Mesabi Range in Minnesota through its process of manufacture and its export until it is delivered in the form of steel for a bridge in Argentina. Such firsthand experiences might enable the child to gain a unified idea of the relation between mankind and the physical forces of his environment, but he cannot visit all places and experience all things. The child must therefore attempt to learn of "the people and the place" through, among others, the vicarious experience of reading.

In order that the facts learned through reading may be retained, organization is necessary. Organization is especially needed when the material that is being read is rich in factual content. When the facts are many and when the organization of the writing is difficult to follow, there is a real need to build an organized overview. The materials of geography are such materials. There are many details. Writers of geographical materials will attest to the fact that the organizational problem is great. It is often difficult for the child, inexperienced in such reading, to follow the organization. The child is confronted with several troublesome adjustment tasks. The first is the problem of giving relative weight to the importance of the topics being discussed. Often the child is unable to isolate the concepts of major importance from the background material used to build up these major concepts. The teacher, through making a careful assignment and through leading the discussion about the material read, can focus attention upon the points of major importance.

Another problem is that the child is confronted with alternative organizations. Should he organize the thoughts that he gains through reading around political areas, or the occupations, or climatic conditions, or other geographical characteristics of those areas? Or should he attempt to organize his thinking around industrial areas, including the geographical characteristics, climatic conditions, and the like, within the industrial areas? Should he, for example, think of the Central Atlantic states and learn of their geographic characteristics, their climates, and the numerous industries of their cities? Or should he think about industries, such as the steel industry, placing areas, cities, and other geographical characteristics within that industry? Probably the child should do both, if he is to get a complete understanding of what he is attempting to study. Certainly he needs help in finding his way through this maze. Thus, large topical units may be one way of helping make such a dual organization. The problem of organization is inherent in reading within the field of geography. If the reading is to be effective, some solution to the problem must be made. As the child gets through the political organization, he may be able to piece together the industrial concepts. Or, if his reading is organized around industrial concepts, he may be able to piece together an idea of the political organization of a given locality. Whichever way the material is organized, the child will need help in seeing this twofold import of geography study.

Moreover, the child must gain an understanding of the general physical characteristics and the climatic conditions of the larger areas; for example, the section of the country under consideration. The teacher must be aware of and must make provision for meeting all of these difficulties of organization that are characteristic of reading the geographical materials.

Frequently, the child is asked to refer to a map, a table, or a figure as many as 100 pages distant from the reading matter that discusses the map or other tool. Skill is required to read running material, refer to a basic study tool, and then relocate the page of reading content and find the place on it once again. It is not uncommon for a page of geography to contain as many as eight maps or other references that require the child to refer to pages other than the one he is reading. For the inexperienced reader, too many referrals tend to break up the continuity of thought and to detract from interest. It is fatiguing also to read several sentences, then page through a book, locate information, then page back again, and skim to find the place, only to read several more lines, and then begin the process again. It is helpful to teach the child early in reading the materials of geography that he should remember the location on the page that he is reading when it is necessary to refer to a map. Thus the skimming process might be eliminated.

The problem of map-text reading is more complicated than discussed above. The child must correlate the information on the map or other basic study tool with the discussion on the page he is reading. Collings [57] has shown that the interrelationships involved in map-text reading require specific skills that are not acquired incidentally and for which definite teaching yields large returns. The problem is to teach the child to interrelate the reading of the map with reading the verbal context that accompanies the map. In all such instances, the discussion on the page is concerned with concepts that are presented in the chart, table, map, or figure. An adequate understanding of both the content of the discussion and the tool referred to requires interrelating the information from both sources.

COMPREHENSION ABILITIES

The social studies deal, among other things, with the development of social institutions, the interrelationships among men, and the relationship between man and the physical forces of his environment. These are large and difficult areas of thinking. It is small wonder that the reading matter dealing with such topics is often both complex and remote to the child [1]. Many of the concepts of history, geography, and other social studies are far removed from the experience of students. The gap between the experience of the child and the realities that he is expected to understand is so wide that it can be bridged only with great difficulty. The need to build a background of understanding, essential to reading, is rarely more acute than in the social studies. The need to relate the material read to the experiences of the child is essential to his understanding of its concepts.

As an outgrowth of complexity of ideas, adjustment to sentence length is required. The sentences in the materials of elementary-school social studies are frequently long and complex. It may be, however, that when dealing with a complex concept, the best way, and possibly the only way, to treat that concept is in a long, complex sentence. Breaking the sentence into two or more parts might break the relationships between the ideas and make the understanding more difficult. Sometimes the use of a complex sentence is the easiest way of relating a complex concept.

Peterson [206] comments upon the unfavorable attitudes that pupils acquire in having to study textbook materials that are inappropriate to their reading capabilities. He suggests that such experiences often color their general attitude toward the entire reading process. She says that teachers using social-studies materials need to be aware of the limitations of the materials and of the specific difficulties the pupils are encountering in reading them. She emphasizes the importance of supplementing passages from textbooks with a wide range of additional material suited to meeting the reading needs as well as the reading capacities of the children.

Understanding of the Conditions and Mores of the Time

Many of the difficulties children have in reading and interpreting accurately the human relationships involved are due to their limited understanding of the locale of which they are reading. The child reading about the problems that confronted the early settlers of our nation finds it difficult to appreciate the lack of adequate transportation, the scarcity of windowpanes, the inadequacy of heating plants, and the vastness of the wilderness. The child tends to interpret those days in light of present-day

America. The presence of different sets of superstitions and social concepts can be appreciated only by the mature reader, and even he realizes his insufficient understanding. The perspective of the child may be somewhat enlarged by building a background of the times and by focusing attention upon differences between his social and physical scene and the social and physical scene about which he is reading. He can be made aware that his understanding is limited and that it can be expanded by extensive reading, by reflection, and by relating what he has read to the nearest approximation in his own experience that he can muster. Teachers should confine the teaching of socialized concepts to those that may be treated richly. Of course, well-made documentary films, accurate television and radio programs, and other instructional aids help make remote situations real.

Reading Critically

Critical reading is the process of evaluating the authenticity and validity of material and of formulating an opinion about it. It is essential for anyone dealing with controversial issues to be able to read critically. Because the social studies deal with human relationships, they naturally discuss many controversial issues. The child will get into difficulty in reading critically in the social studies if he is unable to understand the problem that faces him, remember the problem while reading, and hold himself to the problem. He must judge the pertinency of the material. He must understand the meanings implied as well as stated. He must evaluate the source from which he is reading. He must differentiate the important from the unimportant facts. He must detect statements of fact as opposed to statements of opinion. He must judge the relative accuracy of conflicting statements. He must be able to appraise the authoritativeness and accuracy of the material. He must be able to detect treatments warped by prejudice. He must keep in mind the authors' percepts and intentions, and judge whether in drawing his conclusions the author considered all the facts presented. In order to be more effective in these critical appraisals, the child should develop the habit of viewing his reading in the light of reasonableness and in the light of what he has read and knows about the subject. Michaelis [192] makes similar points in the following statement: "Critical evaluation of the ideas secured through reading is essential. Controversial issues, prejudices, biases, opinions versus facts, varied interpretations, irrelevant ideas, generalizations, inaccuracies, mood and interest of the author, usefulness of ideas, and the like should be noted and discussed thoroughly by the group. Ideas should be checked against other references and sources of data as need arises. Misconceptions and biases of the reader should also be considered. In addition, children should be helped to detect differences between informational and fictional material."

The ability to read critically must be taught. Whenever there is disagreement in the writings of two or more authors, or whenever a child or a group or the teacher think that there is a question concerning the validity of the material, there is an opportunity to teach critical reading. At such times, the teacher should specifically develop the characteristics of critical reading listed above. Effectiveness in reading critically will be dependent upon the extensiveness and the accuracy of meaning backgrounds.

Using Current Materials

The newspaper, magazine, and other periodicals are used as material in the modern social-studies program. In general, many of the adjustments in using current materials stem from the problem of relating current and specific happenings to the broader concepts of which they are only a part. The reader does not have the advantage of historic perspective nor can he estimate accurately the future trend of events. The child must build an understanding that these materials are somewhat transitory and that they need to be interpreted in the light of the mores of his times. The child should be taught that such materials often express current opinion, not established fact, and are sometimes inaccurate.

Using Geographical Materials

Many of the difficulties in reading geographical materials come from the fact that there is a large number of concepts to be learned in reading any one page. These concepts come in rapid succession and are often quite unrelated. The child must either attempt an extraordinarily difficult learning task; or he must select some few concepts to concentrate upon and to learn; or he must neglect their learning entirely, remembering them only long enough to participate in a discussion during the class hour. It would be difficult indeed to make all of these concepts a part of the child's working equipment. Probably what happens is that he reads relatively slowly, remembering as many as he can for short retention, and some few for various reasons are retained for a longer period of time.

Another difficulty in learning geographical concepts, probably related to the first, is that no one concept is elaborated upon sufficiently to permit a full understanding of it. These problems of contraction of presentation make anything more than mere verbalism difficult, if not impossible.

Frequently, a relatively difficult concept is handled in a single sentence; sometimes, two or three concepts are found within a single sentence. One paragraph of 59 words, selected from an intermediate-grade geography book in wide use, contained 12 concepts, or about one concept for every five words. Some of the concepts in that paragraph were important. In fact, some were so important that it would be possible and profitable to spend a week or more of study upon any of them. Obviously, at best, only a sketchy or partial understanding could have been obtained even by a very able reader through the short presentation made.

One more concept difficulty, which seems to be inherent in the study of geography, is that many of the discussions are about places, peoples, and conditions remote in distance to the child. The child, with little sense of distance, cannot get a clear understanding of, for instance, problems of transportation, reasons for the location of industries or population centers, and interrelationships among people. Also the concepts are often remote from the point of view of interest. The child never has been to the places and believes that he never will go to them. In spite of this, curiosity may be and often is aroused by the teacher.

Remoteness in distance and interest is probably closely related to still another difficulty of concept, namely, lack of background sufficient to understand the discussion, be it ever so brief. A child from the Plains states, while reading of the jungles of tropical regions, may visualize them very inadequately or erroneously. In order that the child may visualize the dense foliage of the tropics, many means of background building should be used. The child should read far more than the usual presentation in a geography book; discussions should take place; pictures and slides should be shown; perhaps a motion picture should be viewed. Only after a rich background of knowledge has been built can a meaningful understanding of the *dense foliage of the tropics* be expected. Backgrounds to enable the child of inland localities to picture the expansiveness of the ocean would have to be built by similar procedures, if the child's idea of the ocean is to be at all accurate and meaningful.

When we find that the boy raised in the state of Washington thinks of Salt Lake City as being an eastern city of the United States and that the boy raised in New Jersey thinks of Pittsburgh as a western city of the United States, we have indications of difficulties due to problems of location and distance. Faulty impressions of this sort are apt to be held by any person, child or adult, who has lived in a specific area all his life, who has not done any distant traveling, and who has read somewhat exclusively about his own area. Of course, for the inexperienced, it is not only the matter of distance that creates faulty impressions in reference to locality. A person is quite apt to think (and, of course, incorrectly so) that his locality has advantages enjoyed by no other—the world's most invigorating climate, for example. It is natural for a person to think of his home and his locality as the center of the universe, which, as a matter of fact, it is, for him. It took astronomers thousands of years to reject the world as the center of our solar system. Inasmuch as world distances, in the time it takes to travel them, at least, are shrinking rapidly, and as the peoples of the world become more and more interrelated and interdependent, we should so teach as to expand the child's concept of locality in order that he may be prepared to think more clearly about world happenings. A good way to contrast distances is to plot on a globe the air-hours from the locality of the child to the various localities of the world that he is reading about.

Geography concepts are important concepts and appear to be becoming still more important as the world becomes more highly interrelated. Therefore, although the reading of geography is fraught with many problems, it is an important sort of reading. This highly specialized reading can best be taught through reading geographical materials when the child is actually confronted with the problems that are inherent within those materials. Some of these basic problems in reading geographical materials should be anticipated in the basal reading program, and readiness for meeting them should be developed.

Selected References

Bamman, Henry A. "Reading in Science and Mathematics," *Reading Instruction in Secondary Schools*. Newark, Delaware: International Reading Association, 1964.

Burton, Dwight. "Teaching Students to Read Literature," *Reading Instruction in Secondary Schools*. Newark, Delaware: International Reading Association, 1964.

Figurel, J. Allen, editor. *Improvement of Reading Through Classroom Practice*. Newark, Delaware: International Reading Association Conference Proceedings, 9:31–44, 1964.

Harris, Albert J., editor. *Readings on Reading Instruction*. New York: David McKay Company, Inc., 1963, Chap. 11.

Hunnicutt, C. W., and W. J. Iverson, editors. *Research in the Three R's*. New York: Harper & Brothers, 1958, Chap. 5.

Smith, Henry P., and Emerald V. Dechant. *Psychology in Teaching Reading*. Englewood Cliffs, N.J.: Prentice-Hall, Inc., 1961, Chap. 13.

Spache, George D. *Toward Better Reading*. Champaign, Illinois: Garrard Publishing Company, 1963, Chap. 16.

Strang, Ruth, and D. K. Bracken. *Making Better Readers*. Boston: D. C. Heath and Company, 1957, Chap. 5.

CHAPTER 14

Reading for
Personal Values

. . . Books are no substitute for living, but they can add immeasurably to its richness. When life is absorbing, books can enhance our sense of its significance. When it is difficult, they can give us momentary release from trouble or new insights into our problem [68].

The teacher of grade six, Miss Norris, had spent the summer traveling in Kenya and Uganda in East Africa. Before making the trip, she had read widely expository and story materials. Her motivational readiness to learn about the vast and to her unknown continent had propelled her to read any sort of material on Africa that she could ferret out. Some of it was the high quality she usually demanded, but much of it was not. Yet she read eagerly, expanding her knowledge as she read. The reading prior to the voyage, the voyage itself, and the reading she was doing following the trip enriched her life. For the past three years Miss Norris has worked with children, helping them make good use of their reading abilities in their daily lives. Her own experiences of the summer, during which her reading served her so well each day as she traveled, have inspired her to work more systematically and competently with the children, to widen their reading interests and elevate their reading tastes. During the trip Miss Norris amassed a variety of Africana, with the belief that the objects might serve to stimulate some children to expand their reading interests.

The children who entered the sixth-grade classroom in September found an attractive room, the displays of which immediately challenged them. There were airline maps showing routes to Central and Eastern Africa. There were examples of the handiwork of the people of Kenya and Uganda. There were many pictures, but more significantly the classroom collection of books contained among its resources material of many sorts and on many reading levels about East Africa.

The children found their new teacher bubbling with enthusiasm and wonder over the fabulous journey she had just completed. From time to time, as the days progressed, Miss Norris related incidents of the events and sights of the previous summer. She read aloud from first one book and then another short selections, long ones, and even an entire story. Miss Norris noted that the books so used by her soon became the ones most in demand. She observed that one child's interests motivated him to read about airplanes and air routes throughout the world. Another became interested in the rivers of the world, especially the Nile. Others avidly pursued biographies and adventure stories of the explorers of Eastern and Central Africa. Still others were involved in reading about wildlife conservation, and some of the less able readers were motivated to read easy animal stories. In time periods devoted to independent reading, where choices were the children's own, Miss Norris was pleased to observe that the majority of the children were deep in books that treated some phase of the history, life, and culture of Africa.

Reporting on current news items was a regular activity of the class. Miss Norris realized that contrary to what had been true the previous year, some of the current items, got from newspaper and magazine reading, dealt with Africa and its emerging nations.

During the discussion of choice of field trip, a number of children expressed a wish to visit the United Nations Building on the day the representatives of a new African nation were to be seated.

At a parent-teacher meeting, both fathers and mothers made a special point of telling Miss Norris that they too were reading about Africa and enjoying, secondhand, the tales of her adventures. The ramifications of the influence of a competent teacher are boundless. One father told of the visit of his family to the World's Fair. His son John had insisted that the family go first to the African Village, which all of them appreciated, especially because of the knowledge John had accumulated. They had eaten African food in the treetop restaurant patterned after the famous Tree-Tops of Kenya.

Major goals of the reading program of Miss Norris were to arouse and maintain strong motivations to read. To accomplish these goals she knew she must have a wealth and variety of material on many reading levels readily available, that the children must be actively willing to read widely, and that reading must be pleasant and rewarding to them. She hoped that during this important sixth year permanent reading interests would develop. She was aware that each of the youngsters would come into the new grade with a variety of personal interests. She sensed too that she, like all sixth-grade teachers in America, would influence the reading interests of the children and their attitudes toward reading, both positively and negatively. She knew, as is necessary in all phases of reading instruction, that the instruction must be planned carefully and done systematically if interests were to be extended, deepened, and elevated.

Suggestions to help Miss Norris and other teachers with similar objectives will be presented in the pages to follow.

Interests and Tastes

Attitudes toward reading as a part of life begin very early in the setting of the home. Some children enter first grade with a conception of reading as a useful and pleasant pursuit; others have literally never seen reading used and have never seen someone gain information or enjoyment from reading. Thus, before children have come under the influence of a schoolteacher they display differences in their attitudes toward reading.

In the child's first reading activities, when his parent reads to him, reading tastes and interests are initiated and developed. For some children, this sharing of printed material is limited to hearing the Sunday comics and an occasional story. Other children have been read to many times passages from children's literature, so that by the time they enter school they are already discriminating consumers of reading matter.

Inevitably, values, attitudes, interests, and tastes are further developed during the elementary-school years. And, whether good or bad, they persist. Thus, it is essential from the first days of reading instruction that desirable ones be developed. The gradual development of these learnings is not only important to growth in reading during the elementary years, but also, if rightly made, fosters continued growth after the child is no longer guided by the teacher.

The broad general interests of children of a given age tend to be somewhat similar [209]. It is not surprising to find that third-grade children are interested in animals or that intermediate-grade boys are interested in adventure. The specific interests of children, however, vary greatly from child to child. As Thorndike has pointed out: "No generalization about reading interests of groups will take the place, for the teacher, of a knowledge of the personal pattern of choices of each individual. Any group trends in interest development should serve merely as a framework of general probabilities into which to fit the picture of the individual child" [263].

Clothes may be the primary interest of a 13-year-old girl. She may become so interested in wearing apparel that all of her free time is devoted to window shopping and to looking in newspapers and magazines at pictures and advertisements of clothes. She may have followed fashions and fads of clothing with so much interest that she has a very good knowledge of what people are wearing. It could be said that this interest has given direction to her spare-time activities, and that the interest has given her the drive and motivation for pursuing these activities. This 13-year-old girl, however, may have very poor taste in the clothes she selects for herself. Thus, although her interest in clothes is high, her taste is poor. It is her taste that determines the quality, the beauty, and the appropriateness of what she wears. The interest determines only that clothing is her spare-time activity, not sports. The intensity of the interest determines in no small measure the amount of effort she is willing to expend within that field.

We may think of interest in the field of reading as determining the area or content within which the person will read most frequently. For example, the interest determines whether the child will read adventure stories or biography. Interest also determines how much reading is done within the chosen field and the intensity with which the individual works at his reading. Taste, on the other hand, determines the quality of material he reads within the field of his interest. For example, the child's interest might determine that he read adventure stories. His taste might determine whether he could be best satisfied by reading an adventure-story magazine or a book like *Treasure Island*.

It should be recognized that interests should not be thought of in the narrow confines of fictional reading alone. Broad interests include interests in reading stories about many things and of many types, and they also include reading historical and biographical material, scientific and geographical material, as well as material of other fields of human endeavor [249]. This is attested to by the expansion of literature prepared for children to include well-prepared factual material in these areas. Children's libraries have whole sections devoted to serious accounts in many fields of endeavor. Good taste in reading includes the consideration of the quality of the fictional material read, and also the quality of literature of other types. The child may be interested for example, in reading scientific material. This material may be either fictional or factual. He may satisfy his interest by reading pseudo-scientific material presented in comic-book style. Or he may read widely in science fiction. In either case, his interest should be used at whatever level of taste, to lead him gradually to appreciate material of better scientific quality.

The program designed to develop broad interests and tastes in reading should develop interest in many topics, interests in the materials of several fields of human endeavor, and an intensity of drive that would motivate the individual to read extensively. In addition the program should improve the quality of the materials read in many fields and on many topics.

Present Status of Interests and Tastes

It is difficult to estimate the present status of interests and tastes of the people who are in or have come through the elementary and secondary schools. The indications seem to be that the reading interests and tastes fall far short of what is desired. One does not have to go to research to realize that the schools have not lived up to their full potential in developing extensive reading interests and high quality of tastes. A trip to the corner drugstore with its rental library and rack of current magazines shows a relative uniformity and narrowness of interests and an appalling lack of taste. Visits to the homes of any one community would show a dearth of reading material in many of them and also that the materials that are available are often of relatively inferior quality and sometimes exemplify narrowness and lack of breadth of interests. It must be recognized, however, that limitations in interests and tastes shown in the homes is a reflection of the reading programs of yesteryear, not of the present.

The library is relatively infrequently used by the older individuals of a community. On successive visits to the library few people will be seen withdrawing books. In comparison with the number of people who visit the supermarkets of a community in a day, the number who patronize the library is very small indeed. The truth of this observation is verified by the fact that the branch librarian knows her patrons and even knows something of their interests and tastes; whereas the clerks in the supermarkets do not. A single community has several supermarkets, and only one library. It should be recognized that nearly always one member of the family chooses the food for the day, whereas each individual member usually selects his own reading material. Obviously too, a person could go to the library and withdraw enough books for a week or two. Even so, the difference indicates that little reading is being done in comparison to the amount of eating; and remember this also, one rarely orders a book over the telephone. From these observations it may be concluded that reading interests are relatively few and tastes are relatively immature, facts that research in reading over the years has shown to be true. These findings suggest that schools must place a greater emphasis on a positive program of developing worthwhile, wide, and lasting reading interests and tastes.

Present-day reading attitudes, interests, tastes, and values appear, however, to be improving. There is an upward trend in adult reading. More than 800 million books, including paper-bound editions, are sold annually. It is true that television is in practically all homes in America, but it is equally true that newspapers are there too. One magazine has a circulation so large it is found in at least one out of every ten homes. Statistics on circulation show that other magazines approximate or exceed this figure. Library statistics indicate that the withdrawal of books is increasing, with serious books more popular than in former years.

The attitude of the general public toward all cultural aspects of life is directly related to its attitude toward the cultural aspects of reading [159]. The limited orientation of many segments of our population toward worthwhile literature alone makes it difficult for the school to develop such interests in the children.

Current happenings have an influence upon interests of children. Animal and man are catapulted into outer space, mail is transported by rocket, devastating diseases come under control, and reading interests of boys and girls are influenced thereby. The happenings of the day become a part of the culture of tomorrow and are related to reading interests of children.

EVALUATING INTERESTS

A teacher is never called upon to defend time and effort spent in guiding children as they read widely and well. All who have expectations for children—taxpayers, school board members, supervisors, school officials, parents, teachers, and the children themselves—all are eager to observe children reading actively and interestedly, for the enrichment to lives that reading brings is well appreciated. A major question of teachers deals with how best to help children develop into readers who will read.

A first step in expanding interests is to determine the present interests of each child. Evaluation may be of a number of sorts; the specific type, or types, depends upon the ages of the children, their reading maturities, the available aids, and the predilections and capabilities of the teacher.

Questionnaire

Information may be gained from simple questionnaires. Often the best questionnaire is one devised by the teacher himself, for it may then be made specifically applicable to the particular group of children. A set of questions designed for use one year with one group of children will likely require modifications before being used with other children. An interest questionnaire found useful in grade four by one of the authors follows. The items were adapted from questionnaires by Witty and Kopel [281], Harris [126], and Austin, Bush, and Huebner [8].

Sample Interest Questionnaire

NAME _____ DATE _____

GRADE IN SCHOOL _____ AGE IN YEARS _____ MONTHS _____

1. What do you like to do after school?
2. What do you like to do when it rains?
3. What do you like to do in the summer?
4. What do you like to see on TV?
5. What do you like to see at the movies?
6. What kinds of games do you like to play?
7. What hobbies or collections do you have?
8. What books that you have read do you like best?
9. Do you own any books? _____ What are some of them?
10. What kinds of things would you like to read about?
11. Have you been   Where?
    a. Outside your home town? _____   _____
    b. To another state?   _____   _____
    c. To another country?   _____   _____
    d. On a long vacation trip? _____   _____
12. If you had three wishes and they might all come true, what would you wish?
    1.
    2.
    3.

Write a paragraph telling why you like or dislike one or several of the activities listed in questions 1 to 11.

The responses to these questions furnish the teacher quickly with much knowledge about the children. Fortified with these knowledges the teacher should be able to help each child build upon his present interests.

A much more simplified questionnaire could be worked out for use with primary-grade children, with the teacher reading the questions and re-cording the responses [8].

Conference

Some teachers follow up a questionnaire with a personal interview and are thus able to clarify ambiguous or limited responses. Whenever a teacher elects to carry out an interview, rapport should be established, and the interview should proceed in a relaxed and comfortable fashion in order to be most fruitful.

To confer with each child in a class group, in either an informal or structured way, takes time. It might take several weeks to talk quietly and confidentially with each child for a sufficient interval to ascertain preferences of play, reading, work, hobby, and other free-time activities. Often preferable to an informal conference is a systematically planned one, possibly with a check sheet to guide the teacher during the interview. It is important to obtain much pertinent information relatively quickly and to have a record of the information. Yet the interview should be unhurried and uninterrupted.

The interview is quite as valuable to the child as it is to the teacher. He gains in communicative skill from personal conferences as he enjoys his talk with his teacher about his likes, dislikes, values, and activities. Also a conference helps him clarify his values and concepts.

Observation

The chief and most evaluative technique of any teacher is observation with judgment of behavior. This statement about observation is true what-ever the age of the individual. A teacher sees behavior rather constantly and makes judgments with regard to its significance. Through daily study, reading interests and motivations may be determined. Upon such de-termination planned enrichment may be based.

Interest Autobiographies

In grades three and above, autobiographies about reading activities and interests may be exceedingly informative and useful to the teacher. As a matter of fact, almost any product of the child will indicate interests or concerns. A picture, a story, the choice of current event, a query, a re-sponse to a question, all are revealing. In all cases, the interests shown may serve as a starting point to motivate personal reading.

Anecdotal Records

Inasmuch as it is impossible to keep in mind the indications of interests gleaned from these appraisals, the teacher should keep anecdotal records.

These records should include, not only insightful statements made by the child, but also summary statements recorded by the teacher of the many observations he has made of the child's reading interests. As these accumulate, the teacher should study them to note changes in type or amount of interests, because lessening of interests is symptomatic of a reading difficulty.

Developing Readers Who Will Read

Although the real motivation for reading must come from within the child himself, the teacher, having appraised intrinsic motivations, can help the child pursue interests that have been already established as well as develop new ones. The child is not born with interests. Interests are acquired, including reading interests, and as such are amenable to training. And too, one interest leads to another. For example, a child may be interested in baseball. This interest may lead to reading newspaper accounts of baseball games, which in turn might lead to reading biographies of baseball heroes, which might lead to a trip to the Baseball Hall of Fame in Cooperstown, New York, which might lead to reading about —who knows what?

Wide Reading

In order that the child may encounter many types of reading and thereby sample the field of printed materials more fully than he could through reading a single basal textbook, it is recommended that he should in addition read extensively from other materials. Some of his stimulation to read other materials may well be an outgrowth of the systematic sampling that he encounters in the basal materials. However, the basal material should be recognized as a place of introduction, from which it is expected that the child will branch out into new and untried channels.

There are many ways of stimulating wide reading. When the child encounters in his reading program an excerpt from a larger story or an incident or story from a collection of stories, he should be referred to the book from which the excerpt has come. If his interest has been sufficiently aroused by the excerpt, it will be rather natural for him to follow up that introduction to the book and read the story or other material during the time allotted for independent reading. In the purchase of material for the classroom collection it is wise to include the books from which excerpts have been taken. It will be recognized that the basal program is usually designed to introduce the reading of children's literature, science material, biography, and the like, in order that these materials encourage wide reading in the many fields. At the same time, the teacher can recommend other books by the same author, or upon the same topic, that he knows to be available. The manuals of basic readers have good bibliographies, which often prove helpful in selecting related and appropriate materials. There are also available other bibliographies of children's books, as well as professional treatments on children's literature.

The teacher may stimulate and improve interests and tastes by reading to the children. All teachers at all levels find it desirable to read aloud well-chosen selections to the children. They find it profitable also to have pupils read aloud materials of their own choice. In the first years of reading growth, the teacher must assume almost the entire responsibility for the personal reading. As the child gains in reading proficiency he should assume an increasing amount of this responsibility.

One way in which the teacher may stimulate interest is by reading a part of a story that is available and encourage the children to finish it. If he desires the entire class to read that story, he might stop the reading at a critical dramatic point. If he wants only to introduce a type of material or material of a specific author, he should terminate the reading at the end of an episode. Also the teacher can tell interesting episodes from a book, or interesting facts about a book or an author. He should be sure that books by the author are available and appropriate to the reading levels of the children. Reading and rereading literary materials, especially poetry, help to develop an appreciation of various literary types. In this latter case, the teacher should be careful to select material intrinsically worth while to the children and not simply material he elects to read for his own satisfaction.

Among the most effective ways of encouraging extensive reading is using reading in the pursuit of other interesting class activities. Linguistic, artistic, and dramatic activites foster extensive reading. The dramatization of stories that have been liked, and the search for stories to dramatize, stimulate wide reading and, in turn, develop interests. Portraying the characters of books that have been liked also stimulates interest. One procedure, "Guess Who I Am," in which each child presents his interpretation of a character in a book that has been read, is productive of results and is well liked by the children. The children may have score cards and find out which child can correctly guess the greatest number of characterizations. They do not seem to think of this as an appraisal but as an interesting activity. However, for the teacher it is a way of getting an indication of the extensiveness of reading and the degree of understanding that each child has attained.

An artistic activity that proves effective in stimulating wide reading is depicting, on a mural, the chronology of historical episodes of a certain period. The children search for episodes before planning their mural, so that it may be as authoritative and illustrative of the period as possible. To this purpose, the children read extensively. In this way, both interests and tastes in reading factual material are developed.

Many opportunities should be provided for the children to talk with their teacher and among themselves about the materials they have read. Panel discussions, for which the children read and prepare, develop broad interests. Classroom debates on topics of interest encourage extensive reading. These latter two activities have proved especially profitable in certain of the content fields, such as social studies and science.

Linguistic activities may be stimulated by the use of a period that might be called "Book-Sharing Hour," in which the children tell about or read parts of books that they have liked especially well. The telling or reading may be done in many ways. It may be a period of "I think you would like to read this story because," or "I think you would like to read this newspaper article or about this science experiment because," or "I liked this book because," or "What do you think of my choice?" Through such activities, interests may be expanded and the quality of tastes raised.

In all these activities, based upon wide reading, the teacher should hold the children to high standards of performance. The culminating activity, stemming from reading, should be the children's creation, not the teacher's. If the children prepare a mural, the mural should be carefully planned and well prepared. If a child dramatizes a character he should make a studied estimate of that character. Debates should be well planned and carried out in a studious fashion. In addition, the teacher should guide the reading carefully so as to insure constant growth in the quality of the child's choices and continuous expansion of the child's interests. This is not an easy task, especially when it is considered that the teacher must think in terms of the personal reading interests and abilities of some 30 individuals. The above activities will help the teacher both stimulate and appraise increases in interest and improvement in tastes.

Have Appropriate Materials at Hand

After the first step of determining the nature, scope, and quality of a child's reading interests and other activities, the teacher should make easily accessible the material to satisfy interests. A book, pamphlet, magazine, or newspaper in the community library is less accessible than the book, pamphlet, magazine, or newspaper in the school library, which in turn is less accessible than in the classroom or in the child's desk or hands. As Bracken has expressed it, "The book a youngster needs at any given moment should be only four inches away, not four blocks or four miles" [35]. Further, the ideas in a book on a readability level above that of the child are less accessible to him than are those in a book he can read fluently.

To have appropriate materials readily available requires a large and varied source of supply in the classroom collection and school library. The teacher should be continually building his own knowledge of children's literature. Also he should solicit help from librarian and coworker. The whole field of children's literature is expanding so rapidly that no teacher can expect to keep abreast of all material. Over 1,500 different titles are published annually for children. The teacher requires help from the many resources available to him, including coworkers, librarians, book lists and reviews, and reports about books from the children themselves.

The materials that are needed to develop interests and improve tastes should also include both the basal reader and other basal textbooks and many times as many related materials. The basal books are primarily to give the child the framework or skeleton upon which he must put flesh. If he does not have many opportunities to do related reading, the child will have little chance of getting more than a very incomplete notion of the actual problems with which he is dealing. If his ideas and concepts are to live, if his interests and tastes are to be developed, he must be given the opportunity to read extensively.

There is, as every teacher is aware, a wide range of reading ability in any class. This range is consistent for any grade level. For example, the spread of reading ability in a sixth-grade class is about seven years. This means that there will be within the class children who read effectively material of not more than third-grade difficulty and also children who read effectively material of about ninth-grade difficulty. The challenge is to supply this class with a wealth of material suitable to the various levels of reading ability for each of the content areas and for the personal reading of each child. The materials made available must in addition be selected to cover a wide range of interests and be such that they lend themselves to systematic improvement in reading taste, because it must be remembered that the children vary in level of reading tastes as well as in reading ability itself.

It must be realized that there is no such thing as a book that is suited to a sixth-grade class only. For in reality there is no such thing as a class of sixth-grade readers. There are sixth-grade readers in every class from about the third grade through high school! This fact should be taken into account in supplying materials to any given class. Even though the supply of materials is limited, provision for reading differences can be made through its wise use. Rather than allocating nothing but sixth-grade books to a sixth-grade class, books of readability levels of third, fourth, fifth, sixth, seventh, eighth, and ninth grades should be included. In this way, provision can be made for the nucleus of a class collection of books. There should be a permanent classroom collection of reference books and textbooks of various sorts and at various levels. Included also should be many fictional and factual books from the field of children's literature. There are a number of ways of judging the readability level of material. Material should be appraised in terms of such considerations as its vocabulary content, the length of sentences, the number of prepositional phrases, and the difficulty and remoteness of the concepts. Dale and Chall [63], Lorge [177], Spache [244], and Yoakum [285] have developed formulas to judge material [53]. To appraise the books and other materials of a classroom collection by means of any one of these formulas consumes perhaps more time than the teacher wishes to devote to the task. A more rapid estimate, although somewhat less accurate, can be made by using the books of a basal reading series as a rating scale. The difficulty of a book or selection may be estimated by comparing it with the various books of the basal series. A point can be located that will give a rough estimate of level of difficulty. At this point, in terms of such characteristics as vocabulary, length and complexity of sentences, and difficulty of concepts, material more advanced in the basal series will seem somewhat more difficult, and material earlier in the series will seems somewhat less difficult than the book being rated [143]. Fortified with a knowledge of basal material of several grade designations, a teacher soon becomes able to judge quickly the difficulty of a particular selection. The teacher may revise the estimate of level of difficulty of a selection after he has watched children read it. The final judgment should be made in terms of the reading capabilities of the child who reads the selection with comprehension.

Teacher's Own Motivation

Teachers exert so much influence upon the children they teach that it is wise for the teacher to appraise his own reading attitudes and interests. Odland and Ilstrup pose the question whether "the adults who accept the responsibility of teaching young children the values of reading really consider reading a valuable medium of communication. Can these adults guide children to develop sensitivity and selectivity when, in their own experience, they seem not to consider these intellectual qualities truly important?" [204]

A teacher who feels his own background is weak can deliberately widen, deepen, and improve the quality of his own reading as he helps children widen, deepen, and improve theirs. A wise forward step would be to enroll in a college or university course in children's literature [9]. Such work should do for him what he is attempting to do for the children, cause reading juvenile materials to be fascinating, informative, and rewarding. Another good plan is for several teachers of a school to work cooperatively to build a booklist of juvenile books too good to miss. Then the teachers should read the books on the list. A recently prepared bibliography of children's books that has merit may be found in *Children, Books, and Reading,* a publication of the International Reading Association [68]. Several teachers might work together to annotate such a list. By doing so they would inevitably add to their ability to guide children in personal reading and would also add to the scope of their own personal reading.

Enthusiasm is contagious. Only when a teacher demonstrates day in and day out his own belief in reading as an enjoyable and useful pursuit can he expect to help children build lifetime reading habits. Jacobs emphasizes the importance of "a devotion that is contagious" in the following statement: "[The teacher] is personally so enthusiastic about literature that he generates in others his sense of the values of reading. . . . He so enjoys experiences in reading that he is anxious to lead others to similar pleasures" [145].

Enlist the Aid of Parents

A suggestion a teacher might make to parents in conference or in a PTA talk is that they be readers themselves if they want their children to become readers. Again, it should be stated that enthusiasm and example are contagious. Huus relates an appealing anecdote: "Children who have pleasant experiences with reading at home will want to read. As they see other people reading, it becomes only natural that they also do. A four-year-old, whose lawyer father was always quoting from his legal journals, surprised his family at a dinner party one evening by asking the guests if they had seen the new article about trucks in the latest *Saturday Evening Post.* When they admitted they had not, he said that after dinner he would be glad to show it to them. So when the time came, he produced the magazine, turned to a big double-page spread containing an ad with two huge trailer-trucks, and proudly showed the guests the 'new article' on trucks. Reading? Yes, to him, at his level" [142].

Parents can encourage growth in interests and tastes for their children by themselves showing an interest in materials the child is reading. It is satisfying for the parent to go to the library with his child, show an interest in the books selected, and share further the experience by reading some of the material so that he can participate in a discussion of the contents with his child. These shared experiences are pleasant ones and extraordinarily profitable for the child. Parents probably influence the reading tastes of children more than teachers or librarians do. Often a parent expresses the belief that he should stop reading to his child after the child has developed an independent capability of his own. This is not the case. Sharing books at home in a family circle by means of oral reading should continue as long as the child anticipates the sessions with eager expectancy.

Read Aloud

Whatever the grade level, a day should not pass without the teacher reading aloud to a child, a group, or the entire class. Daily sharing with the children material deemed particularly appropriate, material deemed especially beautiful, or material containing pertinent information will result in increased personal reading by the children. Harris writes, "We can improve interest in reading by helping children enjoy reading [126]. We help children enjoy reading by reading to them. Huus advocates reading "to children regularly, every day, and more than once a day if you can squeeze it in " [142] as a way of improving reading tastes.

Let us hope that the teacher is himself a good oral reader. If he is not, here is another professional attribute he can improve through diligent effort as he helps children become good oral readers. Among the satisfactions teaching brings are the opportunity to use one's knowledge and abilities and the chance to enlarge one's knowledge and improve one's skills. Both of these satisfactions come to the competent teacher of reading.

The search for material to be read aloud should be a careful one [151]. Elements of good children's literature, listed by Johnson and quoted below, should help a teacher in his choice of a good storybook.

1. Children like a quick beginning. In her story *The Puppy Who Wanted a Boy*, Jane Thayer uses a first sentence of seventeen words to give the complete setting of time, characters, problem: "One day Petey, who was a puppy, said to his mother, 'I'd like a boy for Christmas.'"
2. Children like conversation—dialogue which is fast moving and easy to follow.
3. Children like fast story action which contains suspense. They do *not* like description which impedes story action. If an author develops the personalities of his characters through what they say and do, he does not need description.

4. Children like simplicity of plot provided there is substantial content.
5. Children like true-to-life characters with whom they can identify.
6. There should be an economy of episodes, a steady progression to a definite conclusion. The Brothers Grimm sent Cinderella to the ball three times—she needed to go but twice.
7. Quaint expressions, ejaculations, amusing names, occasional exaggerations, and absurdities appeal to the child reader.
8. Choice of words should be appropriate to the spirit of the content and to the child's level of development. A discerning author uses concrete, colorful words depicting vivid sensory impressions.
9. Each story should have originality of content—its own new and distinctive elements. *The Puppy Who Wanted a Boy* introduces a new point of view and a surprise ending. Petey finds not one boy but fifty boys for Christmas.
10. Stories for children must have integrity. Do characters behave as real human beings? Is the story plausible or, if it is fantasy, does the make-believe have its own consistent framework?
11. Great literature for children has spirituality—morality without moralizing. A five-year-old child once said to me, "When I am enchanted, I feel close to heaven" [151].

The books each year that gain Newbery, Caldecott, and other awards meet many of the above criteria. Those teachers who watch each spring for the announcements of award winners and runners-up and who get the books, read them, and share them with children experience true delight.

Provide Time for Reading

It is not enough to submerge children in a reading environment surrounded by books. The capable, enthusiastic, widely read teacher needs also to schedule regular periods during which children may read, read, read, pursuing personal reading interests in materials of their own choice. There are numbers of competing activities for the time of children in after-school hours. The way to insure that children have the opportunity to read independently is to provide for it in the daily and weekly school schedules. Although the years of the upper elementary grades are ones of great reading activity away from school, for many children these years may be made more fruitful in producing readers who will read when personal reading is held in so high estate as to be worthy of schooltime: time to savor books, the "lilt of line," the choice of words or phrase; to browse at the child's own pace, to read sometimes at a gallop, at other times to read slowly to reflect, reread, and restructure creatively.

Often in both popular and professional literature a lament is voiced over the low level of adult reading tastes and the infrequency with which many adults use reading as a leisure-time pursuit, illustrated by the following statement by Eller: "Americans have both the ability and the materials to read if they wish. However, they must have the inclination to read, and the research into the reading actually performed by Americans suggests that this inclination is often lacking" [91]. Let us stimulate the inclination to read by setting up free-reading periods in which the children may pursue and practice reading inclinations.

Build Interests and Tastes Free from Skill-Development Instruction

There should be a clear-cut distinction between reading done in the basal program to develop skills and abilities and reading to expand interests and improve tastes, much of which is achieved during the time set aside for personal reading. McKee emphasizes this point when he says "methods used to help children build an abiding interest in good reading material and a taste for such material must be inherently informal" [188], enabling children to approach a selection as something to be enjoyed in its own right. There is no surer way to stifle expanding interests than to stop the ongoing appreciation of a story or selection in order to engage in drill upon a fundamental of reading or to attempt to extract from children an analysis of content, plot, or characterization. It is unwise to probe and quiz, implying that no learning can go on unless a teacher is asking questions and children are answering them. When a child requires help in recognizing a word or comprehending a concept, the help should be given freely and quickly so that he is enabled to continue to communicate with the author actively and with interest.

Build upon Present Interests and Tastes

Any attempt to help a child improve the literary quality of the material he reads, like expanding reading interests, must be begun at the level revealed by the appraisals of the child. If the tastes are low, start at that level. If on his own the child reads only comic books, bring comic books into the classroom. The tendency of teachers in their eagerness to guide a child toward better quality of reading is to move too rapidly into too difficult books. Only through systematic and expert teaching can a child be led gradually toward better quality of material. The unfortunate truth is that it is possible for a child to read widely and yet never read a really good book [139]. Here, as in so many of the ramifications of building lifetime reading habits, the child requires wise guidance. It is comforting to a teacher to know, in those classes where basal and cobasal readers are used, that those materials are of good literary quality so that in that phase of the program at least the children are reading good materials.

In all of the activities designed to stimulate wide reading, it is necessary for the teacher to give careful guidance based upon his knowledge of the children's present levels of taste. Just as is true in the case of reading tastes, it is necessary to recognize the child's present interest in reading. A child may have a relatively narrow range of interests that leads him to concentrate his reading in a limited field. For example, his sole reading interest might be in animal stories. Although this reading interest is in and of itself highly commendable, it is not wide enough to give the child the many reading experiences and enjoyments that he should have. The teacher could lead such a child by gradual steps from this interest to the selection of materials in closely related fields. The child might be guided into reading *The Jungle Book.* Then he might be encouraged to read other stories by Kipling. Next, he might read other travel tales, and from there it is hard to tell what trails his expanding interests might lead him to follow.

To reiterate, the teacher must first appraise to find out the range of interests and level of tastes, then he must have readily available an increasing gradation of materials dealing with the specific interests of each of the children, and he must provide time for them to follow their inclinations and give counsel that will give direction to their reading.

Present Systematic Lessons

Lessons directed toward elevating reading tastes and expanding reading interests should be planned carefully and systematically. Recommending systematic planning, Burton and Larrick say: "Emphasis on the pleasures of reading in the elementary school does not mean a *laissez-faire* policy of 'surround them with books and sit back.' Instead, it means careful planning to provide for individual differences in an atmosphere that encourages children to wonder and to seek, to contemplate and to evaluate" [45]. Based upon knowledge of each child's reading abilities and interests, the teacher can arrange experiences to expand interests and elevate reading tastes. One way is to integrate the ideas found in reading with the daily experiences of the children. Careful integration of ideas requires thought and attention. Each subject contains a potential for deepening and expanding reading interests. Frequently, it is assumed that the development of reading interests and tastes is limited to reading juvenile fictional material. Such an assumption should not be made. It should be recognized that at the present time the tastes of elementary-school children are being expanded in juvenile fictional material. It is equally important to recognize that children are interested in the wonders of the world about them (science material), in the cultures of the present and past and in interrelationships among men (social-studies material), in their own well-being (health material), in how to make things (industrial arts), in recreation and how they can participate (physical education), and so forth. The concept of children's literature has expanded to include materials drawn from many fields of endeavor, both factual and fictional. Children should be taught to read, enjoy, and demand quality in factual presentations as well as in narrative ones. Children like to attack the problems of everyday living, they like to understand the world about them, and they are willing to put forth effort in order to understand. They like to read factual material factually presented. The program for developing interests and tastes should consider the materials of all fields. Elementary- and high-school children daily read newspapers. Often, when children list material read during independent reading, newspapers head the list [152, 272, 283]. Use should be made of the interests thus displayed in activities of the school reading day.

It is important to interest children in the controversial concerns of the school, community, and nation and to read about them, discuss them, and write about them. Many times a teacher is reluctant to guide the reading into controversial areas. The reluctance causes children to be ill-prepared to read, discuss, reflect about current controversies recorded in newspapers and magazines and discussed over radio and television.

Occasionally, teachers may interest children in specific authors by relating incidents in the life of the author, by displaying his picture, by reading excerpts from biographical material, by giving a well-developed talk about one of his books, or even by inviting him to the school to speak to the children.

In a variety of ways teachers may encourage children to read, including setting up book displays, posting notices of material related to television and radio programs, using television to stimulate reading, using book-related aids, including films, film strips, and recordings. There should be frequent discussion of the feelings aroused and knowledge gained from these aids to teaching and learning [228, 279, 280].

Encourage Use of the Elementary-School Library

All over the country school library facilities are expanding tremendously and may be expected to grow even more rapidly in the decade ahead. In many states school librarians are certified as teaching librarians, a development that enables them to serve children and teachers more effectively. No longer are they regarded largely as custodians of books and as keepers of records.

It is to be recommended that wherever possible the school have a central library that serves two major purposes: (1) a place in which children can go to do independent reading and study; (2) a main source of materials for the classroom collection. When any given topic is to be studied, the teacher will find such a library extremely useful. First, the children can go to the central library to survey it for potential material. The teacher can supplement the reading materials that are gotten by the children by adding those materials he knows to be pertinent and available for the specific topic. These books thus may become a part of the class collection for as long a time as they are needed. In this way, the books may achieve their greatest usefulness. The same book may be used in one class while it is needed there and later in another class. *On Arctic Ice* might be used by an average reader during the study of an Eskimo unit in the fourth grade and also constitute a part of the reading of a poor reader in the sixth grade who was studying arctic travel in a transportation unit. In this way, the book is more effectively used than if it had been located permanently in the classroom collection of either room. The classroom collection might be thought of somewhat like a branch city library.

A wide use should be made of the facilities of the public library. The children should be taught to use public libraries [154]. Trips to the library should be planned. The children should be shown how to use the library and be introduced to the fact that the library is a source from which they may draw materials to satisfy their interests. Perhaps the best way to encourage a child to read extensively and become interested in reading is through teaching him how to use a library and showing him the opportunities and interesting reading that it makes available. The children should be encouraged to have library cards and to learn how to make good use of them. The child should become so well acquainted with the library that he feels at home in it. Harmer [125] found that intensive training in the use of the library and its summer program, accompanied by trips to the library, result in a greater use of the library during the summer vacation and a gain, rather than a loss, in reading capability during the summer period.

The teacher should recognize that the public library is a major source of supplementing the material made available by the public-school system. Many libraries accord school privileges so that a teacher may withdraw many books on a given topic for a considerable period of time. Cooperation between the public library and the public school is to be encouraged.

The reader will sense the many ramifications of library services to children and teachers. The cooperative effort of teacher and librarian in increasing the range of reading interests through guidance of the individual child results in greater reading independence, which in turn produces children who will read. To the prospective teacher, a wise word is to establish, as soon as the year begins, a comfortable rapport with the elementary-school and community librarians. You and your children will be the beneficiaries.

Use Book Lists

A procedure that has stimulated interest in reading, used by intermediate-grade teachers, is to have the children help prepare book orders. Let the children suggest books or types of books to order each year for the classroom collection. Then when the books arrive, allow committees of children to open the packages, make a record of the books, and help get them on the shelves. In no time at all the children will be reading the books!

Another motivational practice is to prepare short book lists, annotated when practicable, for various occasions of the year, such as holidays, or on significant topics, for use by the children. Also it is wise to have short lists at hand for parents who seek help in selecting a book for their child. Sometimes teachers periodically send to parents lists of books that the children would enjoy reading. It is helpful too to prepare a list for summer reading appropriate to a particular child or a group of children. One list might have the title "Books About Horses," another "Books About Space Travel." Some teachers deem it worth while preparing a list to send to parents of adult books on topics the children are dealing with. Miss Norris, the sixth-grade teacher referred to earlier, could no doubt have raised the reading interests of the children by preparing a list for parents. Books written for adults are in the reading fare of many sixth-grade children.

Use Paperbacks

Americans purchase close to 300 million paperbacks each year. Children, as well as adults, buy and read these easy to handle, not too formidable, readily available, and comparatively inexpensive reading materials. There is a great variety of material, covering a wide range of topics and on many different reading levels, in paperback editions. Classroom collections and school libraries should have many paperbacks. Boutwell [34] suggests that a teacher can, with thought, guide children's delight in paperbacks into more valuable channels than was possible with the dime novel and the comic book. He says further, "Paperbacks—abundant pa-

perbacks—available on school racks, through clubs, and in the library
—can vastly extend at little cost the range of subject matter and range
of reading ability within the school" [34]. Boutwell advocates teachers
sponsoring paperback book clubs as a way of stimulating wider reading.
Children in the past have had comic book clubs, which brought many
comic books to many readers.

Use Comic Books

Millions of copies of comic books are read each month by children between the ages of eight and thirteen. It is not unusual to see children who
have been somewhat lackadaisical about reading the materials in the
schoolroom run to the corner drugstore after school, pull a comic off the
shelf, and devour it while sitting uncomfortably on a scale. There can be
no question that this medium of communication offers fascinating reading
to children [238]. The fact that they often turn to comics rather than to
other material may be because action and description of locale and
costume are carried by pictures. All the child has to read is the conversation. It may be due to the element of adventure and excitement. It may
be that the comics stimulate the imagination—that they are the *20,000
Leagues Under the Sea* of today. It may be that, in this scientific age of
the unusual, youth enjoy a new type of imaginative story. Whatever the
reason, comics are popular not only with children but with adults. Children have organized their own *Comic Lend Libraries,* as the following
episode indicates:

> A ten-year-old boy answered the knock on the door and the following
> conversation took place:
> "I have finished mine. Are you ready to trade?"
> "No. I can't trade yet. I have finished reading, but my Dad hasn't read
> it yet."

A solution is to upgrade the general quality of comics to meet the standards of the better comics that are published today. It is possible to
develop tastes and appreciation of comic stories quite as much as developing taste and appreciation of other stories. Children should learn
to evaluate the comics to determine authenticity, accuracy, and literary
merit of presentation. Children should sense that a narrow diet of any
sort is unwholesome; that it would be unfortunate if a child read nothing
but fairy tales, if he read nothing but scientific material, or if he read
nothing but comics. It might be likened to eating hot dogs. There is
nothing intrinsically wrong with a hot dog, but a diet should not consist

entirely of hot dogs if dietary deficiencies are to be avoided. Children surrounded by a wealth of the best in children's literature have been found to limit materially their reading of comics, even though the child can absorb effortlessly by viewing the pictures in a comic book much of the content without the effort involved in reading [246].

Boo¹ ᴿ ᵃʳᵗˢ

Grea. … 'o insure that book reports do not drive children from reading iaᴜ. … draw them to it. Short, varied reports prove stimulating. Long, teᴜ. s, standard reports destroy interest.

A class discussion of ᵉ literary qualities of what has been read, depending on how it is haᵢ 'led by the teacher, can either propel children to read more widely and wisely, or it can stifle reading motivation. One is always concerned about what requiring book reports does to the motivation to read. If the report required is a written one, the child may be gaining experience in expressing himself in written form, in organizing his thoughts, in critical, evaluative, and appreciative thinking. Written reports should be short and should not follow the same form. If the report is oral, the child gains experience in communicating orally, in selecting what he believes will be interesting to his listeners, in organizing his thinking, and, as well, reading to present orally helps develop creative and reflective thinking. Two or more children who have enjoyed a book may wish to collaborate in an oral report on it. Again, reports should be brief. Miller [193] suggests using a three-minute egg timer to limit the length of each report. At each reporting time not more than three or four children should report. Even though the children enjoy turning the egg timer, more than four reports can become boring and perfunctory. When the report is one that is read aloud children are motivated to read well, they develop sensitivity to language, and they learn to choose selections that are stimulating to the audience.

Fifty ways of attracting children to books and gaining their active participation are cited by Amy Jensen [149], including writing, telling, or reading the most humorous incident, the most exciting happening, the most interesting event, the most beautiful description, the most lifelike conversation, the best character description. Other ways of varying reports may be writing a letter to a friend recommending the book, making a list of new unusual words, writing a movie script, constructing a miniature stage setting for part of the story, preparing a book sales talk, participating in an informal, lively panel discussion, comparing or contrasting characters, preparing a picture strip to show steps in a plot, telling an original riddle about the book plot or characters, designing a book jacket, building a bulletin board of reviews of "Books I Think You Will Like," each review signed by the child who wrote it. If there is a class newspaper, there should be a column headed "New Books" and containing reviews written by the children.

Reports may be made in teams, one child reporting to a second at one time, the second to the first at another time. Reports may be put on tape, with one or two selected by a committee to be heard by the entire class. A child in a higher grade may go to a lower grade to tell about a book he enjoyed while in the lower grade. Such a procedure stimulates interest and provides a variety of worthwhile linguistic experiences for the storyteller. The children in the lower grade both enjoy and profit from having the older child come to their room to read or tell a story.

Wide reading may be stimulated by having the children select different topics each week upon which to report: a book that made me chuckle, a mystery I failed to solve, an adventure story, an animal story, an action story, a book about a real boy, a biography, an account of a sport, poetry that is interesting, a story about people in faraway lands, an interesting current event [149]. One way of insuring creativity is to have the child choose a book, read it, and share it with his classmates in whatever way he wishes.

The plea here is for brevity in reporting and for variety of reporting (necessitating variety of reading). A creative teacher produces creativity in children, and both enjoy and profit from their work together.

Recording Growth in Interests

Let the child record his growth in interests. Commercially prepared ways of keeping the child aware of his growing areas of interest in reading have been used by teachers to advantage. *My Reading Design* [202], one such record, allows the child to see graphically the areas he is neglecting and those he is concentrating on. Graphic representations of individual "Reading Trees" have been used successfully by other teachers. It consists of a mimeographed tree with its trunk and branches. The child adds the leaves in the form of titles of books he has read, classifying the books as to the main branch to which they are related. The branches may be named "Animal Stories," "Mystery Stories," "Sports Stories," "Adventure Stories," "Science Selections," and the like. Adding leaves to the many branches of the "Reading Tree" should not become so interesting to the child as to cause him to fail to read sufficiently within any one area. Enough reading should be done within one or several areas to help the child gain the ability to discriminate between the various qualities of writing within the one or several areas.

Attitudes Toward Reading

In addition to developing interests and tastes there are certain attitudes toward reading that are encouraged throughout the reading experiences of the child. The discussion of the role of these attitudes will focus upon: establishing purposes for reading, assuming independence, demanding understanding, being socially responsible, treasuring books. The discussion, then, is illustrative, not exhaustive.

Establishing Purposes for Reading

It is important to inculcate early and to develop throughout the reading program the attitude of independently establishing purposes for reading. The reader who knows what he hopes to gain from reading, whether it be to answer a question or to while away time, is a more effective reader than the one who reads with no well-defined purpose. There are times when a worthwhile purpose for reading is to help time pass quickly and pleasantly.

In pupil-teacher planning, the child examines the reading tasks to see how to attack them, to establish definite goals, and to define reading purposes. In this way the attitude of establishing purposes for reading develops. Even in recreational reading, purposes must be set. The purpose, for example, may be to enjoy the meter or rhythm of a poem, or to study the life of an individual in a biography, or merely to relax. The child must be taught to set purposes whenever he takes up material to read.

Assuming Independence

Assuming independence is an attitude that grows directly out of purposeful reading, whether the reading is part of a study or a recreational situation. Independence enables the reader to rely on his own resources and to institute self-initiated reading activities. Independence is a real yardstick of reading maturity. As in the case of the development of independence in other areas of living, growth results from having the opportunity to be independent. The responsibilities the child is expected to assume should be reasonable ones for him. Independence will be fostered in classes where the children search out their own material in connection with a topical unit or for much of their personal reading.

Demanding Understanding of the Material

It is essential that the child develop the attitude of demanding understanding and the habit of allowing nothing other than a fulfillment of his purpose. Every author assumes his material will be read by an energetic reader who wishes to share his ideas or experience—a reader who demands an understanding of what is read. This orientation is developed by means of having the child participate in reading situations that are important to him and is never encouraged by the "read the next ten pages" assignment method.

The child actively seeking the solution to problems that are important to him will demand understanding and appreciate the contribution that reading can make to the solution of problems. The child wishing to share a story or poem well told by an author will demand understanding. He will wish to relive the action of the story, to see the sights, know the people, and in other ways become emotionally and appreciatively a part of the theme. Only by demanding an understanding of the material can such purposes be achieved. When the teacher senses that the child has failed to comprehend the purport, he can show the child the significance of accurate and complete comprehension.

Other happenings, common in every classroom, provide opportunities for the teacher to stress the importance of an attitude of reading to understand. The attitude of demanding an understanding is developed in such a situation as when a construction activity goes awry due to a failure to read intelligibly. The child learns the desirability of energetically attacking the task of learning to read and recognizes that he must develop the basic skills and abilities essential to the use of this important means of communication if he is to understand what he reads. He realizes the importance of accurate, thoughtful reading in learning situations. The attitude of demanding understanding of what he reads is enhanced also by the creative activities that accompany the reading.

The attitude of demanding accuracy and authenticity and the habit of choosing materials of literary merit are essential to intelligent reading of printed material. Along with development of abilities of appraising material must be developed the need to appraise it critically. At times, it is more important to be concerned with accuracy and authenticity than with the style of writing. At other times, the manner in which something is said is of prime importance. In reading a poem, for example, it is as much the way the ideas are expressed as it is the ideas themselves that make the poem worth reading. What is wanted is that the reader develop the attitude of demanding that the author do something for him, whether it be giving him accurate information or esthetic enjoyment.

Being Socially Responsible

Attitudes of social responsibility in reading situations include cooperating in group reading, assuming responsibility in solving group problems, and recognizing the responsibility for preparing well oral presentations. Also, when listening in an oral-reading situation, it is courteous to attend to the reading. In addition, social responsibility includes such attitudes as avoidance of annoying other people who are reading, wishing to keep material in good order and in good repair, following library customs and rules, sharing reading material and so on. These attitudes are developed when the class community engages in cooperative reading enterprises. A stimulating environment, in which the *esprit de corps* is high, fosters wholesome group reading attitudes. Courtesy is developed in situations in which the children wish to work, to share, and to enjoy reading. It cannot be expected that social responsibility will be developed in round-the-room, unprepared oral-reading situations, where neither the reader nor the listener is comfortable and where respect for the integrity of the individual is often lost. Because in such a situation the reader has had no opportunity to prepare for the reading and because the listener is disinterested, neither the reader nor the listener feels a personal responsibility.

Treasuring Books

Adults show great variability in the pleasure displayed at the sight of a book. Some adults give the book not a second glance. Books make up no part of their lives. Other adults delight at the sight of a book, pick it up, and immediately begin to examine its contents. The same contrast is shown in the approaches that two elementary- or high-school children may make to a new text. One will look at the size of the book and groan; the other will eagerly sample its contents so that almost immediately the book becomes a friend. The latter child has already developed to some degree an attitude of intellectual curiosity. His attitude makes him curious about the contents of books, so that when he enters a library or bookstore he marvels at the treasures it holds. He wonders what the many books contain, what stories their authors have to tell, what factual information the writers wish to communicate, and what topics of interest are treated. He is challenged as well to know who wrote the various books, what the authors are like, and to what extent each book reflects its author's thought and personality.

A library of books is a storehouse of many intellectually profitable and pleasurable experiences to the child who has built an attitude of scholarly

curiosity. Instruction in the early years of school should be given to lead children to develop the attitude of appreciating printed materials of all sorts through realizing their worth to them, to other individuals, and to all mankind. Such understandings are encouraged when the child reads materials important to him.

Encouragement should be given the child who spontaneously displays a fondness for books and reading. A smile, gesture, or word serves as a strong extrinsic incentive, particularly in the beginning days of independent reading. It is very evident that the child in the accompanying picture is interested in books and is on her way to becoming an independent reader.

The products of reading, such as information gained or pleasure experienced, later serve as motivational forces that lead a child to seek other materials to read. In discussing ways of helping a child enjoy reading Gans [99] suggests (1) take time to listen, (2) find out together, (3) share experiences, and (4) be readers on the hunt. Make sure that each child has many happy, satisfying associations with books in order to foster attitudes of treasuring books.

Selected References

Austin, Mary, Clifford L. Bush, and Mildred H. Huebner. *Reading Evaluation.* New York: The Ronald Press Company, 1961, Chap. 2.

Bond, Guy L., and Eva Bond Wagner. *Child Growth in Reading.* Chicago: Lyons and Carnahan, 1955.

Crosby, Muriel, editor. *Reading Ladders for Human Relations,* fourth edition. Washington, D.C.: American Council on Education, 1963.

Dawson, M. A., editor. *Children, Books, and Reading.* Newark, Delaware: International Reading Association, 1964, Chaps. 2 and 10.

DeBoer, John J., and Martha Dallmann. *The Teaching of Reading,* revised edition. New York: Holt, Rinehart and Winston, Inc., 1964, Chaps. 11 and 17.

Hunnicutt, C. W., and W. J. Iverson, editors. *Research in the Three R's.* New York: Harper & Brothers, 1958, Chaps. 6 and 7.

Larrick, Nancy. *Teacher's Guide to Children's Books.* Columbus, Ohio: Charles E. Merrill Books, Inc., 1960.

Russell, David H., and Anna F. Merrill. Children's Librarians Rate the Difficulty of Well-Known Juvenile Books, *Elementary English,* 28:262–68, 1951.

Smith, Nila Banton. *Reading Instruction for Today's Children.* Englewood Cliffs, N.J.: Prentice-Hall, Inc., 1963, Chaps. 12–14.

Strang, Ruth. *Helping Your Child Improve His Reading.* New York: E. P. Dutton Co., Inc., 1962, Chap. 7.

Witty, Paul. "The Role of Interests," *Development in and Through Reading,* The Sixtieth Yearbook of the National Society for the Study of Education, Part I. Chicago: The University of Chicago Press, 1961.

Witty, Paul, *et al.* "Studies of Children's Interests—A Brief Summary," *Elementary English,* 37:469–75, November 1960.

V

THE TEACHER RECOGNIZES INSTRUCTIONAL NEEDS

CHAPTER 15

Appraising Reading Growth

To emphasize the need for valid measurement of the educational goals of instruction, the following incidents, witnessed by one of the authors, are cited:

> In a second-grade classroom, the children were correcting exercises in a workbook. The teacher indicated the correct answer to exercise four, saying, "All those who have the correct answer, put up your right hand." One child proudly and excitedly raised his hand. The teacher called out, "Gary, mark your paper zero. You raised the wrong hand. I said right hand, and you raised your left hand."

> The children of the third-grade in a large elementary school were assembled in the gymnasium, in which the principal stood with a fourth-grade reading book. She had one child after another come up to her to read orally a selection from the fourth-grade book. After a moment of reading, she directed the first child to go to the right, commenting, "You failed to read well enough to work in the fourth-grade next year, so go to the right and be left back." Other children who read orally somewhat better, or possibly with less emotional stress, were sent to the left to join those

who were to be promoted. The process continued until the final child had read, with a sizable number trudging crestfallenly to the right side of the gymnasium and another year in third grade.

Fortunately great gains have been made in appraising growth in reading since these two incidents took place.

It is only through a knowledge of each pupil's development in the fundamental areas of reading that a program, designed to teach the children to read, may be formulated. It is only through a program adjusted to the reading capabilities and needs of the children that reading growth may be optimal and reading disability minimal. To the extent that the reading program is adjusted to known strengths, limitations, and needs of children, growth in reading will be compatible with the potentialities of the children. From the preceding chapters, it should be evident to the reader that the pupil must be, in his development, taken from where he is in any reading attribute on toward greater growth. It is extremely hazardous to allow any gaps in the reading sequence—gaps for the child to hurdle.

Appraisals Used

APPRAISAL IN ASSIGNING MATERIAL

No fifth-grade teacher would think of skipping one third of a class at least a year and some of the children as much as four years. Yet that is what he is actually doing when he attempts to have children, unappraised, read fifth-grade materials. And it is the poorest readers who are accelerated, not the best! At the same time, he is retarding his best readers at least a year and some as much as four years. If the collection of information about the reading capabilities of children does nothing more than show the teacher the range of talent with which he is dealing and where each child is in terms of that range, it is worth whatever time, effort, or cost it entails.

It is through a knowledge of the range of talent to be found in any given class that intelligent distribution of materials can be made. Unfortunately, it is only approximately one teacher in ten in the United States who, when given the opportunity to order material, selects material outside his grade designation. It is the rare school, indeed, which allocates such materials as *My Weekly Reader* according to the reading capabilities of the pupils rather than their grade designations. Materials should actually be distributed in accordance with the reading capabilities of children, and the only way to distribute them that way is through knowledge of what those reading abilities are.

APPRAISAL FOR ORGANIZING CLASS

It is only through a knowledge of the range of talent in any given class that adjustments to that range can be made. The organization of the class for effective use of the printed page is based upon the degree of maturity of each child in the various aspects of reading. The teacher cannot know how to make adequate adjustment to individual differences until he knows the range of reading capabilities he has to deal with. Nor can he know about any child within the class where instruction is to be started until he knows how far along the reading continuum the child has progressed in a particular attribute. The adjustment to range of talent within a class constitutes one of the major problems of reading instruction; it can be answered only insofar as the teacher knows the youngsters he is teaching. As a corollary, to the extent that he knows the children's true reading capabilities, his task is made easier.

Nobody would take 30 youngsters out to the middle of a lake and tell them to jump in unless each knew how to swim. Educationally, we do this sort of thing every day, with results almost as drastic.

APPRAISAL IN PLANNING INSTRUCTION

Another reason the teacher needs to know the results of appraisals is to plan emphases of instruction. He may find, for example, that the children with whom he is working are good readers of literary and social-studies materials, but are somewhat immature readers of science. He rightly decides to give them more experience and instruction in reading science material. Or he may find that the children seem unable to formulate adequate purposes for reading. He decides wisely that more time can be devoted to pupil-teacher planning so that the children may establish the habit of analyzing topics about which they are to read so as to plan the specific goals they wish to achieve. He may find, on the other hand, that some of the children have not established abilities in appreciating what they are reading. They fail to form sensory impressions and find it somewhat difficult to follow the plot. He decides, for this group of children, that instruction should focus attention on developing abilities to read to appreciate. Thus, he inspects the results of the appraisals critically, estimates the needs of his class as a whole and of individuals within the class, and plans instruction to provide the emphases necessary for the well-rounded growth of all of the children.

The teacher needs to know the results of appraisals in order to plan reeducation for those children who have established faulty approaches to reading. He may find, for example, that a few children are slow, laborious readers. A further study indicates that of this few there are several who are word-by-word readers. They have established the habit of reading each word as an isolated entity rather than that of grouping words into usable thought units. He decides that he will have to work with these children so that they may discard the word-by-word approach in favor of an approach using reading by thought units. He finds other children who are rapid but superficial readers—readers that approach all materials superficially. He decides to work with these children, establishing purposes that demand reading to recall specific information. Thus, knowledge of the results of appraisals defines the nature of reeducation needed by specific individuals and indicates the nature of the corrective measures that should be taken.

The appraisals also help in meeting individual needs by locating children in serious difficulty. A study of the appraisals enables the teacher to estimate whether the problem is one that can be met in the classroom, whether the child requires help by a remedial teacher, or whether he should be referred to a reading center or child guidance center for further study and help.

APPRAISALS IN EVALUATING INSTRUCTION

Teachers are continuously using appraisals to evaluate the effectiveness of their own instruction. Every teacher tries varied approaches to reading instruction. At times, he appraises the effectiveness of the new instructional procedure as related to a group or the entire class. At other times, he appraises the effects of a special type of instruction on an individual child. Personal experimentation is appropriate and useful always.

Quite often, the use of appraisals in estimating the influence of instructional changes are broader in scope. Schools are and continually should be volunteering to participate in more carefully designed research efforts. Appraisals are used in a variety of ways in research. Various types of estimates of initial status of the children are necessary in these researches. Appraisals of the results of the experiment are also necessary parts. Both the teachers and the pupils profit from participating in well-designed research. It has been found that the pupils in both experimental and control groups gain in reading growth as a result of the increased interest in instruction that accompanies experimentation. Teachers find that participating in research increases their professional interest in and knowledge about reading instruction. They become involved in the research and await its results with interest.

APPRAISALS IN EVALUATING THE SCHOOL-WIDE
READING PROGRAM

School systems periodically use appraisals to study the results of the citywide instructional program. These studies indicate how well objectives are being met in general and, at the same time, locate areas that need increased emphasis. It may be that the children's reading status in general is satisfactory, but that there seems to be a yearly decrease in voluntary reading in the intermediate grades. As a result, more attention is indicated to personal development reading instruction in the intermediate grades, and an increase in budget for the classroom collections of books, for these grades is needed. There is no question that the children in the intermediate grades in this system will profit from the results of the appraisal. Another school system found that although the children were above average in word-recognition abilities and could read aloud with few errors, their comprehension of what they read was poor. As a result, the entire approach to reading moved from one with a narrow phonetic emphasis to one of a more diversified approach to reading instruction.

The self-evaluation made by school systems allows the administration and teachers alike to be better informed in the consultation with parents and in their interpretation of the reading program to the community. When informed about the effectiveness of instruction, the strengths and needs of the school can be presented more effectively to individuals and groups concerned with education. Education has nothing to hide, but needs the cooperation of an informed community.

Principles of Evaluation

A study of each child's reading growth is basic to adequate adjustment of instruction to his specific needs. It is important to consider principles of evaluation that will help the teacher gain information about the reading attainments and needs of the boys and girls in his class. A list of important guiding principles of evaluation follows:

1. The appraisal should study the broad range of objectives that the reading program is designed to meet. The appraisal should study reading skills, abilities, habits, attitudes, and interests and tastes that constitute the varied developmental goals toward which the child is progressing.
2. A variety of techniques should be used in making appraisals of reading growth. The technique employed in any instance should be decided

by the nature of the outcome that is being appraised. Some techniques are more useful in appraising word recognition than they are for appraising attitudes; and conversely, there are techniques suitable for appraising attitudes that are inefficient in studying skill development.

3. The appraisals should be made in situations as similar to the actual reading one as possible. Whenever a choice between two methods of appraisal is made, the one that encompasses a real reading experience should be chosen, because the application of the skill or ability by the child is usually as important as the skill itself.

4. Whenever possible, standardized test procedures should be used in making appraisals. Such standardized procedures make possible accurate comparisons between skills and abilities.

5. Appraisals should study the learning process itself as well as the present status of the pupils. In addition to knowing present level of performance, it is important to know how the learner is meeting his problems. The appraisals of the learning process help the teacher show the child more efficient ways of learning. For instance, if a child is attempting to remember the factual detail in a large selection by pure recall, the teacher may suggest that he take notes as he proceeds with the reading.

6. The appraisal should demonstrate to the learner his progress toward goals he is seeking. For example, contrasting a tape of his oral reading of a selection taken earlier in the year with one of the same selection taken later often demonstrates dramatically to a child his improved competency in reading. Another way to demonstrate to the child that he is progressing well is to have him silently read an early page of a primer when he has progressed to a first reader. He will be surprised to realize that he can now read with ease material that caused him difficulty earlier.

7. The appraisals should reveal to the learner his strengths, weaknesses, and needs so that he may recognize the necessity for working upon those areas of reading instruction that are still weak. In reading, it is well for the learner to know his relative performance in the skills and abilities he is trying to develop and to identify the ones on which he must focus his study efforts.

8. The learner should assume some responsibility for checking his own strengths and weaknesses. The pupil can, for example, be expected to identify types of material that cause him difficulty. He can check the accuracy of his performance in workbooks. He can keep a record of his expanding interests.

9. Patterns of scores as well as specific scores should be considered in studying the results of appraisals. The study of a profile of many scores contributes more to understanding the reading growth of a child than does the study of the same scores in isolation. The skills and abilities in reading are so interrelated that strength in one area with weakness in another may indicate an unfortunate balance that could cause difficulty if left uncorrected.

10. Test results given in terms of grade norms are useful at elementary-school levels. Norms, expressed by grades, enable the teacher to make comparisons between various test results and also enable him to correlate

the child's indicated levels of performance with suitable instructional materials.

11. Various types of appraisals should be used to complement and verify each other. A standardized test, for example, may demonstrate a high level of comprehension. This result should be verified by determining whether the child is actually able independently to understand material of equal relative difficulty. Or again, a child may score relatively low on a group mental test that requires reading. The teacher knows the child is handicapped in reading and so realizes that the group mental test result represents a minimum estimate of the mental ability of the child. He knows that an individual mental test should be given.

12. Appraisals of reading growth should take place daily. Only by continuous appraisal can the teacher know the instructional needs of children who are growing as rapidly as elementary-school children grow in reading ability. The patterns of scores of children shift rapidly as do also their instructional needs.

13. Periodic surveys should be made of the overall progress of the school, the class, and the child so that adjustments in scheduling, in supplying materials, in supplying technical aid, and in other phases of the curriculum can be made.

14. Appraisals should be extensive enough at all times to identify difficulties at their beginnings, before they can increase and accumulate into disability. The teacher should be a student of all aspects of reading growth to enable him to give a child remedial aid when help is first needed.

15. When disabilities are located, more intensive appraisals are indicated, often including factors other than reading itself. Reading disability is an atypical condition. Most children learn to read with only minor transitory difficulties. The truly disabled reader is frequently found to have limitations in addition to the poor reading. These corollary limitations should be identified and adjustments made, whenever possible.

16. The teacher, through proper administrative channels, should enlist the services of other professional workers to enable him to study the child as thoroughly as seems necessary. Psychological, medical, psychiatric, and neurological services may be needed. If the school does not have these services, the cooperation of the parents or social agencies within the community should be enlisted to procure the services for the child.

17. The results of appraisals should be preserved in well-ordered, usable ways. Because the teacher cannot hope to keep in mind all the information about all the children, he should record the results of appraisals in permanent form. Also, because the present teacher is not the only teacher who will help the child progress toward maturity in reading, such records should be kept in such a way that they can be interpreted by other individuals.

18. The results of appraisals should be made available to those concerned with the reading growth of the child insofar as the results represent suitable useful knowledge for them. The people concerned include not only the present teacher but also the teachers who will have the child in succeeding years, the principal, the parents, and the specialist. The

type of information that should be given to each depends upon the individual receiving the information and his particular concern about the child.

Types of Appraisals

Certain types of appraisal should be made at regular intervals, whereas others should be made continuously throughout the reading program. For example, the primary teacher makes constant, informal appraisals of the child's method of working upon words. When a child makes an error in reading a word or fails to recognize a word, the teacher attempts to find out what caused that error so that he can ascertain the cause of the difficulty. Again, when the intermediate-grade child is seen puzzling over a word for some time, the teacher attempts to judge how the child can improve his attack upon words so that he will not consume so much time in recognizing them. All such estimates constitute very important day-by-day appraisals. Any information that the teacher can secure concerning the level of advancement of the child in the many reading attributes, and any indications he can get as to difficulties in learning, constitute very important appraisals. Reading appraisals, then, are not limited to formal tests, although these are included among the appraisals. Reading appraisals include any means whatsoever that are employed to give information about reading growth.

Certain types of appraisals seem especially suited for giving a clear picture of a child's reading growths. These include standardized tests, workbook tests, teacher-made appraisals, self-inventories, teacher observations, individual conferences, and study of school records. Each of these will be discussed in turn.

STANDARDIZED TESTS

Standardized tests are published tests that may be objectively scored and that furnish norms, making it possible to compare a specific group with a much larger group of similar age or grade. There are many standardized reading tests. Among them can be found tests that measure many of the comprehension abilities, the study skills, general level of word recognition, meaning vocabulary, rate of comprehension, accuracy and speed of oral reading, and ability to read in the subject-matter fields.

Reviews of standardized tests, giving necessary information, may be found in *The Mental Measurements Yearbooks,* edited by Buros [42].

Standardized tests are valuable because of the accuracy with which they measure important outcomes. Most standardized tests have been constructed unusually carefully, so that on repeated testing a pupil gets approximately the same score. The tests are relatively accurate measures of the pupil's ability in the attribute being measured by the test. They also have merit in that they can give a great deal of information in a relatively short time. They are so designed that they may be scored easily. By and large too, they measure important attributes—reading abilities and skills—that have been thought to be of sufficient importance to warrant careful measurement.

The greatest single value in standardized tests is, however, that their norms make possible comparisons of the attainments of a class or of individuals within the class in various important learnings in reading. In other words, the administration of standardized tests makes it easy to tell the levels of the various abilities of a child, or of a class, in relation to the norms of the large number of children that took the test while the test was being standardized. For example, a child's growth in the recognition of words may be compared with his power of comprehension. Or objective comparisons may be made between his effectiveness in one of the comprehension abilities, such as reading to evaluate, and his effectiveness in one of the basic study skills, such as using reference materials. Thus, through the use of standardized tests, it is possible to locate reading strengths and weaknesses of a class or of the instructional needs of an individual within the class. One cautionary remark should be made in regard to the interpretation of the norms of standardized tests. Norms should not be considered ideals of attainment but rather as the performance of average children in average-sized classes with average teachers using average materials. Norms are indications of mediocrity and, therefore, under favorable conditions should be exceeded.

The use of standardized tests gives a rapid means of getting a very great deal of accurate knowledge about the children. It is necessary, however, that care be taken in the selection of the tests. The entire reading-testing program should be considered a unit. Tests should be selected to give a maximum of information with a minimum overlapping between the outcomes measured by them. Cost is a consideration in the selection of tests. However, the testing program is in and of itself rather inexpensive in comparison with the returns that the knowledges of the reading abilities of the children can give. Testing time is another important consideration. The time spent in testing will be repaid through more efficient and more effective instruction many times over when the results are well used. Standardized tests are, on the whole, so designed that they are easy to administer, easy to score, and easy to interpret. A battery of standardized tests should be administered at least once a year, preferably twice a year, and preferably at the beginning of the semester rather than the end.

BASAL READER WORKBOOKS

Inasmuch as workbooks are designed to develop a wide variety of skills and abilities, they are rich in exercises that demand competency in these skills and abilities [135]. These exercises may be used by the teacher to detect the instructional needs of the children. They are related directly to the immediate learnings that the child has been undertaking and are couched in the vocabulary that he is studying at that time. They give, therefore, an indication of the effectiveness with which learning is proceeding to teacher and pupil alike. Many of the exercises are primarily tasks of word recognition and are very helpful in measuring the success with which the child is developing the specific word-recognition techniques he is studying.

A survey of the workbook exercises will show their extensiveness in type and content. Through studying the child's accuracy and ability at performing these tasks, it is possible to know of his day-by-day effectiveness.

The workbooks, although providing relatively rough appraisals, derive their value as an instrument of measurement from the fact that they make it possible to locate a difficulty as soon as it appears. If the child makes few or no mistakes in an exercise within the workbooks, it may be assumed that he is progressing satisfactorily in those attributes that are being practiced. If he makes an undue number of errors, the teacher will find it profitable to study the nature of the errors in order that the proper direct instruction may be given. If a child is consistently in trouble, the teacher should undertake a more thoroughgoing analysis to locate possible difficulties. The teacher, alert to consistent errors made within the workbook, can do much to prevent the accumulation of difficulties that might produce a reading-disability case.

Workbooks include also periodic achievement tests. Although these tests are scored objectively, they do not provide norms. They enable the teacher, however, to determine how an individual child within the group is progressing in comparison with other children of the group. Workbooks also give the teacher an estimate of which children need review on the vocabulary that has been introduced in the basal reading material before they proceed to the next unit of instruction. And at the end of the book, workbooks give an indication whether the child should progress to the next one.

Most workbooks give an index of the pages on which the various reading skills and abilities are taught. By referring to this kind of index, the teacher who wishes to appraise the specific capabilities of a child can find suggestions for types of items that would help him make his own informal appraisals and exercises suggested to correct problems so discovered.

INFORMAL APPRAISALS

Teachers, recognizing the need for continuous study of growth in each of the many attributes that make up effective reading at any level, frequently construct informal appraisals of their own. These tests usually take much the same form as the standardized tests and workbook exercises.

The teacher may use a wide variety of test items, including multiple-choice, completion, matching, true-false, specific answer, objectively scored essay, and problem-situation types. For example, a problem-situation item applicable to reading is the following:

> In which of the following references would you look to find information about the Olympiad?
> _____ 1. *The World Almanac*
> _____ 2. An encyclopedia
> _____ 3. *Who's Who in America*
> _____ 4. A dictionary

The type of item to be used depends upon the reading outcome to be measured.

Teacher-made appraisals have a special value in that they are as flexible as the teacher wishes to make them. When he is emphasizing a given technique in his teaching, he can construct a test to measure progress toward his immediate objective of instruction. Through the use of such procedures, the effectiveness of instruction may, to some extent, be determined immediately. He may ascertain which of the children have failed to profit from the instruction and are in need of more practice and reteaching, and which of the children have reached the objective to the point that further practice would be unwarranted.

The teacher should keep in constant touch with the progress of the pupils. He should appraise the effectiveness with which they react to various types of instruction toward objectives. This will help him adjust his methods of instruction to meet their reading needs. Informal appraisals should be relatively short and simple of operation. Although the short tests within themselves may be somewhat unreliable, their cumulative effect can be made to give very good indications of pupil progress. In order to facilitate the benefits to be derived from teacher-made tests, records should be kept in somewhat permanent form. Frequent review of these records will aid the teacher in following the growth in reading of the 30 children within his class. When he finds that the work and reading habits of any child are consistently low, he can be alert to and provide for the child's reading needs.

The use of a series of basal readers affords an opportunity to appraise informally the levels of reading attainments. The teacher has the child read a short passage from a reader he estimates is about at the child's level. If the child has difficulty, the teacher will have him read a passage from a book at the next lower level. If that material also is too difficult, the child will read from a book of a still lower level, until the teacher locates the level of material, either up or down, that the child can read effectively. The grade designation is shown by the grade designation of the book he reads successfully. Betts has described three levels of attainment informative to teachers. The level of material the child can be expected to read independently, *the independent level,* is one where he makes not more than two errors in every 100 words he reads and where comprehension is good, at least 90 percent. The independent level indicates the difficulty of material the child might be expected to read in supplementary material or in his personal, recreational, or informational reading. The level at which the child can read basal material, under the guidance of a teacher who is thorough in the introductory phases of teaching a lesson, is *the instructional level.* This level is the one used in assigning a child to a reading group. At this level, the child makes not more than five errors in every 100 words he reads, and his comprehension is 75 percent or better. That is, he is able to answer three out of every four questions that deal with the content. The third, *the frustration level,* is the level at which the reading capabilities of the child fail to function, and symptoms of tension may be observed. At this level, the child cannot be expected to understand the content of what he reads well enough to profit from the reading. He makes more than five errors in recognizing words for each 100, and his comprehension is less than 50 percent. Too often, children are required to read materials at their frustration levels. This profits them not at all; it drives them away from reading. Teachers must exercise extreme care to insure that children are not reading at their frustration level, because a prolonged exposure to such reading experiences is detrimental both to their reading growth and to their personal well-being.

TEACHER OBSERVATION

Another important type of appraisal is the informal teacher observation. The good teacher constantly studies the errors and successes, attitudes, interests, independence, and emotional responses of the children within his class. In fact, every day he makes many estimates of their progress in all of the important areas of reading development in which he is interested.

The teacher appraises the child's attack upon new words and helps him develop more effective ones. He estimates how well the child reads for various purposes, and when help is needed, he helps the child make a more adequate adjustment of his reading abilities. He notes those abilities in which the child is most adept and those in which he needs help. He notices the rapidity with which the child gets through his assignments and the accuracy with which he comprehends. He encourages him to read faster when such encouragement is necessary, and to slow down when he travels through his reading at a speed incompatible with his purposes.

The teacher watches the child at work in the library and sees the effectiveness with which he can locate information, how well he reads maps and other pictorial materials. He sees whether the child reads the tabular materials or assiduously avoids them. He notices the books that attract him and ones he avoids. He is interested in the quality of the selection that the child makes for personal reading. He is aware of the number of times the child seeks his help, and he attempts to develop greater independence when he feels that the child seeks council too often.

He notices the child's skill in interpretative oral reading. He also notes his emotional behavior during the oral-reading situation. Is he tense and ill at ease? Or is he relaxed, showing few, if any, signs of emotional strain? The teacher notices the type of errors he makes and whether, due to blockings, they increase as he proceeds with his presentation. The teacher appraises the enthusiasm with which he reads and the nature of the choice that he makes for interpretative oral reading.

The teacher watches the child's vocabulary expand and grow so that he may estimate whether he must give special emphasis on clarifying meanings to the entire class or help a given child. He is constantly alert to inadequacies of background or faulty understandings. He studies the child's effectiveness in reading the materials of the various content fields.

The teacher looks for signs of fatigue, boredom, or discontent. He notices the frequency with which the child chooses reading rather than some other activity that he might undertake. In fact, the teacher is constantly making appraisals of the children's growth, of their limitations, of their attitudes, and of their needs.

As he studies the individual members of his class in the actual processes of learning to read, the teacher develops an understanding of each child— a completeness of understanding that cannot be gained in other ways. He uses, of course, the results of other appraisals to corroborate and supplement his study of the individual. Obviously, for 30 children, he cannot trust his memory to retain accurate impressions of these many observations. So he keeps an informal record of the responses of each child that give significant information. Such information aids materially in sensing the dynamic growth of the children, so that additional instruction can be given to the special needs of the children.

SELF-INVENTORY METHODS

Inventories provide means of appraising the child's attitudes and impressions toward various aspects of the reading program. Inventories may be standardized inventories and questionnaires, or they may be informal teacher-made ones. Either type of inventory may be used to give the teacher insight into the child's present interests, attitudes, and impressions. The teacher may learn the type of material the child likes to read, of books he has enjoyed, about what the child considers to be his major reading strengths and weaknesses, of what in reading he finds difficult, which of his subjects he likes best and the reason he gives for his choices, of how useful he considers reading to be to him, of the uses he makes of reading, of how much he reads in out-of-school hours, and so forth. It is helpful to the teacher to know of the child's feeling with regard to his growth in reading. It is also helpful to learn of the child's expressed interests. Questionnaires designed to inventory the child's interests, attitudes, and impressions have the merit of giving a picture of the child's idea of his present status.

INDIVIDUAL CONFERENCE

At times, in order to supplement observational and other data, the teacher confers individually with the children of his class. Such conferences should be planned in advance in order that he may be sure to have well in mind the additional information he needs to complete his picture of the child. Conferences take time, so it is important for them to be as fruitful as possible. The purpose of a teacher-pupil conference might be to discuss some of the ideas included by the child in his self-inventory of reading interests. The child may have indicated an interest that seemed inconsistent with the interests he has manifested in class. Through the conversational method used in an interview, the teacher may unearth some really important interests and attitudes of which he had no intimation.

Interviews are personal and enable the teacher to demonstrate to the child that he is concerned with his welfare. A child quickly senses the fact that his teacher is interested in him. Through the use of the interview, the teacher is frequently able to establish feelings of friendship within the child that make him aware of the fact that he is getting personal attention. Rapport built in this way is very beneficial to the mutual effectiveness of the teacher and pupil working together upon the problem of improving growth in reading.

SCHOOL RECORDS

Reading growth is developmental and cumulative in nature. Present learnings depend upon previous ones. A study of school records enables the teacher to view the child's present status with historical perspective. By means of such a longitudinal study, the teacher is able to detect that the child may now be progressing at a rate that is accelerated over his past performance. This acceleration may have resulted from the fact that a fortunate reading characteristic has relatively recently begun to be used. The school records indicate gross changes now occurring and other fluctuating tendencies.

Information concerning the child's mental ability, previous grade scores in academic areas, family, number of siblings, absence from school, periods of illness, sensory limitations, comments of previous teachers, records of parent interviews, and many other pertinent facts are tabulated on permanent records. An inspection of this information helps the teacher gain insights about the youngster and his capabilities, environment, and his longitudinal progress in learning to read. This information aids materially in adapting instruction to meet specific needs of the dynamic growth of the children to whom reading instruction is being given.

Appraisals Used to Evaluate Major Objectives

The contention has been made throughout this book that from the very start of reading instruction in the primary grades, all teachers should be concerned with developing reading ability in some very important fundamental areas, so that at any educational level the teacher may deal solely with more mature aspects of the same attributes that have been considered by the teachers at earlier levels. In other words, again, the point of view upon which this presentation is based is that growth in reading is developmental; it is not a series of discrete stages or hurdles over which a child must progress, finishing one type of instruction one year and then going into another type the next year. In appraising reading development, measurement is made of growth in each of the fundamental areas, for measurement within one area alone will not acquaint the teacher with the progress of the child.

Although the attributes are related one to the other, the relationships are not close enough to insure that a person who is mature in one aspect of reading will be equally mature in his development in all, or any, of the others. Consequently, frequent appraisal of the child's growth in each of these areas is needed. It may be seen, thus, that the task of appraisal in reading is somewhat difficult. Such appraisals, however, are very important, for through a knowledge of the level of maturity of a child in each of these attributes the teacher can intelligently guide his further growth.

VOCABULARY DEVELOPMENT

There are many instruments designed to measure the ability of the child to recognize words and attach meanings to those words. They are usually constructed in a multiple-choice form of two types. In one type, the child has a key word upon which he is being measured. He is supposed to show his understanding of that word by selecting its synonym from several response words. As may be seen, the child must not only recognize the word upon which he is being tested and know its meaning, but he must also recognize and know the meaning of the synonym. Usually, the synonym is a much easier word to recognize and understand than is the word upon which the child is being tested. Another type of test, of which there are several variations, is one in which the child is to select among four or more words the one that best describes a picture or an explanatory sentence. In the first three grades, the vocabulary tests are usually of the picture sort.

Another type of test designed to measure the meaning vocabulary of the child is one such as the Durrell-Sullivan Reading Capacity and Achievement Tests [85], in which the examiner reads the word and the child is requested to select from several pictures the correct one to illustrate the word. In this case, meaning vocabulary is isolated from word recognition because the child does not have to recognize the word visually. Usually, in reading instruction, it is enough to know the level at which the child can recognize and interpret words accurately. So, for the most part, it is not necessary to try to separate word recognition from word meaning, because it is the combining that is used in effective reading.

By and large, vocabulary tests are good and cover the field rather well. However, it is not until the upper grades that standardized tests appear for measuring vocabulary in the subject-matter fields. The tests measure the vocabulary of mathematics, science, social studies, and literature. These special vocabulary tests are useful, because they furnish norms whereby a teacher may compare a given child's development in the vocabularies of the various content subjects.

Although the teacher should notice and study the meaning-vocabulary development of the children under his care, he will do well to use standardized tests to supplement and verify his estimates. As in the case of other standardized tests, the vocabulary tests have been carefully constructed and tried out. Each item has been analyzed to justify its inclusion within the test. As a result of careful construction, standardized tests measure much more accurately than the teacher can possibly appraise by informal means. The teacher-made tests have the advantage of measuring the vocabulary the child is using in his basal work, whereas the standardized test measures vocabulary development in general. Both types of tests should be a part of the appraisal of vocabulary growth.

WORD-RECOGNITION TECHNIQUES

In appraising growth in word-recognition techniques, practically every type of appraisal not only can be used but should be used. Probably the most useful appraisal for the improvement of instruction is the daily observation of the teacher. The teacher observes when the child is failing to use context clues and immediately gives him exercises to help him to develop that ability and habit. The teacher notices when he is overemphasizing or underemphasizing sounding of words, or phonetic analysis, and instigates measures to cause him to employ these analytical techniques when needed and to avoid their use when the word can be recognized by more rapid techniques. Daily observational appraisals of this sort give direction to instruction in reading.

In order to supplement the observations of word difficulties and of failure to establish important techniques, the teacher studies completed workbook exercises to make analyses of errors. By making such analyses, it is possible to determine, for example, if the child tends to neglect the beginnings of words, making an undue proportion of his errors in these important initial parts, or whether in multiple-choice exercises he tends to select relatively frequently the reversed form of the word. In a like manner, the typical errors each child makes may be located so that instruction may be directed toward helping each child overcome his typical errors.

The teacher may have found that the class, as a whole, is weak in a certain fundamental analytical technique. For example, he may have found that the children are rather poor at locating and using small words within compound words. Hence, he should give some direct instruction upon this ability. After the instruction has been given, he appraises its outcome. He will want to know which children have learned the ability well and which ones need more practice with it. The best means of measuring the effectiveness of that instruction and in locating the children who need more instruction is through the use of a teacher-made test. The test may consist of more exercises of compound words—ones that have not been directly taught—to find out how easily and accurately the children recognize these words. One way of constructing such a test would be to use multiple-choice questions in which a group of compound words make up the response words from which the child is to select the correct one.

If a child consistently demonstrates weakness in word recognition, then the teacher may resort to individual conference or individual study, having the child read a little to him in order to locate errors and to discuss them with the child. This type of appraisal is used only for a child who has marked disability.

There are standardized tests to help the teacher ascertain the level of general maturity of the ability to recognize words. These tests make it possible for the teacher to compare the level of maturity of the children he is teaching with the level of maturity of a much larger population.

To the child in serious difficulty with word-recognition, there are diagnostic tests that may be given.

At the upper-grade levels, teacher observation, study of workbook exercises, and teacher-made tests will bring to light the flexibility the child displays in recognizing new and unfamiliar words and the extent to which he is able to avoid slow, laborious techniques, using them only when absolutely necessary. As a matter of fact, the intermediate-grade child may use much the same techniques as did the primary child in recognizing very difficult words. In certain cases he too will be found to have marked shortcomings in his attack. For example, it is not uncommon to find a youngster in the upper grades, a poor reader to be sure, employing immature techniques, such as resorting to spelling attack or piecemeal observation, when he should recognize the word as made up of two or three usable elements. When these types of difficulties are encountered in the upper grades, individual help in overcoming them should be undertaken. If the difficulties are serious enough, such a child should receive remedial help outside the classroom.

COMPREHENSION ABILITIES

There are many opportunities for appraising growth in the various comprehension abilities. Use may be made of all the types of appraisals. There is no area that is better covered by standardized tests than the one of comprehension abilities. There are tests to measure reading to get the general significance, reading to predict outcomes, reading to organize, reading to follow directions, reading to note details, reading to retain factual information, reading to evaluate, reading to interpret, reading for appreciation, and reading for power of comprehension.

In those abilities for which there are standardized tests, such tests should be used periodically. However, even when annual or semiannual testing programs are employed, the teacher must, in addition, make continuous appraisals of growth in these abilities. He must estimate upon which abilities the child needs further experience in order that such training and experience may be provided. In those abilities for which there are no standardized tests, it is incumbent upon the teacher to make his own appraisals. He will find it necessary to make a considerable use of teacher observations and teacher-made tests. He will, in addition, study the completed workbook exercises in order to ascertain how the child is progressing.

It is, however, in appraising comprehension abilities that the standardized tests find much of their usefulness. They enable the teacher, through the use of cumulative records, to follow the child's developmental growth in their abilities over a period of years. The teacher can relate growth in any given ability to the previous growth the child has demonstrated in that ability and know whether he has been able to accelerate that growth through careful instruction and added practice. Through the use of standardized tests, he can also compare the child's relative performance in the various comprehension abilities one with another. This comparison, of course, is made possible because standardized tests have norms. In his own appraisals, the teacher is able merely to say that a child seems to be as well equipped in one type of reading as in another. When he uses standardized test results, he is able to make such a comparison with a greater degree of certainty. Every teacher should have a profile of comprehension abilities for each child within his class. These profiles should be available to him at the beginning of the year, so that he can plan his instruction in terms of (1) the class needs, and (2) individual needs.

The standardized tests in appraising comprehension ability give good indications of the suitability of material from the standpoint of level of difficulty. It will be remembered that throughout the discussions of reading interests, as well as growth in comprehension abilities, the importance of suiting material to the reading level of the child has been stressed. It is through the knowledge gained from the use of standardized tests, supplemented by teacher observation, that the best adjustment of material to the individual pupil can be made.

In addition to the specific types of comprehension abilities, the teacher should appraise the basic comprehension abilities. He should note the proficiency with which a child is able to read in thought units. This information can be got by noticing the phrasing the child uses in prepared oral-reading situations as well as in the exercises in workbooks that are designed to develop reading by thought units.

The teacher should appraise also the child's sentence sense. How well he can understand sentences of various degrees of complexity should be studied. This appraisal can be made in relationship to discussions in which the understanding of a relatively difficult sentence is the key to the answer to a specific question. When the child makes an error, often the error results from failure to understand the interrelationships of the words and concepts within the sentence. Exercises designed to develop sentence sense are suggested in teacher's manuals and are included in workbooks. The performance of children on these exercises gives information about their capabilities in this basic comprehension ability. The understanding of paragraph and larger selections may be appraised in similar ways.

SPEED OF COMPREHENSION

Because the rate of comprehension is not a single attribute, it is somewhat difficult to appraise. A person uses various speeds of reading. The problem is one of adjusting the speed of reading to the material and to the purpose at hand. It could be likened to speed of locomotion of an individual along the ground. The individual's speed could be timed when he is in a track suit sprinting the 100-yard dash. It could be timed as he is leisurely walking through a forest, listening to the wind rustling the leaves and enjoying the solitude of the forest. It could be timed as he ascends a mountainside with a heavy pack on his back. It could be timed as he is walking along a path, tabulating the flora, or as he is hurrying down that same path to pick up an article he left behind, or as he is running to catch a communters' train so as not to be late to work. Obviously, the speed of locomotion varies markedly as the situation changes. To measure his speed of running the 100-yard dash and to compare that speed with track records may be interesting. However, it tells only how fast he can run the 100-yard dash when conditions are just right. An individual who had a relatively fast rate at running the 100-yard dash might not be able to go at all fast in comparison with others while he was carrying a pack up a mountainside. He might, walking along a path tabulating flora, get to the end of the path more quickly, but it is questionable whether he would arrive with the best understanding of the plant life if he did so.

So it is with reading. To measure the speed of reading easy narrative materials is interesting, but it is not enough. It tells only how fast the person is able to read easy narrative materials. It does not tell about the rapidity with which he can read material of greater difficulty. It does not tell about the rapidity with which he can read for more exact purposes. It does not tell whether he attempts to read too rapidly or too slowly for most effectively meeting his purpose. It does not tell the degree of flexibility he has attained. These are quite as important appraisals of speed of reading as the speed with which the reader can race through material simple in purpose and easy in content. Probably, in fact, the most important aspect of speed is the flexibility with which the reader can and does adjust his speed of reading to fit his purpose and to the type of comprehension required to meet that purpose. Can he skim rapidly? Can he read slowly and carefully to evaluate the material? These are the more crucial questions.

Teacher-made timed performance tests may be used to supplement standardized test results. The teacher can gain much information concerning the rates of comprehension of the individuals of his class by timing the reading of selected passages within different types of material for various purposes.

When it is found that one child, or a group of children, are reading for a particular purpose too slowly, instruction and practice should be given to enable the work to be done more rapidly. Through other timed tests and records of numbers of words read in previous tests, the teacher can stimulate the children to read more rapidly. If a child is slow in several types of reading, he is probably a corrective problem and should be given remedial work.

It may be found that one child, or a group of children, reads too rapidly for a special purpose or in a specific type of material. Under such circumstances, the teacher should hold him or them to a high level of comprehension and explain that they can meet the level of comprehension only by reading more carefully and somewhat more slowly. It is probably not that they get through the material too rapidly, but that they comprehend too little, and that a balance must be made between the two.

The real problem, thus, is to get the child to read as rapidly as he can and still read the material with the understanding and the accuracy that is commensurate with his purpose. Because standardized tests are not available for measuring these aspects of speed of reading, the teacher will find it helpful to consider any one child's achievement in comparison with the general achievement of the class.

STUDY SKILLS

In the primary grades, the appraisal of the basic study skills, such as the use of table of contents, use of dictionaries, use of indexes, use of basic reference materials, use of the library, and use of reading graphic and tabular material, must of necessity be informal. The basic study skills as such have not yet matured to the point where they have been completely isolated or easily detected. The child has, however, been making a good use of certain of the basic study skills. He has learned to use the table of contents of a book. He has learned to use the library, although he has not learned to use many of the tools of the library. He depends, for the most part, for his location of books upon going to the shelves where he knows books suitable to him are located. The child probably has learned to use the dictionary to some extent, especially if picture dictionaries are available, and if he has had experience in making a dictionary of his own. It would not be correct to say that he has not developed any ability in the basic study skills, because he has.

Use of study skills is an important outcome of reading even in the early grades and is one that should be appraised. There are two means by which this outcome can best be appraised, namely, teacher observation and teacher-made tests. The teacher, of course, informally observes the skill with which the child locates material while working on topical units. Very likely, the child for the most part, has used the table of contents as his source. He has also gone to the central library or classroom collection of books and has selected the types of books that might be expected to deal with a topic. The teacher has observed how pertinent are his choices. The teacher has seen him open a book to the table of contents and glance through it to determine the part of the book that might be most likely to give the information he is seeking. When the teacher has noticed a child at a loss to know how to go about locating the material upon his phase of the larger topic, he gives the child assistance.

From time to time, the teacher uses a second method of appraisal. He places children in situations, somewhat controlled, that demand the use of specific study skills and watches to see how well they meet the situation. Such problem situations are, in reality, a type of teacher-made test, one depending upon performance rather than upon pencil-and-paper work. For example, the teacher in first grade may say: "John has just told us an interesting story about his trip to the farm. In our readers there is a story about another boy's trip to the farm. Open your books and see if you can find the story." Whereupon the teacher observes which children thumb through the book somewhat aimlessly and which ones use the table of contents and page numbers of their books to locate the story. This is, of course, an appraisal of an immature phase of growth in the study skills, but it does, nonetheless, measure learnings of study skills.

In the upper grades, the appraisals take more definite form. The teacher sets up more difficult problems and situations for the youngsters to meet—situations, for instance, in which at one time they must refer to the dictionary to derive the pronunciations or meanings of words; at another time, in which they must refer to an encyclopedia or other basic reference to find information. The teacher ranks the various members of the class as he watches the approach they make to these exercises in locating information in dictionaries and encyclopedias. At another time, the teacher may set up the problem of locating a specific fact within a book to see whether the children attempt to use the table of contents to locate the fact or refer directly to the index. The teacher can, of course, prepare pencil-and-paper tests that appraise the rapidity with which the children look up a given set of words or the skill the children show in ascertaining which would be the most likely key words to use in referring to an index to locate information on a specific topic.

Another area that can be appraised through problems and teacher observation is the child's use of the library. Does he refer to the card catalogue? Or does he wander around the library looking at book titles? Or does he seek advice from the librarian?

Workbooks contain many exercises designed to give experience with various study skills. The teacher may use these exercises as a means of determining growth and development in these skills.

In addition, there are standardized tests, which measure basic study skills. Here again, standardized-test results may be used to obtain information as to a given child's relative ability in various types of study skills. They may give more evidence of the child's growth in the study skills than can be secured in any other way, with the possible exception of teacher-made performance tests.

Probably many of the appraisals of level of maturity of reading graphic and tabular materials, such as maps, graphs, charts, and tables, will take place in connection with the school subjects. In reading about social-studies concepts, which the primary child does, it is necessary from time to time for him to refer to simple maps. The map may be of a hypothetical community, showing the location of the grocery store, the fire department, and the post office. Or it may be of the school. Or the map may be one of the United States, upon which, for example, the child locates the nation's capital. Inasmuch as the primary child reads maps—and during any one week of school rather frequently, too—it is well to appraise the development of this skill.

There is a need in the study of numbers to read simple charts, graphs, and tabular materials. The teacher must appraise the child's growth in performing these kinds of reading. However, the appraisal of reading pictorial and tabular materials should be informal teacher observation and teacher-made tests. It is not necessary in the primary grades to measure more objectively the beginnings of these difficult learnings.

In the upper grades, however, more exact appraisals are necessary. The workbook materials of the basal reader give opportunities for judging the day-by-day growth in reading pictorial and tabular materials. A rather liberal use should be made of teacher-made tests, both of performance and of paper-and-pencil types. Teacher observation, of course, should be continued.

There are standardized tests for measuring more mature aspects of these abilities, which are suitable for use at the upper-elementary level. These tests are designed to measure the same sort of skills the teacher has been appraising by less exact methods in the earlier grades; but they measure the applications of these skills in the reading of more difficult types of maps, graphs, charts, tables, and in other basic study skills.

The teacher should be aware of the fact that the study skills that are related to one subject-matter area are not necessarily those related to another. Krantz [167] has shown that the appraisal of study skills related to the social studies does not necessarily indicate the child's proficiency in the study skills related to science or to other areas. The study skills appear to be rather specific to the fields to which they relate. They do not appear to be generally applicable. Therefore, the appraisal of a particular study skill should include items taken from several content fields if an overall estimate of a child's level in that skill is to be obtained.

ORAL READING

There are standardized tests for measuring the speed and accuracy with which a child can read passages aloud. These tests are usually power tests, with short passages getting more difficult as one progresses through the test. In tabulating the score, both speed and number of errors are used to give a single score of competence in oral reading. Such a test does not and cannot give an indication of the quality of interpretation. The relative abilities of the children on quality of oral interpretation must be appraised subjectively by the teacher. Many teachers in working with a class build *esprit de corps* to the extent that the class may help in making the judgments of growth in interpretative oral reading. Under such conditions the teacher may estimate the strengths and weaknesses of the children by means of a rating scale that helps him locate the special problem upon which each child should be working in his oral reading. The children know what factor in oral reading each child is working on in his oral presentation and judge whether he has improved in it. Among the factors teachers include in such rating scales are the following: quality of voice; pitch; intensity or force; timing; rate; conversationalness; accuracy of interpretation; accuracy of word recognition; poise; posture; and freedom from tension. The best materials in which to measure interpretative oral reading are materials that are frequently read aloud, as, for example, news items and story materials. Usually, the appraisals should be made upon material that the child has prepared for presentation. However, from time to time, some of the better oral readers may be appraised on their ability to do sight oral reading.

SUBJECT-MATTER AREAS

In measuring reading in the subject-matter areas, the teacher must, for the most part, use estimates of the effectiveness with which the children are able to read the books of the subject-matter fields. If a given child seems to get along well in most of his subjects but has difficulty in one of them, the teacher will find it expedient to explore the effectiveness with which he can read the materials of that field. Of course, he may have difficulty in reading the materials because he does not know the subject, or it may be that he is not interested in that subject. But it is often true that his lack of learning results from his inability to read the materials. For example, the child may be able to read the materials of arithmetic and science fairly effectively, but he may be in difficulty in his social-studies reading. The teacher, upon exploring the reason for his difficulty, may find that he does not read rapidly enough to cover the materials of a given topic in the social studies, that he has become discouraged, and that he has adopted the attitude that there is little use in reading any of the social-studies material because he does not have time to read it all. The teacher should immediately offer suggestions for meeting his problem. On the other hand, the child's difficulty in reading social-studies material might have been related to some other reading adjustment. Teacher appraisals should be made of the child's effectiveness in meeting all the specialized adjustments needed for reading in the subject-matter areas.

In locating the source of difficulty within a content field, the teacher has available the possibility of using analysis of the work done in the workbook of that field, if such workbooks are used. He may talk with the youngster to find out how he goes about reading in the content subject with which he has demonstrated some weakness. Through such interviews, insight may be gained that will show that the child is hampered by some misunderstanding in regard to the nature of the reading task. Especially will this be true when there is constant appraisal so that the child does not get too seriously in difficulty before his trouble is detected.

INTERESTS, TASTES, AND VALUES

Just as in the other areas of reading, the child's development of attitudes, tastes, and values is gradual, having no clearly defined levels of attainment for any given grade. The teacher must study the children carefully and continuously to note those who rely upon their own resources more thoroughly day by day and those who seem to be developing habits of greater dependence. Is a given child becoming more and more self-reliant in his reading? Does he establish his own purposes for reading? Does he demand understanding of what he reads? Does he appreciate the reasonableness of the content of the materials? Is he socially responsible in group-reading situations? The methods of appraisal are of two types. One type of appraisal is day-by-day observation of the children at work, at which time, for example, the teacher may note whether they come to him or other members of the class for help when they could, unaided have found the solution to their reading problem. The teacher notes whether they are effective in locating materials on given topics or whether they seem to grope around, finding material as if by chance or not at all. He notes whether they tend to resort to reading as a tool to answer their questions, allow the questions to go unanswered, or use more difficult means of finding the information. Such appraisals may be made at any time during any and every reading activity.

From time to time, the teacher may wish to resort to a second means of appraisal, namely, teacher-prepared problem-situation tests. One example of a situation set up to appraise the competence of children in doing independent work is that of giving them topics to look up in the library and having them list the steps by which they located the information. Analysis may then be made of the reports to see if there was any tendency toward dependence upon others and to note any confusion concerning how to go about the problem.

A teacher in the early grades may allot time in which the children have freedom of choice of material to read and appraise the degree to which they are self-reliant in making the selection. The child who is immature might come to the teacher and say, "Do you think this would be a good book for me to read?" A child still more immature might say, "I can't find anything to read. Can you find something for me?"

A habit essential to effective reading is that of engaging in reading activities for increasingly remote goals. The mature reader can both study several days on a problem without further suggestions from the teacher and establish his own purposes for reading. He also can initiate many of his own reading activities. This performance gives the teacher an effective means of appraising growth.

The teacher can make a relatively long-time assignment. Children with a small degree of independence will come to him relatively soon for further help. Children with an average amount of self-reliance will continue until some new phase of the problem enters to make the task sufficiently difficult so that they lack the independence to meet it. The truly independent readers will meet this new phase, adjust their goals, and proceed, and they will continue their work in socially acceptable ways. The habit of working independently was used as an example in this discussion. Other habits and attitudes can be appraised in a similar manner.

The appraisal of reading interests and tastes and the use of reading in establishing values was discussed in an earlier chapter and will not be treated here. Nonetheless, it is important for the teacher to recognize the value of appraising these outcomes of reading instruction in the overall evaluation of a child's capabilities.

RECORD OF APPRAISALS

Although it is realized that the teacher must and does make many appraisals in reading, especially those in day-by-day growth, it is apparent that any help that can be given him in understanding the level of development of the children in his class should be given. It should be recognized also that standardized tests give information on many skills and abilities that are somewhat difficult for the teacher to appraise. It is through a cumulative account of standardized-test results, teacher appraisals, results of inventories, and the like, that a complete picture of the reading growth of a given child can be obtained. In order that this information may be kept in usable form, a profile record should be kept by the teacher of each child's growth in reading. The teacher may wish to prepare a form for this record that meets his specific needs. In preparing such a form, it is important to have it flexible so that the teacher can record many sorts of appraisals. These recordings should be made at each testing period in order that a quick comparison may be made of the child's present growth in comparison with previous growths. Provision should be made on the form for recording the results of interviews, questionnaires, and teacher observations. In addition to these results, it is important to record the dates of interviews, observations, and tests, as well as the names of any testing instruments used. Then the profile will have meaning to other teachers who may have need to examine it.

The teacher will find it helpful to keep for each child an individual file in which he may place the test blanks of the children as well as any slips of paper upon which he has recorded a behavioral record. A profile may be mimeographed on the inside of a manila folder. Then each year the folder may be sent along to the new teacher, who will have the benefit of the previous teacher's knowledge about the reading growth and interests of the child. Such cumulative records enable teachers to understand the child's reading development far better than do appraisals restricted to a single year.

Selected References

Austin, Mary, Clifford L. Bush, and Mildred H. Huebner. *Reading Evaluation.* New York: The Ronald Press Company, 1961, Chaps. 1 and 2.

Bond, Guy L., and Miles A. Tinker. *Reading Difficulties: Their Diagnosis and Correction.* New York: Appleton-Century-Crofts, Inc., 1957, Chaps. 7, 8, and 9.

McKim, Margaret G., and Helen Caskey. *Guiding Growth in Reading,* second edition. New York: The Macmillan Company, 1963, Chap. 13.

Russell, David H. *Children Learn to Read,* second edition. Boston: Ginn and Company, 1961, Chap. 16.

Tinker, Miles A., and Constance M. McCullough. *Teaching Elementary Reading,* second edition. New York: Appleton-Century-Crofts, Inc., 1962, Chap. 16.

Vernon, M. D. *Backwardness in Reading.* New York: Cambridge University Press, 1960.

CHAPTER 16

Adjusting to
Individual Needs

"Four Masters: **An Allegory"** *by Margaret LaPray**

The first master to inherit thirty orange trees said, "All of these trees were planted at approximately the same time. I will therefore show no favoritism. I will treat them exactly alike. All trees will be trimmed exactly eighteen inches from the extremity of each branch." One third of the trees were of sufficient growth so that the results were positive. The trees flourished. One third of the lesser trees were barbed. Healing rains and favorable weather aided their recovery. One third of the scrawniest trees were limp and lifeless looking. Five of the last group failed to recover.

The first master said, "I have no remorse. I can honestly say I have been FAIR."

The second master to inherit thirty orange trees said, "The puniest trees need my love and attention; the others are quite able to take care of themselves." So saying he gave extra amounts of water to the dry lifeless trees and in so doing he stunted the growth of the remaining trees. The flooded grove was soggy. Soon the gentle wind, the warm sun, and the extended time dried the swampy area.

* Margaret LaPray, "Four Masters: An Allegory," in *The Reading Teacher,* September 1963, pp. 8–9. Reprinted with permission of Margaret LaPray and the International Reading Association.

347

The second master said, "See the even growth of the trees. My puny trees are no longer weak, they grow even as the other trees in the grove. This is the right and only way."

The third master to inherit thirty orange trees said, "Of most importance are the three tallest, strongest, and sturdiest trees. These trees are the hope of the future. They will be the most productive, consequently they deserve most of my attention. After numerous soil tests of the three individual trees, enriching chemical supplements were prescribed. Because these elements were good for the chosen three, the master decided to enrich all the trees. A few trees were burned. Many green leaves turned yellow and then brown. The master squinted and shook his head. Next the quiet rain, pure air, and days of time tempered the rich soil. The trees recovered and even produced.

The third master said, "Because of this formula I now have three of the tallest, sturdiest, and most productive trees in the country. All of my trees produced. I will write out my special chemical elements for others to follow."

The fourth and last master to inherit thirty orange trees said, "I will not use the basic methods of systematic pruning, spraying, deep watering, and soil enrichment. These are outmoded programs. I will treat each tree as an individual; as I find the tree needs pruning, spraying, watering and enriching, I will see that this care is given INDIVIDUALLY. This master spent half of the night reading individual soil tests and keeping accurate records. According to the master's plan each tree was given half a day of individual attention. By the time the master was one third of the way through the grove the remaining trees suffered from lack of attention. Some trees were diseased. Some grew in distorted shapes. These trees required more first aid than the original program provided. The fourth master worked later and later.

The last master said, "Look at this tree I am now developing. How gratifying my labor is." True as he worked on each tree individually the change was observable.

A sage walked by and overheard the masters. "Fools," he said. "Trees have common, individual and group needs; to pay attention to any one of of these to the exclusion of the others is disastrous. He who improves the basic program contributes; he who eliminates the basic program detracts. The master who understands the application of these four statements is a master indeed" [169].

Instruction designed to develop so complex an ability as reading must be adjusted to meet individual needs. The complex learnings that make up reading are developmental—new learnings are rooted in and depend upon previous learnings, and, in turn, these new learnings become the background basic to subsequent learnings. Each child goes through the developmental sequence of learning to read at his unique rate and in his own way. It is the child who learns to read. The child learns to read with

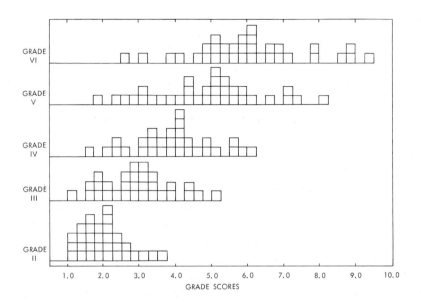

Figure 2. *Level of comprehension scores of pupils in grades two to six (tests given at the beginning of the year).*

his mental capabilities, his interests, his motivations, his values, his energy, his eyes, his ears, and his personal and social development. Variation in any one of these influences not only the rate at which he learns but the way by which he learns.

No two children, each with his own rate of growth in reading, could be expected to require the same time to develop any one aspect of the reading sequence. Nor, for that matter, could they be expected to progress through the entire reading sequence at the same rate.

Extent of Variation Expected

The range of scores and the frequency of each score at the beginning of the year for a class of second-, third-, fourth-, fifth-, and sixth-grade pupils in level of comprehension are presented in Figure 2. The test given to the second-grade class was the Gates Primary Test; the test given to the third-grade class was the Gates Advanced Primary Test; the level of comprehension measure for grades four, five, and six was obtained from the Gates Reading Survey Test. The pupils who scored the lowest possible score were retested using the Gates Primary Test. In the figure, each block represents a child. As can be seen by counting the blocks, the second-grade class has 31 members, the third grade 30, and so on. It was

349

the policy of the school, in which the children were tested, to have approximately 30 children in each class. In any given case, the level of comprehension test score, given in quarter-grade units, indicates the level of paragraph difficulty the child can comprehend. A grade score of 2.0, for example, indicates that a child who earned 2.0 can read paragraphs of beginning second-grade difficulty with understanding. Were such a child given paragraphs of third-grade level of difficulty he would not be able to read them effectively.

The graphed results of this one attribute of reading comprehension show that the reading program in this school is progressing well on the average. It is clear that there is a wide range of ability within each of the five classes. It may be seen that there is an increasingly larger range as the higher grades are reached. The graph shows that the score of most of the pupils in each class cluster around the median score for that grade and that fewer children are represented by scores toward the extremes in either direction from the median score. Parenthetically, it might be added that the better the teaching of reading in any class and in any school, the greater will be the individual differences in achievement. The only way to keep children alike in reading is not to teach any of them. Then none is able to read. The minute reading instruction is begun, some children will progress more rapidly than others. The differences between the poorest and best pupils will grow increasingly larger in each grade. Figure 2 presents comparative data from class to class in level of comprehension. Should data with regard to any other attribute of reading be so presented, sizable differences in achievement in it would also be depicted. Whatever reading skill or ability is examined, large differences in achievement are found within a grade and from grade to grade.

Current Administrative Adjustments

The problem of range of capability, graphically presented in Figure 2, has brought about many administrative arrangements for organizing classes for instruction in reading. Some of these ways will be discussed.

ADJUSTMENT BY PROMOTION POLICIES

Data, such as those presented in Figure 2, show that a policy of advancing able readers and failing to promote less able ones does not meet the instructional problems in reading. There are children in beginning second grade who academically are suited to read with understanding middle third-grade paragraphs but who are by no means advanced third-grade readers [282]. They have achieved well in reading in first grade. They have, however, not progressed through the developmental learnings of grades two and three. They could not possibly be expected to profit if so large a segment of instruction is omitted; they might be forever handicapped in learning to read. Or, to cite another example, there are two children in the sixth grade who are academically no better in power of comprehension than the typical beginning third-grade child. No one would recommend that these children, large in size and mature in interests, be placed in the third grade. Actually, they are two sixth-grade pupils, who read poorly. These two six-graders should be kept with, or near, their own age group, and adjustments of materials and instruction should be made to meet their needs. Table 1 shows what happened when a rigorous promotion policy was in operation in Dayton, Ohio, in 1912 [112].

TABLE 1 Age-Grade Distribution of 11,769 Children in the Elementary Schools of Dayton, Ohio, During the School Year of 1912–1913*

	AGE												THREE OR MORE YEARS
GRADE	5	6	7	8	9	10	11	12	13	14	15	16	17	OVERAGE
I	309	1308	451	128	52	11	6	4	2	1				3.3%
II		203	906	372	115	52	30	8		2				5.5
III			188	823	455	169	73	45	19	2	2			7.9
IV				168	621	414	224	133	43	19	2	2		11.1
V				2	179	475	307	236	111	51	6	1		12.3
VI					4	148	439	344	166	69	16	5	1	7.6
VII						8	158	430	318	159	26	5		2.8
VIII							8	104	334	221	84	10	2	1.6

* Used with permission of the Research Division of the Board of Education, Dayton, Ohio, 1914.

This table shows that the range in chronological age of children in any given grade was extreme. In the third grade, for example, there were children seven years of age and a few who were over 13. These extreme differences in chronological age resulted from the attempt to keep children academically equal by promotional policies. The children who could not read second-grade material were retained in first grade until they could. Children in the second grade were retained there until they had made the learnings expected of the typical child in grade two, and so forth. This practice attempted, albeit unsuccessfully, to lower the range of reading capability at any grade level so that all children within that grade would be approximately equal in reading. The decision a school system has to make is whether it is more effective to adjust to differences in chronological age or to differences in reading capability [166].

In Dayton in 1912 the decision was made to attempt to keep the children equal in reading and to allow chronological age to vary. As a result children of ages seven to 13 or over were housed in the same classroom. These children had entirely different interests, did not play well together, and certainly were not in a learning situation conducive to educational accomplishment. In the United States, in general, the decision has been made to keep children of similar ages together. This decision does not mean that a modest amount of retardation or acceleration is unwise.

The assumption made in rigorous promotion policies is that a child who is having difficulty in reading would profit more from repeating a grade than he would advancing with his classmates to the more difficult work in the higher grade. Cook [58] found that children profit more by advancing with their age group than by remaining behind. All that appeared to be accomplished by failures was the hoarding of the poor readers in the lower grades.

ADJUSTMENT BY ASSIGNMENT TO SPECIAL
READING CLASSES

Some school systems have adopted the policy of assigning children of like reading capability, regardless of grade designation, to the same room for reading instruction. Certainly, there is nothing seriously wrong with grouping for instruction, for one class during the day, children of ages nine to twelve. However, other results of such a policy should be carefully considered. Many students of reading think it unfortunate that the teacher who teaches the skills and abilities of reading and who is acquainted with the developmental needs of the children does not have them during the remainder of the school day. Reading is done in connection with topical-unit work, with study in the content fields, and with independent reading. The regular classroom teacher continues to teach reading as he is engaged in working with the children in other activities of the school day. He must know what each child is achieving in basal reading in order to instruct him at other times. And, conversely, he locates the child's reading needs as he observes the child read throughout the day. Most authorities deem it wise to have the teacher who gives the basic instruction in reading also teach the children during the rest of the school day.

Furthermore, most educators have concluded that reshuffling the children for reading instruction is not profitable, because rates of growth in reading vary so dramatically. Shortly after the original assignment to an instructional group, reassignments would have to be made if children of like levels of reading development are actually to be kept together [12]. Some of the youngest of the fourth-grade children would have advanced so rapidly as to be superior to the slower sixth-grade children with whom they had been grouped.

Another problem in connection with assigning children to a different room to work on reading with a different teacher and different classmates is that it is perplexing to decide on which attribute of reading achievement to assign the children to the rooms. Should the assignment be based on the results of a test that measures ability to comprehend rapidly the general significance of a paragraph? Should it be on the ability to read to appraise the worth of a passage? Or to appreciate characterization or plot of a story? Should it be on the basis of size of sight vocabulary? Or upon the basis of knowledge of visual, structural, and phonetic elements? Or upon a general estimate of the child's overall reading ability? Whatever basis of assignment is used, the children will vary in all the others, and will soon vary in that one as well.

Many experts have concluded that the teacher who has the children throughout the day should be the one who gives the basic instruction in reading for it is he who has the most accurate knowledge of the varied reading needs of each child in his class. It is a well-known fact that a child in the intermediate grade varies as much as two or three years in his ability to do different types of reading and in each of the underlying skills. There is marked variation from child to child and sizable variation in achievement in various aspects of reading for any given child.

ADJUSTMENT BY HOMOGENEOUS GROUPING

An arrangement sometimes advocated in school systems that have several classes of each grade is to group the poor readers in one class, the average readers in other classes, and the superior ones in another. Although this plan has some rather attractive-appearing features [12, 113, 114, 165], the consensus of opinion is that it does not provide a lifelike situation. It is contended that maintaining an intellectually stimulating environment is difficult when the entire class consists of the lowest third of the reading population. Capable children need to learn to lead and to contribute in activities that encompass a larger, less homogeneous proportion of the school population. In heterogeneous grouping, able youngsters afford stimulation for the less able ones. It is much easier to stimulate creative work in a class that has some capable youngsters in it than in one that consists of only the lowest group. For these and other reasons, the majority of schools have felt it unwise in the elementary school to group children according to ability even on the basis of an overall estimate of reading capability.

Referring again to Figure 2, it should be noted that there is progress from year to year even for children who are finding reading most difficult. By comparing the lower end of the sixth-grade distribution with the second-grade distribution, it may be seen that the two poorest readers in level of comprehension in the beginning sixth-grade class are above the median score of the second-grade class. By comparing median scores, one grade with the next, it may be seen that positive progress is taking place in this aspect of reading comprehension. Unquestionably, in this school good teaching is being done. There is some evidence that adjustments to individual instructional needs are being made.

Many ungraded primary or continuous-growth programs have several of the same characteristics as have homogeneous grouping plans. Frequently, the children are separated into classrooms where the expectation for one classroom is to complete the primary reading program in two years. Another classroom is expected to complete it in three years, the third is expected to complete the work after four years. This is ability-grouping teamed with promotional policies of retardation and acceleration. Many children have grown nicely in reading capability under this sort of administrative arrangement. In general, however, it may be stated that the weaknesses inherent in homogeneous grouping and in promotional retardation and acceleration are operative, but to a somewhat lesser degree in ungraded primary and continuous-growth programs. Teachers working within the framework of such plans report that they continue to have the problem of individual differences in reading, and they find themselves handling groups within their classes just as they do in more heterogeneous arrangements. Nonetheless, there can be no question that these plans make somewhat less the differences in reading ability encountered by any one teacher. It appears that these arrangements do not have as much in their disfavor as their opponents claim nor as much in their favor as their proponents believe. As in the homogeneous classrooms, the basic problem of adjusting to individual differences still exists; that is, the teacher must use instructional practices that meet the various needs of the children he is teaching.

INDIVIDUALIZED INSTRUCTION

Individualized instruction was discussed in the chapter on current approaches to teaching reading, at which time the methodological procedures were described. Individualized instruction is a way of organizing a class for reading instruction. Under this approach the child is taught to read individually, or occasionally in groups [144], in material he has selected. Theoretically, each child reads a different selection, and instruction is given individually for five or ten minutes each week. Many authorities question whether as complex a set of skills and abilities as are involved in reading can be taught within so short a time as five or ten minutes per week. Fundamental to individualized reading is a great variety of reading material and a permissive class atmosphere that enables freedom of choice of material for basic instructional purposes. The advocates of this method feel that children take a greater interest in reading and read more widely than under more traditional methods and that the children discover on their own many of the techniques involved in reading and that, through conferences, the teacher can show them the needed alterations in their reading approaches.

It is difficult to see how so permissive a reading atmosphere can provide for basal reading instruction in the skills and abilities essential to mature reading. For personal reading, a permissive atmosphere with independent, individual reading is far more appropriate, although, even here, experts in children's literature feel that the personal reading should be guided to a greater extent than is suggested in individualized programs [208].

For the basic reading instruction and for instruction in topical units, this plan appears unworkable [198]. For one thing, reading is a complex process that must be taught systematically. For another, no teacher can keep in mind the reading needs of each child from week to week for the ten minutes, at most, of instruction he is able to allot to a given child. Nor does he have time to teach even one selection to each child each week, for, it will be recalled, the steps in teaching a selection include teacher preparation, building readiness, introducing new vocabulary, setting purposes, reading silently, discussing, developing reading skills and abilities, and using the products of reading. And too, children of elementary-school ages are not expected to be mature enough to work alone for an entire week with only ten minutes or so of individual conference and instruction in the development of reading skills and abilities.

ABILITY GROUPING WITHIN THE CLASSROOM

Although it is recognized that no classroom organization or administrative device will solve completely the problem of adjusting to instructional needs, it is apparent that some form of organization is required. Jarolimek [147] found that 97 percent of the teachers in his study used some form of grouping to adjust to individual differences in reading. He found further that the grouping was confined to the period of basal reading instruction. He found little apparent adjustment to differences in reading ability in the reading situations in other aspects of the curriculum. Rather, he observed that in over 90 percent of the classes single textbooks were being used in doing the basic work in the content areas. For many children the textbooks were on a frustration level, for some on an instructional level, and for some on an independent reading level.

In adjusting to individual differences in the classroom by means of ability grouping, the teacher must decide how many groups to use. The time available for teaching basic reading is not unlimited, nor are the energies of the teacher. The teacher might like to separate the class into six instructional groups or even more, but he is aware that he can use only an hour daily for basic instruction in reading and would be able to devote only ten minutes average instructional time for each of the six groups. For three groups there would be 20 minutes available to handle the instructional phases of reading. Most teachers and most school systems have come to the conclusion that three instructional groups is an effective number [268]. Therefore, many classrooms throughout the nation are organized into three groups for instruction in reading; the poorest readers in the lowest group, the middle group made up of the average readers, and the best readers in the top group. There are protests against grouping children so arbitrarily. Burrows [43], for example, says: "No democratic-minded person in our society defends the caste system. Yet in our schools we are still operating such a system. In thousands of classrooms across the country children of poor reading performance live under a stigma quite akin to that of being an Untouchable. Even when a poor group is labeled the 'Brownies' or the 'Chipmunks,' no one is fooled."

Always present, but by no means always apparent, in studying children in school is the desire of each child to be a participating, contributing member of his class. In any teaching situation, consideration must be given to the motivations of the child. Usually, the child in reading difficulty is unable to participate in a satisfying way in class activities. Sornson [243] indicates that a youngster's social and personal adjustment becomes less satisfactory as his reading difficulties develop. She found the attitudes of parents, teachers, and the children themselves worsened in comparison with attitudes toward children more successful in reading. Each child requires opportunities to succeed as well as chances to participate actively in the pursuits of the school day, including learning to read. Fortunately, in the modern school and available to today's teachers are improved materials, improved methods of teaching and appraising, and better understanding of children.

Criticisms are voiced against ability grouping on a fixed basis, where a child is classified at the beginning of the school year, or for that matter, at the beginning of his school life, and where the classification never changes. The child stays somewhat indefinitely in the group to which he is assigned. Such a track system is criticized because of the damage to the personal integrity of the individuals who make up the lower groups and the loss of opportunity to work with others by those who constitute the upper group. Buswell [48] found that grouping for reading within the classroom affected the level of aspiration of the children; even when engaging in activities other than reading, the children tended to aspire to work with other members of their own group or with members of the next higher group and not with members of a lower reading group or a group two levels higher. The children in the top group did not choose children from lower reading groups as workers on any project.

MULTIPLE-FLEXIBLE GROUPING

Differences in rate of achievement in reading and in instructional needs are complex and sizable whatever system of adapting to individual differences is used. Therefore, adjustment to individual differences cannot be solved by any one method of organization alone. Multiple-flexible grouping, interest groups, individualized instruction, and diagnostic teaching should all have a part in teaching method, separately or in combination, when and where appropriate in meeting the reading needs of children [38]. Each plan has its strengths and limitations. Adjustment to individual differences will be accomplished most adequately by using the various approaches in the situations and for the learnings to which they are most suited.

During basic instruction in reading, the teacher must work closely with the children if the skills and abilities are to expand and grow. Some form is recommended of multiple-flexible grouping according to range of talent and capabilities. This grouping arrangement enables the teacher to introduce new words systematically and teach the other skills and abilities. Groups are arranged so that a child can move readily from one group to another as it becomes apparent that he will profit from the reassignment. And too, at times a given child may work with two instructional groups. The groups need not be clearly defined. This flexibility of grouping avoids unfortunate categorizing of children and permits adjustments to individual differences.

To avoid further unfortunate categorizing and labeling, it is recommended that the groups be named for a member who is, for a short time, the group leader. Group leaders should change fairly often. And too, the children should not be seated in any geographical double-row arrangement by groups, but should be seated according to physical needs. Those children who have any hearing loss should be placed in a favorable location within the room. The children with visual difficulties should be seated according to their visual needs. Other special needs of the children should be considered in planning seating arrangements.

In summary, for basic instruction, group organization should be dynamic, not static. The groups should be flexible. Often the entire class should work together [214].

An Illustration of Effective Procedures of Grouping for Basal Instruction

The distribution of the reading capabilities of the fifth-grade class, shown in Figure 3, is presented below.

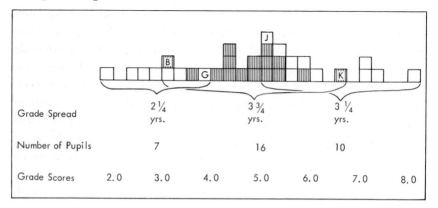

Figure 3.   *Level of comprehension scores of pupils by groups in a fifth-grade class (tests given at the beginning of the year).*

The middle group has been shaded to indicate the three-group separation that was made by the teacher, Mr. Thorpe. The first initials of some children have been included so that they may be identified for later discussion. Use of the findings of observation and appraisals of several attributes of reading, in addition to level of comprehension, resulted in placing children in a group other than the one they would have been placed in had level of comprehension been the only consideration. Taking more information into account to determine grouping has the effect of increasing the variation in level of comprehension in each of the three groups. Grouping decisions never should be made on the results of one reading attribute alone. Teachers consider several important characteristics in grouping children for instruction. Level of comprehension is just one of the considerations used by Mr. Thorpe. He used information about the children's word-recognition capabilities, information got from teacher observation and from other test results, including mental tests results. The ability to work independently and general maturity of each child were appraised informally by Mr. Thorpe.

It will be noted in Figure 3 that the most advanced group of ten children ranges from a grade score of 5.0 to 8.25, or a total of 3¼ years, rather than the 2¾ years it would have ranged had level of comprehension alone been used in making the grouping decision. The 16 children in the middle group range 3¾ years in level of comprehension, the lowest group of seven children ranges 2¼ years. Mr. Thorpe purposely assigned only seven children to the lowest group, believing the instructional problems with this group were more complex. For one thing, these children lack independence; each child requires more detailed instruction than the children in the other groups. With fewer children in the lowest group, all of whom are somewhat distractable, Mr. Thorpe needs to watch fewer children as they work independently at their seats while he works with another group in the reading circle. After all, the teacher has only two eyes and his energy is not boundless.

In forming the groups, Mr. Thorpe used level of comprehension as the most important single attribute of reading proficiency, because it most nearly represented, of all the information available, the level of difficulty of material the children could read understandingly. On the basis of additional information, he decided that certain children would profit more from instruction in a group other than the one to which they would have been assigned had level of comprehension been the sole criterion.

J, Jack, for example, was assigned to group one rather than group two, because he demonstrated a high degree of independence in reading. Although Jack has some difficulty in paragraph understanding, Mr. Thorpe felt that this limitation, so important in level of comprehension, could be corrected effectively as instruction progressed in the daily basal instruction in group one. In general, this bright boy would profit more in overall reading development by working in the most advanced group.

K, Kathy, who on the basis of level of comprehension would have been assigned to the most advanced group, was placed in the middle group for the time being so that she might get the advantage of specific instruction in certain word-recognition techniques in which she had shown weakness. Kathy has difficulty with syllabication and with locating root words in affixed words. It was felt by the teacher that this girl needed the concentrated instruction that the middle group would receive in these skills. Mr. Thorpe thought that Kathy might develop these word-recognition techniques quickly, in which case she would be placed in the upper group. Occasionally, when a new skill was introduced in the upper group, he had Kathy work with that group too.

B, Betty, was placed in the middle group, even though on the basis of level of comprehension she would be the poorest reader in that group, because she had excellent word-recognition skills, was a diligent worker, and a capable child. Betty recently had moved from an underprivileged area to the area served by this school. Her family is bilingual. Betty had a limited background of experience and a meager vocabulary of English words. Mr. Thorpe felt that this child was limited in level of comprehension because of the language inadequacy rather than any limitation in skill development. As a matter of fact, her skill development was superior to her comprehension ability. Mr. Thorpe knew that many opportunities in the course of teaching the selections in the middle group would present themselves to give Betty training in applying her high degree of reading skill in comprehension tasks.

G, Gerald, is an attractive, capable boy who is finding satisfactions in the classroom through mischievous behavior. He is not, however, a behavioral problem. He is a slow word-by-word reader. On the level of comprehension test, in which time is not a factor, Gerald scored well in relation to his general reading capability. Mr. Thorpe judged that the work that would be most profitable to Gerald would be that of group three, where the focus would be on building sight vocabulary, reading in thought units, and developing rapid word-recognition techniques.

Mr. Thorpe knew that the assignments to groups were tentative and that he would continually consider the possibility of change in group placement not only for the children discussed above but also for any of the other children whose reading patterns or rates of growth altered during the year. He was aware also that the grouping was for basic instruction only. However, to some extent, the grouping would carry over to other reading activities. The supplementary reading would often be attuned to the material being handled in basal-reading group instruction. He was careful to see that there was adequate supplementary material to meet the range of reading capability within all the groups, because he would not be working directly with the children in preparatory activities as he did when teaching the reading of basal material.

Although the supplementary materials should in general be on the independent reading levels of the children, the basic material used for a group is on the instructional level that best fits that group. The poorer readers within any group can read the basal material with profit even though it is somewhat difficult for them, because the teacher is showing them how to read that material and is preparing them for reading it. It should be noted that during basal instruction the poorest reader in a group is reading material that for him is difficult, and the most able reader in the group reads material that for him is relatively easy. A teacher, therefore, in the directly related supplementary reading gives the able reader more material with which he has to tussle than he does to the less able reader, because the less able reader needs to gain the fluency that comes about from reading material that is relatively easy for him. On the other hand, to gain power the capable child should have reading experiences that challenge all his reading capability. These generalizations are true no matter which of the reading groups is under consideration.

Mr. Thorpe recognized that instructional needs differ because the children in his class are different. He recognized too that children have similar instructional needs, because in many ways they are similar. They are, in the first place, children. Each is a person who needs to progress successfuly in reading growth. All children tend to respond similarly to success and to failure, although the response varies somewhat. Indeed, it is the rare child who does not evidence real delight when he is successful in a reading situation. Children need to establish similar learnings to become mature readers; they need to progress through sequences that are the same in many respects. They differ, however, in the length of time and in the expenditure of effort required to establish a given learning. Even under the usual uniform instruction, more than nine out of ten children learn to read well because they are alike in so many respects. It is not possible to forecast with accuracy which child will be the tenth —the child who gets into difficulty. He may be an intellectually able child, or he may be a child handicapped with poor hearing. He may the child who for any of many reasons fails to establish a learning essential in the reading sequence or the child who overemphasizes a necessary learning.

Recognizing the developmental needs, Mr. Thorpe knew that each child should be made to feel himself a successful participating member of the class community in which he would spend so much of his day. Mr. Thorpe was aware that the grouping he had established for basic instruction in reading should in no way keep any child from being a member of other activities of the school day nor should it keep him from entering into the related activities that accompany basic instruction. Mr. Thorpe, therefore, decided, inasmuch as the middle group was the largest, numbering about half the class, that most of the expanded reading should be an outgrowth of the topics introduced in the basic reader of the middle group. In addition to their own basic material, he had the children of the advanced group read the material that the middle group was studying. All the children worked together planning and doing the activities related to expanding the topic of the unit that stemmed from the basic program of the middle group. Mr. Thorpe wisely provided some materials suited to the lowest group, dealing with the same topic, which was read prior to the discussion and as extended reading growing out of the discussion. Thus, the children of the lowest group were able not only to enter into the planning of the activities but also had the opportunity to read in relation to the topic under consideration. It was possible more often for children in the upper group to use the central library and the classroom collection of books to locate additional material to extend their reading on the topic. Thus, they became resource workers, enriching the topic for all the children and, as well, gaining experience in independent library research. Mr. Thorpe had added material to the classroom collection of books so that material was readily accessible for all the children to read, whatever their capability.

Frequently, during the planning discussions, the children formed interest groups to pursue various phases of the topic. The class, under Mr. Thorpe's guidance, was subdivided into committees according to the natural divisions of the topic itself. For this phase of the reading program, thus, grouping arrangements quite different than the usual ones occurred. Hurley [141], among others, subscribes to grouping according to the natural divisions of a topic. Hurley says: "Considerable experimenting has gone forward to find valid bases for grouping children for learning. Examination of motives behind children's habits as they seek to belong to natural and spontaneous groups has given promising clues. These include, among others: grouping to learn a certain skill; grouping to work with friends; grouping to have fun." A child becomes a member of a given committee on the basis of his interests or of a specific purpose and on the availability of material at his level of accomplishment. He must be in a group that is dealing with a phase of the topic for which there are materials that he can read comfortably. Each child must be able to contribute to the group thinking as a result of his reading. Each child works somewhat independently of the teacher. Consequently, he must rely on his own resources and those of other members of his committee. It is interesting to note that the best and poorest reader within the class might conceivably be on the same committee (in the same interest group), each making a contribution to the group.

It must be noted that all the children within the class must be studying the same topic in order for all of them to work on committees related to the topic. If materials written on varying levels of reading difficulty and dealing with the same content are made available, this extended reading is a natural outgrowth of the topics introduced. Where such materials are not available, occasionally topics introduced in the basic material of groups other than the middle group should be used so that the children even in the lowest group can feel that their basic reading is important to the class. However, usually those topics would not be studied as completely as those of the middle group.

Reading related to a central theme, explored by the class as a whole, motivates the children to do the supplementary work. The teacher's problem is not one of forcing the children to read; quite the contrary, his problem is to keep these supplementary reading activities from dominating the work of the day to the extent that other important content areas are neglected. The motivation for reading comes from the children themselves when they are reading on a topic in which they know they are going to use the results creatively—and when they sense that to the degree they gain information and understanding, they will be able to contribute to the ongoing classroom work and its creative expression.

Mr. Thorpe organized the time devoted to basic reading instruction so that he could work directly with each group while the remaining members of the class were engaged in other educationally worthwhile activities directly related to that instruction. Three strands of reading work went forward simultaneously: instruction in the skills and abilities, using the basic reader itself; skill development activities, using either teacher-prepared exercises or the basic reader workbooks; and independent reading related to the topic, using supplementary materials dealing with the expanded topic. The latter two phases were done independently of the teacher. These phases are commonly called, miscalled rather, seatwork. Mr. Thorpe's task was to insure that purposes for these strands of instruction were understood and accepted by the children. Under this type of well-planned instruction disciplinary problems rarely occur. Nonetheless, a teacher knows he must be alert to the possibility that a child might finish the exercises before the time came for his group to work directly with the teacher. He would then suggest to the child that he could use the available time for either more reading on the topic or for working upon the creative outcomes of the topic.

Mr. Thorpe set aside time in the daily schedule for personal-development reading. Some of the children wished to pursue further phases of the topic being explored in the basic reading program. He neither discouraged nor encouraged this practice. The fact is that he often felt it was more advantageous to the children to suggest that, during this free-reading time, they read material they themselves had selected for its personal interest to them. Mr. Thorpe was not adverse to guiding children into reading he believed would expand their interests beyond the everyday happenings of classroom instruction. His goal in this instruction was to enrich the children's reading lives, to stimulate their curiosity about books, and to enable them to dip more deeply into the abundance of material that is available now at every age and every reading capability level. He wished to encourage the children to explore the reading world.

There was no grouping planned for recreational, personal reading. However, from time to time the children grouped themselves to explore and discuss cooperatively materials dealing with common interests. Often this transient, spontaneous grouping crossed other more formal organizational lines. In a well-conducted classroom these spontaneous groups will not be restricted to any reading group demarcation. Because all groups do recreational reading at the same time and because the children are accustomed to working in interest groups in connection with the basic-reader reading; because formal grouping in basic reading is flexible, and because sharing books discovered and especially enjoyed in personal reading is customary; and because the children work together in the content areas, the stigma of differences in reading capabilities vanishes.

Diagnostic Teaching

It will be noted from the above illustration that Mr. Thorpe not only had his class well organized for reading instruction and not only had created a stimulating environment for reading growth, but he was also a diagnostic teacher. Diagnostic teaching is a necessary element in adequate adjustment to individual differences in reading. Diagnostic teaching is based on an understanding of the reading strengths and needs of each child and an understanding of each child's status in the characteristics related to reading instruction and a use of those understandings to modify instructional procedures so that the teaching is adjusted to the needs of the children.

A given child may find some learnings difficult and time-consuming and others relatively quick and easy. When the learning curves for any children are compared, differences show up, and irregularities within any one child's learning curves appear as well. One such irregularity, for example, might result from the fact that the child found the use of context clues easy to establish, but the use of initial elements difficult. For this child, the first of these learnings was accomplished easily and rapidly and the second only slowly and laboriously. The learning curve of a second child, on the other hand, might show irregularities resulting from the fact that he established the use of context clues as an aid to word recognition slowly and only as a result of special help from the teacher, whereas he learned quickly and with no special difficulty the use of initial elements. Such irregularities within the learning patterns of each child, coupled with differences between children's general rate of learning, constitute one of the most serious problems in teaching reading, that of adjusting to individual needs. In order to meet the differing rates of learning among children and the irregularities of rate of learning typical of each child, a teacher must make individual adjustments while teaching reading.

The best of grouping procedures, the supply and appropriateness of materials, the extensiveness of library resources, and the programs of appraisals are means of giving well-prepared teachers a reasonable chance of adjusting instruction to the various capabilities and needs of children. Most children get along remarkably well in reading in accordance with their capacities for such learning. Even so, however, all children are helped if the teacher recognizes their minor deviations from effective reading growth and adjusts to them. Naturally, some children require more extensive study than others. Reading disabilities are prevented and general reading growth is enhanced when the teacher studies each child's reading progress and gives corrective help when needed before minor confusions accumulate into major difficulties.

In studying the children, the teacher considers all sources of information available to him in order to explore the nature of reading adjustments that should be made. For those children who do not have serious reading problems, the adjustments can be made during regular instruction. For those few children who are in serious difficulty, a more thorough diagnostic appraisal is required. These children will usually not number more than three in a class of 30. These are the children who need a more thorough diagnosis of their learning difficulties and who require a more intensive program of remediation or adjustment than is given to other children within the classroom. The diagnoses are always directed toward formulating methods of improvement.

In Mr. Thorpe's fifth-grade class there were three children to whom he gave the Bond-Clymer-Hoyt Diagnostic Reading Tests, in addition to the group mental test and the Gates Reading Survey Test. Their profiles are shown in Figure 4. In each case, the mental grade was obtained from the results of the mental test; the vocabulary knowledge, level of comprehension, and speed of comprehension grade scores from the Gates Survey Test; the grade scores for total word recognition, recognition of isolated

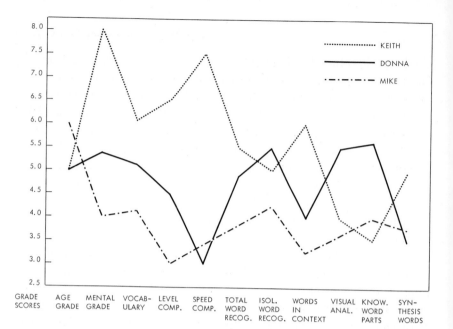

| GRADE SCORES | AGE GRADE | MENTAL GRADE | VOCAB-ULARY | LEVEL COMP. | SPEED COMP. | TOTAL WORD RECOG. | ISOL. WORD RECOG. | WORDS IN CONTEXT | VISUAL ANAL. | KNOW. WORD PARTS | SYN-THESIS WORDS |

Figure 4. *Profiles of mental and reading test results of three children in grade five.*

words, recognition of words in context, visual analysis, knowledge of visual, structural, and phonetic elements, and ability to synthesize words from the Bond-Clymer-Hoyt Diagnostic Reading Tests. Although these three children are in the same fifth-grade class, a study of the profile variability, depicted in this graphic presentation of test results, shows that the instructional needs of the children are different. More detailed descriptions of these three children follow.

A CHILD WITH POOR WORD-RECOGNITION SKILLS

Keith is intellectually one of the most able members of this fifth-grade class. He is successful in his schoolwork, is a leader, makes outstanding contributions in class, reads the fifth-grade textbooks of the content areas without difficulty. He does considerable personal reading and selects books slightly above the fifth-grade level of difficulty. He reads them rapidly and understands them well.

On Keith's cumulative record folder were recorded the results of a Stanford-Binet Test of Intelligence, given in the final month of the previous year. Mr. Thorpe noted a discrepancy between the results of this individual test, which showed an intelligence quotient of 135, and the results of the group test, which indicated an IQ of 120. Such a discrepancy between verbal group tests and individual Stanford-Binet scores is not unusual in the case of an able child who is deficient in reading ability.

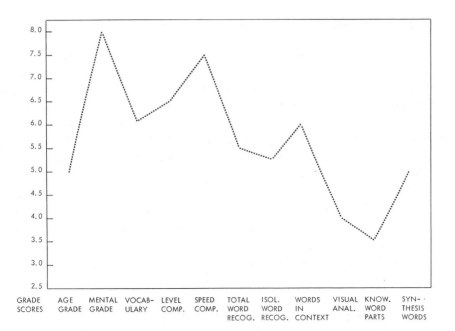

Figure 5. *Profile of Keith, an able boy with poor word-recognition skills.*

Clymer [55] has shown that verbal group tests mismeasure large numbers of poor readers. In the fifth-grade population with which he worked, he found the children who read in the lowest third were grossly underestimated by the results of the usual verbal group tests of intelligence. Barnes [15] found similar results, showing that reading ability influences paper-and-pencil aptitude test results in general.

The survey test in reading revealed a much lower score on the vocabulary section of the test than upon level of comprehension and speed. Mr. Thorpe wondered about these inconsistencies and decided to study Keith's reading capability further by giving him the Bond-Clymer-Hoyt Diagnostic Reading Tests. He planned to give the diagnostic tests to several children, including Donna and Mike, whose patterns of reading growth were causing him concern.

Upon studying the results of the diagnostic tests, Mr. Thorpe was surprised to see that Keith is in need of specific help with reading. As can be seen from the graph, he is in difficulty in use of word-recognition techniques. He is decidedly low in visual analysis; in knowledge of visual, phonetic, and structural elements; and in ability to synthesize in contrast to general level of comprehension and speed of reading. He uses context clues well, but his recognition of isolated words is comparatively poor.

The Stanford-Binet test result shows that Keith has a mental age similar to that of the typical eighth-grade child. His word-recognition skills are,

367

in general, approximately equal to a fourth-grade child. Actually, thus, Keith is a disabled reader. His high intellectual ability has enabled him to use his relatively ineffective word-recognition skills efficiently, so that comprehension and speed are rather good in spite of his basic reading inadequacy. Without careful appraisal, his limitation in the word-recognition techniques might have passed unnoticed by Mr. Thorpe, although he might have suspected from informal observation that there was a possible difficulty in this area.

Mr. Thorpe had noticed, even prior to studying the diagnostic test results, that in oral reading sessions Keith tends to skip or to slur, without accurately pronouncing, unusual names and words. Nonetheless, he is a reasonably good oral reader.

Had the word-recognition inadequacies of this capable boy passed unnoticed and unremedied, it is reasonable to suppose that as he progressed to higher grades he would have got into serious trouble. As the vocabulary burden increased with the addition of technical words in the content fields and as more multisyllabic words appeared in his everyday reading, it would be expected that Keith would use ways other than reading to achieve scholastically, and his achievement in reading would become progressively poorer, as compared with his intellect, for when such basic incapacities are left uncorrected, the trouble accumulates and reading disability often results. To say the least, if he had been allowed to continue without establishing more adequate word-recognition skill, he would continue to be a less effective reader than he might otherwise have been. There are many college students with intellectual capability equal to Keith's who are, nonetheless, ineffective students because such inadequacies in their reading patterns were not discovered and corrected within the classroom by their intermediate-grade classroom teachers.

A WORD-BY-WORD READER

Donna, another member of this fifth-grade class, is a girl slightly above average in mental ability. She tries hard, spells well, writes carefully and legibly, and cooperates well in her attempt to contribute to class discussions. To Mr. Thorpe, Donna seems uncomfortable and unhappy in reading situations. She rarely reads for recreation. In fact, she has said that she does not enjoy reading, either in or out of class.

Mr. Thorpe is already aware that Donna's unduly high levels of aspiration stem from pressures she experiences at home. Her parents hold her to unrealistic standards of performance, failing to realize the unreasonableness of their expectations and failing to appreciate how hard their daughter tries to satisfy them.

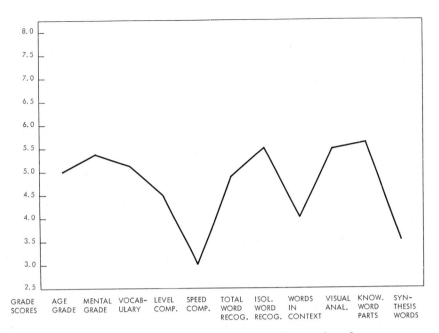

Figure 6. *Profile of Donna, a slow, word-by-word reader.*

A study of the survey tests indicates that Donna has a relatively high reading vocabulary score, but that her speed of reading is about that of the average youngster who is beginning third grade, and her comprehension score is equal to a 4.5 grade norm. Mr. Thorpe decided to include her in the group to be given the diagnostic tests.

The results of the diagnostic tests reveal Donna to be very poor in recognizing words in context, in contrast to her ability to recognize words in isolation. Her ability to use context clues is equivalent to that of the average child beginning fourth grade, whereas her ability to break words into usable elements is equal to that of the average child halfway through the fifth grade. Her ability to synthesize words is poor.

Mr. Thorpe tested Donna further with informal oral reading procedures. Also, he observed her behavior in the classroom. He senses that she is somewhat slow at completing assignments and that she reads orally word by word. When she finishes reading a passage orally, she answers only fairly well the comprehension questions based upon what she has read. He has noted that, at times, when she is having difficulty recognizing a word she seems to sound it out fairly well, but is inept at finally pronouncing the word. Her score on ability to synthesize corroborated this observation.

Donna depends entirely too much upon high skill in visual analysis and phonetic knowledges. She does not use context adequately. She is unable to group words into thought units. As a result, she reads very slowly with limited comprehension.

From these test results and observations, Mr. Thorpe concluded that Donna is a word-by-word reader in need of instruction designed to develop the ability to use context clues and to group words into thought units. He determined to provide Donna with specific instruction she needed to overcome her weaknesses. In no respects, other than speed of reading and ability to group words into thought units, is Donna so far away from the class group that she could not be taught adequately in the typical class situation. Mr. Thorpe will avoid exercises for her that are designed to further emphasize the analytical techniques and will give her many opportunities to participate in those exercises designed to teach phrasing and use of context clues. When Donna becomes proficient in the use of these rapid techniques, her slow speed of reading will have been remedied.

Just a routine sort of corrective work would not have helped Donna. But when her problem was identified and the proper corrective work given, it could be expected that her achievement in reading would progress in keeping with her general capability. However, Mr. Thorpe planned to keep careful track of her progress over the first several weeks of school. If the classroom remedial procedures did not seem to be correcting her reading defect, she would be recommended for more prolonged and specific remedial help than he was able to provide in the classroom. Donna is another child who, if left unremedied, would become more and more seriously handicapped in reading as she progressed into the reading demands of higher grades.

It should be added that Mr. Thorpe scheduled a conference with Donna's parents to discuss her work in reading and to seek their understanding of her instructional needs. He planned to acquaint her parents with what he was attempting to do for Donna and to enlist their cooperation in helping her overcome her great concern for satisfying their unrealistic standards of success. Donna is a child of high average ability and cannot be expected to make exceptionally high scholastic achievements. She can be expected to do well, however.

A SLOW-LEARNING CHILD

Mike is the oldest child in the fifth-grade class. He repeated the second grade. He does not apply himself well. Already this year he has caused much trouble in the class. On the school playground he uses his physical strength to get his way. In fact, he is regarded by the other children as being somewhat of a bully.

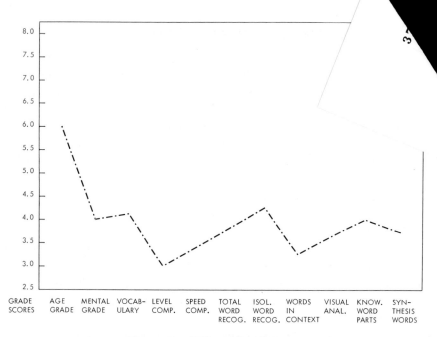

| GRADE
SCORES | AGE
GRADE | MENTAL
GRADE | VOCAB-
ULARY | LEVEL
COMP. | SPEED
COMP. | TOTAL
WORD
RECOG. | ISOL.
WORD
RECOG. | WORDS
IN
CONTEXT | VISUAL
ANAL. | KNOW.
WORD
PARTS | SYN-
THESIS
WORDS |

Figure 7. *Mike, a slow learner.*

Mike's score on the group mental test indicates that he has low scholastic promise. His IQ is 68. Mr. Thorpe plans to request that an individual test of intelligence be given to him to determine more accurately his level of intellectual functioning.

The score Mike made on the vocabulary section of the survey test is slightly higher than the mental test result. In the comprehension section of the Gates Reading Survey Test he made only a score of 3.0. He attempted enough items, although many incorrectly, to get a speed score of 3.4. Even though Mr. Thorpe recognized that poor learning ability is Mike's major handicap, he included him in the diagnostic testing group to find out if there were special limitations upon which he could work to help Mike show better progress in reading.

The results of the diagnostic tests tended to verify the other findings. Mike is relatively high in word-recognition skills. This demonstration of strength is not surprising inasmuch as he has had one more year in which to build these skills, for it will be remembered that he repeated second grade. Undoubtedly, all of his teachers drilled him in word recognition in an attempt to help him improve his reading skills. He is, however, low in ability to use context clues. In and of itself, this result of the diagnostic testing did not seem unusual, because the use of context clues depends upon attending to meaning. Mike, with his limited mental ability, and one extra year of instruction, could be expected to have developed pass-

371

ably well some of the mechanics of reading, but he could never be expected to do well with the intellectually more demanding aspects of reading [146]. Mr. Thorpe concluded that Mike is reading about as well as could be expected in view of his mental ability, that his skills in word recognition are adequate, and that his major problems in reading are in comprehension abilities. In order to build a background, he planned to give Mike concrete experiences. He felt Mike should do considerable rereading of material for new purposes. He might first read a passage, for example, to get a general notion of what it was about, and then read it again to get some specific details to help him with a construction activity in connection with reading.

Mr. Thorpe's study of Mike in the classroom, the analysis of the test findings and informal appraisals caused him to query whether Mike's instructional needs might better be met in a special education class. Consequently, he requested that a more thoroughgoing psychological study of Mike be made.

There are children in any classroom, such as Keith, Donna, and Mike, who have persistent reading problems and who should have an intensive study of their problems. In diagnosing reading problems, the teacher finds answers to the following questions:

1. *Is the child's basic problem really one of reading?*
   For Keith and Donna, the answer is Yes. For Mike, the answer is No.

In answering this question, the teacher must decide whether the child is or is not learning to read as well as can be expected of him, even though he is one of the poorer readers. Is he reading up to his mental capability? Does he have a physical limitation that is impeding his progress? Has he come from an environment that is slowing his reading growth? And so on. This basic query and its answer is not concerned with the reading status of the child; it is concerned with what his status could or should be. It is not how advanced he is in reading, but how well he reads in comparison with the opportunity he has had to learn to read. The teacher should know that many children, slow in reading development, could not be expected to be higher for a variety of reasons. Their reading patterns show no irregularities that limit their reading growth and that could be assumed to be correctable by remedial instruction. These children are not disabled readers. What they need is tended to by adequate techniques of adjusting to individual differences—in general, taking the children from where they are and encouraging them to continue to progress. The disabled reader, on the other hand, is not living up to what could be expected of him. He has an irregular reading pattern. There are conditions within his reading profile that impede or make impossible his future reading growth. These are the children who need carefully designed remedial help. The vast majority of them can and should get that help in the classroom, however.

2. *Does the child need a diagnosis requiring more time,*
   equipment, and training than the teacher has?

The answer to this question revolves around the estimated complexity of the child's reading problem, the possibility of there being limiting conditions or emotional difficulties, and the availability of resource helpers. A thorough diagnosis with accompanying suggestions to the teacher quite often enables the teacher to help the child reinstate himself in reading.

3. *Should the child be given remedial or corrective work in the*
   classroom, by a remedial teacher, in the Reading Center,
   or in a Child Study Clinic?

The answer to this question is based upon the complexity of the reading problem. The teacher must consider the amount of time he can legitimately devote to the one child, possibly at the expense of the other children in his classroom. In every case where the correction can reasonably be made within the classroom, the teacher should assume that responsibility. With a child who has a stubborn reading disability that will take considerable time and skilled careful tutoring to correct, the problem should be handled by a remedial teacher or in the Reading Center. If the reading problem is further complicated by personal difficulties or marked physical limitations, the child should be referred to a Child Study Clinic.

4. *What is the specific nature of the reading training the child needs?*

To obtain an answer to this question the teacher locates the area of reading instruction in which the basic problem lies. Is the basic problem in word recognition, in comprehension, in fluency? Or what is the area of difficulty? Then, within the area, the teacher must decide, through diagnosis, the specific nature of the difficulties. Suppose the basic problem is one of word recognition, then what type of word-recognition difficulty is involved? That is, quite specifically, the teacher decides what is wrong with the child's reading. After studying the diagnosis, the teacher should formulate a program of instruction specifically designed to overcome the reading difficulties found.

In addition to diagnosing the reading problem, a study should be made of the type of instruction the child has been receiving. Burt and Lewis [44] have indicated that in remedial work it is necessary to understand not only the child but also the methods previously used with him. Methods that have been unsuccessful should be avoided in the new work. Experience with children in difficulty has indicated that the teacher should study the instructional approaches with any given child and use those that for him seem to produce successful results.

5. *What level and type of material should be used to correct the difficulty?*

The answer to this question will depend not only upon the child's general reading level but also upon the nature of the difficulty to be corrected. Keith reads on a relatively high level in comparison to his skill development. If he is to show improvement, the material should be of a level of difficulty similar to his grade level in the skills that are to be improved rather than at his level of comprehension ability. Donna requires training in use of context clues, reading in thought units, comprehension abilities, and fusion, so the materials for her should present few if any word-recognition difficulties. Donna already has a tendency to depend too much on word-recognition techniques to the exclusion of thoughtful reading. For her, material will be needed that is considerably easier than her high level of skill development might indicate.

6. *What interests of the child can be utilized to motivate his learning?*

Keith needs relatively easy material that is intellectually stimulating to him. Fortunately, there is an ever-increasing amount of material written with a high interest but low readability level. If a child is to maintain interest in reading the material, it must be in a format that does not appear too juvenile to him. Workbooks emphasize skill development and have a format that looks relatively mature. Probably, workbook material would fit Keith's instructional needs most adequately.

The teacher will find that in selecting reading material for a disabled reader, it is frequently possible to use a present interest of the child. Mr. Thorpe, in working with Keith, should make every effort to get material that he can read on the topics that grow out of the basic reading instruction. When material is not available on a child's particular interest, the teacher will need to stimulate interest in a topic on which he has the requisite material. No compromise should be made with the level of difficulty of material used in correcting a child's reading disability. It is essential that the material given the child with a reading difficulty be of a level he *can* read rather than material that meets his specific interests but is too difficult for him to read. In working with Keith, Mr. Thorpe decided to motivate him by having him evaluate material of fourth-grade difficulty to determine its suitability for other boys of his age. He asked

Keith to report on the content of the material so that he could classify it according to subject matter. Keith reported that some of the material was "all right," but that other material was "too babyish for boys of my age to read." As Keith read the materials to make the judgments his word-recognition capabilities improved.

7. *What techniques may be used to demonstrate to*
   the child that he is making progress?

Most disabled readers are discouraged readers. Many have rejected reading; some are antagonistic toward reading. Motivating a child who is in reading difficulty is a task of no mean proportions. Yet he must expend effort in reading if learning is to result. A productive way of keeping motivation on a high level is to acquaint the child with his progress. There are numbers of teaching techniques that may be used to demonstrate progress. In the case of Donna, for example, a chart showing the increase of speed of comprehension might be used. Or, tape recordings could demonstrate to Donna her improvement in phrasing in oral reading as she learned to reject the word-by-word habit in favor of reading in thought units.

8. *Are there conditions within the child that can be corrected?*
   Or are there conditions to which the program must adjust?

The teacher should ascertain whether there are any correctible visual, auditory, or other limitations that are adversely influencing reading achievement. The correction of such limitations should enable the child to learn more effectively. In certain cases, the teacher will find it necessary to adjust instructional procedures to the limiting condition. If, for example, the child has a physical condition that makes him tire easily, the length of the work period should be shortened.

Differences in mental capability must be considered and adjustments made to them. Anderson [6], for example, found that the methods should be somewhat related to the intellectual capability of the youngster. High-ability youngsters profit more from meaningful methods; low-ability youngsters profit more from repetitive drill procedures.

9. *Are there environmental conditions that constitute*
   a threat to ecective remediation?

To answer this question it is necessary to know the reading situations the child faces throughout the school day and at home. In the case of Donna, there were unfortunate pressures exerted upon her at home, which, if possible, should be eliminated. Seeking cooperation of her parents should help. It is the rare parent who does not try to cooperate when he is acquainted with the problem the child faces and with the solution being attempted by the teacher. In fact, parents are often pleased to learn that their child is being helped with his reading problem, and they are eager to cooperate in the way the teacher suggests.

At school, it is important that appropriate adjustments be made to the child's reading limitations. In all reading situations, the materials should be at the proper level of difficulty. If, throughout the major portion of the day, the child is attempting to read material that is too difficult for him, it is impossible to motivate his reading, to keep him encouraged about it, and to correct his problem. It is not possible for him to learn when he is using material he cannot read. Learning does not take place by means of osmosis, up through the arms to the central nervous system merely by holding a book.

10. *Are the teaching procedures and materials producing results?*

This question is not answered on the original diagnosis, but inasmuch as diagnosis is continuous, the teacher has this question in mind somewhat constantly. Whenever the remediation proves effective the child's instructional needs alter. When, for example, Keith learns more effective means of recognizing unfamiliar words, his instructional need might shift to a need for broadening his comprehension abilities to bring them more nearly in line with his mental capabilities. Of course, comprehension might improve somewhat automatically as word recognition improved. But one could not know this without continuous study of the progress made.

Using the knowledge of the results of all the means of appraisal at his disposal the teacher is able to modify his instructional practices and so adjust instruction to the individual needs of the children. There are many opportunities to make the needed adjustments. During the introductory phases of teaching a selection, certain types of instructional adjustments can be made. During the guidance of silent reading, other adjustments are possible. In the follow-up phases of teaching a selection, when exercises designed to develop skills and abilities are given, still other opportunities for adjusting instruction to individual needs present themselves.

During the introductory phases of teaching a selection, the teacher will give the child who has a limited meaning vocabulary more opportunities to participate in the discussion of the pictures and concepts in those discussions in which vocabulary and concepts are being emphasized, thereby encouraging the expansion of his meaning vocabulary. When the teacher notices that a child has a specific type of word-recognition problem, he will give that child an unusual number of opportunities to participate when new words are introduced. When establishing the purposes for reading, the teacher may adjust the purpose for a given child, to give him the experience he needs in a comprehension ability. He may, for example, in the case of a child who has difficulty in recalling facts that are presented, suggest that the child write a list of some specific items of information in the given passage to present to the children at a later time. While discussing the concepts presented in a selection, after silent reading, the teacher may call upon a child known to have a weakness in a certain type of comprehension to see whether or not he has read understandingly. If a misconception is located, the teacher may use this as an instructional opportunity to explore with the child how the misconception arose. In the development of skills and abilities and in the use of skill-development books, after the children have read a selection, the teacher may excuse a child who is somewhat prone to being overanalytical from an analytical type of follow-up exercise or from doing an analytical page in the skill-development book. The teacher also, from time to time, prepares material for specific children, or even a specific child, to extend the experiences with a reading goal beyond those that would be given to children who are growing typically.

The teacher who so thoroughly studies the day-by-day performance of each child in his class is a diagnostic teacher—one who analyzes the child's needs and makes immediate adjustments in instruction to strengthen each child's reading growth. Such teaching is difficult teaching, but therein lies the artistry so necessary in teaching the child to read.

Selected References

Bond, Guy L., and Bertha Handlan. *Adapting Instruction in Reading to Individual Differences*. Minneapolis: The University of Minnesota Press, 1952.

Bond, Guy L., and Miles A. Tinker. *Reading Difficulties: Their Diagnosis and Correction*. New York: Appleton-Century-Crofts, Inc., 1957, Chap. 3.

DeBoer, John J., and Martha Dallmann. *The Teaching of Reading*, revised edition. New York: Holt, Rinehart and Winston, Inc., 1964, Chap. 12.

Goodlad, John L., and Robert H. Anderson. *The Nongraded Elementary School*. New York: Harcourt, Brace and World, Inc., 1963.

McKim, Margaret G., and Helen Caskey. *Growth in Reading*, second edition. New York: The Macmillan Company, 1963, Chap. 14.

Rasmussen, Margaret, editor. *Toward Effective Grouping*. Washington: Association for Childhood Education International, 1962.

Robinson, H. M. *Why Pupils Fail in Reading*. Chicago: The University of Chicago Press, 1946.

Smith, Henry P., and Emerald V. Dechant. *Psychology in Teaching Reading*. Englewood Cliffs, N.J.: Prentice-Hall, Inc., 1961, Chaps. 9 and 15.

Strang, Ruth, Constance M. McCullough, and Arthur E. Traxler. *The Improvement of Reading*, third edition. New York: McGraw-Hill Book Company, 1961, Chaps. 14 and 15.

Umans, Shelley. *New Trends in Reading Instruction*. New York; Bureau of Publications, Teachers College, 1961, Chap. 3.

BIBLIOGRAPHY

1. Aaron, I. E. "Developing Reading Competencies Through Social Studies and Literature," *Reading As an Intellectual Activity*, International Reading Association Proceedings, 8:107–10. New York: Scholastic Magazines, Inc., 1963.
2. ———. "Using Basal Materials Effectively," *Improvement of Reading Through Classroom Practice*, International Reading Association Conference Proceedings, 9:73–74. Newark: International Reading Association, 1964.
3. Agnew, Donald C. *The Effect of Varied Amounts of Phonetic Training on Primary Reading*. Durham, North Carolina: Duke University Press, 1939.
4. Allen, R. Van, and Gladys C. Halversen. *The Language Experience Approach*. Boston: Ginn and Company, 1961.
5. Anderson, I. H., and W. F. Dearborn. *The Psychology of Teaching Reading*. New York: The Ronald Press Company, 1952.
6. Anderson, P. S. *The Effects of Teacher Attitude Toward Learning Theories and Toward Children on Pupil Achievement in Fourth-Grade Arithmetic and Reading*. Unpublished Ph.D. dissertation, University of Minnesota, 1959.
7. Artley, A. Sterl. "Phonic Skills in Beginning Reading," *Education*, May 1962.

8. Austin, Mary C., Clifford L. Bush, and Mildred H. Huebner. *Reading Evaluation.* New York: The Ronald Press Company, 1961.
9. ———, and Coleman Morrison. *The First R.* New York: The Macmillan Company, 1963.
10. ———, *et al. The Torch Lighters—Tomorrow's Teachers of Reading.* Cambridge, Massachusetts: Harvard University Press, 1961.
11. Bailey, Myrtle. *Success in Reading.* Minneapolis: T. S. Denison, 1963.
12. Balow, I. H. "Does Homogeneous Grouping Give Homogeneous Groups?" *Elementary School Journal,* 63:28–32, October 1962.
13. ———. "Lateral Dominance Characteristics and Reading Achievement in the First Grade," *Journal of Psychology,* 55:323–28, April 1963.
14. Bamman, Henry A. "Developing Reading Competencies Through Mathematics and Science," *Reading as an Intellectual Activity,* International Reading Association Conference Proceedings, 8:110–12. New York: Scholastics Magazines, Inc., 1963.
15. Barnes, K. F. *The Influence of Reading Ability on Performance on Certain Aptitude Tests.* Unpublished Ph.D. dissertation, University of Minnesota, 1950.
16. Betts, Emmett A. "Reading: Linguistic and Psychological Bases," *Improvement of Reading Through Classroom Practice,* International Reading Association Conference Proceedings, 9:20–23. Newark, Delaware: International Reading Association, 1964.
17. ———, and A. S. Austin. *Visual Problems of School Children.* Chicago: The Professional Press, Inc., 1941.
18. Bloomfield, Leonard, and Clarence Barnhart. *Let's Read; A Linguistic Approach.* Detroit: Wayne State University Press, 1961.
19. Bond, Austin D., *et al. Looking at Science.* Chicago: Lyons & Carnahan, 1963.
20. Bond, Eva. *Reading and Ninth-Grade Achievement.* New York: Bureau of Publications, Teachers College, 1938.
21. Bond, E. A. *Tenth-Grade Abilities and Achievements.* New York: Bureau of Publications, Teachers College, 1940.
22. Bond, Guy L. *The Auditory and Speech Characteristics of Poor Readers.* New York: Bureau of Publications, Teachers College, 1935.
23. ———"Teaching Selections in Reading," *The Road to Better Reading.* Bureau of Secondary Curriculum Development. Albany, New York: The State Education Department, 1953, 30–41.
24. ———, *et al. Days of Adventure.* Chicago: Lyons & Carnahan, 1962.
25. ———, *et al. Fun with Us.* Chicago: Lyons & Carnahan, 1962.
26. ———, *et al. Teachers' Edition, Fun with Us.* Chicago: Lyons & Carnahan, 1962.
27. ———, *et al. Fun To Do Book.* Chicago: Lyon & Carnahan, 1962.
28. ———, *et al. Happy Times.* Chicago: Lyons & Carnahan, 1962.
29. ———, and Eva Bond. *Developmental Reading.* New York: The Macmillan Company, 1941.
30. ———, and Leo C. Fay. "A Comparison of the Performance of Good and Poor Readers on the Individual Items of the Stanford-Binet Scale, Forms L and M," *Journal of Educational Research,* 43:475–79, 1950.

31. ———, and Bertha Handlan. *Adapting Instruction to Individual Differences*. Minneapolis: University of Minnesota Press, 1952.

32. ———, and Miles A. Tinker. *Reading Difficulties: Their Diagnosis and Correction*. New York: Appleton-Century-Crofts, Inc., 1957.

33. ———, and Eva Bond Wagner. *Child Growth in Reading*. Chicago: Lyons & Carnahan, 1955.

34. Boutwell, William D. "Bringing Readers and Books Together Successfully —Through Paperback Book Clubs and School Stores," *Reading As an Intellectual Activity*, International Reading Association Conference Proceedings, 8:168–73. New York: Scholastic Magazines, Inc., 1963.

35. Bracken, Dorothy K. in Mildred Dawson (ed.), *Children, Books, and Reading*. Newark, Delaware: International Reading Association, 1964, p. 55.

36. Brazziel, William F., and Mary Terrell. "For First-Graders: A Good Start in School," *Elementary School Journal*, 62:352–55, April 1962.

37. Bremer, Neville. "First-Grade Achievement Under Different Plans of Grouping," *Elementary English*, 35:324–26, May 1958.

38. Briggs, Daniel. "Grouping Guidelines," *Improvement of Reading Through Classroom Practice*, International Reading Association Conference Proceedings, 9:53–55. Newark, Delaware: International Reading Association, 1964.

39. Brogan, Peggy, and Lorene Fox. *Helping Children Read*. New York: Holt, Rinehart and Winston, Inc., 1961.

40. Brown, Gertrude S., *et al. Your Country and Mine*. New York: Ginn and Company, 1960.

41. Burks, Harold F., and Paul Bruce. "The Characteristics of Poor and Good Readers As Disclosed by the Wechsler Intelligence Scale for Children," *Journal of Educational Psychology*, 46:488–93, December 1955.

42. Buros, O. (ed.). *Fourth Mental Measurements Yearbook*. Highland Park, New Jersey: Gryphon Press, 1953.

43. Burrows, A. T. "Caste System or Democracy in Teaching Reading," *Elementary English*, 25:145–48, 1950.

44. Burt, C., and R. B. Lewis. "Teaching Backward Readers," *British Journal of Psychology*, 16, 1946.

45. Burton, Dwight L., and Nancy Larrick. "Literature for Children and Youth," *Development In and Through Reading*, Sixtieth Yearbook of the National Society for the Study of Education, Part I. Chicago: University of Chicago Press, 1961.

46. Buswell, Guy T. "The Process of Reading," *The Reading Teacher*, 13:108–15, December 1959.

47. Buswell, Margaret M. *The Reading Ability of Entering First-Grade Pupils*. Unpublished Master's thesis, University of Minnesota, 1947.

48. ———. *The Relationship Between the Social Structure of the Classroom and the Academic Success of the Pupils*. Unpublished Ph.D. dissertation, University of Minnesota, 1950.

49. Carlson, T. R. *The Relationships Between Speed and Accuracy of Comprehension of Reading*. Unpublished Ph.D. dissertation, University of Minnesota, 1946.

50. Carmichael, L., and W. F. Dearborn. *Reading and Visual Fatigue*. Boston: Houghton Mifflin Company, 1947.

51. Causey, O. S. *The Reading Teacher's Reader*. New York: The Ronald Press Company, 1958.
52. Chall, Jeanne. "Different Approaches to Beginning Reading," *Reading As an Intellectual Activity*, International Reading Association Conference Proceedings, 8:250–54. New York: Scholastic Magazines, Inc., 1963.
53. ———. *Readability: An Appraisal of Research and Applications*. Columbus, Ohio: The Ohio State University, 1958.
54. ———. Roswell, Florence G., and Susan Hahn Blumenthal. "Auditory Blending Ability a Factor in Success in Beginning Reading," *The Reading Teacher*, 17:113–18, November 1963.
55. Clymer, Theodore W. *The Influence of Reading Ability on the Validity of Group Intelligence Tests*. Unpublished Ph.D. dissertation, University of Minnesota, 1952.
56. ———. "The Utility of Phonic Generalizations in the Primary Grades," *The Reading Teacher*, 16:252–58, January 1963.
57. Collings, M. R. *Children's Procedures in Interpreting Reading Matter Accompanied by Maps*. Unpublished Ph.D. dissertation, Wayne University, 1954.
58. Cook, Walter W. *Grouping and Promotion in the Elementary Schools*. Series on Individualization of Instruction, No. 2. Minneapolis: University of Minnesota Press, 1941.
59. Crookes, T. G., and Margaret Greene. "Some Characteristics of Children with Two Types of Speech Disorders," *British Journal of Educational Psychology*, 33:31–40, February 1963.
60. Crosby, Muriel (ed.). *Reading Ladders for Human Relations*. Washington, D.C.: American Council of Education, fourth edition, 1963.
61. Cutts, Warren G. *Research in Reading for the Middle Grades*. Washington, D.C.: Superintendent of Documents, Government Printing Office, Catalog No. FS 5.230:30009, 1963.
62. Dale, E. "Is There a Substitute for Reading?" *The News Letter*. Columbus, Ohio: Bureau of Educational Research, The Ohio State University, April 1945, 3–4.
63. ———, and J. Chall. "Formula for Predicting Readability," *Educational Research Bulletin*, 27:11–20, 37–45. Columbus, Ohio: The Ohio State University, 1948.
64. Darby, O. N. "The Uses and Abuses of Oral Reading," *Elementary School Journal*, 51:380–88, March 1951.
65. Darrow, Helen Fisher, and Virgil M. Hawes. *Approaches to Individualized Reading*. New York: Appleton-Century-Crofts, 1960.
66. Davis, David C. "Phonemic Structural Approach to Initial Reading Instruction," *Elementary English*, 31:218–23, March 1964.
67. Dawson, Martha E. *A Study of Vocabulary Size of Third-Grade Pupils in Relation to Home Environmental Factors*. Unpublished Ed. D. thesis, Indiana University, 1956.
68. Dawson, Mildred A. *Children, Books and Reading*. Newark, Delaware: International Reading Association, 1964.
69. Dawson, Mildred A., and H. A. Bamman. *Fundamentals of Basic Reading Instruction*. New York: David McKay Company, Inc., 1963.

70. Dechant, Emerald V. *Improving the Teaching of Reading.* Englewood Cliffs, New Jersey: Prentice-Hall, Inc., 1964.
71. Delacato, Carl H. *The Diagnosis and Treatment of Speech and Reading Problems.* Springfield, Illinois: Charles C Thomas, 1963.
72. Dewey, John. *Construction and Criticism.* New York: Columbia University Press, 1930.
73. Dixon, Norman R. "Listening: Most Neglected of the Language Arts," *Elementary English,* 31:285–88, March 1964.
74. Doctor, Robert L. "A Comparison of the Effectiveness of Workbook and Non-Workbook Types of Follow-up Materials," *Challenge and Experiment in Reading,* International Reading Association Conference Proceedings, 7:156–59. New York: Scholastic Magazines, Inc., 1962.
75. Dolch, Edward W. "How Much Word Knowledge Do Children Bring to Grade One?" *Elementary English,* 13:177–83, May 1963.
76. ———. *Teaching Primary Reading,* third edition. Champaign, Illinois: Garrard Press, 1960.
77. Downing, John A. "The Augmented Roman Alphabet for Learning To Read," *The Reading Teacher,* 16:325–36, March 1963.
78. ———. *Experiments with an Augmented Alphabet for Beginning Readers.* New York: Educational Records Bureau, 1962.
79. ———. "Teaching Reading with i/t/a in Britain," *Phi Delta Kappan,* XLV, No. 7: 322–29, April 1964.
80. Durkin, Dolores. "Children Who Learned To Read at Home," *Elementary School Journal,* 62:15–18, January 1961.
81. ———. "Early Readers—Reflections After Six Years of Research," *The Reading Teacher,* 18:3–7, October 1964.
82. ———. *Phonics and the Teaching of Reading.* New York: Bureau of Publications, Teachers College, 1962.
83. Durrell, Donald D. *Improving Reading Instruction.* Yonkers: World Book Company, 1956.
84. ———. "Success in First Grade Reading," *Journal of Education,* 140, February 1958.
85. ———, and H. B. Sullivan. *Durrell-Sullivan Reading Capacity and Achievement Tests.* Yonkers: World Book Company, 1945.
86. Eames, T. H. "A Comparison of the Ocular Characteristics of Unselected and Reading Disability Groups," *Journal of Educational Research,* 25:211–15, 1932.
87. ———. "Physical Factors in Reading," *The Reading Teacher,* 16:427–32, May 1962.
88. Edgerton, Ronald B. "How Difficult Are Children's Encyclopedias?" *Elementary School Journal,* 55:219–25, December 1954.
89. Edmiston, R. W., and Bessie Peyton. "Improving First Grade Achievement by Readiness Instruction," *School and Society,* 71:230–32, April 1950.
90. Edson, W. H. *A Study of the Relationships Between Visual Characteristics and Specific Silent Reading Abilities.* Unpublished Ph.D. dissertation, University of Minnesota, 1950.
91. Eller, William. "Reading Interest: A Function of the Law of Effect," *The Reading Teacher,* 13:115–20, December 1959.

92. Evans, N. Dean. "Individualized Reading—Myths and Facts," *Elementary English*, 39:580–83, October 1962.

93. Fay, Leo C. "Responsibility for and Methods of Promoting Growth in Reading in Content Areas," *Better Readers in Our Times*, International Reading Association Conference Proceedings, I. New York: Scholastic Magazines, Inc., 1956.

94. ———. *The Relationship Between Specific Reading Skills and Selected Areas of Sixth-Grade Achievement*. Unpublished Ph.D. dissertation, University of Minnesota, 1948.

95. Fernald, G. M. *Remedial Techniques in Basic School Subjects*. New York: McGraw-Hill Book Company, Inc., 1943.

96. Fries, Charles C. *Linguistics and Reading*. New York: Holt, Rinehart and Winston, Inc., 1963.

97. Gans, Roma. *A Study of Critical Reading Comprehension in the Intermediate Grades*. New York: Bureau of Publications, Teachers College, 1940.

98. ———. *Common Sense in Teaching Reading*. New York: The Bobbs-Merrill Company, Inc., 1963.

99. ———. "Reading Is Fun." *Parent Teacher Series*, 10:1–45, 1954.

100. Gates, Arthur I. "Basal Principles in Reading Readiness Teaching," *Teachers College Record*, 40: 495–506, 1949.

101. ———. "How Can One Tell What Practices Seem Most Promising?" *Improvement of Reading Through Classroom Practice*, International Reading Association Conference Proceedings, 9:23–24. Newark, Delaware: International Reading Association, 1964.

102. ———. *The Improvement of Reading*, third edition. New York: The Macmillan Company, 1947.

103. ———. "The Necessary Mental Age for Beginning Reading," *Elementary School Journal*, 37:497–508, 1937.

104. ———. "Results of Teaching a System of Phonics," *The Reading Teacher*, 14:248–52, March 1961.

105. ———. "Vocabulary Control in Basal Reading Material," *The Reading Teacher*, 15:81–85, November 1961.

106. ———. "The Word Recognition Ability and the Reading Vocabulary of Second- and Third-Grade Children," *The Reading Teacher*, 15:443–48, May 1962.

107. ———, Guy L. Bond, and David H. Russell. *Methods of Determining Reading Readiness*. New York: Bureau of Publications, Teachers College, 1939.

108. ———, Guy L. Bond. *Reading Readiness*. Teachers College Record, 37:679–85, 1936.

109. Gesell, Arnold, and Frances L. Ilg. *The Child from Five to Ten*. New York: Harper & Brothers, 1946.

110. Gilbert, Luther C. "Functional Motor Efficiency of the Eyes and Its Relation to Reading," *University of California Publications in Education*, 11:159–232, 1953.

111. ———. "Speed of Processing Visual Stimuli and Its Relation to Reading," *Journal of Educational Psychology*, 55:8–14, February 1959.

112. Goodenough, F. L. *Mental Testing*. New York: Rinehart and Company, 1949.
113. Goodlad, John L. "Classroom Organization," in C. W. Harris (ed.). *Encyclopedia of Educational Research*, third edition. New York: The Macmillan Company, 1960, 221–26.
114. ———, and Robert H. Anderson. *The Nongraded Elementary School*. New York: Harcourt, Brace and World, Inc., 1963.
115. Gray, W. S. *On Their Own in Reading*. Chicago: Scott, Foresman and Company, 1960.
116. Grisby, O. J. "An Experimental Study of the Development of Concepts of Relationship in Pre-School Children As Evidenced by Their Expressive Ability," *Journal of Experimental Education*, I:144–62, 1932.
117. Groff, Patrick J. "Children's Attitudes Toward Reading and Their Critical Reading Abilities in Four Content-type Materials," *Journal of Educational Research*, 55:314–18, April 1962.
118. ———. "Comparison of Individualized and Ability Grouping Approaches to Reading Achievement," *Elementary English*, 40:258–64, March 1963.
119. ———. "A Study of Handedness and Reading Achievement," *The Reading Teacher*, 16:31–34, September 1962.
120. Gunderson, Doris V. *Research in Reading Readiness*. Washington, D.C.: Superintendent of Documents, Government Printing Office, Catalog No. 5.230:30013, 1964.
121. ———. *Research in Reading at the Primary Level*. Washington, D.C.: Superintendent of Documents, Government Printing Office, Catalog No. 5.230:30008, 1963.
122. Halcomb, James F. "Reading: The Language Experience Approach," *Challenge and Experiment in Reading*, International Reading Association Conference Proceedings, 7:72–74. New York: Scholastic Magazines, Inc., 1962.
123. Hampleman, Richard S. "A Study of the Comparative Reading Achievements of Early and Late School Starters," *Elementary English*, 36:331–34, May, 1959.
124. Hanson, C. W. *Factors Associated with Superior and Inferior Achievement in Problem Solving in Sixth-Grade Achievement*. Unpublished Ph.D. dissertation, University of Minnesota, 1943.
125. Harmer, William R. *The Effect of a Library Training Program on Summer Loss or Gain in Reading Abilities*. Unpublished Ph.D. dissertation, University of Minnesota, 1959.
126. Harris, Albert J. *Effective Teaching of Reading*. New York: David McKay Company, Inc., 1962.
127. ———. *Readings on Reading Instruction*. New York: David McKay Company, Inc., 1963.
128. ———. *How To Increase Reading Ability*, fourth edition. New York: Longman's Green and Company, 1961.
129. Harrison, M. L., and J. B. Stroud. *Harrison-Stroud Reading Readiness Profile*. Boston: Houghton Mifflin Company, 1950.
130. Hartung, Maurice, *et al. Seeing Through Arithmetic*. Chicago: Scott, Foresman and Company, 1957.

131. Hay, Julie, and Charles E. Wingo. *Reading with Phonics.* Philadelphia: J. B. Lippincott Company, 1948.

132. Heilman, Arthur W. *Teaching Reading.* Columbus, Ohio: Charles E. Merrill Books, Inc., 1961.

133. Henig, Max S. "Predictive Value of a Reading-Readiness Test and of Teacher's Forecasts, *Elementary School Journal,* 50:41–46, September 1949.

134. Henry, S. "Children's Audiograms in Relation to Reading Attainment," *Journal of Genetic Psychology,* 70:211–31, 1947; 71:3–63, 1948.

135. Herrick, Virgil E. "Basal Instructional Materials in Reading," *Development In and Through Reading,* The Sixtieth Yearbook of the National Society for the Study of Education. Chicago: University of Chicago Press, 1961.

136. Hester, Kathleen B. *Teaching Every Child to Read,* second edition. New York: Harper & Row, 1964.

137. Hildreth, Gertrude. *Teaching Reading.* New York: Holt, Rinehart and Winston, Inc., 1958.

138. ———, and N. L. Griffiths. *Metropolitan Reading Readiness Test.* Yonkers, New York: World Book Company, 1950.

139. Huck, Charlotte S. "A Comprehensive Literature Program," *Children, Books, and Reading.* Newark, Delaware: International Reading Association, 1964, pp. 111–22.

140. Hunnicutt, C. W., and W. J. Iverson (eds.). *Research in the Three R's.* New York: Harper & Brothers, 1958.

141. Hurley, B. D. *Curriculum for Elementary School Children.* New York: The Ronald Press Company, 1957.

142. Huus, Helen. "Developing Interest and Taste in Literature in the Elementary Grades," *Reading As an Intellectual Activity,* International Reading Association Conference Proceedings, 8:46–50. New York: Scholastic Magazines, Inc., 1963.

143. Inskeep, James Edward, Jr. "*A Comparison of Several Methods of Estimating Readability of Elementary School Reading Material.* Unpublished Ph.D. dissertation, University of Minnesota, 1960.

144. Jacobs, Leland B. "Individualized Reading Is Not a Thing!" *Individualized Reading Practices,* Alice Miel (ed.), Practical Suggestions for Teaching, No. 14. New York: Bureau of Publications, Teachers College, 1958.

145. ———. "The Individual and His World of Books," *Education,* 74:523–26, May 1954.

146. Jan-Tausch, James. "Concrete Thinking As A Factor in Reading Comprehension," *Challenge and Experiment in Reading,* International Reading Association Conference Proceedings, 7:161–64. New York: Scholastic Magazines, Inc., 1962.

147. Jarolimek, J. *A Study of Current Practices in Individualizing Instruction in Minnesota Schools.* Unpublished Ph.D. dissertation, University of Minnesota, 1955.

148. ———. *Social Studies in Elementary Education.* New York: The Macmillan Company, 1959.

149. Jensen, Amy Elizabeth. "Attracting Children to Books," *Elementary English,* 33:332–39, October 1956.

150. Jetton, Trula M. "The Basal Reader—A Tool for Meeting Individual Differences," *Improvement of Reading Through Classroom Practice*, International Reading Association Conference Proceedings, 9:72–73. Newark, Delaware: International Reading Association, 1964.

151. Johnson, Eleanor M. "What Is Happening to Children's Storybooks?" *The Reading Teacher*, 17:178–81, December 1963.

152. Johnson, H. *Teaching of History*. New York: The Macmillan Company, 1940.

153. Johnson, R. A. E. *The Relationship Between Reading Ability and the Use of Communication Media by Adolescents*. Unpublished Ph.D. dissertation, University of Minnesota, 1954.

154. Karlin, Robert. "Library-Book Borrowing vs. Library-Book Reading," *The Reading Teacher*, 16:77–81, November 1962.

155. ———. "Physical Growth and Success in Undertaking Beginning Reading," *Journal of Educational Research*, 51:191–201, November 1957.

156. ———. "The Prediction of Reading Success and Reading Readiness Tests," *Elementary English*, 34:320–22, May 1957.

157. Karlsen, Bjorn. "Children's Reading and the Linguistic Structure of Languages," *The Reading Teacher*, 18:184–87, December 1964.

158. Karp, Mark. "Silent Before Oral Reading," *Elementary School Journal*, 44:102–04, October 1944.

159. Kasdon, Lawrence M. "Early Reading Background of Some Superior Readers Among College Freshmen," *Journal of Educational Research*, 52:151–53, December 1958.

160. Keislar, Evan. "Conference on Perceptual and Linguistic Aspects of Reading," *The Reading Teacher*, 18:43–49, October 1964.

161. Kerfoot, James F. "The Vocabulary in Primary Arithmetic Texts," *The Reading Teacher*, 14:177–80, January 1961.

162. Klausmeier, H. J., K. Dresden, H. C. Davis, and W. A. Wittich. *Teaching in the Elementary School*. New York: Harper & Brothers, 1956.

163. Koenker, R. *Characteristic Differences Between Excellent and Poor Achievers in Sixth-Grade Division*. Unpublished Ph.D. dissertation, University of Minnesota, 1941.

164. Kolson, Clifford J. *The Vocabulary of Kindergarten Children*. Unpublished Ed.D. thesis, University of Pittsburgh, 1960.

165. ———. "Workable Approach to Grouping," *Clearing House*, 36:539–42, May 1962.

166. Kowitz, G. T., and C. M. Armstrong, "The Effect of Promotion Policy on Academic Achievement," *Elementary School Journal*, 61:435–43, May 1961.

167. Krantz, L. *The Relationship of Reading Abilities and Basic Skills of the Elementary School to Success in the Interpretation of the Content Materials in High School*. Unpublished Ph.D. dissertation, University of Minnesota, 1955.

168. Lamoreaux, L. A., and Dorris M. Lee, *Learning To Read Through Experience*. New York: Appleton-Century-Crofts, Inc., 1943.

169. LaPray, Margaret. "Four Masters: An Allegory," *The Reading Teacher*, 17:8–9, September 1963.

170. Larrick, Nancy. *Teacher's Guide to Children's Books.* Columbus, Ohio: Charles E. Merrill Books, Inc., 1960.
171. Lazar, M. *Individualization of Instruction in Reading.* Bureau of Reference, Research and Statistics, Educational Research Bulletin No. 1. New York: Board of Education, 1941.
172. ———, Marcella K. Draper, and Louise H. Schwietart. *A Practical Guide to Individualized Reading.* New York: Bureau of Educational Research, Board of Education of the City of New York, Publication No. 40, October 1960.
173. Lee, D. M. "Developing Experience Charts," *Instructor,* 71:85–86, March 1962.
174. ———, and R. Van Allen. *Learning to Read Through Experience.* New York: Appleton-Century-Crofts, Inc., 1963.
175. Lee, J. M., and W. W. Clark. *Lee-Clark Reading Readiness Tests.* Los Angeles: California Test Bureau, 1951.
176. Lefevre, Carl A. "Contributions of Linguistics to Reading," *Changing Concepts of Reading Instruction,* International Reading Association Conference Proceedings, 6:245–49. New York: Scholastic Magazines, Inc., 1961.
177. Lorge, I. "Predicting Readability," *Teachers College Record,* 45:404–19, 1944.
178. Madden, Richard. "Workbooks! Tools or Crutch?" *NEA Journal,* 45:94–95, February 1956.
179. MacKinnon, A. R. "Reading and Five-Year-Old Children," *Changing Concepts of Reading Instruction,* International Reading Association Conference Proceedings, 6:164–67. New York: Scholastic Magazines, Inc., 1961.
180. Mazurkiewisz, Albert J. "The Bethlehem i/t/a Study," *Improvement of Reading Through Classroom Practice,* International Reading Association Conference Proceedings, 9:265–67. Newark, Delaware. International Reading Association, 1964.
181. McCracken, Glenn. "Have We Over-emphasized the Readiness Factor?" *Elementary English,* 29: 271–75, May 1952.
182. ———. "The New Castle Reading Experiment—A Terminal Report," *Elementary English,* 30:13–21, January 1953.
183. ———. *The Right To Learn.* Chicago: Henry Regnery Company, 1959.
184. ———, and Charles C. Walcutt. *Basic Reading.* Philadelphia: J. B. Lippincott Company, 1963.
185. McCullough, Constance. *Changing Concepts of Reading Instruction,* International Reading Association Conference Proceedings, 6:13–22. New York: Scholastic Magazines, Inc., 1961.
186. ———. "Opinions Differ on Individualized Reading," *NEA Journal,* 47: 163, March 1958.
187. McDowell, J. B. "Report on the Phonetic Method of Teaching Children To Read, *Catholic Education Review,* 51:506–19, October 1953.
188. McKee, Paul. *The Teaching of Reading in the Elementary School.* Boston: Houghton Mifflin Company, 1948.

189. McKillop, A. S. *The Relationship Between the Reader's Attitude and Certain Types of Reading Response*. New York: Bureau of Publications, Teachers College, 1952.
190. McKim, Margaret C., and Helen Caskey. *Guiding Growth in Reading*, second edition. New York: The Macmillan Company, 1963.
191. Meek, Lois H. *Study of Learning and Retention in Young Children*. New York: Bureau of Publications, Teachers College, 1925.
192. Michaelis, J. U. *Social Studies for Children in a Democracy*. Englewood Cliffs, New Jersey: Prentice-Hall, Inc., 1957.
193. Miller, Edith F. *Stimulate Reading*, Grade Teacher, 8:134–35, April 1962.
194. Mills, Robert E. "An Evaluation of Techniques for Teaching Word Recognition, *Elementary School Journal*, 56:221–25, January 1956.
195. Monroe, Marion. "The Use of Picture Dictionaries in the Primary Grades," *Elementary English*, 31:340–45, April 1964.
196. ———. *Children Who Cannot Read*. Chicago: University of Chicago Press, 1932.
197. ———, and Bernice Rogers. *Foundations for Reading*. Chicago: Scott, Foresman and Company, 1964.
198. Morrison, Coleman. "Individualized Reading: Some Unanswered Questions," *Improvement of Reading Through Classroom Practice*, International Reading Association Conference Proceedings, 9:93–94. Newark Delaware: International Reading Association, 1964.
199. Mott, C., and L. B. Baisden. *The Children's Book on How To Use Books and Libraries*. New York: Charles Scribner's Sons, 1955.
200. Murphy, Helen A. *Evaluation of Specific Training in Auditory and Visual Discrimination on Beginning Reading*. Unpublished Ph.D. dissertation, Boston University, 1943.
201. ———, and D. D. Durrell. *Murphy-Durrell Diagnostic Reading Readiness Test*. Yonkers: World Book Company, 1949.
202. *My Reading Design*. North Manchester, Indiana: Reading Circle, Inc.
203. Odland, R. N. *A Comparative Study of Word Recognition Abilities of Good and Poor Readers in Third Grade*. Unpublished Ph.D. dissertation, University of Minnesota, 1958.
204. ———, and Therese Ilstrup. "Will Reading Teachers Read?" *The Reading Teacher*, 17:83–87, November 1963.
205. O'Donnell, Roy. "Awareness of Grammatical Structure and Reading Comprehension," *High School Journal*, 45:184–88, February 1962.
206. Peterson, E. M. *Aspects of Readability in the Social Studies*. New York: Bureau of Publications, Teachers College, 1954.
207. Pincus, Morris, and Frances Morganstern. "Should Children Be Taught To Read Earlier?" *The Reading Teacher*, 18:37–42, October 1964.
208. Pooley, Robert C. "Reading and Language Arts," *Development In and Through Reading*, The Sixtieth Yearbook of the National Society for the Study of Education, Part I, 35–53, 1961.
209. Porterfield, O. V., and Harry Schlichting. "Peer Status and Reading Achievement," *Journal of Educational Research*, 54: 291–97, April 1961.
210. Powell, Marvin, and Kenneth M. Parsley, Jr., "The Relationship Between First Grade Reading Readiness and Second Grade Reading Achievement," *Journal of Educational Research*, 54:229–33, February 1961.

211. Purcell, Barbara A. "Methods of Teaching Reading—A Report on a Tri-state Survey," *Elementary School Journal,* LVIII:449–53, May 1958.
212. Putnam, Lillian R. "Controversial Aspects of Individualized Reading," *Improvement of Reading Through Classroom Practice,* International Reading Association Conference Proceedings, 9:99–100. Newark, Delaware: International Reading Association, 1964.
213. Rambusch, Nancy McCormick. *Learning How To Learn: An American Approach to Montessori.* Baltimore: Helicon Press, 1962.
214. Rasmussen, Margaret (ed). *Toward Effective Grouping.* Washington: Association for Childhood Education International, 1962.
215. Robinson, H. Alan. "A Study of the Techniques of Word Identification," *The Reading Teacher,* 16:238–42, January 1963.
216. Robinson, H. M. *Why Pupils Fail in Reading.* Chicago: University of Chicago Press, 1946.
217. ———, and C. B. Huelsman, Jr. "Visual Efficiency and Progress in Learning To Read." *Clinical Studies in Reading:* II Supplementary Educational Monograph No. 77. Chicago: University of Chicago Press, 1953.
218. Romano, Michael J. "Reading and Science: A Symbolic Relationship," *Education,* 81:273–76, January 1961.
219. Rowan, Helen (ed.). " 'Tis Time He Should Begin To Read," *Carnegie Corporation of New York Quarterly,* April 1961.
220. Russell, David H. "Arithmetic Power Through Reading," *Instruction in Arithmetic.* Boston: Ginn and Company, 1960.
221. ———. *Children Learn To Read.* Boston: Ginn and Company, 1961
222. ———. "Six Studies of Children's Understanding of Concepts," *Elementary School Journal,* 63:255–60, May 1963.
223. ———. "Continuity in the Reading Program," *Development In and Through Reading,* The Sixtieth Yearbook of the National Society for the Study of Education, Part I. Chicago: University of Chicago Press, 1961.
224. ———, and Anna F. Merrill. "Children's Librarians Rate the Difficulty of Well-Known Juvenile Books," *Elementary English,* 28: 262–68, 1951.
225. Sartain, Harry W. "Individualized Reading in Perspective," *Changing Concepts of Reading Instruction,* International Reading Association Conference Proceedings, 6:84–87. New York: Scholastic Magazines, Inc., 1961.
226. ———. "The Roseville Experiment with Individualized Reading," *The Reading Teacher,* 13:277–81, March 1960.
227. Schneider, Herman and Nina. *Science in Our World.* Boston: D. C. Heath and Company, 1961.
228. Scott, Lloyd, F. "Television and School Attainment," *Phi Delta Kappan,* 38:25–28, October 1956.
229. Seegers, J. Conrad, and Robert H. Seashore. "How Large Are Children's Vocabularies?" *Elementary English,* 26:181–94, April 1949.
230. Sheldon, William D. "Teaching the Very Young To Read," *The Reading Teacher,* 16:163–69, December 1962.
231. Shores, J. Harlan. "Reading Science Materials for Two Distinct Purposes," *Elementary English,* 37:461–68, December 1960.
232. ———, and J. L. Saupe. "Reading for Problem-solving in Science," *Journal of Educational Psychology,* 44:149–58, March 1953.

233. Simpson, Dorothy M. *Perceptual Readiness and Beginning Reading.* Unpublished Ph.D. dissertation, Purdue, 1960.
234. Sister M. Caroline. *Breaking the Sound Barrier.* New York: The Macmillan Company, 1960.
235. Sister M. Herculane. "A Survey of the Flexibility of Rates and Techniques According to Purpose," *Journal of Developmental Reading,* 4:207–10, 1961.
236 Sister Mary Edward. "A Modified Linguistic Versus a Composite Basal Reading Program," *The Reading Teacher,* 17:511–15, April 1964.
237. Sister Miriam, O.P. "Context Clues in Primary Reading," *The Reading Teacher,* 230–34, April 1958.
238. Slover, Vera. "Comic Books vs. Story Books," *Elementary English,* May 1959.
239. Smith, Dora V. "Literature and Personal Reading," *Reading in the Elementary School,* The Forty-eighth Yearbook of the National Society for the Study of Education, Part II. Chicago: University of Chicago Press, 1949.
240. Smith, M. K. "Measurement of the Size of General English Vocabulary Through the Elementary Grades and High School," *Genetic Psychology Monographs,* 24:311–45, 1941.
241. Smith, Nila B. "Patterns of Writing in Different Subject Areas," *Journal of Reading,* 8:31–36; 95–102, October, November 1964.
242. ———. *Reading Instruction for Today's Children.* Englewood Cliffs, New Jersey: Prentice-Hall, Inc., 1963.
243. Sornson, H. H. *A Longitudinal Study of the Relationship Between Various Child Behavior Ratings and Success in Reading.* Unpublished Ph.D. dissertation, University of Minnesota, 1950.
244. Spache, George D. "A New Readability Formula for Primary-Grade Reading," *Elementary School Journal,* 52:410–13, 1953.
245. ———. "Is This a Breakthrough in Reading? *The Reading Teacher,* 15:258–62, January, 1962.
246. ———. *Toward Better Reading.* Champaign, Illinois: Garrard Publishing Company, 1963.
247. Sparks, Paul E., and Leo C. Fay. "An Evaluation of Two Methods of Teaching Reading," *Elementary School Journal,* 57:386–90, April 1957.
248. Staiger, Ralph C. "Agreements About Phonics," *Elementary English,* 31:204–06, 209, March 1964.
249. Stanchield, Jo M. "The Reading Interests of Eighth-Grade Boys," *Journal of Developmental Reading,* 5:256–65, 1962.
250. Stranger, Margaret, and Ellen K. Donahue. *Prediction and Prevention of Reading Difficulties.* New York: Oxford University Press, 1937.
251. Stauffer, Russell G. "Critical Thinking and the Educated Guess," *Changing Concepts of Reading Instruction,* International Reading Association Conference Proceedings, 6:173–7. New York: Scholastic Magazines, Inc., 1961.
252. Stewart, David K. "Values and Limitations of Basal Readers," *Materials for Reading,* Supplementary Educational Monographs, 86:51–56. Chicago: University of Chicago Press, 1956.

253. Strang, Ruth. "Relationships Between Certain Aspects of Intelligence and Certain Aspects of Reading," *Educational and Psychological Measurement,* 3:355–59, 1943.

254. ———. *Helping Your Child Improve His Reading.* New York: E. P. Dutton and Co., Inc., 1962.

255. ———, and D. K. Bracken. *Making Better Readers.* Boston: D. C. Heath and Company, 1957.

256. ———. C. M. McCullough, and A. E. Traxler. *The Improvement of Reading,* third edition. New York: McGraw-Hill Book Company, 1961.

257. Strickland, Ruth G. "Concern for Research on Linguistics and Reading," *Reading As an Intellectual Activity,* International Reading Association Conference Proceedings, 8:183–85. New York: Scholastic Magazines, Inc., 1963.

258. ———. *The Language of Elementary School Children: Its Relationship to the Language of Reading Textbooks and the Quality of Reading of Selected Children.* Indiana University, 38: No. 4, July 1962.

259. Sutton, Marjorie Hunt. "Readiness for Reading at the Kindergarten Level," *The Reading Teacher,* 18:234–39, January 1964.

260. Tanyzer, Harold J., and Albert J. Mazurkiewicz. *i/t/a Early-to-read Program.* New York: Initial Teaching Alphabet Publications, Inc., 1963.

261. Thompson, Martha. "The Purposes of Workbooks and Teacher's Guides," *Materials for Reading.* Supplementary Educational Monographs, 86:71–74. Chicago: University of Chicago Press, 1957.

262. Thorndike, Edward L. "Reading As Reasoning: A Study of Mistakes in Paragraph Reading, *Journal of Educational Research,* 8:323–32, June 1917.

263. Thorndike, Robert L. *Children's Reading Interests: A Study Based on a Fictitious Annotated Titles Questionnaire.* New York: Bureau of Publications, Teachers College, 1941.

264. Tinker, Miles A. "A Study of Eye Movements in Reading," *Psychological Bulletin,* 43:93–120, 1946.

265. ———. "Motor Efficiency of the Eye As a Factor in Reading," *Journal of Educational Psychology,* 29:167–74, 1938.

266. ———, and Constance McCullough. *Teaching Elementary Reading,* second edition. New York: Appleton-Century-Crofts, Inc., 1962.

267. Tooze, R. *Your Children Want To Read.* Englewood Cliffs. New Jersey: Prentice-Hall, Inc., 1957.

268. Umans, Shelley. *New Trends in Reading Instruction.* New York: Bureau of Publications, Teachers College, 1963.

269. Van Riper, C. "The Speech Pathologist Looks at Reading," *The Reading Teacher,* 17:505–10, April 1964.

270. Veatch, Jeannette. *Individualizing Your Reading Program.* New York: G. P. Putnam and Sons, 1959.

271. Vernon, M. D. *Backwardness in Reading.* New York: Cambridge University Press, 1960.

272. Wardeberg, H. L. *The Relationship of Reading Ability to Newspaper Reading Done by Adolescents.* Unpublished Ph.D. dissertation, University of Minnesota, 1953.

273. Wesley, E. B. *Teaching the Social Studies in Elementary Schools*, revised edition. Boston: D. C. Heath and Company, 1952.

274. Whipple, Gertrude. "The Language of Maps and Globes," *NEA Journal*, November, 1959.

275. Wilson, Rosemary Green. "A Linguistic Approach to Beginning Reading Based on Fries' Principles," *Improvement of Reading Through Classroom Practice*, International Reading Association Conference Proceedings, 9:225–26. Newark, Delaware: International Reading Association, 1964.

276. Winston, Gertrude C. "Oral Reading and Group Reading," *Elementary English*, April 1963.

277. Witty, Paul. "A Forward Look in Reading," *Elementary English*, 38:151–64, March 1961.

278. ———. "Individualized Reading: A Postscript," *Elementary English*, 31:211–17, March 1964.

279. ———. "The Role of Interest," *Development In and Through Reading*, The Sixtieth Yearbook of the National Society for the Study of Education, Part I. Chicago: University of Chicago Press, 1961.

280. ———, and associates. "Studies of Children's Interests—A Brief Summary," *Elementary English*, 37:469–75, November 1960.

281. ———, and David Kopel. *Reading and the Educative Process*. Boston: Ginn and Company, 1939.

282. Woestehoff, E. S. *The Specific Reading Proficiencies of Pupils Having Normal and Accelerated Reading Growth*. Unpublished Ph.D. dissertation, University of Minnesota, 1958.

283. Wollmar, M. H. B. *Children's Voluntary Reading*. New York: Bureau of Publications, Teachers College, 1949.

284. Worthington, Louise Willson. "Oral Reading? Certainly!" *Contributions in Reading*, No. 19. Boston: Ginn and Company.

285. Yoakum, G. A. "The Reading Difficulty of School Ttextbooks," *Elementary English Review*, 22:304–09, 1945.

NAME INDEX

Aaron, I. E., 91, 282, 379
Adams, Fay, 258, 259
Agnew, Donald C., 82, 379
Allen, R. Van, 49, 86, 92, 379, 388
Anderson, I. H., 40, 379
Anderson, P. S., 375, 379
Anderson, Robert H., 353, 377, 385
Armstrong, C. M., 351, 387
Artley, A. S., 151, 379
Austin, A. S., 26, 380
Austin, Mary C., 92, 293, 294, 315, 346, 380

Bailey, Myrtle, 18, 380
Baisden, L. B., 232, 289, 389
Balow, I. H., 26, 34, 352, 353, 380
Bamman, Henry A., 262, 286, 380, 382
Barnes, K. F., 367, 380
Barnhart, Clarence, 83, 380
Bell, Kate, 263
Betts, Emmett A., 26, 83, 380
Bloomfield, Leonard, 83, 380
Blumenthal, Susan Hahn, 86, 382
Bond, Austin D., 263, 380
Bond, Eva, 183, 380
Bond, E. A., 21, 380

Bond, Guy L., 20, 26, 29, 31, 32, 33, 101, 103, 104, 105, 106, 110, 127, 128, 131, 166, 173, 183, 255, 263, 279, 315, 346, 377, 380–81, 384
Boutwell, William D., 307–8, 381
Bracken, D. K., 286, 298, 381, 392
Brazziel, William F., 25, 381
Bremer, Neville, 25, 381
Briggs, Daniel, 357, 381
Brogan, Peggy, 92, 381
Brown, Gertrude S., 258, 259, 381
Bruce, Paul, 25, 381
Burks, Harold F., 25, 381
Buros, O., 326, 381
Burrows, A. T., 356, 381
Burt, C., 25, 373, 381
Burton, Dwight L., 286, 304, 381
Bush, Clifford L., 293, 294, 315, 346, 380
Buswell, Guy T., 26, 381
Buswell, Margaret M., 19, 357, 381

Carlson, T. R., 220, 221, 381
Carmichael, L., 221, 381
Caskey, Helen, 80, 346, 377, 389
Causey, O. S., 132, 382

395

SUBJECT INDEX